Volvo 740 & 760 Automotive Repair Manual

by Matthew Minter, Bob Henderson and John H Haynes

Member of the Guild of Motoring Writers

Models covered:
Volvo 740, GL, GLE and GLT; 2316 cc
Volvo 740 Turbo and 760 Turbo; 2316 cc
Volvo 760 GLE; 2849 cc
1982 through 1988
Does not include diesel engine information

(10U2 – 1550)

ABCDE
FGHI

Haynes Publishing Group
Sparkford Nr Yeovil
Somerset BA22 7JJ England

Haynes North America, Inc
861 Lawrence Drive
Newbury Park
California 91320 USA

Acknowledgements

We are grateful for the help and cooperation of Volvo of North America Corporation for their assistance with technical information, certain illustrations and vehicle photos, and the Champion Spark Plug Company who supplied the illustrations of various spark plug conditions.

A book in the **Haynes Automotive Repair Manual Series**

Printed in the USA

ISBN 1 85010 550 2

Library of Congress Catalog Card Number 89-83488

Contents

1
2
3
4
5
6
7
8
9
10
11
12

Volvo 760 Turbo Sedan

Volvo 740 Turbo Wagon

About this manual

Its purpose

The purpose of this manual is to help you get the best value from your vehicle. It can do so in several ways. It can help you decide what work must be done, even if you choose to have it done by a dealer service department or a repair shop; it provides information and procedures for routine maintenance and servicing; and it offers diagnostic and repair procedures to follow when trouble occurs.

It is hoped that you will use the manual to tackle the work yourself. For many simpler jobs, doing it yourself may be quicker than arranging an appointment to get the vehicle into a shop and making the trips to leave it and pick it up. More importantly, a lot of money can be saved by avoiding the expense the shop must pass on to you to cover its labor and overhead costs. An added benefit is the sense of satisfaction and accomplishment that you feel after having done the job yourself.

Using the manual

The manual is divided into Chapters. Each Chapter is divided into numbered Sections, which are headed in bold type between horizontal lines. Each Section consists of consecutively numbered paragraphs.

Photographs are keyed to the Section and Paragraph (for example, photo 3.12 means Section 3, Paragraph 12). Figures are numbered consecutively through each Chapter with a Section reference in the caption.

Procedures, once described in the text, are not normally repeated. When it is necessary to refer to another Chapter, the reference will be given as Chapter and Section number i.e. Chapter 1/16). Cross references given without use of the word ''Chapter'' apply to Sections and/or paragraphs in the same Chapter. For example, ''see Section 8'' means in the same Chapter.

Reference to the left or right side of the vehicle is based on the assumption that one is sitting in the driver's seat, facing forward.

Even though extreme care has been taken during the preparation of this manual, neither the publisher nor the author can accept responsibility for any errors in, or omissions from, the information given.

NOTE

A Note provides information necessary to properly complete a procedure or information which will make the steps to be followed easier to understand.

CAUTION

A Caution indicates a special procedure or special steps which must be taken in the course of completing the procedure in which the **Caution** is found which are necessary to avoid damage to the assembly being worked on.

WARNING

A Warning indicates a special procedure or special steps which must be taken in the course of completing the procedure in which the **Warning** is found which are necessary to avoid injury to the person performing the procedure.

Introduction to the Volvo 740 and 760

The Volvo 760 Sedan was introduced in 1982, followed by the 740 in 1984. Station Wagon versions became available for the 1986 model year. The models represent the top of the Volvo range; besides the solidity and attention to safety characteristic of the marque, they are luxuriously equipped.

Engines available in the 760 range are a 2.8 liter V6 and a turbocharged 2.3 liter four-cylinder, both with fuel injection. The turbocharged engine is also available in the 740 range, other options being the same engine without the turbo.

Both manual and automatic transmissions are available throughout the range. The manual transmission may be 5-speed, or 4-speed plus overdrive. The automatic transmission may be 4-speed or 3-speed plus overdrive. Power is transmitted to the rear wheels through a traditional live rear axle. A limited slip differential is available as an optional extra.

Braking is by discs front and rear, the handbrake acting on separate drums on the rear wheels. Anti-lock braking (ABS) is available on later models. Steering is power-assisted on all models.

The home mechanic will find the vehicles well-constructed and pleasant to work on, provided that tools and facilities appropriate to the vehicle are available.

General dimensions, weights and capacities

Dimensions

Wheelbase	2.770 m (9ft 1.1 in)
Overall length	4.785 m (15 ft 8.4 in)
Overall width	1.760 m (5 ft 9.3 in)
Track	1.460 m (4 ft 9.5 in)
Overall height	1.430 m (4 ft 8.3 in)

Weights

Curb weight (depending on equipment):

740	1270 to 1460 kg (2800 to 3219 lb)
760	1330 to 1500 kg (2932 to 3307 lb)
Gross vehicle weight	See type designation plate (under hood)

Capacities (approx)

Engine oil (drain and refill, including filter change):

B23/B230	3.85 litres (6.8 pints) — plus 0.6 litre (1 pint) for Turbo oil cooler if drained
B28	6.5 litres (11.4 pints)

Cooling system:

B23/B230	9.5 litres (16.7 pints)
B28	10.0 litres (17.6 pints)
Fuel tank	60 or 82 litres (13.2 or 18.0 gallons) depending on model and year

Manual gearbox:

M46 (4-speed plus overdrive)	2.3 litres (4.0 pints)
M47 (5-speed)	1.3 litres (2.3 pints)

Automatic transmission (drain and refill):

AW 71	3.9 litres (6.9 pints)
ZF 4HP 22	2.0 litres (3.5 pints)

Rear axle:

1030	1.3 litres (2.3 pints)
1031	1.6 litres (2.8 pints)

Jacking, towing and wheel changing

Jacking

Use the jack supplied with the vehicle only for wheel changing during roadside emergencies. For repair or maintenance, use a pillar jack or floor jack under one of the jacking points. To raise both rear wheels it is permissible to jack up under the final drive casing, but use a block of wood as an insulator. To raise both front wheels, remove the engine undertray and place the jack below the center of the front axle crossmember.

If the whole vehicle is being raised on a four-point lift, place the lifting arms as shown in the illustration. If the front lifting arms are placed below the jacking points, the vehicle may become nose heavy.

Never crawl under a vehicle supported solely by a jack — always supplement the jack with axle stands. These may be placed under the jacking points, the rear axle tube or the front crossmember. Do not use four axle stands under the jacking points, however — as with the four-point lift, the vehicle could become nose heavy.

For many procedures, an alternative to jacking is to use ramps or to place the vehicle over a pit. Make sure that ramps and axle stands are adequately rated for the weight of the vehicle and in good condition. Never perform any fuel system work while in a pit.

Towing

Towing eyes are provided at both front and rear of the vehicle (photos). The rear towing eye should be used only for emergency towing of another vehicle: for trailer towing a properly installed towing hitch is required.

Vehicles with automatic transmission must not be towed further than 20 miles (30 km) or faster than 12 mph (20 km/h). If these conditions cannot be met, or if transmission damage has already occurred, the driveshaft must be removed or the vehicle towed with its rear wheels off the ground.

When being towed, insert the ignition key and turn it to position II. This will unlock the steering and allow lights and direction indicators to be used. If the engine is not running, greater effort will be required to operate steering and brakes.

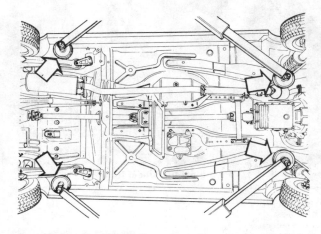

Support points (arrowed) for a four-point lift, or when using four axle stands

Pry out the cover plate . . .

. . . for access to the front towing eye

Wheel changing

Park on a firm flat surface if possible. Apply the handbrake and engage reverse gear or P. Chock the wheel diagonaly opposite the one being removed.

Remove the wheel cover, when applicable, for access to the wheel nuts. Pry the trim off if necessary using a screwdriver. Loosen the wheel nuts half a turn each using the lug wrench (photos).

If the car is fairly new, the wheels and tries will have been balanced on the vehicle during production. To maintain this relationship, mark the position of the wheel relative to the hub. (This is not necessary if the tire is to be removed for repair or replacement, since the balance will inevitably be altered). Some wheels are positively located by a pin on the hub, again making marking unnecessary.

Engage the jack head in the jacking point nearest the wheel being removed (photo). Turn the jack handle clockwise to lower the foot of the jack to the ground. If the ground is soft or uneven, place a plank or block under the foot of the jack to spread the load.

Jack up the vehicle until the wheel is clear of the ground. Remove the wheel nuts and lift the wheel off the studs. Installed the new wheel onto the studs and secure it with the nuts. Tighten the nuts until they are snug, but do not tighten them fully yet.

Lower the vehicle and remove the jack. Perform the final tightening of the wheel nuts in criss-cross sequence. The use of a torque wrench is strongly recommended, especially when light alloy wheels are installed. See Chapter 10 Specifications for the recommended tightening torque.

Install the wheel cover, when applicable, and stow the tools. If a new wheel has been brought into service, check the tire pressure at the first opportunity.

Prying off the wheel trim

Loosening the wheel nuts

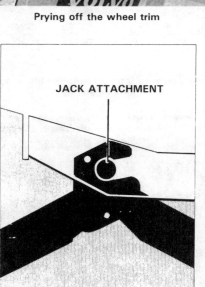

Jack head engagement with the jacking point

Jack head engaged in the jacking point

Vehicle identification numbers

When ordering spare parts, always give as much information as possible. Quote the car model, year of manufacture and if necessary the chassis number.

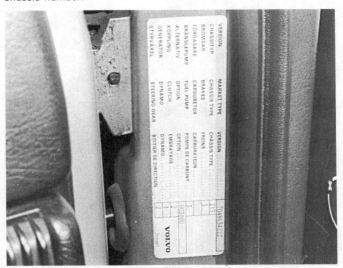

The service plate provides information needed when buying certain spare parts

The locations of the various identification plates are shown in the accompanying diagram. The information to be found on the service plate is normally sufficient for routine maintenance and repair requirements (photo). It is interpreted as follows:

Part	Manufacturer	Code
Brakes	Girling front and rear	1
	Girling front and ATE rear	2
	DBA front, ATE rear	3
Carburettor	SU	2
	Pierburg	3
	Solex	5
Fuel pump	Bosch	3
	AC-Delco	4
	Sofabex	5
Clutch	Fichtel & Sachs	2
	Verto/Valeo	3
Alternator	Bosch	1
Steering box	Cam Gear	2
	Zahnrad Fabrik (ZF)	3

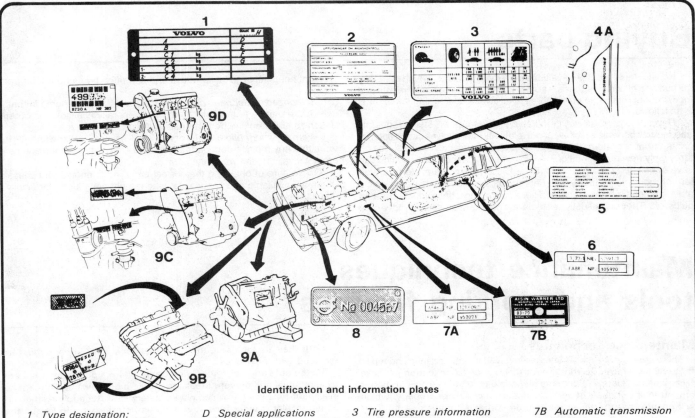

Identification and information plates

1	*Type designation:*	
A	*Type approval*	
B	*Vehicle identification number*	
C1	*Gross vehicle weight*	
C2	*Gross train weight*	
C3	*Front axle weight*	
C4	*Rear axle weight*	

D Special applications
E Market code
F Color code
G Trim level
H Country of origin Emission control decal (not UK)

3 Tire pressure information
4 Type designation, model year and chassis number
5 Service plate
6 Final drive ratio, type and serial number
7A Manual transmission number

7B Automatic transmission number
8 Body number
9A Engine number (Diesel)
9B Engine number (B 28)
9C Engine number (B 23)
9D Engine number (B 230)

Buying parts

Replacement parts are available from many sources, which generally fall into one of two categories – authorized dealer parts departments and independent retail auto parts stores. Our advice concerning these parts is as follows:

Retail auto parts stores: Good auto parts stores will stock frequently needed components which wear out relatively fast, such as clutch components, exhaust systems, brake parts, tune-up parts, etc. These stores often supply new or reconditioned parts on an exchange basis, which can save a considerable amount of money. Discount auto parts stores are often very good places to buy materials and parts needed for general vehicle maintenance such as oil, grease, filters, spark plugs, belts, touch-up paint, bulbs, etc. They also usually sell tools and general accessories, have convenient hours, charge lower prices and can often be found not far from home.

Authorized dealer parts department: This is the best source for parts which are unique to the vehicle and not generally available elsewhere (such as major engine parts, transmission parts, trim pieces, etc.).

Warranty information: If the vehicle is still covered under warranty, be sure that any replacement parts purchased – regardless of the source – do not invalidate the warranty!

To be sure of obtaining the correct parts, have engine and chassis numbers available and, if possible, take the old parts along for positive identification.

Maintenance techniques, tools and working facilities

Maintenance techniques

There are a number of techniques involved in maintenance and repair that will be referred to throughout this manual. Application of these techniques will enable the home mechanic to be more efficient, better organized and capable of performing the various tasks properly, which will ensure that the repair job is thorough and complete.

Fasteners

Fasteners are nuts, bolts, studs and screws used to hold two or more parts together. There are a few things to keep in mind when working with fasteners. Almost all of them use a locking device of some type, either a lockwasher, locknut, locking tab or thread adhesive. All threaded fasteners should be clean and straight, with undamaged threads and undamaged corners on the hex head where the wrench fits. Develop the habit of replacing all damaged nuts and bolts with new ones. Special locknuts with nylon or fiber inserts can only be used once. If they are removed, they lose their locking ability and must be replaced with new ones.

Rusted nuts and bolts should be treated with a penetrating fluid to ease removal and prevent breakage. Some mechanics use turpentine in a spout-type oil can, which works quite well. After applying the rust penetrant, let it work for a few minutes before trying to loosen the nut or bolt. Badly rusted fasteners may have to be chiseled or sawed off or removed with a special nut breaker, available at tool stores.

If a bolt or stud breaks off in an assembly, it can be drilled and removed with a special tool commonly available for this purpose. Most automotive machine shops can perform this task, as well as other repair procedures, such as the repair of threaded holes that have been stripped out.

Flat washers and lockwashers, when removed from an assembly, should always be replaced exactly as removed. Replace any damaged washers with new ones. Never use a lockwasher on any soft metal surface (such as aluminum), thin sheet metal or plastic.

Fastener sizes

For a number of reasons, automobile manufacturers are making wider and wider use of metric fasteners. Therefore, it is important to be able to tell the difference between standard (sometimes called U.S. or SAE) and metric hardware, since they cannot be interchanged.

All bolts, whether standard or metric, are sized according to diameter, thread pitch and length. For example, a standard 1/2 — 13 x 1 bolt is 1/2 inch in diameter, has 13 threads per inch and is 1 inch long. An M12 — 1.75 x 25 metric bolt is 12 mm in diameter, has a thread pitch of 1.75 mm (the distance between threads) and is 25 mm long. The two bolts are nearly identical, and easily confused, but they are not interchangeable.

In addition to the differences in diameter, thread pitch and length, metric and standard bolts can also be distinguished by examining the bolt heads. To begin with, the distance across the flats on a standard bolt head is measured in inches, while the same dimension on a metric bolt is sized in millimeters (the same is true for nuts). As a result, a standard wrench should not be used on a metric bolt and a metric wrench should not be used on a standard bolt. Also, most standard bolts have slashes radiating out from the center of the head to denote the grade or strength of the bolt, which is an indication of the amount of torque that can be applied to it. The greater the number of slashes, the greater the strength of the bolt. Grades 0 through 5 are commonly used on automobiles. Metric bolts have a property class (grade) number, rather than a slash, molded into their heads to indicate bolt strength. In this case, the higher the number, the stronger the bolt. Property class numbers 8.8, 9.8 and 10.9 are commonly used on automobiles.

Strength markings can also be used to distinguish standard hex nuts from metric hex nuts. Many standard nuts have dots stamped into one side, while metric nuts are marked with a number. The greater the number of dots, or the higher the number, the greater the strength of the nut.

Metric studs are also marked on their ends according to property class (grade). Larger studs are numbered (the same as metric bolts),

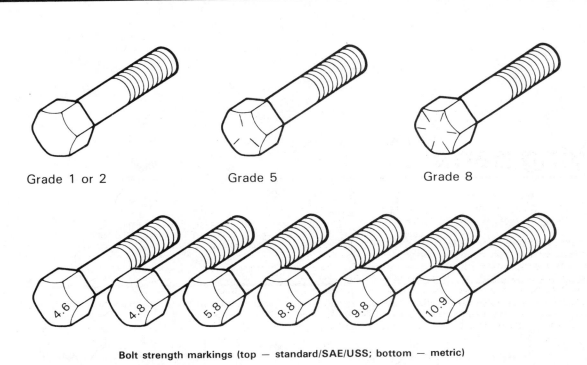

Grade 1 or 2   Grade 5   Grade 8

4.6   4.8   5.8   8.8   9.8   10.9

Bolt strength markings (top — standard/SAE/USS; bottom — metric)

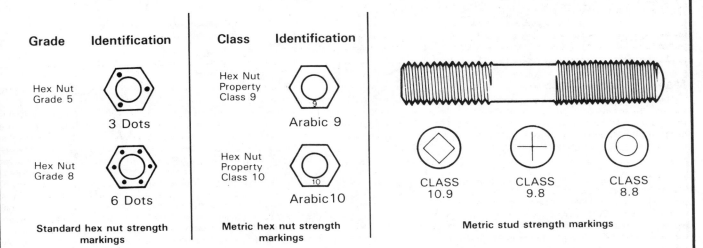

Grade	Identification
Hex Nut Grade 5	3 Dots
Hex Nut Grade 8	6 Dots

Standard hex nut strength markings

Class	Identification
Hex Nut Property Class 9	Arabic 9
Hex Nut Property Class 10	Arabic 10

Metric hex nut strength markings

CLASS 10.9   CLASS 9.8   CLASS 8.8

Metric stud strength markings

while smaller studs carry a geometric code to denote grade.

It should be noted that many fasteners, especially Grades 0 through 2, have no distinguishing marks on them. When such is the case, the only way to determine whether it is standard or metric is to measure the thread pitch or compare it to a known fastener of the same size.

Standard fasteners are often referred to as SAE, as opposed to metric. However, it should be noted that SAE technically refers to a non-metric *fine thread* fastener only. Coarse thread non-metric fasteners are referred to as USS sizes.

Since fasteners of the same size (both standard and metric) may have different strength ratings, be sure to reinstall any bolts, studs or nuts removed from your vehicle in their original locations. Also, when replacing a fastener with a new one, make sure that the new one has a strength rating equal to or greater than the original.

Tightening sequences and procedures

Most threaded fasteners should be tightened to a specific torque value (torque is the twisting force applied to a threaded component such as a nut or bolt). Overtightening the fastener can weaken it and cause it to break, while undertightening can cause it to eventually come loose. Bolts, screws and studs, depending on the material they are made of and their thread diameters, have specific torque values, many of which are noted in the Specifications at the beginning of each Chapter. Be sure to follow the torque recommendations closely. For fasteners not assigned a specific torque, a general torque value chart is presented here as a guide. These torque values are for dry (unlubricated) fasteners threaded into steel or cast iron (not aluminum). As was previously mentioned, the size and grade of a fastener determine the amount of torque that can safely be applied to it. The figures listed here are approximate

Metric thread sizes	Ft-lb	Nm/m
M-6	6 to 9	9 to 12
M-8	14 to 21	19 to 28
M-10	28 to 40	38 to 54
M-12	50 to 71	68 to 96
M-14	80 to 140	109 to 154

Pipe thread sizes		
1/8	5 to 8	7 to 10
1/4	12 to 18	17 to 24
3/8	22 to 33	30 to 44
1/2	25 to 35	34 to 47

U.S. thread sizes		
1/4 — 20	6 to 9	9 to 12
5/16 — 18	12 to 18	17 to 24
5/16 — 24	14 to 20	19 to 27
3/8 — 16	22 to 32	30 to 43
3/8 — 24	27 to 38	37 to 51
7/16 — 14	40 to 55	55 to 74
7/16 — 20	40 to 60	55 to 81
1/2 — 13	55 to 80	75 to 108

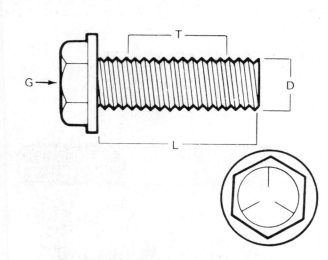

Standard (SAE and USS) bolt dimensions/grade marks

    G   Grade marks (bolt strength)
    L   Length (in inches)
    T   Thread pitch (number of threads per inch)
    D   Nominal diameter (in inches)

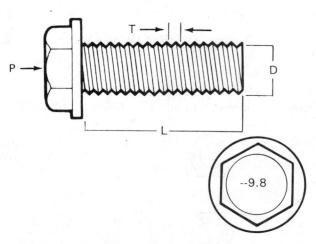

Metric bolt dimensions/grade marks

    P   Property class (bolt strength)
    L   Length (in millimeters)
    T   Thread pitch (distance between threads in millimeters)
    D   Diameter

for Grade 2 and Grade 3 fasteners. Higher grades can tolerate higher torque values.

Fasteners laid out in a pattern, such as cylinder head bolts, oil pan bolts, differential cover bolts, etc., must be loosened or tightened in sequence to avoid warping the component. This sequence will normally be shown in the appropriate Chapter. If a specific pattern is not given, the following procedures can be used to prevent warping.

Initially, the bolts or nuts should be assembled finger-tight only. Next, they should be tightened one full turn each, in a criss-cross or diagonal pattern. After each one has been tightened one full turn, return to the first one and tighten them all one-half turn, following the same pattern. Finally, tighten each of them one-quarter turn at a time until each fastener has been tightened to the proper torque. To loosen and remove the fasteners, the procedure would be reversed.

Component disassembly

Component disassembly should be done with care and purpose to help ensure that the parts go back together properly. Always keep track of the sequence in which parts are removed. Make note of special characteristics or marks on parts that can be installed more than one way, such as a grooved thrust washer on a shaft. It is a good idea to lay the disassembled parts out on a clean surface in the order that they were removed. It may also be helpful to make sketches or take instant photos of components before removal.

When removing fasteners from a component, keep track of their locations. Sometimes threading a bolt back in a part, or putting the washers and nut back on a stud, can prevent mix-ups later. If nuts and bolts cannot be returned to their original locations, they should be kept in a compartmented box or a series of small boxes. A cupcake or muffin tin is ideal for this purpose, since each cavity can hold the bolts and nuts from a particular area (i.e. oil pan bolts, valve cover bolts, engine mount bolts, etc.). A pan of this type is especially helpful when working on assemblies with very small parts, such as the carburetor, alternator, valve train or interior dash and trim pieces. The cavities can be marked with paint or tape to identify the contents.

Whenever wiring looms, harnesses or connectors are separated, it is a good idea to identify the two halves with numbered pieces of masking tape so they can be easily reconnected.

Gasket sealing surfaces

Throughout any vehicle, gaskets are used to seal the mating surfaces between two parts and keep lubricants, fluids, vacuum or pressure contained in an assembly.

Many times these gaskets are coated with a liquid or paste-type gasket sealing compound before assembly. Age, heat and pressure can sometimes cause the two parts to stick together so tightly that they are very difficult to separate. Often, the assembly can be loosened by striking it with a soft-face hammer near the mating surfaces. A regular hammer can be used if a block of wood is placed between the hammer and the part. Do not hammer on cast parts or parts that could be easily damaged. With any particularly stubborn part, always recheck to make sure that every fastener has been removed.

Avoid using a screwdriver or bar to pry apart an assembly, as they can easily mar the gasket sealing surfaces of the parts, which must remain smooth. If prying is absolutely necessary, use an old broom handle, but keep in mind that extra clean up will be necessary if the wood splinters.

After the parts are separated, the old gasket must be carefully scraped off and the gasket surfaces cleaned. Stubborn gasket material can be soaked with rust penetrant or treated with a special chemical to soften it so it can be easily scraped off. A scraper can be fashioned from a piece of copper tubing by flattening and sharpening one end. Copper is recommended because it is usually softer than the surfaces to be scraped, which reduces the chance of gouging the part. Some gaskets can be removed with a wire brush, but regardless of the method used, the mating surfaces must be left clean and smooth. If for some reason the gasket surface is gouged, then a gasket sealer thick enough to fill scratches will have to be used during reassembly of the components. For most applications, a non-drying (or semi-drying) gasket sealer should be used.

Hose removal tips

Warning: *If the vehicle is equipped with air conditioning, do not disconnect any of the A/C hoses without first having the system depressurized by a dealer service department or an air conditioning specialist.*

Hose removal precautions closely parallel gasket removal precautions. Avoid scratching or gouging the surface that the hose mates against or the connection may leak. This is especially true for radiator hoses. Because of various chemical reactions, the rubber in hoses can bond itself to the metal spigot that the hose fits over. To remove a hose, first loosen the hose clamps that secure it to the spigot. Then, with slip-joint pliers, grab the hose at the clamp and rotate it around the spigot. Work it back and forth until it is completely free, then pull it off. Silicone or other lubricants will ease removal if they can be applied between the hose and the outside of the spigot. Apply the same lubricant to the inside of the hose and the outside of the spigot to simplify installation.

As a last resort (and if the hose is to be replaced with a new one anyway), the rubber can be slit with a knife and the hose peeled from the spigot. If this must be done, be careful that the metal connection is not damaged.

If a hose clamp is broken or damaged, do not reuse it. Wire-type clamps usually weaken with age, so it is a good idea to replace them with screw-type clamps whenever a hose is removed.

Tools

A selection of good tools is a basic requirement for anyone who plans to maintain and repair his or her own vehicle. For the owner who has few tools, the initial investment might seem high, but when compared to the spiraling costs of professional auto maintenance and repair, it is a wise one.

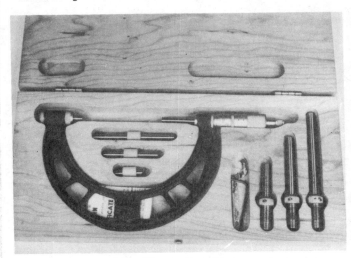

Micrometer set

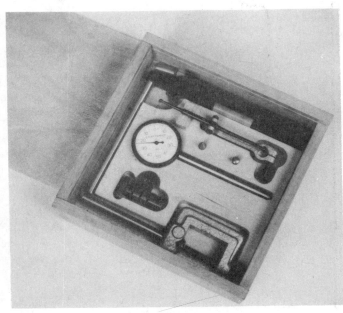

Dial indicator set

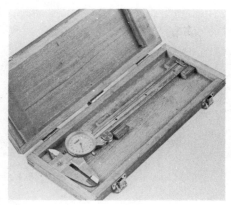

Dial caliper

Hand-operated vacuum pump

Timing light

Compression gauge with spark plug hole adapter

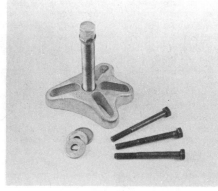

Damper/steering wheel puller

General purpose puller

Hydraulic lifter removal tool

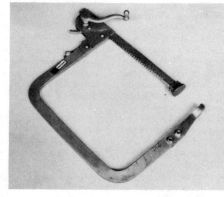

Valve spring compressor

Valve spring compressor

Ridge reamer

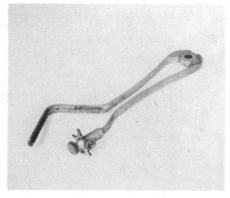

Piston ring groove cleaning tool

Ring removal/installation tool

Ring compressor

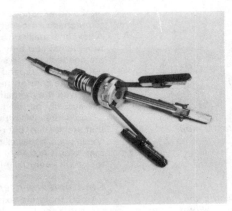

Cylinder hone

Brake hold-down spring tool

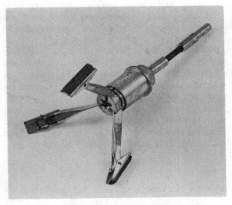

Brake cylinder hone

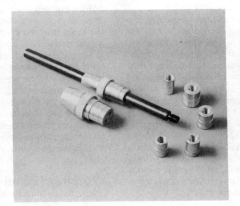

Clutch plate alignment tool

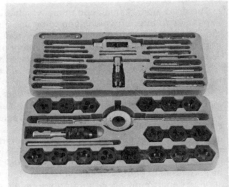

Tap and die set

To help the owner decide which tools are needed to perform the tasks detailed in this manual, the following tool lists are offered: *Maintenance and minor repair, Repair/overhaul* and *Special*.

The newcomer to practical mechanics should start off with the maintenance and minor repair tool kit, which is adequate for the simpler jobs performed on a vehicle. Then, as confidence and experience grow, the owner can tackle more difficult tasks, buying additional tools as they are needed. Eventually the basic kit will be expanded into the repair and overhaul tool set. Over a period of time, the experienced do-it-yourselfer will assemble a tool set complete enough for most repair and overhaul procedures and will add tools from the special category when it is felt that the expense is justified by the frequency of use.

Maintenance and minor repair tool kit

The tools in this list should be considered the minimum required for performance of routine maintenance, servicing and minor repair work. We recommend the purchase of combination wrenches (box-end and open-end combined in one wrench). While more expensive than open end wrenches, they offer the advantages of both types of wrench.

Combination wrench set (1/4-inch to 1 inch or 6 mm to 19 mm)
Adjustable wrench, 8 inch
Spark plug wrench with rubber insert
Spark plug gap adjusting tool
Feeler gauge set
Brake bleeder wrench
Standard screwdriver (5/16-inch x 6 inch)
Phillips screwdriver (No. 2 x 6 inch)
Combination pliers — 6 inch
Hacksaw and assortment of blades
Tire pressure gauge
Grease gun
Oil can
Fine emery cloth
Wire brush

Battery post and cable cleaning tool
Oil filter wrench
Funnel (medium size)
Safety goggles
Jackstands (2)
Drain pan

Note: *If basic tune-ups are going to be part of routine maintenance, it will be necessary to purchase a good quality stroboscopic timing light and combination tachometer/dwell meter. Although they are included in the list of special tools, it is mentioned here because they are absolutely necessary for tuning most vehicles properly.*

Repair and overhaul tool set

These tools are essential for anyone who plans to perform major repairs and are in addition to those in the maintenance and minor repair tool kit. Included is a comprehensive set of sockets which, though expensive, are invaluable because of their versatility, especially when various extensions and drives are available. We recommend the 1/2-inch drive over the 3/8-inch drive. Although the larger drive is bulky and more expensive, it has the capacity of accepting a very wide range of large sockets. Ideally, however, the mechanic should have a 3/8-inch drive set and a 1/2-inch drive set.

Socket set(s)
Reversible ratchet
Extension — 10 inch
Universal joint
Torque wrench (same size drive as sockets)
Ball peen hammer — 8 ounce
Soft-face hammer (plastic/rubber)
Standard screwdriver (1/4-inch x 6 inch)
Standard screwdriver (stubby — 5/16-inch)
Phillips screwdriver (No. 3 x 8 inch)
Phillips screwdriver (stubby — No. 2)

Pliers — vise grip
Pliers — lineman's
Pliers — needle nose
Pliers — snap-ring (internal and external)
Cold chisel — 1/2-inch
Scribe
Scraper (made from flattened copper tubing)
Centerpunch
Pin punches (1/16, 1/8, 3/16-inch)
Steel rule/straightedge — 12 inch
Allen wrench set (1/8 to 3/8-inch or 4 mm to 10 mm)
A selection of files
Wire brush (large)
Jackstands (second set)
Jack (scissor or hydraulic type)

Note: *Another tool which is often useful is an electric drill motor with a chuck capacity of 3/8-inch and a set of good quality drill bits.*

Special tools

The tools in this list include those which are not used regularly, are expensive to buy, or which need to be used in accordance with their manufacturer's instructions. Unless these tools will be used frequently, it is not very economical to purchase many of them. A consideration would be to split the cost and use between yourself and a friend or friends. In addition, most of these tools can be obtained from a tool rental shop on a temporary basis.

This list primarily contains only those tools and instruments widely available to the public, and not those special tools produced by the vehicle manufacturer for distribution to dealer service departments. Occasionally, references to the manufacturer's special tools are inluded in the text of this manual. Generally, an alternative method of doing the job without the special tool is offered. However, sometimes there is no alternative to their use. Where this is the case, and the tool cannot be purchased or borrowed, the work should be turned over to the dealer service department or an automotive repair shop.

Valve spring compressor
Piston ring groove cleaning tool
Piston ring compressor
Piston ring installation tool
Cylinder compression gauge
Cylinder ridge reamer
Cylinder surfacing hone
Cylinder bore gauge
Micrometers and/or dial calipers
Hydraulic lifter removal tool
Balljoint separator
Universal-type puller
Impact screwdriver
Dial indicator set
Stroboscopic timing light (inductive pick-up)
Hand operated vacuum/pressure pump
Tachometer/dwell meter
Universal electrical multimeter
Cable hoist
Brake spring removal and installation tools
Floor jack

Buying tools

For the do-it-yourselfer who is just starting to get involved in vehicle maintenance and repair, there are a number of options available when purchasing tools. If maintenance and minor repair is the extent of the work to be done, the purchase of individual tools is satisfactory. If,

on the other hand, extensive work is planned, it would be a good idea to purchase a modest tool set from one of the large retail chain stores. A set can usually be bought at a substantial savings over the individual tool prices, and they often come with a tool box. As additional tools are needed, add-on sets, individual tools and a larger tool box can be purchased to expand the tool selection. Building a tool set gradually allows the cost of the tools to be spread over a longer period of time and gives the mechanic the freedom to choose only those tools that will actually be used.

Tool stores will often be the only source of some of the special tools that are needed, but regardless of where tools are bought, try to avoid cheap ones, especially when buying screwdrivers and sockets, because they won't last very long. The expense involved in replacing cheap tools will eventually be greater than the initial cost of quality tools.

Care and maintenance of tools

Good tools are expensive, so it makes sense to treat them with respect. Keep them clean and in usable condition and store them properly when not in use. Always wipe off any dirt, grease or metal chips before putting them away. Never leave tools lying around in the work area. Upon completion of a job, always check closely under the hood for tools that may have been left there so they won't get lost during a test drive.

Some tools, such as screwdrivers, pliers, wrenches and sockets, can be hung on a panel mounted on the garage or workshop wall, while others should be kept in a tool box or tray. Measuring instruments, gauges, meters, etc. must be carefully stored where they cannot be damaged by weather or impact from other tools.

When tools are used with care and stored properly, they will last a very long time. Even with the best of care, though, tools will wear out if used frequently. When a tool is damaged or worn out, replace it. Subsequent jobs will be safer and more enjoyable if you do.

Working facilities

Not to be overlooked when discussing tools is the workshop. If anything more than routine maintenance is to be carried out, some sort of suitable work area is essential.

It is understood, and appreciated, that many home mechanics do not have a good workshop or garage available, and end up removing an engine or doing major repairs outside. It is recommended, however, that the overhaul or repair be completed under the cover of a roof.

A clean, flat workbench or table of comfortable working height is an absolute necessity. The workbench should be equipped with a vise that has a jaw opening of at least four inches.

As mentioned previously, some clean, dry storage space is also required for tools, as well as the lubricants, fluids, cleaning solvents, etc. which will soon become necessary.

Sometimes waste oil and fluids, drained from the engine or cooling system during normal maintenance or repairs, present a disposal problem. To avoid pouring them on the ground or into a sewage system, pour the used fluids into large containers, seal them with caps and take them to an authorized disposal site or recycling center. Plastic jugs, such as old antifreeze containers, are ideal for this purpose.

Always keep a supply of old newspapers and clean rags available. Old towels are excellent for mopping up spills. Many mechanics use rolls of paper towels for most work because they are readily available and disposable. To help keep the area under the vehicle clean, a large cardboard box can be cut open and flattened to protect the garage or shop floor.

Whenever working over a painted surface, such as when leaning over a fender to service something under the hood, always cover it with an old blanket or bedspread to protect the finish. Vinyl covered pads, made especially for this purpose, are available at auto parts stores.

Safety first!

Regardless of how enthusiastic you may be about getting on with the job at hand, take the time to ensure that your safety is not jeopardized. A moment's lack of attention can result in an accident, as can failure to observe certain simple safety precautions. The possibility of an accident will always exist, and the following points should not be considered a comprehensive list of all dangers. Rather, they are intended to make you aware of the risks and to encourage a safety conscious approach to all work you carry out on your vehicle.

Essential DOs and DON'Ts

DON'T rely on a jack when working under the vehicle. Always use approved jackstands to support the weight of the vehicle and place them under the recommended lift or support points.

DON'T attempt to loosen extremely tight fasteners (i.e. wheel lug nuts) while the vehicle is on a jack — it may fall.

DON'T start the engine without first making sure that the transmission is in Neutral (or Park where applicable) and the parking brake is set.

DON'T remove the radiator cap from a hot cooling system — let it cool or cover it with a cloth and release the pressure gradually.

DON'T attempt to drain the engine oil until you are sure it has cooled to the point that it will not burn you.

DON'T touch any part of the engine or exhaust system until it has cooled sufficiently to avoid burns.

DON'T siphon toxic liquids such as gasoline, antifreeze and brake fluid by mouth, or allow them to remain on your skin.

DON'T inhale brake lining dust — it is potentially hazardous (see *Asbestos* below)

DON'T allow spilled oil or grease to remain on the floor — wipe it up before someone slips on it.

DON'T use loose fitting wrenches or other tools which may slip and cause injury.

DON'T push on wrenches when loosening or tightening nuts or bolts. Always try to pull the wrench toward you. If the situation calls for pushing the wrench away, push with an open hand to avoid scraped knuckles if the wrench should slip.

DON'T attempt to lift a heavy component alone — get someone to help you.

DON'T rush or take unsafe shortcuts to finish a job.

DON'T allow children or animals in or around the vehicle while you are working on it.

DO wear eye protection when using power tools such as a drill, sander, bench grinder, etc. and when working under a vehicle.

DO keep loose clothing and long hair well out of the way of moving parts.

DO make sure that any hoist used has a safe working load rating adequate for the job.

DO get someone to check on you periodically when working alone on a vehicle.

DO carry out work in a logical sequence and make sure that everything is correctly assembled and tightened.

DO keep chemicals and fluids tightly capped and out of the reach of children and pets.

DO remember that your vehicle's safety affects that of yourself and others. If in doubt on any point, get professional advice.

Asbestos

Certain friction, insulating, sealing, and other products — such as brake linings, brake bands, clutch linings, torque converters, gaskets, etc. — contain asbestos. *Extreme care must be taken to avoid inhalation of dust from such products since it is hazardous to health.* If in doubt, assume that they *do* contain asbestos.

Fire

Remember at all times that gasoline is highly flammable. Never smoke or have any kind of open flame around when working on a vehicle. But the risk does not end there. A spark caused by an electrical short circuit, by two metal surfaces contacting each other, or even by static electricity built up in your body under certain conditions, can ignite gasoline vapors, which in a confined space are highly explosive. Do not, under any circumstances, use gasoline for cleaning parts. Use an approved safety solvent.

Always disconnect the battery ground (–) cable *at the battery* before working on any part of the fuel system or electrical system. Never risk spilling fuel on a hot engine or exhaust component.

It is strongly recommended that a fire extinguisher suitable for use on fuel and electrical fires be kept handy in the garage or workshop at all times. Never try to extinguish a fuel or electrical fire with water.

Torch (flashlight in the US)

Any reference to a ''torch'' appearing in this manual should always be taken to mean a hand-held, battery-operated electric light or flashlight. It DOES NOT mean a welding or propane torch or blowtorch.

Fumes

Certain fumes are highly toxic and can quickly cause unconsciousness and even death if inhaled to any extent. Gasoline vapor falls into this category, as do the vapors from some cleaning solvents. Any draining or pouring of such volatile fluids should be done in a well ventilated area.

When using cleaning fluids and solvents, read the instructions on the container carefully. Never use materials from unmarked containers.

Never run the engine in an enclosed space, such as a garage. Exhaust fumes contain carbon monoxide, which is extremely poisonous. If you need to run the engine, always do so in the open air, or at least have the rear of the vehicle outside the work area.

If you are fortunate enough to have the use of an inspection pit, never drain or pour gasoline and never run the engine while the vehicle is over the pit. The fumes, being heavier than air, will concentrate in the pit with possibly lethal results.

The battery

Never create a spark or allow a bare light bulb near a battery. They normally give off a certain amount of hydrogen gas, which is highly explosive.

Always disconnect the battery ground (–) cable *at the battery* before working on the fuel or electrical systems.

If possible, loosen the filler caps or cover when charging the battery from an external source (this does not apply to sealed or maintenance-free batteries). Do not charge at an excessive rate or the battery may burst.

Take care when adding water to a non maintenance-free battery and when carrying a battery. The electrolyte, even when diluted, is very corrosive and should not be allowed to contact clothing or skin.

Always wear eye protection when cleaning the battery to prevent the caustic deposits from entering your eyes.

Mains electricity (household current in the US)

When using an electric power tool, inspection light, etc., which operates on household current, always make sure that the tool is correctly connected to its plug and that, where necessary, it is properly grounded. Do not use such items in damp conditions and, again, do not create a spark or apply excessive heat in the vicinity of fuel or fuel vapor.

Secondary ignition system voltage

A severe electric shock can result from touching certain parts of the ignition system (such as the spark plug wires) when the engine is running or being cranked, particularly if components are damp or the insulation is defective. In the case of an electronic ignition system, the secondary system voltage is much higher and could prove fatal.

Routine maintenance

The maintenance schedules below are basically those recommended by the manufacturer. Servicing intervals are determined by mileage or time elapsed — this is because fluids and systems deteriorate with age as well as with use. Follow the time intervals if the appropriate mileage is not covered within the specified period.

Vehicles operating under adverse conditions need more frequent maintenance. Adverse conditions include climatic extremes, full-time towing or taxi work, driving on unpaved roads, and a high proportion of short journeys. In such cases the engine oil and filter should be changed every 3000 miles (5000 km) or three months, whichever comes first.

Weekly, every 250 miles (400 km), or before a long journey

Check tire pressures and inspect tires (Chapter 10, Sec 32)
Check engine oil level (Chapter 1, Sec 2 or 48)
Check coolant level (Chapter 2, Sec 2)
Check brake fluid level (Chapter 9, Sec 3)
Top up washer reservoir(s) (Chapter 12, Sec 28)
Inspect engine bay and under vehicle for leaks
Check function of lights, horn, wipers, etc.

Every 6000 miles (10,000 km) or six months, whichever comes first

Replace engine oil and filter (Chapter 1, Secs 2 and 3/48 and 49)
Check power steering fluid level (Chapter 10, Sec 3)
Check coolant antifreeze concentration (Chapter 2, Sec 2)
Replace spark plugs (Chapter 4, Sec 3)
Inspect battery (Chapter 12, Sec 3)
Check idle speed and CO level (Chapter 3, Sec 8)
Inspect tires thoroughly (Chapter 10, Sec 32)
ABS: check that spare wheel well drain is clear

Every 12,000 miles (20,000 km) or twelve months, whichever comes first

In addition to the work previously specified
Check operation of power brake booster (Chapter 9, Sec 6)
Check handbrake adjustment (Chapter 9, Sec 7)
Check automatic transmission selector adjustment (Chapter 6, Sec 39)
Grease hood hinges
Check front wheel bearing adjustment (Chapter 10, Sec 4)
Check security and condition of steering and suspension components (Chapter 10, Sec 2)

Check brake pad wear (Chapter 9, Secs 4 and 5)
Inspect brake hydraulic lines and hoses (Chapter 9, Sec 8)
Check tightness of trailing arm nuts, control arm, strut and steering gear fastenings, and front axle crossmember bolts. (First 12,000 miles only). (Chapter 10, Sec 2)
Check clutch adjustment (when applicable) (Chapter 5, Sec 3)
Check transmission oil level (Chapter 6, Sec 2 or 28)
Inspect driveshaft, center bearing and universal joints (Chapter 7, Sec 2)
Check condition and security of exhaust system (Chapter 3, Sec 19)
Check rear axle oil level (Chapter 8, Sec 3)
Check condition of fuel lines
Thoroughly inspect engine for fluid leaks
Check condition of underseal and paintwork (Chapter 11, Sec 2)
Inspect in-line fuel filter (carburetor models) (Chapter 3, Sec 2)
Check condition and tension of accessory drivebelts(s) (Chapter 4, Sec 2)
Lubricate distributor felt pad (B28E engine only) (Chapter 4, Sec 2)
Inspect distributor cap, rotor and HT leads (Chapter 4, Sec 2)
Check turbo boost pressure switches (when applicable) (Chapter 3, Sec 45)
Check turbo tamperproof seals (when applicable) on wastegate actuator rod
Check operation of kickdown cable (automatic transmission) and adjust if necessary (Chapter 6, Sec 31)

Every 24,000 miles (40,000 km) or two years, whichever comes first

In addition to the work previously specified
Replace automatic transmission fluid (Chapter 6, Sec 29)
Replace fuel filter (Chapter 3, Sec 7)
Replace air cleaner element (Chapter 3, Sec 5)
Clean crankcase ventilation hoses, flame trap, etc (Chapter 1, Sec 5 or 51)
Check valve clearances, (Chapter 1, Sec 4 or 50)
Perform a compression test (Chapter 1, Sec 45 or 96)
Replace coolant (Chapter 2, Secs 3 to 5)
Replace brake fluid by bleeding (Chapter 9, Sec 9); at the same time consider replacing rubber seals and flexible hoses as a precautionary measure

Every 48,000 miles (80,000 km) or four years, whichever comes first

In addition to the work previously specified
Replace camshaft drivebelt (B 23/B 230 engines) (Chapter 1, Sec 6)

Note: *The vehicles on pages 19 through 23 are right-hand drive models. Vehicles sold in North America are left-hand drive, so brake, clutch and steering components are on the opposite side.*

Under-hood view of a Volvo 760 GLE

1 Battery
2 Ignition control unit
3 Ignition coil
4 Air conditioning compressor
5 Engine oil dipstick
6 Suspension turrets
7 Identification plate
8 Ignition vacuum advance valve
9 Brake fluid reservoir
10 Power brake booster
11 Engine oil filler cap
12 Air control valve
13 Fuel distributor
14 Automatic transmission dipstick
15 Vacuum pump
16 Air conditioner receiver/drier
17 Fuel filter
18 Coolant expansion tank
19 Air cleaner
20 Windshield washer filler cap
21 Hood catches
22 Radiator
23 Power steering reservoir
24 Left-hand rocker cover
25 Inlet manifold
26 Air intake
27 Compressor drivebelt
28 Radiator top hose
29 Throttle cable

Under-hood view of a Volvo 760 Turbo

1 Windshield washer filler cap
2 Air cleaner
3 Airflow meter
4 Coolant expansion tank
5 Suspension turrets
6 Identification plate
7 Brake and clutch fluid reservoir
8 Power brake booster
9 Turbocharger
10 Turbo air outlet
11 Bypass valve
12 Bypass valve hose
13 Engine oil filler cap
14 HT leads
15 Clutch master cylinder
16 Auxiliary air valve
17 Vacuum delay valve
18 Engine oil dipstick
19 Throttle linkage
20 Air conditioner receiver/drier
21 Ignition coil
22 Power steering pump and reservoir
23 Fuel pressure regulator
24 Ignition distributor
25 Radiator top hose
26 Battery
27 Hood catches
28 Intercooler
29 Radiator

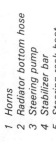

Front underside view of a Volvo 760 GLE

1 Horns
2 Radiator bottom hose
3 Steering pump
4 Stabilizer bar
5 Steering rack boot
6 Tie-rods
7 Control arms
8 Radius rods
9 Brake calipers
10 Transmission dipstick/filler tube
11 Transmission drain plug
12 Exhaust pipe
13 Transmission fluid cooler lines
14 Steering hydraulic unions
15 Jacking plate
16 Engine oil drain plug
17 Refrigerant lines (air conditioning)

Front underside view of a Volvo 760 Turbo

1 Horn	7 Tie-rods	13 Clutch slave cylinder	19 Damper
2 Refrigerant lines (air conditioning)	8 Control arms	14 Transmission filler/level plug	20 Driveshaft flange
3 Oil cooler hoses	9 Radius rods	15 Transmission drain plug	21 Exhaust pipe
4 Vacuum tank	10 Brake calipers	16 Transmission mounting	22 Steering intermediate shaft
5 Stabilizer bar	11 Engine oil drain plug	17 Overdrive solenoid	23 Steering hydraulic unions
6 Steering rack boots	12 Brace	18 Overdrive	24 Jacking plate
			25 Radiator bottom hose

Rear underside view of a Volvo 760 Turbo

1 Mud deflector	6 Shock absorber	10 Panhard rod	15 Muffler
2 Main fuel tank	lower mountings	11 Rear axle	16 Subframe
3 Trailing arm brackets	7 Spring pans	12 Rear axle drain plug	17 Driveshaft
4 Rear jacking points	8 Spare wheel well	13 Torque rod	18 Fuel tank breather
5 Trailing arms	9 Stabilizer bar	14 Exhaust pipe	

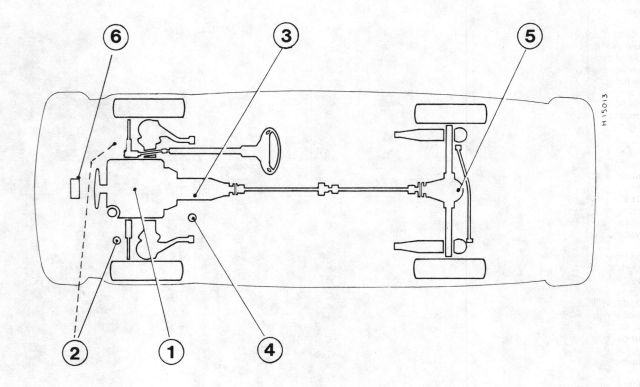

Recommended lubricants and fluids

Component or system	Lubricant type or specification
1 Engine oil	Multigrade engine oil, viscosity range 10W/30 to 15W/50, to API SF/CC, SF/CD or better
2 Cooling system	Volvo coolant type C and clean water
3 Manual transmission:	
Temperate climate	Volve Thermo Oil
Cold climate	ATF type F or G
4 Automatic transmission:	
Models up to 1983	ATF type F or G
1984 and later models	ATF type Dexron® II D
5 Rear axle:	
Except limited slip differential	Gear oil SAE 90 EP to API GL 5 or 6
Limited slip differential	Special Volvo oil (No 1 161 276-9), or gear oil as above with Volvo additive (No 1 161 129-0)
6 Power steering	ATF type A, F or G
Brake hydraulic system	Brake fluid to DCT 4

Note: *The above are general recommendations. Lubrication requirements may vary in climatic extremes and/or under severe conditions of use. Consult a Volvo dealer, or the operations handbook supplied with the vehicle*

Conversion factors

Length (distance)

	X		=		X		=	
Inches (in)	X	25.4	=	Millimetres (mm)	X	0.0394	=	Inches (in)
Feet (ft)	X	0.305	=	Metres (m)	X	3.281	=	Feet (ft)
Miles	X	1.609	=	Kilometres (km)	X	0.621	=	Miles

Volume (capacity)

	X		=		X		=	
Cubic inches (cu in; in³)	X	16.387	=	Cubic centimetres (cc; cm³)	X	0.061	=	Cubic inches (cu in; in³)
Imperial pints (Imp pt)	X	0.568	=	Litres (l)	X	1.76	=	Imperial pints (Imp pt)
Imperial quarts (Imp qt)	X	1.137	=	Litres (l)	X	0.88	=	Imperial quarts (Imp qt)
Imperial quarts (Imp qt)	X	1.201	=	US quarts (US qt)	X	0.833	=	Imperial quarts (Imp qt)
US quarts (US qt)	X	0.946	=	Litres (l)	X	1.057	=	US quarts (US qt)
Imperial gallons (Imp gal)	X	4.546	=	Litres (l)	X	0.22	=	Imperial gallons (Imp gal)
Imperial gallons (Imp gal)	X	1.201	=	US gallons (US gal)	X	0.833	=	Imperial gallons (Imp gal)
US gallons (US gal)	X	3.785	=	Litres (l)	X	0.264	=	US gallons (US gal)

Mass (weight)

	X		=		X		=	
Ounces (oz)	X	28.35	=	Grams (g)	X	0.035	=	Ounces (oz)
Pounds (lb)	X	0.454	=	Kilograms (kg)	X	2.205	=	Pounds (lb)

Force

	X		=		X		=	
Ounces-force (ozf; oz)	X	0.278	=	Newtons (N)	X	3.6	=	Ounces-force (ozf; oz)
Pounds-force (lbf; lb)	X	4.448	=	Newtons (N)	X	0.225	=	Pounds-force (lbf; lb)
Newtons (N)	X	0.1	=	Kilograms-force (kgf; kg)	X	9.81	=	Newtons (N)

Pressure

	X		=		X		=	
Pounds-force per square inch (psi; lbf/in²; lb/in²)	X	0.070	=	Kilograms-force per square centimetre (kgf/cm²; kg/cm²)	X	14.223	=	Pounds-force per square inch (psi; lbf/in²; lb/in²)
Pounds-force per square inch (psi; lbf/in²; lb/in²)	X	0.068	=	Atmospheres (atm)	X	14.696	=	Pounds-force per square inch (psi; lbf/in²; lb/in²)
Pounds-force per square inch (psi; lbf/in²; lb/in²)	X	0.069	=	Bars	X	14.5	=	Pounds-force per square inch (psi; lbf/in²; lb/in²)
Pounds-force per square inch (psi; lbf/in²; lb/in²)	X	6.895	=	Kilopascals (kPa)	X	0.145	=	Pounds-force per square inch (psi; lbf/in²; lb/in²)
Kilopascals (kPa)	X	0.01	=	Kilograms-force per square centimetre (kgf/cm²; kg/cm²)	X	98.1	=	Kilopascals (kPa)
Millibar (mbar)	X	100	=	Pascals (Pa)	X	0.01	=	Millibar (mbar)
Millibar (mbar)	X	0.0145	=	Pounds-force per square inch (psi; lbf/in²; lb/in²)	X	68.947	=	Millibar (mbar)
Millibar (mbar)	X	0.75	=	Millimetres of mercury (mmHg)	X	1.333	=	Millibar (mbar)
Millibar (mbar)	X	0.401	=	Inches of water (inH₂O)	X	2.491	=	Millibar (mbar)
Millimetres of mercury (mmHg)	X	0.535	=	Inches of water (inH₂O)	X	1.868	=	Millimetres of mercury (mmHg)
Inches of water (inH₂O)	X	0.036	=	Pounds-force per square inch (psi; lbf/in²; lb/in²)	X	27.68	=	Inches of water (inH₂O)

Torque (moment of force)

	X		=		X		=	
Pounds-force inches (lbf in; lb in)	X	1.152	=	Kilograms-force centimetre (kgf cm; kg cm)	X	0.868	=	Pounds-force inches (lbf in; lb in)
Pounds-force inches (lbf in; lb in)	X	0.113	=	Newton metres (Nm)	X	8.85	=	Pounds-force inches (lbf in; lb in)
Pounds-force inches (lbf in; lb in)	X	0.083	=	Pounds-force feet (lbf ft; lb ft)	X	12	=	Pounds-force inches (lbf in; lb in)
Pounds-force feet (lbf ft; lb ft)	X	0.138	=	Kilograms-force metres (kgf m; kg m)	X	7.233	=	Pounds-force feet (lbf ft; lb ft)
Pounds-force feet (lbf ft; lb ft)	X	1.356	=	Newton metres (Nm)	X	0.738	=	Pounds-force feet (lbf ft; lb ft)
Newton metres (Nm)	X	0.102	=	Kilograms-force metres (kgf m; kg m)	X	9.804	=	Newton metres (Nm)

Power

	X		=		X		=	
Horsepower (hp)	X	745.7	=	Watts (W)	X	0.0013	=	Horsepower (hp)

Velocity (speed)

	X		=		X		=	
Miles per hour (miles/hr; mph)	X	1.609	=	Kilometres per hour (km/hr; kph)	X	0.621	=	Miles per hour (miles/hr; mph)

Fuel consumption*

	X		=		X		=	
Miles per gallon, Imperial (mpg)	X	0.354	=	Kilometres per litre (km/l)	X	2.825	=	Miles per gallon, Imperial (mpg)
Miles per gallon, US (mpg)	X	0.425	=	Kilometres per litre (km/l)	X	2.352	=	Miles per gallon, US (mpg)

Temperature

Degrees Fahrenheit = ($°C \times 1.8$) + 32

Degrees Celsius (Degrees Centigrade; °C) = ($°F - 32$) x 0.56

*It is common practice to convert from miles per gallon (mpg) to litres/100 kilometres (l/100km), where mpg (Imperial) x l/100 km = 282 and mpg (US) x l/100 km = 235

Troubleshooting

Introduction

The vehicle owner who does his or her own maintenance according to the recommended schedules should not have to use this section of the manual very often. Modern component reliability is such that, provided those items subject to wear or deterioration are inspected or replaced at the specified intervals, sudden failure is comparatively rare. Problems do not usually just happen as a result of sudden failure, but develop over a period of time. Major mechanical failures in particular are usually preceded by characteristic symptoms over hundreds or even thousands of miles. Those components which do occasionally fail without warning are often small and easily carried in the vehicle.

With any troubleshooting, the first step is to decide where to begin. Sometimes this is obvious, but on other occasions a little detective work will be necessary. The owner who makes half a dozen haphazard adjustments or replacements may be successful in curing a fault (or its symptoms), but he will be none the wiser if the fault recurs and he may well have spent more time and money than was necessary. A calm and logical approach is better in the long run. Always take into account any warning signs or abnormalities that may have been noticed in the period preceding the fault — power loss, high or low gauge readings, unusual noises or smells, etc — and remember that failure of components such as fuses or spark plugs may only be indications of an underlying fault.

The pages which follow here are intended to help in cases of failure to start or breakdown on the road. There is also a Fault Diagnosis Section at the end of each Chapter which should be consulted if the preliminary checks prove unfruitful. Whatever the fault, certain basic principles apply. These are as follows:

Verify the fault. This is simply a matter of being sure that you know what the symptoms are before starting work. This is particularly important if you are investigating a fault for someone else who may not have described it very accurately.

Don't overlook the obvious. For example, if the vehicle won't start, is there gas in the tank? (Don't take anyone else's word on this particular point, and don't trust the fuel gauge either!) If an electrical fault is indicated, look for loose or broken wires before digging out the test gear.

Cure the disease, not the symptom. Substituting a dead battery with a fully charged one will get the vehicle started, but if the underlying cause is not attended to, the new battery will go the same way. Similarly, changing oil-fouled spark plugs for a new set will get you moving again, but remember that the reason for the fouling (if it wasn't simply an incorrect grade of plug) will have to be established and corrected.

Don't take anything for granted. Particularly, don't forget that a new' component may itself be defective (especially if it's been rattling round in the trunk for months), and don't leave components out of a fault diagnosis sequence just because they are new or recently installed. When you do finally diagnose a difficult fault, you'll probably realize that all the evidence was there from the start.

Electrical faults

Electrical faults can be more puzzling than mechanical failures, but they are no less susceptible to logical analysis if the basic principles

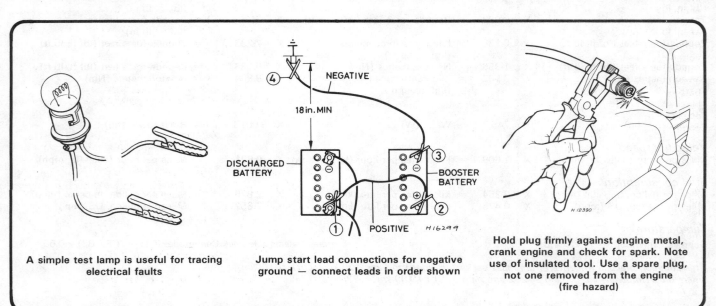

A simple test lamp is useful for tracing electrical faults

Jump start lead connections for negative ground — connect leads in order shown

Hold plug firmly against engine metal, crank engine and check for spark. Note use of insulated tool. Use a spare plug, not one removed from the engine (fire hazard)

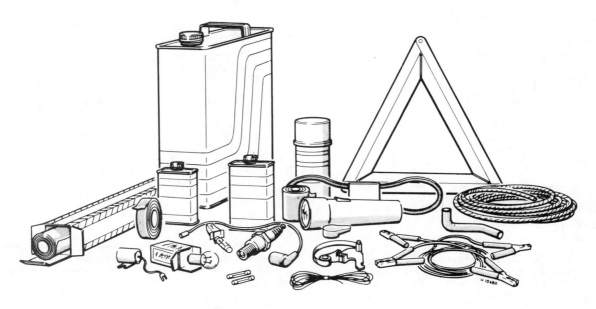

Carrying a few spare parts can save you a long walk

of operation are understood. Vehicle electrical wiring exists in extremely unfavorable conditions — heat, vibration and chemical attack — and the first things to look for are loose or corroded connections and broken or chafed wires, especially where the wires pass through holes in the body or are subject to vibration.

All metal-bodied vehicles in current production have one terminal of the battery grounded, ie connected to the vehicle body, and in nearly all modern vehicles it is the negative (-) terminal. The various electrical components — motors, bulb holders etc — are also connected to ground, either by a lead or directly by the mount. Electric current flows through the component and then back to the battery via the body. If the component mounting is loose or corroded, or if a good path back to the battery is not available, the circuit will be incomplete and malfunction will result. The engine and/or transmission are also grounded by flexible metal straps to the body or subframe; if the straps are loose or missing, starter motor, alternator and ignition trouble may result.

Assuming the ground to be satisfactory, electrical faults will be due either to component malfunction or to defects in the current supply. Individual components are dealt with in Chapter 12. If wires are broken or cracked internally this results in an open-circuit, and the easiest way to check for it is to bypass the suspect wire temporarily with a length of wire having an alligator clip or suitable connector at each end. Alternately, a 12V test light can be used to verify the presence of supply voltage at various points along the wire and the break can be isolated.

If a bare portion of a live wire touches the body or other grounded metal part, the electricity will take the low-resistance path back to the battery: this is known as a short-circuit. Hopefully a short-circuit will blow a fuse, but otherwise it may cause burning of the insulation (and possibly further short-circuits) or even a fire. This is why it is not a good idea to bypass persistently blowing fuses.

Spare parts and tool kit

Most vehicles are supplied only with sufficient tools for tire changing; the Maintenance and minor repair tool kit detailed in Tools and working facilities, with the addition of a hammer, is probably sufficient for most repairs. In addition a few items which can be installed without too much trouble in the event of a breakdown should be carried. Experience and available space will modify the list below, but the following may save having to call for professional assistance:

Spark plugs, clean and correctly gapped
HT lead and plug cap — long enough to reach the plug furthest from the distributor
Distributor rotor
Drivebelt(s) — emergency type may suffice

Spare fuses
Set of light bulbs
Roll of insulating tape
Length of wire
Flashlight
Battery jumper leads
Tow-rope
Ignition waterproofing aerosol
Can of engine oil
Sealed can of brake fluid

If spare fuel is carried, a can designed for the purpose should be used to minimize risks of leakage and collision damage. A first aid kit and a warning triangle are obviously sensible items to carry in addition to the above.

Engine will not start

Engine fails to turn when starter operated

Dead battery (recharge, use jumper leads, or push start)
Battery terminals loose or corroded
Battery ground to body defective
Engine ground strap loose or broken
Starter motor (or solenoid) wiring loose or broken
Automatic transmission selector in wrong position, or inhibitor switch defective
Ignition/starter switch defective
Major mechanical failure (seizure)
Starter or solenoid internal fault (see Chapter 12)

Starter motor turns engine slowly

Partially discharged battery (recharge, use jumper leads, or push start)
Battery terminals loose or corroded
Battery ground to body defective
Engine ground strap loose
Starter motor (or solenoid) wiring loose
Starter motor internal fault (see Chapter 12)

Starter motor spins without turning engine

Flywheel gear teeth damaged or worn
Starter motor mounting bolts loose

Engine turns normally but fails to start

Damp or dirty HT leads and distributor cap (crank engine and check for spark)
No fuel in tank (check for delivery at start injector)
Fouled or incorrectly gapped spark plugs (remove, clean and regap)
Other ignition system fault (see Chapter 4)
Other fuel system fault (see Chapter 3)
Poor compression (see Chapter 1)
Major mechanical failure (eg camshaft drive)

Engine fires but will not run

Air leaks at intake manifold
Fuel starvation (see Chapter 3)
Ballast resistor defective, or other ignition fault (see Chapter 4)

Engine cuts out and will not restart

Engine cuts out suddenly — ignition fault

Loose or disconnected LT wires
Wet HT leads or distributor cap
Coil failure (check for spark)
Other ignition fault (see Chapter 4)

Engine misfires before cutting out — fuel fault

Fuel tank empty
Fuel pump defective or filter blocked (check for delivery)
Fuel tank filler vent blocked (suction will be evident on releasing cap)
Other fuel system fault (see Chapter 3)

Engine cuts out — other causes

Serious overheating
Major mechanical failure (eg camshaft drive)

Engine overheats

Loose or broken drivebelt
Coolant loss due to internal or external leakage (see Chapter 2)
Thermostat defective
Low oil level
Brakes binding
Radiator clogged
Electric cooling fan not operating correctly
Engine coolant passages clogged
Ignition timing incorrect or automatic advance malfunctioning
Mixture too weak

Note: *Do not add cold water to an overheated engine or damage may result*

Low engine oil pressure

Warning light illuminated with engine running

Oil level low or incorrect grade
Defective sending unit
Wire to sending unit grounded
Engine overheating
Oil filter clogged or bypass valve defective
Oil pressure relief valve defective
Oil pick-up strainer clogged
Oil pump worn or mounts loose
Worn engine bearings

Note: *Low oil pressure in a high-mileage engine at idle is not necessarily a cause for concern. Sudden pressure loss at speed is far more significant. In any event, check the sending unit before condemning the engine.*

Engine noises

Pre-ignition during acceleration

Incorrect grade of fuel
Ignition timing incorrect
Distributor defective or worn
Excessive carbon build-up in engine
Crankcase ventilation system blocked (can also cause oil leaks)

Whistling or wheezing noises

Leaking vacuum hose
Leaking manifold gasket
Blown head gasket

Tapping or rattling

Incorrect valve clearances
Worn valve gear
Worn timing chain or belt
Broken piston ring (ticking noise)

Knocking or thumping

Unintentional mechanical contact (eg fan blades)
Worn drivebelt
Peripheral component defective (alternator, water pump etc)
Worn connecting rod bearings (regular heavy knocking, perhaps less under load)
Worn main bearings (rumbling and knocking, perhaps worsening under load)
Piston slap (most noticeable when cold)

Chapter 1 Engine

Contents

1

Specifications

Part A: In-line engine

General

Engine type	4-stroke, 4-cylinder in-line, ohc, spark ignition, water-cooled
Identification:	
B23FT	Fuel injection, turbocharged, up to 1984
B230F	Fuel injection, normally aspirated, from 1985 model year
B230FT	Fuel injection, turbocharged, from 1985 model year
Bore	96 mm (3.782 in) nominal
Stroke	80 mm (3.152 in)
Cubic capacity	2316 cc (141.4 cu in)
Compression ratio:	
B23FT and B230FT	8.7:1
B230F	9.8:1
Compression pressure:	
Overall value	131 to 160 psi
Variation between cylinders	29 psi max
Firing order	1-3-4-2 (No 1 at front)

Cylinder head

Warp limit — acceptable for use:	
Lengthwise	0.50 mm (0.020 in)
Across	0.25 mm (0.010 in)
Warp limit — acceptable for refinishing:	
Lengthwise	1.00 mm (0.040 in)
Across	0.50 mm (0.020 in)
Height:	
New	146.1 mm (5.756 in)
Minimum after refinishing	145.6 mm (5.736 in)

Cylinder bores

Standard sizes:	
C	96.00 to 96.01 mm (3.7824 to 3.7828 in)
D	96.01 to 96.02 mm (3.7828 to 3.7832 in)
E	96.02 to 96.03 mm (3.7832 to 3.7836 in)
G	96.04 to 96.05 mm (3.7840 to 3.7844 in)
First oversize	96.30 mm (3.7942 in)
Second oversize	96.60 mm (3.8060 in)
Wear limit	0.1 mm (0.004 in)

Pistons

Running clearance	
B23	0.05 to 0.07 mm (0.0020 to 0.0028 in)
B230	0.01 to 0.03 mm (0.0004 to 0.0012 in)

Piston rings

Clearance in groove:	
Top compression	0.060 to 0.092 mm (0.0024 to 0.0036 in)
Second compression	0.040 to 0.072 mm (0.0016 to 0.0028 in)
Oil control	0.030 to 0.065 mm (0.0012 to 0.0026 in)
End gap (in 96.00 mm/3.7795 in bore):	
Compression rings, B23	0.40 to 0.65 mm (0.016 to 0.026 in)
Compression rings, B230	0.30 to 0.55 mm (0.012 to 0.022 in)
Oil control	0.30 to 0.60 mm (0.012 to 0.024 in)

Piston pins

Fit in connecting rod	Light thumb pressure
Fit in piston	Firm thumb pressure

Valve clearances (intake and exhaust)

Checking value:	
Cold engine	0.30 to 0.40 mm (0.012 to 0.016 in)
Warm engine	0.35 to 0.45 mm (0.014 to 0.018 in)
Setting value:	
Cold engine	0.35 to 0.40 mm (0.014 to 0.016 in)
Warm engine	0.40 to 0.45 mm (0.016 to 0.018 in)
Adjusting shims available	3.30 to 4.50 mm (0.1299 to 0.1772 in) in steps of 0.05 mm (0.0020 in)

Intake valves

Head diameter	44 mm (1.733 in)
Stem diameter:	
New	7.955 to 7.970 mm (0.3134 to 0.3140 in)

Wear limit . . . . 7.935 mm (0.3126 in)
Valve head angle* . . . . 44° 30'

Exhaust valves
Head diameter . . . . 35 mm (1.379 in)
Stem diameter (B230 F):
  New . . . . 7.945 to 7.960 mm (0.3130 to 0.3136 in)
  Wear limit . . . . 7.925 mm (0.3122 in)
Stem diameter (B23 and 230 FT):
  32 mm (1.26 in) from head . . . . Same as B230 F
  16 mm (0.63 in) from tip:
    New . . . . 7.965 to 7.980 mm (0.3138 to 0.3144 in)
    Wear limit . . . . 7.945 mm (0.3130 in)
Valve head angle* . . . . 44° 30'

* Valves are Stellite coated and cannot be machined

Valve seat inserts
Diameter (standard):
  Intake . . . . 46.00 mm (1.8124 in)
  Exhaust . . . . 38.00 mm (1.4972 in)
Oversizes available . . . . + 0.25 and 0.50 mm (0.0098 and 0.0197 in)
Fit in cylinder head . . . . 0.17 mm (0.0067 in) interference
Valve seat angle . . . . 45° 00'

Valve guides
Length . . . . 52 mm (2.048 in)
Internal diameter . . . . 8.000 to 8.022 mm (0.3152 to 0.3160 in)
Height above cylinder head:
  Intake . . . . 15.4 to 15.6 mm (0.606 to 0.614 in)
  Exhaust . . . . 17.9 to 18.1 mm (0.705 to 0.713 in)
Stem-to-guide clearance:
  New (intake) . . . . 0.030 to 0.060 mm (0.0012 to 0.0024 in)
  New (exhaust) . . . . 0.060 to 0.090 mm (0.0024 to 0.0035 in)
  Wear limit (intake and exhaust) . . . . 0.15 mm (0.0059 in)
Fit in head . . . . Press (9000 N/2025 lbs minimum)
External oversizes available . . . . 3 (marked by grooves)

Valve springs
Diameter . . . . 25.9 mm (1.02 in)
Free length . . . . 45.5 mm (1.79 in)
Length under load of:
  280 to 320 N (63 to 72 lbs) . . . . 38.0 mm (1.50 in)
  710 to 790 N (160 to 178 lbs) . . . . 27.5 mm (1.08 in)

Tappets (cam followers)
Diameter . . . . 36.975 to 36.995 mm (1.4568 to 1.4576 in)
Height . . . . 30.000 to 31.000 mm (1.182 to 1.221 in)
Shim clearance in tappet . . . . 0.009 to 0.064 mm (0.0004 to 0.0025 in)
Tappet clearance in cylinder head . . . . 0.030 to 0.075 mm (0.0012 to 0.0030 in)

Camshaft
Identification letter (stamped on end):
  B23FT . . . . T
  B230F . . . . M
  B230FT . . . . T
Maximum lift:
  T . . . . 9.9 mm (0.3901 in)
  M
    Intake . . . . 9.5 mm (0.374 in)
    Exhaust . . . . 10.5 mm (0.414 in)
Bearing journal diameter . . . . 20.950 to 29.970 mm (1.1791 to 1.1799 in)
Bearing running clearance:
  New . . . . 0.030 to 0.071 mm (0.0012 to 0.0028 in)
  Wear limit . . . . 0.15 mm (0.0059 in)
  Endplay . . . . 0.1 to 0.4 mm (0.004 to 0.016 in)

Auxiliary shaft
Bearing journal diameter:
  Front . . . . 46.975 to 47.000 mm (1.8508 to 1.8518 in)
  Center . . . . 43.025 to 43.050 mm (1.6951 to 1.6961 in)
  Rear . . . . 42.925 to 42.950 mm (1.6912 to 1.6922 in)
Bearing running clearance . . . . 0.020 to 0.075 mm (0.0008 to 0.0030 in)
Endplay . . . . 0.20 to 0.46 mm (0.008 to 0.018 in)

Crankshaft — B23
Run-out . . . . 0.05 mm (0.0019 in) max
Endplay . . . . 0.25 mm (0.0098 in) max

Main bearing journal diameter:
    Standard . . . .   63.451 to 63.464 mm (2.4999 to 2.5004 in)
    First undersize. . . . .   63.197 to 63.210 mm (2.4899 to 2.4904 in)
    Second undersize . . . .   62.943 to 62.956 mm (2.4800 to 2.4805 in)
Main bearing running clearance . . . .   0.028 to 0.083 mm (0.0011 to 0.0033 in)
Main bearing out-of-round . . . .   0.07 mm (0.0028 in) max
Main bearing taper . . . .   0.05 mm (0.0020 in) max
Connecting rod bearing journal diameter:
    Standard . . . .   53.987 to 54.000 mm (2.1270 to 2.1276 in)
    First undersize. . . . .   53.733 to 53.746 mm (2.1170 to 2.1175 in)
    Second undersize . . . .   53.479 to 53.492 mm (2.1070 to 2.1075 in)
Connecting rod bearing running clearance . . . .   0.024 to 0.070 mm (0.0009 to 0.0028 in)
Connecting rod bearing out-of-round . . . .   0.05 mm (0.0019 in) max
Connecting rod bearing taper . . . .   0.05 mm (0.0019 in) max

Crankshaft — B230

Run-out . . . .   0.025 mm (0.0009 in) max
Endplay . . . .   0.080 to 0.270 mm (0.003 to 0.011 in)
Main bearing journal diameter:
    Standard . . . .   54.987 to 55.000 mm (2.1665 to 2.1670 in)
    First undersize. . . . .   54.737 to 54.750 mm (2.1556 to 2.1571 in)
    Second undersize . . . .   54.487 to 54.500 mm (2.1467 to 2.1473 in)
Main bearing running clearance . . . .   0.024 to 0.072 mm (0.0009 to 0.0028 in)
Main bearing out-of-round . . . .   0.004 mm (0.0002 in) max
Main bearing taper . . . .   0.004 mm (0.0002 in) max
Connecting rod bearing journal diameter:
    Standard . . . .   48.984 to 49.005 mm (1.9300 to 1.9307 in)
    First undersize. . . . .   48.734 to 48.755 mm (1.9201 to 1.9209 in)
    Second undersize . . . .   48.484 to 48.505 mm (1.9102 to 1.9110 in)
Connecting rod bearing running clearance . . . .   0.023 to 0.067 mm (0.0009 to 0.0026 in)
Connecting rod bearing out-of-round . . . .   0.004 mm (0.0002 in) max
Connecting rod bearing taper . . . .   0.004 mm (0.0002 in) max

Connecting rods

Side clearance:
    B23 . . . .   0.15 to 0.35 mm (0.006 to 0.014 in)
    B230 . . . .   0.25 to 0.45 mm (0.010 to 0.018 in)

Flywheel

Run-out . . . .   0.02 mm (0.0008 in) per 100 mm (3.9 in) diameter

Lubrication system

Oil capacity (drain and refill):
    Engine only . . . .   3.6 qts
    Engine and oil filter . . . .   4.1 qts
    For Turbo oil cooler add . . . .   0.6 qt
Oil type . . . .   See Recommended lubricants and fluids
Oil pressure (warm engine @ 2000 rpm) . . . .   36 to 87 psi

Oil pump

Type . . . .   Gear, driven from intermediate shaft
Clearances:
    Endplay . . . .   0.02 to 0.12 mm (0.0008 to 0.0047 in)
    Gear side clearance . . . .   0.02 to 0.09 mm (0.0008 to 0.0035 in)
    Backlash . . . .   0.15 to 0.35 mm (0.0059 to 0.0138 in)
    Driving gear bearing clearance . . . .   0.032 to 0.070 mm (0.0013 to 0.0028 in)
    Idler gear bearing clearance . . . .   0.014 to 0.043 mm (0.0006 to 0.0017 in)
Relief valve spring free length . . . .   39.20 mm (1.544 in)
Relief valve spring length under load of:
    46 to 54 N (10 to 12 lbf) . . . .   26.25 mm (1.034 in)
    62 to 78 N (14 to 18 lbf) . . . .   21.00 mm (0.827 in)

## Torque specifications*	Nm	Ft-lbs
Cylinder head bolts: **Note:** *Replace bolts if center section shows signs of stretching*		
Stage 1	20	15
Stage 2	60	43
Stage 3	Tighten 90° further	Tighten 90° further
Main bearing caps	110	81
Connecting rod bearing caps (B23):		
New bolts	70	52
Used bolts	63	47
Connecting rod bearing caps (B230)**:		
Stage 1	20	14
Stage 2	Tighten 90° further	Tighten 90° further

Flywheel/driveplate (use new bolts)	70	51
Spark plugs (dry threads)	25 ± 5	18 ± 4
Camshaft sprocket	50	36
Intermediate shaft sprocket	50	36
Camshaft bearing caps	20	15
Crankshaft pulley/sprocket bolt (B23)	165	120
Crankshaft pulley/sprocket bolt (B230):		
Stage 1	60	43
Stage 2	Tighten 60° further	Tighten 60° further
Oil pan bolts	11	8

* Oiled threads unless otherwise stated
** Replace bolts if length exceeds 55.5 mm (2.185 in)

Part B: V6 engine
General
Engine type	4-stroke, V6, ohc (one per head), spark ignition, water-cooled
Identification:	
B28F	Continuous injection (CI) system, to 1986
B280F	LH-Jetronic fuel injection, 1987 on
Bore	91 mm (3.583 in) nominal
Stroke	73 mm (2.874 in)
Cubic capacity	2849 cc (173.8 cu in)
Compression ratio	
B28F	8.8:1
B280F	9.5:1
Compression pressure:	
Overall value	116 to 160 psi
Variation between cylinders	29 psi max
Firing order	1-6-3-5-2-4 (No 1 LH rear)

Cylinder head
Warp limit — acceptable for use	0.05 mm (0.002 in) per 100 mm (3.9 in) length
Warp limit — acceptable for refinishing	No refinishing allowed
Height (new)	111.07 mm (4.376 in)

Cylinder liners
Bore:	
Grade 1 (takes grade A piston)	91.00 to 91.01 mm (3.5854 to 3.5857 in)
Grade 2 (takes grade B piston)	91.01 to 91.02 mm (3.5857 to 3.5861 in)
Grade 3 (takes grade C piston)	91.02 to 91.03 mm (3.5861 to 3.5865 in)
Liner protrusion above block:	
Checking value (used seals)	0.14 to 0.23 mm (0.0055 to 0.0091 in)
Setting value (new seals)	0.16 to 0.23 mm (0.0063 to 0.0091 in)
Liner seal thickness:	
B28F	
Blue mark	0.070 to 0.105 mm (0.0028 to 0.0041 in)
White mark	0.085 to 0.120 mm (0.0034 to 0.0047 in)
Red mark	0.105 to 0.140 mm (0.0041 to 0.0055 in)
Yellow mark	0.130 to 0.165 mm (0.0051 to 0.0065 in)
B280F	
Orange mark	0.098 to 0.134 mm (0.0039 to 0.0053 in)
White mark	0.118 to 0.154 mm (0.0046 to 0.0061 in)
Blue mark	0.138 to 0.194 mm (0.0054 to 0.0076 in)
Yellow mark	0.130 to 0.165 mm (0.0051 to 0.0065 in)

Pistons
Diameter (matched to liners):	
B28F	
Grade A	90.970 to 90.980 mm (3.5842 to 3.5846 in)
Grade B	90.980 to 90.990 mm (3.5846 to 3.5850 in)
Grade C	90.990 to 91.000 mm (3.5850 to 3.5854 in)
B280F	
Grade A	90.920 to 90.930 mm (3.5822 to 3.5826 in)
Grade B	90.930 to 90.940 mm (3.5826 to 3.5830 in)
Grade C	90.940 to 90.950 mm (3.5830 to 3.5834 in)
Clearance in bore	0.020 to 0.040 mm (0.0008 to 0.0016 in)
Piston pin bore:	
Blue mark	23.510 to 23.573 mm (0.9262 to 0.9287 in)
White mark	23.507 to 23.510 mm (0.9261 to 0.9262 in)
Red mark	23.504 to 23.507 mm (0.9260 to 0.9261 in)

Piston pins
Diameter:	
Blue mark	23.497 to 23.500 mm (0.9257 to 0.9259 in)
White mark	23.494 to 23.497 mm (0.9256 to 0.9257 in)

Red mark	23.491 to 23.494 mm (0.9255 to 0.9256 in)
Clearance in connecting rod	0.020 to 0.041 mm (0.0008 to 0.0016 in)
Clearance in piston	0.010 to 0.016 mm (0.0004 to 0.0006 in)

Piston rings

Clearance in groove:	
Top compression	0.045 to 0.074 mm (0.0018 to 0.0029 in)
Second compression	0.025 to 0.054 mm (0.0010 to 0.0021 in)
Oil control	0.009 to 0.0233 mm (0.0004 to 0.0092 in)
End gap (in 91.00 mm/3.5827 in bore):	
Top and second compression	0.40 to 0.60 mm (0.016 to 0.024 in)
Oil control	0.40 to 1.45 mm (0.016 to 0.057 in)

Valve clearances

Intake:	
Cold engine	0.10 to 0.15 mm (0.004 to 0.006 in)
Warm engine	0.15 to 0.20 mm (0.006 to 0.008 in)
Exhaust:	
Cold engine	0.25 to 0.30 mm (0.010 to 0.012 in)
Warm engine	0.30 to 0.35 mm (0.012 to 0.014 in)

Intake valves

Head diameter	
B28F	44 mm (1.73 in)
B280F	45.3 mm (1.78 in)
Stem diameter:	
26.5 mm (1.04 in) from head	7.965 to 7.980 mm (0.3136 to 0.3142 in)
Just below keeper groove	7.975 to 7.990 mm (0.3140 to 0.3146 in)
Valve head angle	
B28F	29.5°
B280F	44.5°

Exhaust valves

Head diameter	
B28F	37 mm (1.46 in)
B280F	38.5 mm (1.51 in)
Stem diameter:	
32 mm (1.26 in) from head	7.945 to 7.960 mm (0.3128 to 0.3134 in)
Just below keeper groove	7.965 to 7.980 mm (0.3136 to 0.3142 in)
Valve head angle	44.5°

Valve seat inserts

Fit in cylinder head	0.070 to 0.134 mm (0.0028 to 0.0053 in) interference
Oversizes available	3
Valve seat angles:	
Intake	
B28F	Compound (60° — 30° — 15°)
B280F	45°
Exhaust	45°

Valve guides

Internal diameter	8.000 to 8.022 mm (0.3150 to 0.3158 in)
Fit in cylinder head	0.052 to 0.095 mm (0.0020 to 0.0037 in) interference
External oversizes available	3 (marked by grooves)

Valve springs

Free length	47.1 mm (1.8543 in)
Length under load:	
230 to 266 N (52 to 60 lbs)	40.0 mm (1.5748 in)
613 to 689 N (138 to 155 lbs)	30.0 mm (1.811 in)

Rocker gear

Rocker arm clearance on shaft	0.012 to 0.054 mm (0.0005 to 0.0021 in)

Camshafts

Identification letter	
B28F	F
B280F	S
Identification number:	
B28F	
Left	615 or 977
Right	616 or 978
B280F	
Left	486 or 979
Right	487 or 980

Maximum lift (at lobe)
  B28F
    Intake . . . . 5.44 mm (0.2142 in)
    Exhaust . . . . 5.94 mm (0.2340 in)
  B280F
    Intake . . . . 5.96 mm (0.2348 in)
    Exhaust . . . . 5.43 mm (0.2139 in)
Bearing journal diameters:
  1 . . . . 40.440 to 40.465 mm (1.5933 to 1.5943 in)
  2 . . . . 41.040 to 41.065 mm (1.6169 to 1.6180 in)
  3 . . . . 41.640 to 41.665 mm (1.6406 to 1.6416 in)
  4 . . . . 42.240 to 42.265 mm (1.6642 to 1.6652 in)
Bearing running clearance . . . . 0.035 to 0.085 mm (0.0014 to 0.0034 in)
Endplay:
  New . . . . 0.070 to 0.144 mm (0.0028 to 0.0057 in)
  Wear limit . . . . 0.5 mm (0.020 in)

Crankshaft

Run-out (measured on center journals) . . . . 0.02 mm (0.0008 in)
Endplay . . . . 0.070 to 0.270 mm (0.0028 to 0.0106 in)
Main bearing running clearance . . . . 0.038 to 0.088 mm (0.0015 to 0.0035 in)
Connecting rod bearing running clearance . . . . 0.030 to 0.080 mm (0.0012 to 0.0031 in)
Rear seal diameter:
  Standard . . . . 79.926 to 80.000 mm (3.1490 to 3.1520 in)
  Undersize . . . . 79.726 to 79.800 mm (3.1412 to 3.1441 in)
Main bearing journal diameter:
  Standard . . . . 70.043 to 70.062 mm (2.7596 to 2.7604 in)
  Undersize . . . . 69.743 to 69.762 mm (2.7478 to 2.7486 in)
Main bearing out-of-round . . . . 0.007 mm (0.0003 in) max
Main bearing taper . . . . 0.01 mm (0.0004 in) max
Main bearing shell thickness:
  Standard . . . . 1.961 to 1.967 mm (0.0772 to 0.0774 in)
  Oversize . . . . 2.111 to 2.117 mm (0.0831 to 0.0833 in)
Rear main bearing journal width:
  Standard . . . . 29.20 to 29.25 mm (1.1504 to 1.1524 in)
  First oversize . . . . 29.40 to 29.45 mm (1.1583 to 1.1603 in)
  Second oversize . . . . 29.50 to 29.55 mm (1.1623 to 1.1642 in)
  Third oversize . . . . 29.60 to 29.65 mm (1.1662 to 1.1682 in)
Thrust washer thickness:
  Standard . . . . 2.30 to 2.35 mm (0.0906 to 0.0925 in)
  First oversize . . . . 2.40 to 2.45 mm (0.0945 to 0.0965 in)
  Second oversize . . . . 2.45 to 2.50 mm (0.0965 to 0.0984 in)
  Third oversize . . . . 2.50 to 2.55 mm (0.0984 to 0.1004 in)
Connecting rod bearing journal diameter:
  B28F
    Standard . . . . 52.267 to 52.286 mm (2.0578 to 2.0585 in)
    Undersize . . . . 51.967 to 51.986 mm (2.0459 to 2.0467 in)
  B280F
    Standard . . . . 59.971 to 59.990 mm (2.3628 to 2.3636 in)
Connecting rod bearing journal out-of-round . . . . 0.007 mm (0.0003 in) max
Connecting rod bearing journal taper . . . . 0.01 mm (0.0004 in) max

Connecting rods

Side clearance (between each pair of rods) . . . . 0.20 to 0.38 mm (0.008 to 0.015 in)
Connecting rod bearing shell thickness:
  Standard . . . . 1.842 to 1.848 mm (0.0725 to 0.0728 in)
  Oversize . . . . 1.992 to 1.998 mm (0.0784 to 0.0787 in)

Flywheel

Run-out . . . . 0.05 mm (0.0020 in) max

Lubrication system

Oil capacity (drain and refill):
  B28F
    Engine only . . . . 6.3 qts
    Engine and oil filter . . . . 6.9 qts
  B280F
    Engine only . . . . 5.8 qts
    Engine and oil filter . . . . 6.3 qts
Oil type . . . . See Recommended lubricants and fluids
Oil pressure (warm engine):
  At 900 rpm . . . . 14.5 psi minimum
  At 3000 rpm . . . . 58 psi

Oil pump

Type	Gear, chain-driven from crankshaft sprocket
Clearances:	
Endplay	0.025 to 0.084 mm (0.0010 to 0.0033 in)
Gear side clearance	
B28F	0.110 to 0.185 mm (0.0043 to 0.0073 in)
B280F	0.020 to 0.095 mm (0.0007 to 0.0037 in)
Backlash	0.17 to 0.27 mm (0.0067 to 0.0106 in)
Driving gear bearing clearance	0.015 to 0.053 mm (0.0006 to 0.0021 in)
Idler gear bearing clearance	0.015 to 0.051 mm (0.0006 to 0.0020 in)
Relief valve spring free length	89.5 mm (3.524 in)
Relief valve spring length under load of 88 N (20 lbf)	56.5 to 60.5 mm (2.226 to 2.383 in)

Torque specifications*

	Nm	Ft-lbs
Connecting rod bearing caps	45 to 50	33 to 37
Crankshaft pulley nut	240 to 280	177 to 206
Camshaft sprocket	70 to 90	52 to 66
Flywheel (use new bolts)	45 to 50	33 to 37
Spark plugs (dry threads)	12 ± 2	9 ± 1.5
Rocker cover	15	11
Cylinder head bolts (see text):		
Stage 1	60	43
Loosen, then Stage 2A	20	15
Stage 2B	Tighten 106° further	Tighten 106° further
Stage 3 (after warm-up and cooling)	Tighten 45° further	Tighten 45° further
Main bearing nuts (see text):		
Stage 1	30	22
Loosen, then Stage 2A	30 to 35	22 to 26
Stage 2B	Tighten 73 to 77° further	Tighten 73 to 77° further
Oil pump to block	10 to 15	7 to 11
Timing cover bolts	10 to 15	7 to 11

Oiled threads unless otherwise stated

PART A: IN-LINE ENGINE

1   General information

The four-cylinder engine is of the overhead camshaft type. The cylinders are in line and the engine is mounted vertically and is in a north-south attitude in the engine bay. Cooling is by water.

Drive to the camshaft is by toothed belt and sprockets. The camshaft drivebelt also drives an auxiliary shaft, which in turn drives the oil pump and (on B23 engines) the distributor. Other accessories are driven from the crankshaft pulley by V-belts.

The cylinder block is of cast iron and the cylinder head of aluminium alloy, with pressed-in valve guides and valve seats. The cylinder head is of the crossflow type, the intake ports being on the left-hand side and the exhaust ports on the right.

The crankshaft runs in five shell type main bearings; the connec-

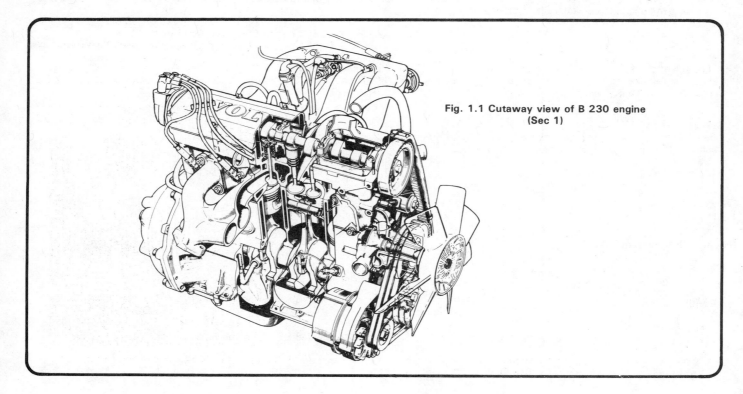

Fig. 1.1 Cutaway view of B 230 engine
(Sec 1)

ting rod bearings are also of the shell type. Crankshaft endplay is taken by thrust flanges on No 5 main bearing (B23) or by separate thrust washers on No 3 main bearing (B230). The camshaft runs in plain bearings machined directly in the cylinder head.

Valve actuation is direct, the camshaft being located above the valves. The cam lobes depress bucket type tappets; valve clearance is determined by the thickness of the shim in the recess in the top of each tappet.

The lubrication system is of the full-flow, pressure-feed type. Oil is drawn from the oil pan by a gear type pump, driven from the auxiliary shaft. Oil under pressure passes through a full-flow filter before being fed to the various shaft bearings and to the valvegear. On some models an external oil cooler is fitted, mounted next to the radiator. Turbo models also have an oil feed and return for the turbocharger bearings.

Although the B230 engine series represents a considerable advance on the B23, with many engine components having been redesigned, from the mechanic's point of view the two engine types are almost identical. Significant differences will be found in the Specifications or in the appropriate section of text.

2 Maintenance and inspection

1   Every 250 miles (400 km), weekly, or before a long journey, check the oil level as follows.
2   With the vehicle parked on level ground, and with the engine having been stopped for a few minutes, open and prop the hood. Withdraw the dipstick, wipe it on a clean rag and re-insert it fully. Withdraw it again and read the oil level relative to the marks on the end of the stick.
3   The oil level should be in between the MAX and MIN marks on the dipstick. If it is at or below the MIN mark, top up (via the oil filler cap) without delay. The quantity of oil required to raise the level from MIN to MAX on the dipstick is approximately 1 quart. Do not overfill.
4   The rate of oil consumption depends on leaks and on the quantity of oil burnt. External leakage should be obvious. Oil which is burnt may enter the combustion chambers through the valve guides or past the piston rings; excessive blow-by past the rings can also force oil out

via the crankcase ventilation system. Driving conditions also affect oil consumption.
5   Every 6000 miles (10,000 km) or six months, whichever comes first, drain the engine oil immediately after a run. Park the vehicle on level ground, position a drain pan of adequate capacity under the oil pan and remove the drain plug. Allow the oil to drain for at least 15 minutes.
6   Clean the drain plug, the plug washer (if present) and the drain plug seat on the oil pan. Install and tighten the drain plug, then fill the engine with the correct grade and quantity of oil.
7   Before running the engine, replace the oil filter as described in Section 3. When the engine is next started, there may be a delay in the extinguishing of the oil pressure warning light while the new filter fills with oil. Run the engine and check for leaks from the filter and drain plug, then stop the engine and check the oil level.
8   Every 24,000 miles (40,000 km nominal) or two years, check the valve clearances and adjust if necessary. See Section 4.
9   At the same interval, inspect the crankcase ventilation system hoses, breathers etc and clean or replace them as necessary. See Section 5.
10 Every 48,000 miles (80,000 km) or four years, replace the camshaft drivebelt (Section 6).
11 Regularly inspect the engine for leaks of oil, fuel or coolant, and repair as necessary.

3 Oil filter — replacement

1   The oil filter is located low down on the right-hand side of the engine block. Access is particularly bad on Turbo models.
2   Raise and support the front of the vehicle, and remove the engine undertray if necessary. Place a drain pan below the filter.
3   Unscrew the filter from its seat using a chain or strap wrench (photo). If a suitable wrench is not available, drive a large screwdriver through the filter casing and use that as a lever to unscrew it. Be prepared for oil spillage.
4   Discard the old filter, remembering it is full of oil. Wipe clean the filter seat on the block.
5   Smear clean engine oil or grease onto the sealing ring of the new filter. Screw the new filter into position (photo).
6   Tighten the new filter by hand only, three-quarters of a turn beyond the point where the sealing ring contacts the seat (or as instructed by the manufacturer). If the filter is overtightened, it will be extremely difficult to remove.
7   Run the engine and check for oil leaks from around the base of the filter. Tighten a little further if necessary.
8   Stop the engine. Install the undertray, then lower the vehicle and check the oil level.

4 Valve clearances — check and adjustment

1   Disconnect or remove items such as spark plug wires, vacuum/

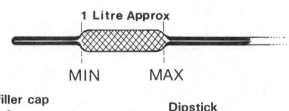

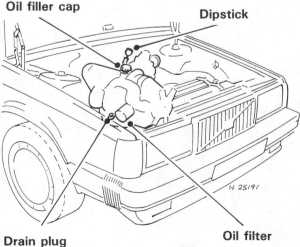

Fig. 1.2 Lubrication system maintenance points and dipstick markings (Sec 2)

Fig. 1.3 Engine oil drain plug (arrowed) (Sec 2)

3.3   Removing the oil filter with a strap wrench (looking from below)

3.5   Installing a new oil filter

4.2   Camshaft cover, showing all ten securing nuts

breather/boost pressure hoses, and if necessary the throttle cable, in order to gain access to the camshaft cover. Also unbolt the auxiliary air valve from the camshaft cover, where applicable.

2   Remove the securing nuts and lift off the camshaft cover. Note the location of the ground strap, the spark plug wire clip and similar items (photo). Recover the gasket.

3   Using a wrench on the crankshaft pulley center bolt, bring the engine to TDC, No 1 cylinder firing. (This will be easier if the spark plugs are removed.) No 1 piston is at TDC when the notch on the crankshaft pulley is in line with the figure O on the timing scale, and the cam lobes for No 1 cylinder (at the front) are both pointing obliquely upwards.

4   With the engine in this position, measure and record the clearance between the base of the front cam lobe and the tappet shim beneath it. Insert various thicknesses of feeler gauges until a firm sliding fit is obtained (photo). This thickness is the clearance for No 1 exhaust valve. Write it down.

5   Repeat the measurement and recording on the second cam from the front. This gives No 1 intake valve clearance.

6   Turn the crankshaft 180° (half a turn) clockwise so that the cam lobes for No 3 cylinder are pointing obliquely upwards. Measure and record the clearances for these two valves. The exhaust valve is always nearer the front.

7   Turn the crankshaft a further 180° and deal with No 4 cylinder, then 180° again for No 2.

8   Compare the clearances recorded with those given in the Specifications. If the recorded clearances are within limits, commence reassembly (paragraph 16). Otherwise, adjust the clearances as follows.

9   Gather together a small screwdriver or scriber, a pair of long-nosed pliers and a stout open-end wrench or square section screwdriver.

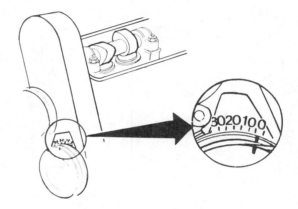

Fig. 1.4   Pulley and cam lobe positions — No 1 at TDC and firing (Sec 4)

These will substitute for the special tools normally required to change the shims with the camshaft in position. (Alternatively, the camshaft can be removed, but this involves, but this involves much extra work).

10   With the cam lobes in the same position as for checking, depress the tappet with the wrench or screwdriver. Only press on the edge of the tappet. Flick the shim out of the top of the tappet with the small screwdriver and remove it with the long-nosed pliers. Release the tappet (photos).

4.4   Measuring No 1 exhaust valve clearance

4.10A   Freeing a tappet shim — the tappet is being held down with a square section screwdriver

4.10B   Extracting the shim. Here an open-end wrench is being used to depress the tappet

4.11   Original shim thickness is engraved on the underside

4.16   Installing the rubber plug at the rear of the camshaft

4.17   A new camshaft cover gasket in position

11   The correct thickness of shim must now be calculated. First the thickness of the old shim must be known. It may be engraved on the underside (photo), but ideally the actual thickness should be measured with a micrometer or vernier gauge. This will take account of any wear.

12   The required shim thickness can now be calculated as shown in this example:

Specified clearance (A) = 0.40 mm (0.016 in)
Measured clearance (B) = 0.28 mm (0.11 in)
Original shim thickness (C) = 3.95 mm (0.156 in)
Shim thickness required = C − A + B = 3.83 mm (0.151 in)

In this example the shim to be installed would have to be 3.85 mm or 3.80 mm, giving clearances of 0.38 mm or 0.43 mm respectively.

13   Lubricate a new shim of the required thickness. Depress the tappet and insert the shim, marked side downwards. Release the tappet and check that the shim is properly located.

14   Repeat the operations on the adjacent tappet, if necessary, then proceed to the other valves, each time turning the crankshaft to position the cam lobes upwards. Do not turn the crankshaft while shims are missing from tappets, as the cam lobes may jam in them.

15   When all the required shims have been installed, turn the crankshaft through several complete turns, then check all the clearances again.

16   Make sure that the rubber plug to the rear of the camshaft (B23

only) is securely installed and in good condition. Replace it if necessary (photo).

17   Install the camshaft cover, using a new gasket (photo). Install and tighten the nuts, remembering to install the spark plug wire bracket and ground strap.

18   Reconnect the spark plug wires, vacuum hoses etc, then run the engine and check that there are no oil leaks from the camshaft cover.

5   Crankcase ventilation system — general information

1   The crankcase ventilation system directs oil fumes and blow-by gases from the lower crankcase into the induction system, so that they may be drawn into the engine and burnt. Typical hose layouts are shown in Figs. 1.5 and 1.6

2   It is important to keep the hoses, flame taps, restrictors etc, clean and in good condition. Obstruction of the system can cause a build-up of pressure within the crankcase, with subsequent failure of oil seals. Leaks in the system can cause rough or erratic idling, besides being a source of pollution.

3   Do not atempt to remove the long oil drain hose from below the oil trap, as the oil pan must be removed in order to install it correctly.

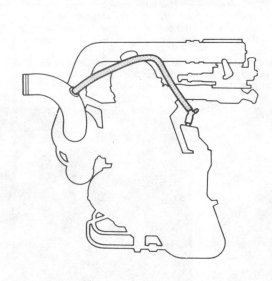

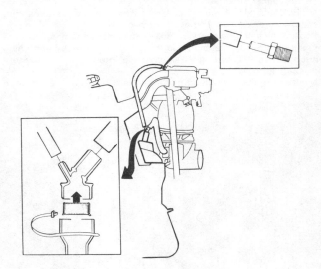

Fig. 1.5   Typical crankcase ventilation hose routing — Turbo (Sec 5)

Fig. 1.6   Typical crankcase ventilation hose routing — normally aspirated (Sec 5)

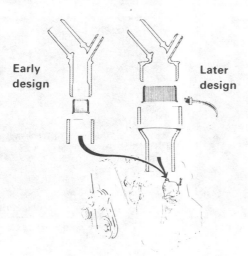

Fig. 1.7   Details of crankcase ventilation oil and flame traps (Sec 5)

6   Camshaft drivebelt — removal, installation and tensioning

1   Remove the fan clutch and fan assembly, the fan shroud, and the accessory drivebelts. Refer to Chapter 2 if necessary. On B230 engines, also remove the water pump pulley.
2   Unbolt and remove the camshaft drivebelt cover. (On B230 engines, just remve the top half of the cover.)
3   Using a wrench on the crankshaft pulley center bolt, bring the engine to TDC, No 1 firing. This is indicated when the mark on the camshaft sprocket is in line with the mark on the camshaft cover or the drivebelt backplate. At the same time the marks on the crankshaft sprocket guide plate and the oil seal housing will be in line. (The pulley mark cannot be used even if the pulley is still in place, since the timing scale is on the drivebelt cover.) Although it is not critical, the position of the auxiliary shaft sprocket timing mark should also be noted (photos).
4   On B230 engines, remove the starter motor or the flywheel bottom cover plate. Have an assistant jam the ring gear teeth, then loosen the crankshaft pulley bolt without disturbing the set position of the crankshaft. Remove the bolt and the pulley, then remove the lower half of the camshaft drivebelt cover.
5   On B23 engines, if the crankshaft pulley was not removed with the accessory drivebelts, remove it now (photo).
6   Loosen the belt tensioner nut. Pull on the belt to compress the tensioner spring. Lock the tensioner in this position, either by tightening the nut again or by inserting a nail or similar into the hole in the tensioner shaft (photos).
7   Mark the running direction of the belt if it is to be re-used, then

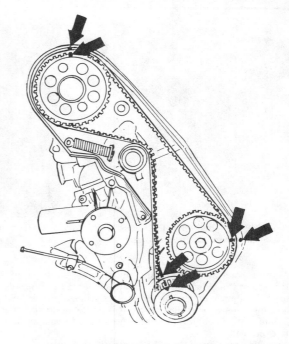

Fig. 1.8   Sprocket alignment marks (arrowed) — No 1 at TDC and firing. Auxiliary shaft marks are not critical (Sec 6)

slip it off the sprockets and tensioner roller and remove it. Do not rotate the crankshaft, camshaft or auxiliary shaft with the bolt removed.
8   Spin the tensioner roller and check for roughness or shake; replace if necessary.
9   Do not contaminate the drivebelt with oil, nor kink it or fold it sharply.
10   Before installing, make sure that all three sprockets are in the correct positions (paragraph 3). Slip the belt over the sprockets and around the roller, observing the correct running direction if the old belt is being re-used.
11   Recheck the alignment of the sprocket marks, then release the belt tensioner by loosening the nut or pulling out the nail (photo). Tighten the tensioner nut.
12   On B230 engines, install the drivebelt lower cover and the crankshaft pulley. Make sure that the dowel (guide pin) on the sprocket engages with the hole in the pulley. Jam the ring gear teeth and tighten the pulley bolt to the specified torque. Install the starter motor or flywheel cover.
13   On all engines, rotate the crankshaft two full turns clockwise. Stop at TDC, No 1 firing, and check that the various timing marks still align. Loosen and retighten the tensioner nut.

6.3A   Timing marks — camshaft (A), auxiliary shaft (B) and crankshaft (C)

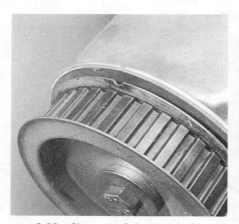

6.3B   Close-up of the camshaft sprocket and cover marks

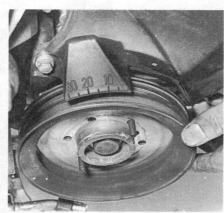

6.5   Removing the crankshaft pulley

6.6A Loosen the tensioner nut . . .

6.6B . . . and insert a nail or rivet (arrowed) to restrain the spring

6.11 Pulling out the rivet to release the tension

14 Install the drivebelt cover (or the top section), then install the accessory drivebelts, pulleys, fan etc.

15 Run the engine to operating temperature, then switch it off. Bring the engine to TDC, No 1 firing. Remove the access plug from the front of the drivebelt cover, loosen the tensioner nut once more and then retighten it. Install the access plug (photo).

16 If a new belt has been installed, repeat paragraph 15 after approximately 600 miles (1000 km).

7 Major operations possible with the engine installed

1 The following items may be relatively easily removed with the engine in place:
  (a) Camshaft drivebelt
  (b) Camshaft
  (c) Cylinder head and valve train
  (d) Crankshaft/auxiliary shaft front oil seals
  (e) Flywheel/clutch (after removal of gearbox)
  (f) Crankshaft rear oil seal (after removal of flywheel)
  (g) Engine mounts

2 It is possible to remove the oil pan with the engine installed, but the amount of preparatory work is formidable — see Section 16. With the oil pan removed, the oil pump, pistons and connecting rods may be dealt with.

3 The engine must be removed for removal of the crankshaft and main bearings.

8 Engine disassembly and reassembly — general information

1 If the engine has been removed from the car for major overhaul, or if individual components have been removed for repair or replacement, observe the following general hints on disassembly and reassembly.

2 Thoroughly clean the exterior of the engine using a degreasing solvent. Clean away as much of the external dirt and grease as possible before disassembly.

3 As parts are removed, clean them with solvent. Blow out all passages with compressed air.

4 Avoid working with the engine or any of the components directly on a concrete floor, as grit presents a real source of trouble.

5 Wherever possible, work should be carried out with the engine on an engine stand or the individual components on a strong bench. If the work must be done on the floor, cover it with a board or sheets of newspaper.

6 Have plenty of clean, lint-free rags available and also some containers or trays to hold small items. This will help during reassembly and also prevent possible losses.

7 Always obtain a complete set of gaskets if the engine is being completely dismantled, or all those necessary for the individual component

Guide pin

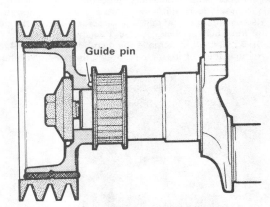

Fig. 1.9 Crankshaft pulley and sprocket details — B 230 engine (Sec 6)

6.15 The tensioner nut access plug

or assembly being worked on. Keep the old gaskets, using them as patterns to make replacements if new ones aren't available.

8   When possible reinstall nuts, bolts and washers in their locations after removal as this helps to protect the threads and avoids confusion or loss.

9   During reassembly thoroughly lubricate all components, where appropriate, with engine oil, but avoid contaminating the gaskets and joint mating faces.

10. Besides gaskets, seals and so on, a selection of cable ties will be needed to replace those which have to be cut when working on and around the engine.

11 Engine undertray removal is necessary for virtually all operations requiring access to the underside of the engine.

9 Camshaft — removal and installation

Note: *If a new camshaft is to be installed, the lubrication system must be flushed with two consecutive oil and filter changes before removing the old camshaft. Drain the oil and replace the filter, then run the engine for 10 minutes. Fresh oil and a new filter must be provided for the new camshaft. Failure to observe this may cause rapid wear of the new camshaft.*

1   Remove the camshaft drivebelt (Section 6). The belt may stay on the lower sprockets.

2   Hold the camshaft sprocket from turning with a suitable tool inserted through the holes in its face, or by clamping an old drivebelt around it. Loosen the camshaft sprocket bolt. Do not allow the camshaft to move, or piston/valve contact may occur (photo).

3   Remove the sprocket bolt and the sprocket itself. Note the position of any front plates, backplates and washers (photos).

4   On B230 engines, remove the distributor (Chapter 4, Section 4).

5   Remove the camshaft cover, noting the position of the spark plug

wire bracket and the ground strap. Recover the gasket.

6   Make identification marks if necessary, then progressively slacken the camshaft bearing cap nuts (photo). The camshaft will rise up under the pressure of the valve springs — be careful that it does not stick and then suddenly jump up. Remove the bearing caps.

7   Lift out the camshaft complete with front oil seal. Be careful of the lobes, which may have sharp edges (photo).

8   To measure the camshaft endplay, temporarily remove all the tappets and shims in order for proper installation. Install the camshaft and the rear bearing cap; measure the endplay between the cap and the camshaft flange (photo). Excessive endplay, if not due to wear of the camshaft itself, can be corrected by replacing the rear bearing cap. Install the tappets and shims to their original locations on completion.

9   Begin installation by liberally oiling the tappets, shims, the camshaft bearings and caps and the cam lobes. Use clean engine oil, or special camshaft lubricant if supplied with a new shaft.

10 Install the camshaft in approximately the correct position for No 1 firing (No 1 lobes both pointing obliquely upwards). Apply sealant to the head mating surfaces of the front and rear bearing caps (photo). Install all the bearing caps in their correct positions and pull them down by tightening the nuts a little at a time. When all the caps are seated, tighten the nuts to the specified torque.

11 Lubricate a new oil seal and install it on the front of the camshaft, lips inwards. Tap it in with a piece of tube until it is seated (photo).

12 Install the camshaft sprocket and associated components. Hold the sprocket and tighten the bolt to the specified torque.

13 Install the distributor if it was removed.

14 Install and tension the camshaft drivebelt (Section 6).

15 If any new parts have been installed, check the valve clearances (Section 4).

16 Install the camshaft cover, using a new gasket.

17 If a new camshaft has been installed, run it in at moderate engine speeds for a few minutes (neither idling nor racing), or as directed by the manufacturer.

9.2   Restrain the sprocket and loosen the bolt

9.3A   Removing the bolt, washer and front plate . . .

9.3B   . . . the camshaft sprocket itself . . .

9.3C   . . . and the sprocket backplate. Other engines may differ slightly

9.6   Loosening a camshaft bearing cap nut

9.7   Removing the camshaft

9.8 Measuring camshaft endfloat

9.10 Installing the camshaft front bearing cap. Sealant is on shaded areas

9.11 Installing a new oil seal

10 Cylinder head — removal and installation

1 Disconnect the battery negative cable.
2 Drain the cooling system (Chapter 2, Section 3).
3 Disconnect or remove spark plug wires, vacuum/breather hoses etc, to gain access to the camshaft cover.
4 Disconnect the radiator top hose from the thermostat housing.
5 Remove the fan and fan shroud.
6 Remove all accessory drivebelts and the water pump pulley (Chapter 2, Section 7).
7 On B230 engines, remove the distributor cap.
8 Remove the camshaft drivebelt cover. (If the cover is in two sections, just remove the upper section.)
9 Bring the engine to TDC, No 1 firing, then remove the camshaft drivebelt and tensioner — see Section 6. (The drivebelt can stay on the lower sprockets.) Do not rotate the crankshaft or camshafts from now on.
10 On B230 engines, unbolt and remove the camshaft sprocket and the spacer washer. Also remove the camshaft drivebelt tensioner stud.
11 Remove the bolts which secure the drivebelt backplate to the cylinder head.
12 Remove the nuts which secure the intake and exhaust manifolds to the cylinder head. Pull the manifolds off their studs to the sides of the engine bay, supporting them if necessary. Recover the gaskets.
13 Remove the camshaft cover. Carefully scrape off the gasket.
14 Loosen the cylinder head bolts, half a turn at a time to begin with,

in the order shown in Fig. 1.10. Remove the bolts. Obtain new bolts for reassembly if the old ones appear stretched.
15 Lift off the cylinder head. On B230 engines it will be necessary to bend the drivebelt backplate forwards a little.
16 Set the head down on a couple of wooden blocks to avoid damage to protruding valves. Carefully scrape off the old head gasket.
17 Begin installation by placing a new head gasket on the cylinder block. Make sure it is the right way up — all the bolt holes, oilways etc must line up (photo).
18 Make sure that the camshaft to set to the No 1 firing position — both cam lobes for No 1 cylinder pointing obliquely upwards. Lower the head into position.
19 Oil the threads of the cylinder head bolts. Install the bolts and tighten them, in the sequence shown in Fig. 1.11, to the specified Stage 1 torque.
20 In the same sequence tighten the bolts to the Stage 2 torque, then go around again and tighten the bolts through the angle specified for Stage 3. (If the engine is on the bench, it may be preferable to leave Stage 3 tightening until after engine installation.) No further tightening is required.
21 The remainder of installation is a reversal of the removal procedure. Use new gaskets etc where necessary.
22 Check the valve clearances (Section 4) before starting the engine. Also refer to Section 44, most of which applies.

10.17 A new head gasket in position

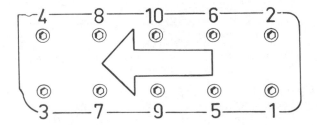

Fig. 1.10 Cylinder head bolt loosening sequence (Sec 10)

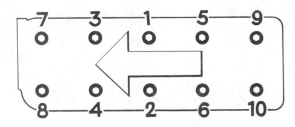

Fig. 1.11 Cylinder head bolt tightening sequence (Sec 10)

11.2 Unbolting the auxiliary shaft sprocket — a large screwdriver can be used to immobilize the sprocket while loosening the bolt

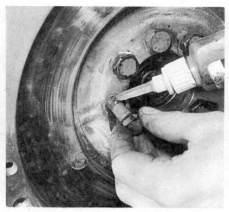

12.5A Applying thread locking compound to a flywheel bolt

12.5B Jam the ring gear and tighten the bolts

11 Oil seals (front) — replacement

1   Remove the camshaft drivebelt (Section 6)
2   Restrain and unbolt the appropriate sprockets for access to the failed seal (photo). If necessary, also remove the drivebelt tensioner and backplate.
3   Carefully remove the seal by prying it out with a small screwdriver or hooked tool. Do not damage the shaft sealing face.
4   Clean the seal seat. Examine the shaft sealing face for wear or damage which could cause premature failure of the new seal.
5   Lubricate the new oil seal. Install the seal over the shaft, lips inwards, and tap it in with a seal driver or piece of tube.
6   Install the other components that were removed. Install a new camshaft drivebelt if the old one was oil-soaked or worn.

Fig. 1.12 Driveplate and washers (Sec 12)

12 Flywheel/driveplate — removal and installation

Flywheel

1   Remove the transmission (Chapter 6, Section 4).
2   Remove the clutch pressure plate and driven plate (Chapter 5, Section 10).
3   Make alignment marks so that the flywheel can be installed in the same position relative to the crankshaft.
4   Unbolt the flywheel and remove it. Do not drop it, it is heavy. Obtain new bolts for reassembly.
5   Install by reversing the removal operations. Use new bolts, tightened to the specified torque, with thread locking compound (photos).
6   Install the clutch as described in Chapter 5.

Driveplate

7   Remove the automatic transmission (Chapter 6, Section 37).
8   Proceed as above from paragraph 3, ignoring the references to the clutch. Note the location and orientation of the large washers on each side of the driveplate.

13 Oil seal (crankshaft rear) — replacement

1   Remove the flywheel or driveplate (Section 12).
2   Note whether the old seal is flush with the end of its carrier, or recessed into it.
3   Carefully pry out the old oil seal. Do not damage the carrier or the surface of the crankshaft.
4   Clean the oil seal carrier and the crankshaft. Inspect the crankshaft for a wear groove or ridge left by the old seal (photo).
5   Lubricate the carrier, the crankshaft and the new seal. Install the seal, lips inwards, and use a piece of tube (or the old seal, inverted)

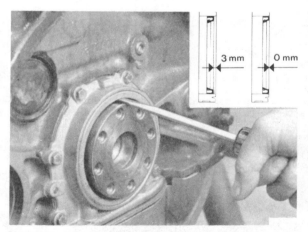

Fig. 1.13 Levering out the rear oil seal. Note recessed depth (inset) (Sec 13)

to tap it into place. If there is any wear on the crankshaft sealing surface, drive the new seal in a little deeper than the old one. The seal may be recessed up to 6 mm (0.24 in) within the carrier.
6   Install the flywheel or driveplate.

14 Flywheel ring gear — replacement

Note: *The driveplate ring gear cannot be replaced separately.*
1   Remove the flywheel (Section 12).
2   Drill through the old ring gear at the root of two teeth. Do not drill into the flywheel.

13.4 Wear groove left by the old oil seal

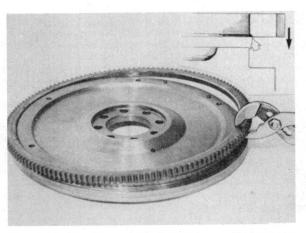

Fig. 1.14 Installing the flywheel ring gear. Inset shows
chamfer (Sec 14)

3   Split the ring gear, using a chisel above the drilled hole. Wear eye
protection when doing this. Lever the ring gear off the flywheel and
clean up its seat.
4   Heat the new ring gear to 230°C (446°F) in an oven or oil bath,
or with a flame. If using a flame, place scraps of 40/60 solder (40%
tin, 60% lead) on the ring gear to show when the correct temperature
has been reached. The solder will melt at 220 to 230°C (428 to 446°F).
Do not overheat the gear, or its temper will be lost.
5   Using tongs, install the gear to the flywheel, with the inner chamfer
towards the flywheel. Tap the gear into place if necessary with a brass
drift, then allow it to cool.
6   Install the flywheel.

15 Pilot bearing — removal and installation

Note: A pilot bearing is only installed on manual transmission models.
1   Remove the clutch pressure and driven plates (Chapter 5).
2   Pry out the bearing retaining circlip (photo).
3   Extract the bearing with a slide hammer or similar tool (photo).

4   When installing, drive the bearing into place with a seal driver or
piece of tubing which contacts its outer race. Install the circlip.
5   Install the clutch components.

16 Oil pan — removal and installation

Note: Read through this procedure first to see what is involved. Some
readers will prefer to remove the engine
1   Raise the front of the vehicle on ramps, support it securely on
jackstands or drive it over a pit.
2   Drain the engine oil. Install the drain plug for safe keeping.
3   Disconnect the battery negative cable.
4   Remove the splash guard from below the engine.
5   Disconnect the exhaust downpipe from the silencer.
6   Remove the nuts which secure the engine mounts to the crossmember.
7   Mark the relationship of the steering intermediate shaft to the steering gear input shaft. Release the clamp bolts and disconnect the shaft
from the steering gear.
8   Support the engine from above, either with a hoist or with an ad-

15.2 Removing the pilot bearing circlip

15.3 Extracting the pilot bearing

justable support resting on the inner fenders or suspension turrets. Check the security of the support arrangements.

9 Release the fan shroud and remove the engine oil dipstick, then raise the engine slightly to take the weight off the mounts. On the B230 engine, be careful not to crush the distributor against the firewall.

10 Remove the engine mounts on the left-hand side. Cut the cable tie which secures the power steering hose nearby. Also remove the intake manifold bracing strut (not on carbureted engines).

11 Remove the bolts which secure the front crossmember to the body.

12 Remove the flywheel/driveplate bottom cover plate.

13 Pull the front crossmember downwards to give adequate clearance below the oil pan. Disconnect or move aside power steering hoses as necessary.

14 Remove the oil pan securing bolts. Separate the oil pan from the block — if it is stuck, tap it with a soft-faced hammer. Do not lever between the mating faces.

15 Lower the oil pan, twist it to free it from the oil pump pick-up and remove it.

16 Clean the oil pan internally. Remove all traces of gasket from the oil pan and block faces.

17 Begin installation by sticking a new gasket to the oil pan with grease.

18 Position the oil pan on the block, being careful not to move the gasket. Secure the oil pan with two bolts in opposite corners.

19 Install all the oil pan bolts and tighten them progressively to the specified torque.

20 The remainder of installation is a reversal of the removal procedure. Check that the drain plug is tight, then refill the engine with oil on completion.

17 Oil pump — removal and installation

1 Remove the oil pan (Section 16).

2 Remove the two bolts which secure the oil pump. Note that one of these bolts also secures the oil trap drain hose guide. Remove the pump and the guide.

3 Separate the oil pump delivery pipe from the pump. Remove the seals from each end of the pipe.

4 Begin installation by installing the delivery pipe, with new seals, to the pump (photo).

5 Position the pump on the block, engaging the pump drivegear and the delivery pipe at the same time (photo).

6 Install the two bolts and the drain hose guide. Tighten the bolts.

7 Make sure that the oil drain hose is correctly positioned, then install the oil pan.

18 Pistons and connecting rods — removal and installation

1 Remove the cylinder head (Section 10), the oil pan (Section 16) and the oil pump (Section 17).

Fig. 1.15 Removing the oil pan (Sec 16)

17.4 Installing the delivery pipe to the oil pump. New seal (arrowed) is in the pump.

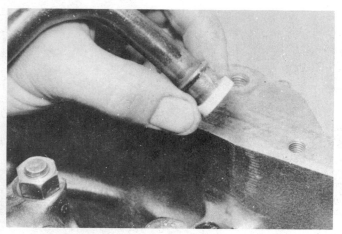

17.5 Installing the delivery pipe and a new seal to the block

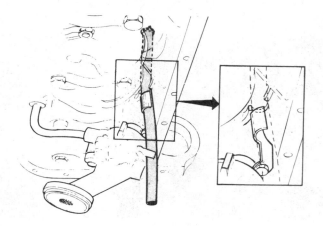

Fig. 1.16 Correct positioning of oil drain hose (Sec 17)

2   Completely remove the ridge at the top of each cylinder with a ridge reaming tool. Follow the manufacturer's instructions provided with the tool. Failure to remove the ridge before attempting to remove the piston/connecting rod assemblies may result in piston breakage.

3   Turn the crankshaft to bring a pair of connecting rod caps into an accessible position. Check that there are identification numbers or marks on each connecting rod and cap; paint or punch suitable marks if necessary, so that each rod can be installed in the same position.

4   Remove two connecting rod nuts or bolts. Tap the cap with a soft-faced hammer to free it. Remove the cap and bearing shell.

5   Push the connecting rod and piston up and out of the bore. Recover the other half bearing shell if it is loose.

6   Install the cap to the connecting rod so that they do not get mixed up. Keep the bearing shells in their original positions if there is any chance that they will be re-used.

7   Repeat the operations on the remaining connecting rods and pistons, turning the crankshaft as necessary to gain access to the connecting rod caps.

8   Examine the bores and the pistons (Sections 30 and 31). Also inspect the crankshaft journals (Section 29). If it is decided that the engine will have to be removed for further attention, the cylinder head must be installed first, using at least six bolts to secure it.

9   Begin installation by deglazing the bores with a glaze buster hone. (Stuff rags into the bores first to protect the crankshaft, and be sure to remove all traces of abrasive.) The object is to give a cross-hatch finish to the bore which will help new rings to bed in quickly.

10   Oil a piston and its bore. Make sure that the top half of the bearing shell is installed to the connecting rod and the bottom half to the cap (photo). Also check that the piston ring gaps are evenly spaced.

11   Attach a piston ring compressor to the piston. Insert the piston and connecting rod into their bore, making sure that the arrow on the piston crown points towards the front of the engine. Tap the piston crown with a wooden hammer handle so that the piston enters the bore. If it sticks, do not force it, but release the ring compressor and check the rings (photos).

12   Check that the bearing shell is still secure in the connecting rod. Oil the crankpin and seat the connecting rod onto it. Install the cap with its shell, and tighten the nuts or bolts to the specified torque (photos).

13   Repeat the operations on the other three pistons, turning the crankshaft as necessary to receive the crankpins.

14   Check that the crankshaft is still free to rotate. Some stiffness is to be expected if new shells have been installed, but binding or tight spots should be investigated.

15   Install the oil pump, the oil pan and the cylinder head.

19   Engine mounts — removal and installation

1   Disconnect the battery negative terminal.

2   Remove the nuts from the mount to be removed (photo).

3   Connect a hoist to the engine, or support it in some other way. Do not jack up directly onto the oil pan, as damage may result.

4   Take the weight off the mount and remove it. It may be necessary to move aside power steering hoses, and (on fuel injection engines) to remove the intake manifold bracing strut.

5   Install by reversing the removal operations.

20   Methods of engine removal

The engine is removed by lifting it out of the engine compartment, with or without the transmission.

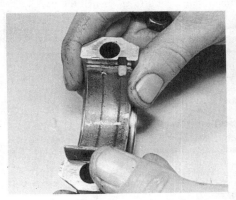

18.10   Installing a bearing shell to a connecting rod cap — be sure the tab on the bearing fits into the recess on the cap

18.11A   Installing a piston into its bore

18.11B   Arrow on piston crown must face front of engine. Letters (D) are grade marks

18.12A   Installing the connecting rod cap . . .

18.12B   . . . and tightening the nuts

19.2   The engine right-hand mount — Turbo shown, others are more accessible

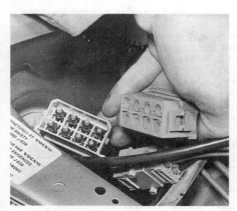

21.11 Disconnecting an engine wiring harness multi-plug

21.22 Disconnecting the oil cooler hoses

21.23 Disconnecting the vacuum tank

21 Engine — removal (alone)

1   Disconnect the battery negative terminal. Either remove the hood, or open it to its widest setting.
2   Drain the cooling system and remove the radiator. Refer to Chapter 2 if necessary.
3   On Turbo models, remove the intercooler and associated hoses (Chapter 3). Also remove the airflow meter-to-turbo hose.
4   On carburetor models, remove the air cleaner (Chapter 3).
5   On all models, remove the air cleaner hot air ducting.
6   On B230 engines, remove the distributor cap and spark plug wires. On B23 engines, remove the coil-to-distributor HT lead.
7   Disconnect the throttle cable.
8   Disconnect the brake servo vacuum hose.
9   Disconnect the fuel supply and return pipes. Be prepared for fuel spillage.
10   Disconnect the various crankcase ventilation, vacuum and pressure sensing hoses. Make notes or identifying marks if there is any possibility of confusion later.
11   Disconnect the engine wiring harness electrical connector, again making notes if necessary (photo).
12   Disconnect the starter motor feed wire, then remove the battery completely.
13   Disconnect the engine ground strap(s).
14   Disconnect the air conditioning compressor clutch wiring harness connector.
15   Remove the power steering pump without disconnecting the hoses and wire it up out of the way. See Chapter 10 if necessary.
16   Disconnect the heater hoses at the rear of the engine.
17   Remove the starter motor (Chapter 12).
18   Disconnect the exhaust downpipe from the manifold or turbo exit.
19   If the engine is equipped with an oil cooler, unbolt its mounting bracket.
20   Raise and support the vehicle. Remove the engine undertray, if not already done.
21   Drain the engine oil and remove the oil filter.
22   If the engine is equipped with an oil cooler, disconnect the flexible hoses at their unions with the rigid pipes (photo). The contents of the oil cooler will drain out of the open unions. Remove the oil cooler.
23   Disconnect the hose from the vacuum tank (photo), then unbolt and remove it.
24   Remove those engine-to-transmission nuts and bolts which are accessible from below. Also remove the flywheel/driveplate bottom cover.
25   On automatic transmission models, unbolt the torque converter from the driveplate. Turn the crankshaft as necessary to gain access. Make alignment marks for reference when installing.
26   Remove the air conditioning compressor drivebelt (Chapter 2, Section 7).
27   Remove the nuts which secure the air conditioning compressor bracket to the engine. Move the compressor aside without disconnecting the refrigerant hoses. It will rest in the space vacated by the battery.
28   Disconnect the two ignition sensor multi-plugs at the firewall. Identify the plugs to avoid confusion when installing. (This only applies

to the Motronic system.)
29   Support the transmission from below, using a floor jack if one is available. Pad the jack head with rags or wood.
30   Attach a hoist to the engine using the lifting eyes provided. Jack the engine up slightly to take the weight off the engine mounts.
31   Remove the nuts which secure the engine mounts to the frame.
32   Remove the remaining engine-to-transmission nuts and bolts.
33   Check that no wires, hoses etc have been overlooked. Raise the engine and pull it forwards off the transmission, at the same time raising the jack under the transmission. Do not allow the weight of the transmission to hang on the input shaft.
34   Once the engine is clear of the transmission, carefully lift it out of the engine compartment and take it to the bench (photo).

22 Engine — removal (with transmission)

1   Proceed as in the previous Section, paragraphs 1 to 16, 18 to 23 and 26 to 28.
2   Disconnect the wires from the starter motor solenoid.
3   Remove the exhaust downpipe completely.

Manual transmission

4   Remove the clutch slave cylinder (without disconnecting the hydraulic hose) or disconnect the clutch cable, as applicable. See Chapter 5.
5   Disconnect the gear lever — see Chapter 6, Sections 4 and 21.

Automatic transmission

6   Disconnect the kickdown and control linkages — see Chapter 6, Section 37.

All models

7   Mark and disconnect the electrical connectors from the transmission.
8   Unbolt the driveshaft from the rear of the transmission.
9   Support the transmission. Unbolt the crossmember from the transmission and from the side rails and remove it.
10   Unbolt the bracing strut from below the bellhousing (when installed).
11   Attach a hoist or support fixture to the engine using the eyes provided to take the weight off the engine mounts.
12   Remove the nuts which secure the engine mounts to the frame.
13   Check that no attachments have been overlooked. Raise the engine, at the same time lowering the support under the transmission, until the whole assembly can be lifted from the engine compartment.

23 Engine — separation from transmission

1   Remove the starter motor.
2   Remove the bellhousing-to-engine nuts and bolts. Also remove the flywheel/driveplate bottom cover plate (if applicable).

21.34 Lifting out the engine

24.2A Removing the oil cooler adaptor nut . . .

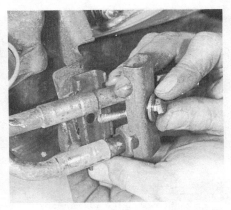

24.2B . . . and the pipe bracket

Manual transmission

3 With the aid of an assistant, slide the transmission off the engine. Once it is clear of the dowels, do not allow it to hang on the input shaft.

Automatic transmission

4 Unbolt the torque converter from the driveplate, turning the crankshaft to gain access from below or through the starter motor hole. Make alignment marks for reference when reassembling.
5 With the aid of an assistant, slide the transmission off the engine. Make sure that the torque converter stays in the bellhousing.

24 Engine — disassembling for overhaul

1 With the engine removed for disassembly, remove external components as follows, referring to other Chapters when necessary:
 (a) Alternator and brackets (Chapter 12)
 (b) Exhaust manifold, with turbocharger if equipped (Chapter 3)
 (c) Fan and water pump (Chapter 2)
 (d) Distributor (Chapter 4)
 (e) Intake manifold with carburetor or injection components (Chapter 3)
 (f) Turbo bypass valve (Chapter 3, Section 46)
 (g) Spark plugs (Chapter 4)
 (h) Clutch pressure and driven plates (Chapter 5)
 (j) Ignition sensors and bracket (Chapter 4)
 (k) Auxiliary air valve or air control valve (not carburetor models) (Chapter 3, Section 34 or 46)
2 If the engine is equipped with an oil cooler, remove the plumbing and the oil filter adaptor. The adaptor is secured by a large central nut and the pipes by a bracket (photos).
3 Unbolt the coolant distribution pipe.
4 Remove the dipstick. Unbolt the dipstick tube bracket and pull the tube out of the block (photo).

5 Unbolt the crankcase ventilation system oil trap and pull out the long drain hose. Working through that hole, lift up the oil pump drivegear/shaft and remove it (photo).
6 If not already done, remove the camshaft drivebelt cover. Jam the flywheel ring gear and loosen the crankshaft pulley/sprocket center bolt.
7 Remove the camshaft drivebelt and tensioner (Section 6).
8 Unbolt and remove the camshaft and auxiliary shaft sprockets, then remove the camshaft drivebelt backplate.
9 Remove the cylinder head (Section 10).
10 Remove the crankshaft pulley (or pulley boss), the sprocket and guide plates.
11 Remove the flywheel or driveplate (Section 12).
12 Remove the oil pan and oil pump (Sections 16 and 17).
13 Remove the pistons and connecting rods (Section 18).
14 Remove any pressure switches, transducers etc from the cylinder block.

25 Auxiliary shaft — removal

1 With the engine disassembled as described in the previous Section, unbolt and remove the front oil seal housing (photo). Note the cable clips attached to the bottom studs. Remove the gasket.
2 Withdraw the auxiliary shaft, being careful not to damage the bearings in the block (photo).

26 Crankshaft and main bearings — removal

1 With the pistons and connecting rods removed, position the engine with the crankshaft facing up (engine upside down).

24.4 Removing the dipstick tube

24.5 Unbolting the oil trap

25.1 Removing the front oil seal housing

25.2 Removing the auxiliary shaft

26.2 Removing the rear oil seal housing

26.5 Removing the rear main bearing cap

2   Remove the front and rear oil seal housings (if not already done) (photo).
3   If it is possible that the existing main bearing shells will be re-used, the crankshaft endplay should be measured now to make sure that it is within limits. See Section 38, paragraph 9.
4   Inspect the main bearing caps for identifying numbers or marks. Paint or punch marks if necessary. They must be installed in their original positions.
5   Remove the main bearing cap bolts. Lift off the main bearing caps, tapping them with a soft-faced hammer if necessary to free them. Keep the bearing shells with their caps if they may be re-used (photo).
6   Lift out the crankshaft. Do not drop it, it is heavy (photo).
7   On B230 engines, recover the two half thrust washers from each side of the center main bearing. (On B23 engines, No 5 bearing shells have integral thrust flanges.)
8   Remove the upper half main bearing shells from their seats in the crankcase by pressing the end of the shell furthest from the locating tab. Again, keep the shells in order if they are to be re-used.

27 Inspection and overhaul — general information

With the engine completely stripped, clean all the components and examine them for wear. Each part should be checked, and where necessary replaced or overhauled as described in the following Sections. Replace main and connecting rod bearings as a matter of course, unless you know that they have had little wear and are in perfect condition.

If in doubt as to whether to replace a component which is still just serviceable, consider the time and effort which will be incurred should it fail at an early date. Obviously the age and expected life of the vehicle must influence the standards applied. Gaskets, oil seals and O-rings must all be replaced as a matter of course. Flywheel bolts must be replaced because of the high stresses to which they are subjected.

Some other bolts may be re-used if they do not show signs of stretching — see Specifications or the appropriate Section. Take the opportunity to replace the engine freeze plugs while they are easily accessible. Knock out the old plugs with a hammer and chisel or punch. Clean the plug seats, smear the new plugs with sealant and tap them squarely into position.

28 Oil pump — inspection and overhaul

1   Remove the Allen screws which hold the two halves of the pump together (photo).
2   Remove the pick-up pipe and gear cover from the gear housing. Be prepared for the ejection of the relief valve spring (photo).
3   Remove the relief valve spring and plunger (or ball on early models) and the pump gears (photos).
4   Clean all components, paying particular attention to the pick-up screen, which is partly obscured by its housing. Inspect the gears, housing and gear cover for signs of wear or damage.
5   Measure the relief valve spring, and if possible compare its characteristics with those in the Specifications. Replace it if it is weak or distorted. Also inspect the plunger or ball for scoring or other damage.
6   Install the gears to the casing. Using a straight-edge and feeler blades, check the gear side clearance and endplay (photos). Also check the backlash between the teeth. If the clearances are outside the specified limits, replace the pump.
7   If the clearances are satisfactory, lubricate the gears. Lubricate and install the relief valve plunger (or ball) and spring (photo). Pack the pump with petroleum jelly, filling all voids between the gears, cavity and cover. If this isn't done, the pump may fail to prime when the engine is started.
8   Install the pick-up pipe and gear cover. Install and tighten the Allen screws.

26.6 Lifting out the crankshaft

28.1 Undoing the oil pump Allen screws

28.2 Separating the pick-up pipe and cover from the pump body

28.3A Removing the oil pump idler gear . . .

28.3B . . . and the driving gear

28.6A Measuring oil pump gear side clearance . . .

28.6B . . . and gear endplay

28.7 Installing the relief valve plunger

29 Crankshaft and bearings — inspection

1 Examine the crankpin and main journal surfaces for scoring or scratches. Measure the journals in several places, using a micrometer, to check for out-of-round and taper. Limits are given in the Specifications. If the journals are scored or out of limit, the crankshaft must be reground and undersize bearings installed.

2 Inspect the bearing shells for signs of general wear, pitting and scratching. Replace them as a matter of course unless they are in perfect condition.

3 On engines with separate thrust washers, these should be replaced if the crankshaft endplay is excessive.

4 An accurate method of determining bearing wear is by the use of Plastigage. Reinstall the crankshaft in the main bearings and lay a strip of Plastigage across the journal or shell, which must be dry. Install the bearing cap, tightening the bolts/nuts to the specified torque. On removal of the cap the width of the filament is checked against a scale which shows the bearing running clearance. This clearance is then compared with that given in the Specifications (photos). The connecting rod bearings can be checked this way, too.

5 If the crankshaft is suspected of being cracked it should be taken to a suitably equipped workshop for crack testing.

6 Replace the pilot bearing now, while it is accessible — see Section 15.

29.4A Plastigage filament (arrowed) on a bearing shell

29.4B Checking the width of the crushed filament

30 Cylinder block and bores — inspection and overhaul

1   The cylinder bores must be checked for taper, ovality, scoring and scratches. Start by examining the top of the bores; if these are worn, a slight ridge will be found which marks the top of the piston ring travel. If the wear is excessive, the engine will have had a high oil consumption rate accompanied by blue smoke from the exhaust.

2   If available, use an inside dial gauge to measure the bore diameter just below the ridge and compare it with the diameter at the bottom of the bore, which is not subject to wear. If the difference is more than 0.1 mm (0.004 in), the cylinders will normally require reboring with new oversize pistons installed.

3   Aftermarket oil control rings can be obtained for fitting to the existing pistons if it is felt that the degree of wear does not justify a rebore. However, any improvement brought about by such rings may be only temporary.

4   If new pistons or piston rings are to be installed in old bores, deglaze the bores as described in Section 18.

5   If there is a ridge at the top of the bore, remove it with a ridge reamer (Section 18). If the ridge is left, the piston ring may hit it and break.

6   Thoroughly examine the crankcase and cylinder block for cracks and damage and use a piece of wire to probe the oil passages and water jacket to ensure they are unobstructed.

31 Pistons and connecting rods — inspection and overhaul

1   Check that each piston and connecting rod carry identification and orientation marks, so that they may be reassembled correctly.

2   Remove one of the circlips which secure the piston pin. Push the piston pin out of the piston and connecting rod (photos).

3   Examine the pistons for scoring, burning and cracks. If new pistons of standard size are required, note that four grades are available — see Specifications. The grade letter is stamped on the piston crown and adjacent to each bore.

4   Measure the diameter of each piston, at 90° to the piston pin and about 7 mm (0.28 in) above the bottom of the skirt. Subtract the diameter from the bore measurement (Section 30) to give the piston running clearance in the bore. Clearance limits are given in the Specifications.

5   If new rings are to be installed to the existing pistons, expand the old rings over the top of the pistons. The use of two or three old feeler blades will be helpful in preventing the rings dropping into empty grooves. Note that the oil control ring is in three sections.

6   Before installing the new rings to the pistons, insert them into the cylinder bore and use a feeler gauge to check that the end gaps are within the specified limits (photo). If an end gap is too small, carefully file the ends of the ring.

7   Clean out the piston ring grooves using a piece of old piston ring as a scraper. Be careful not to scratch the aluminium surface of the pistons. Protect your fingers — piston ring edges are sharp (photo).

8   Check the vertical clearance of the new rings in their grooves. Replace the piston if the clearance is excessive.

9   Check the fit of the piston pin in the connecting rod bushing and in the piston. If there is perceptible play, a new bushing or an oversize piston pin must be installed. Consult a Volvo dealer or other specialist.

10 Install the rings to the piston, starting with the oil control ring sections (photo). Observe the TOP marking on the second compression ring (photo). The other rings can be installed either way up unless they are marked. Do not expand the compression rings too far or they will break — use a ring expander tool or feeler blades as described in paragraph 5.

11 Oil the piston pin. Reassemble the connecting rod and piston, making sure the rod is installed facing the right direction, and secure the piston pin with the circlip.

31.2A Removing a piston circlip

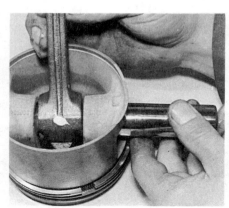

31.2B Pulling out the piston pin

31.6 Measuring a piston ring end gap

31.7 Cleaning a piston ring groove

31.10A Installing the oil control ring sections

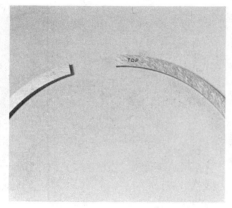

31.10B TOP marking on second compression ring

Fig. 1.17   Checking piston ring side clearance (Sec 31)

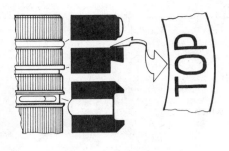

Fig. 1.18   Piston ring profiles (Sec 31)

32   Camshaft and tappets — inspection

1   Inspect the cam lobes and the camshaft bearing journals for scoring or other visible evidence of wear. Once the surface hardening of the lobes has been penetrated, wear will progress rapidly.

2   Measure the bearing journals with a micrometer and check for ovality and taper. The bearing running clearances can be established by installing the camshaft to the head and using Plastigage (Section 29). If the bearing caps and seats in the head are damaged, the head will have to be replaced.

3   Check the camshaft endplay as described in Section 9.

4   Inspect the tappets for scuffing, cracking or other damage; measure their diameter in several places with a micrometer. Tappet clearance in the bore can be established by measuring bore diameter and subtracting tappet diameter from it. Replace the tappets if they are damaged or worn.

5   Inspect the tappet shims for visible damage; replace them if they are obviously worn. A selection of new shims should be available in any case for setting the valve clearances.

33   Auxiliary shaft — inspection

1   Inspect the shaft bearing journals and gears for wear or damage. Measure the journals with a micrometer. Replace the shaft if it is worn or damaged.

2   If the auxiliary shaft bearings in the block are damaged, have them replaced by a Volvo dealer or other specialist.

34   Flywheel/driveplate — inspection

1   Inspect the flywheel/driveplate for cracks or other damage. Pay particular attention to the clutch friction face of the flywheel — see Chapter 5, Section 12.

2   If the driveplate is damaged, it must be replaced. Small cracks or moderate scoring on the flywheel friction face can be removed by machining; this is specialist work. Large cracks or deep scores will necessitate replacement.

3   Inspect the flywheel ring gear and replace it if necessary (Section 14).

4   Flywheel run-out may be checked during engine rebuilding, when the flywheel is mounted on the crankshaft.

35   Cylinder head — disassembly

1   If not done during removal, unbolt and remove the camshaft sprocket and backplate.

2   Unbolt and remove the thermostat housing and the engine lifting eye. Remove the thermostat and gasket.

3   Progressively loosen the camshaft bearing cap nuts. The camshaft will be lifted by valve spring pressure as this is done. Be careful that it does not spring up suddenly.

4   With the spring pressure relieved, remove the nuts and the camshaft bearing caps. Keep the caps in order: they are numbered 1 to 5, the numbers being on the thermostat side.

5   Lift out the camshaft with its oil seal(s).

6   Have ready a box divided into eight segments, or some other means of keeping matched components together.

7   Lift out the tappets and shims, keeping them identified for position (photo).

8   Remove the rubber rings from the valve stem tips.

9   Tap each valve stem sharply, using a light hammer and drift, to free the spring keepers.

10   Install a valve spring compressor to one valve. Compress the spring until the keepers are exposed. Lift out the keepers — a small screwdriver, a magnet or a pair of tweezers may be useful (photo). Carefully release the spring compressor and remove it.

11   Remove the valve spring retainer and the valve spring. Pull the valve out of its guide (photo). If the valve stem tip has been hammered or otherwise damaged so that it will not pass through the guide, do not

35.7   Removing a tappet

35.10   Extracting a keeper with a magnet

35.11   Removing a valve

35.12 Removing the inlet valve stem oil seal

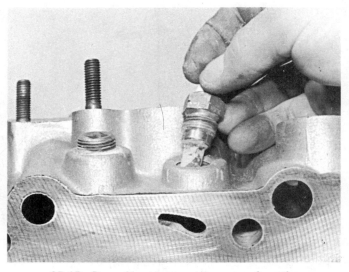

35.15 Removing a temperature sensor from the cylinder head

force it, but deburr the end with a fine file.

12 If it is an intake valve which has been removed, pull off the valve stem oil seal with a pair of long-nosed pliers (photo).

13 Remove the valve spring lower seat. If there is much carbon build-up around the outside of the valve guide, this will have to be scraped off before the seat can be removed.

14 Repeat paragraphs 10 to 13 on the other valves. Remember to keep all matched components together if they are to be re-used.

15 Remove the temperature sensor(s) and thermotime switch (as applicable), identifying them if necessary (photo).

36 Cylinder head — overhaul

1   With the cylinder head disassembled as described in the previous Section, use a scraper or wire brush to remove carbon from the combustion chambers and posts. Be careful not to scratch or gouge the head, especially on gasket mating faces.

2   Remove all traces of gasket from the mating faces and wash the head with solvent.

3   Use a straight-edge and feeler blade to check that the cylinder head surface is not distorted. If it is, it must be resurfaced by an automotive machine shop.

4   If the engine is still in the car, clean the piston crowns and cylinder bore upper edges, but make sure that no carbon drops between the pistons and bores. To do this, locate two of the pistons at the top of their bores and seal off the remaining bores with paper and masking tape. Press a little grease between the two pistons and their bores to collect any carbon dust; this can be wiped away when the piston is lowered. To prevent carbon build-up, polish the piston crown with metal polish, but remove all traces of the polish afterwards.

5   Examine the heads of the valves for pitting and burning, especially the exhaust valve heads. Replace any valve which is badly burnt. **Caution:** *Exhaust valves on Turbo engines contain sodium and must not be mixed with other scrap metal. Consult a Volvo dealer for safe disposal of these valves.*

6   Inspect the valve seats for pitting, burning or cracks. Have the seats recut or replaced if necessary. Light pitting can be removed by valve grinding.

7   Check the fit of the valves in their guides, if possible using a dial gauge to measure play at the valve head when it is held 1 to 2 mm (0.04 to 0.08 in) off its seat. Limits are given in the Specifications. If replaceing the valves does not improve the fit, the guides must be replaced. This is another specialist job.

8   If the old valves are in good condition, remove the carbon from them. This is most easily done by gripping the valve stem in an electric drill chuck, mounting the drill securely and spinning the valve against a wire brush or scraper. Wear eye protection.

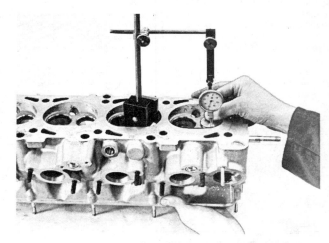

Fig. 1.19 Measuring valve play in the guide (Sec 36)

9   Valve grinding should now be carried out, either to mate new components together or to improve the fit of the old ones. Place the cylinder head upside down on a couple of wooden blocks.

10 Smear a trace of coarse carborundum paste on the seat face and press a suction grinding tool onto the valve head. With a semi-rotary action, grind the valve head to its seat, lifting the valve occasionally to redistribute the grinding paste. When a dull matt even surface is produced on both the valve seat and the valve, wipe off the paste and repeat the process with fine carborundum paste as before. A light spring placed under the valve head will greatly ease this operation. When a smooth unbroken ring of light grey matt finish is produced on both the valve and seat, the grinding operation is complete (photos).

11 Remove all traces of grinding paste from the valves, seats and guides, using first a solvent-soaked rag, then a clean rag, finally compressed air (if available). It is important that no grinding paste is left in the engine.

12 Measure the free length of the valve springs, and if possible check their load/length characteristics — see Specifications. Replace the springs if they are obviously weak or distorted, or if they have seen much service.

13 Replace the intake valve stem oil seals as a matter of course.

36.10A Applying grinding paste to a valve

36.10B Grinding in a valve

37.2 Installing a valve spring lower seat — some models use a flat seat instead of a dished one

37 Cylinder head — reassembly

1 Install the temperature sensors and similar items to their positions in the head. Apply a non-hardening thread sealer or Teflon tape to the threads.

2 Oil the stem of one valve and insert it into its guide. Install the spring lower seat, dished side up (photo).

3 On an intake valve, install the valve stem oil seal, pushing it onto the valve guide with an appropriately sized socket. Be careful not to damage the seal lips on the valve stem: if a protective sleeve is supplied with the seals, cover the keeper grooves with it when fitting the seal.

4 Install the valve spring and retainer (photos). Compress the spring and install the two keepers, using a dab of grease on each to hold them in position. Carefully release the compressor.

5 Cover the valve stem with a cloth and tap it sharply with a light hammer to verify that the keepers are properly seated.

6 Repeat paragraphs 2 to 5 on the other valves. (Stem oil seals are not fitted to exhaust valves).

7 Install new rubber rings to the valve stem tips (photo).

8 Oil the tappets and insert them into their bores. Install a shim to each tappet (photo). Record the thickness of shims installed for reference later.

9 Oil the camshaft lobes and bearings. Install the camshaft and the bearing caps, applying sealant to the mating faces of the front and rear caps.

10 Install the bearing cap nuts and pull down the caps by progressively tightening the nuts. When all the caps are seated, tighten the nuts to the specified torque.

11 Lubricate and install a new front oil seal, lips inwards. Seat it with a seal driver or piece of pipe.

12 Install the camshaft sprocket and plates. Secure the sprocket with the bolt and washer. Restrain the sprocket with a strap wrench or similar tool when tightening the bolt. (On the B230 engine the sprocket will have to be removed again when installing the cylinder head, so do not bother to tighten the bolt fully.)

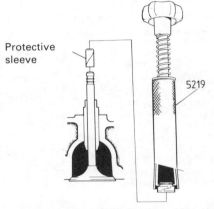

Protective sleeve

5219

Fig. 1.20 Tool 5219 for installing the valve stem oil seals — a deep socket will do (Sec 37)

13 Check the valve clearances and adjust them if necessary as described in Section 4, turning the camshaft sprocket by hand or with a strap wrench.

14 Install the thermostat, using a new gasket, and the engine lifting eye.

38 Crankshaft and main bearings — installation

1 Wipe the bearing shell locations in the crankcase and main bearing caps with a clean lint-free rag.

2 Install the main bearing shells to their locations (the same locations as previously occupied if they are being re-used). Press the shells into the webs so that the tangs engage in the recesses provided. All

37.4A Installing a valve spring . . .

37.4B . . . and the spring retainer

37.7 Installing a rubber ring to the valve stem tip

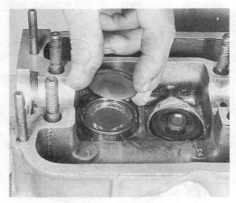

37.8   Installing a shim to its tappet

38.4   Oiling a main bearing shell

38.7   Tightening a main bearing cap bolt

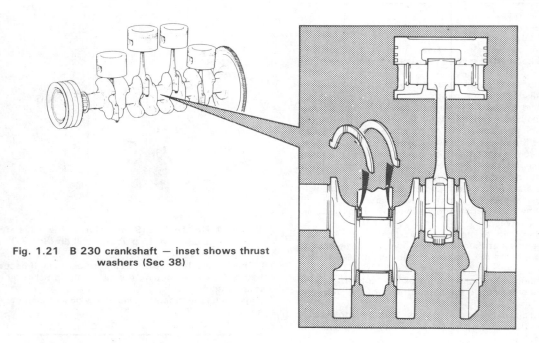

Fig. 1.21   B 230 crankshaft — inset shows thrust washers (Sec 38)

the shells are the same, except for No 5 shells on the B23 engine which have thrust flanges.

3   On the B230 engine, smear some grease on the smooth sides of the half thrust washers. Place the washers in position on each side of the center bearing in the crankcase. The slotted sides of the washers face outwards. Set the camshaft into place and measure the bearing clearance as described in Section 29. Remove the crankshaft.

4   Oil the bearing shells in the crankcase (photo).

5   Wipe clean the crankshaft journals, then lower it into position with the help of an assistant. Make sure that the shells (and thrust washers, when applicable) are not displaced.

6   Inject oil into the crankshaft oil passages. Oil the shells in the main bearing caps and install the caps, each in its correct position and facing the right way.

7   Install the main bearing cap bolts and tighten them progressively to the specified torque (photo).

8   Rotate the crankshaft. Some stiffness is to be expected with new components, but there must be no tight spots or binding.

9   Check the crankshaft endplay, levering it back and forth and placing a dial indicator on the flywheel mounting face. On the B23 engine, endplay can also be checked by inserting a feeler gauge between the crankshaft web and No 5 bearing flange.

10   Install the rear oil seal carrier, using a new gasket. Trim the protruding ends of the gasket level with the oil pan mating face (photos).

11   Install a new rear oil seal as described in Section 13.

39   Auxiliary shaft — installation

1   Lubricate the auxiliary shaft bearing surfaces and insert the shaft into the block, being careful not to damage the bearings.

2   Install the front oil seal housing, using a new gasket. Trim the ends of the gasket level with the oil pan mating face. Some of the housing bolts cannot be installed yet because they also secure the camshaft drivebelt backplate.

3   Install new oil seals in the front oil seal housing, lips inwards and lubricated. Use a seal driver or piece of pipe to seat the seals (photo).

40   Engine — reassembly after overhaul

1   Install the oil pressure switch and any other senders or transducers to the block.

2   Install the pistons and connecting rods (Section 18).

3   Install the oil pump, delivery pipe and drain hose guide (Section 17).

4   Install the oil trap drain hose, making sure that it is inserted fully into its hole and that it is secured towards its lower end by the guide (photo). It is impossible to install this hose after the oil pan has been installed.

5   Install the oil pan, using a new gasket (photos). Tighten the bolts

38.10A Installing a rear oil seal carrier gasket

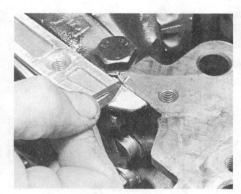

38.10B Trimming the ends of the gasket

39.3 Front oil seals and housing in position. Four bolt holes (arrowed) are shared with drivebelt backplate

40.4 Oil trap drain hose correctly installed. The guide is secured by an oil pump bolt (arrowed)

40.5A Reinstalling the oil pan

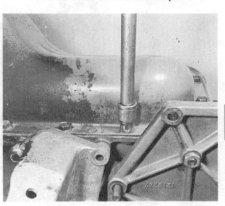

40.5B Be sure to tighten the oil pan bolts to the specified torque or the gasket may be damaged

progressively to the specified torque.

6 Install the flywheel or driveplate (Section 12), making sure that it is in the correct position.

7 Install the crankshaft sprocket and guide plates, and the pulley or pulley boss. Install the pulley bolt, jam the ring gear teeth and tighten the bolt to the specified torque (photos).

8 Install the cylinder head (Section 10).

9 Install the water pump, using a new gasket.

10 Install the camshaft drivebelt backplate, the auxiliary shaft and camshaft sprockets, and the drivebelt and tensioner (Section 6). Install the drivebelt cover.

11 Install the oil pump drivegear/shaft, making sure it engages with the oil pump end with the auxiliary shaft gear (photo).

12 Install a new O-ring to the crankcase ventilation system oil trap. Install and secure the trap (photos).

13 Install the dipstick tube and secure its bracket. Insert the dipstick.

14 Install the coolant distribution pipe.

15 When applicable, install the oil cooler adaptor, using a new O-ring (photo).

16 Install the remaining external components listed in Section 24, paragraph 1. If preferred, delicate items such as the distributor and alternator may be left until the engine has been installed in the vehicle.

17 Make sure that the ignition sensor bracket is in place before mating the transmission to the engine, since it is impossible to install it afterwards.

41 Engine — reconnection to transmission

Automatic transmission

1 Make sure that the torque converter is fully engaged in the trans-

40.7A Installing the crankshaft sprocket rear guide plate . . .

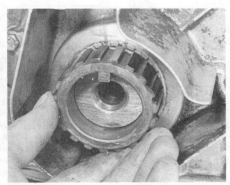

40.7B . . . the sprocket itself . . .

40.7C . . . the front guide plate and the pulley boss . . .

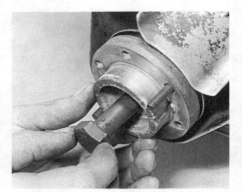

40.7D . . . and the pulley bolt

40.11 Installing the oil pump drivegear

40.12A Installing a new O-ring to the oil trap

40.12B Reinstalling the oil trap

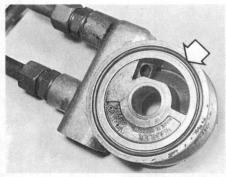

40.15 Oil cooler adaptor — O-ring arrowed

mission. Put a thin coat of grease or anti-seize compound on the torque converter locating lug.

2   Connect the transmission to the engine, engaging the locating dowels. Install a couple of bellhousing-to-engine nuts and bolts.

3   Insert the torque converter-to-driveplate bolts, turning the crankshaft to gain access. Install all of the bolts finger tight at first, then tighten them in cross-cross sequence to the specified torque (Chapter 6 Specifications).

Manual transmission

4   Make sure that the clutch is correctly centered and that the clutch release components are installed in the bellhousing. Put a thin coating of grease or anti-seize compound on the input shaft splines.

5   Mate the transmission to the engine. Rotate the crankshaft or the input shaft if necessary to align the input shaft and clutch driven plate splines. Do not allow the weight of the transmission to hang on the input shaft.

6   Engage the transmission on the engine dowels. Install a couple of bellhousing-to-engine nuts and bolts.

All models

7   Install the remaining bellhousing nuts and bolts, and (when applicable) the flywheel/driveplate bottom cover plate. Tighten the nuts and bolts a little bit at a time until the specified torque is reached.

8   Install the starter motor.

42 Engine — installation (with transmission)

1   Installation is essentially a reversal of the procedure in Section 22, with the following additional points.

2   On automatic transmission models, adjust the gear selector mechanism (Chapter 6, Section 30).

3   Refill the engine with oil and coolant.

4   Refill the manual transmission or automatic transmission with lubricant if necessary.

5   Refer to Section 44 before starting the engine.

43 Engine — installation (alone)

1   Make sure that the clutch is properly centered, or that the torque converter is fully engaged in the transmission. Put a light coat of grease or anti-seize compound on the transmission input shaft or the torque converter locating lug.

2   Lower the engine into position; have an assistant watch to see that no pipes, wires etc, are trapped.

3   On manual transmission models, rock the engine from side to side, or rotate the crankshaft slightly, to encourage the input shaft to enter the clutch driven plate. Do not allow the engine to hang on the input shaft.

4   When the bellhousing is engaged on the engine dowels, insert a couple of engine-to-bellhousing nuts and bolts and snug them up.

5   The remainder of installation is now a reversal of the procedure in Section 21.

6   Refill the engine with oil and coolant.

7   Refer to Section 44 before starting the engine.

44 Initial start-up after overhaul or major repair

1   Make a final check to ensure that everything has been reconnected to the engine and that no rags or tools have been left in the engine bay.

2   Check that the accessory drivebelts are correctly tensioned.

3   Check that engine oil and coolant levels are correct.

4   Start the engine. This may take a little longer than usual as fuel is pumped up to the engine.

5   Check that the oil pressure light goes out when the engine starts.

6   Run the engine at a fast idle (approximately 2000 rpm) and check for leaks of oil, fuel and coolant. Also check power steering and (when applicable) transmission fluid cooler unions for leaks. Some smoke and odd smells may be expected as assembly lubricant burns off exhaust components.

7   Bring the engine to operating temperature. Check that the throttle cable is correctly adjusted, then check the idle speed and mixture (Chapter 3, Section 8).

8   On automatic transmission models, check the adjustment of the kickdown cable (Chapter 6, Section 31).

9   Stop the engine and allow it to cool. Recheck the oil and coolant levels and top up if necessary.

10   If new bearings, pistons etc, have been installed, the engine should be run in at restricted speeds and loads for the first 600 miles (1000 km) or so. After this mileage the camshaft drivebelt should be re-tensioned (Section 6) and the valve clearances rechecked (Section 4). At the same time it will be beneficial to change the engine oil and filter. There is no need to retighten the cylinder head bolts.

45 Compression check

1   When engine performance is down, or if misfiring occurs which cannot be attributed to the ignition or fuel system, a compression test can provide diagnostic clues. If the test is performed regularly it can give warning of trouble before any other symptoms become apparent.

2   The engine must be at operating temperature, the battery must be fully charged and the spark plugs must be removed. The services of an assistant will also be required.

3   Disable the ignition system by disconnecting the coil LT wire. In-stall the compression tester to No 1 spark plug hole. (The type of tester which screws into the spark plug hole is preferred.)

4   Have the assistant hold the throttle wide open and crank the engine. Record the highest reading obtained on the compression tester.

5   Repeat the test on the remaining cylinders, recording the pressure developed in each.

6   Desired pressures are given in the Specifications. If the pressure in any cylinder is low, pour a teaspoonful of clean engine oil into the spark plug hole and repeat the test.

7   If the addition of oil temporarily improves the compression pressure, this indicates that rings, bore or piston wear was responsible for the pressure loss. No improvement suggests that leaking or burnt valves or a blown head gasket may be to blame.

8   A low reading from two adjacent cylinders is almost certainly due to the head gasket between them having blown.

9   On completion of the test, install the spark plugs and reconnect the coil LT wire.

46 Troubleshooting — engine

Symptom	Reason(s)
Engine fails to start	Discharged battery
	Loose battery connection
	Loose or broken ignition leads
	Moisture on spark plugs, distributor cap, or HT leads
	Incorrect spark plug gaps
	Cracked distributor cap or rotor
	Other ignition system fault
	Dirt or water in fuel
	Empty fuel tank
	Faulty fuel pump
	Other fuel system fault
	Faulty starter motor
	Low cylinder compressions
Engine idles erratically	Intake manifold air leak
	Leaking head gasket
	Incorrect valve clearances
	Worn camshaft lobes
	Faulty fuel pump
	Loose crankcase ventilation hoses
	Idle adjustment incorrect
	Uneven cylinder compressions
Engine misfires	Spark plugs worn or incorrectly gapped
	Dirt or water in fuel
	Idle adjustment incorrect
	Burnt valve
	Leaking cylinder head gasket
	Distributor cap cracked
	Incorrect valve clearances
	Uneven cylinder compressions
	Worn carburetor
	Other fuel or ignition system fault
Engine stalls	Idle adjustment incorrect
	Intake manifold air leak
	Ignition timing incorrect
Excessive oil consumption	Worn pistons, cylinder bores or piston rings
	Valve guides and valve stem seals worn
	Oil leaks
Engine backfires	Idle adjustment incorrect
	Ignition timing incorrect
	Incorrect valve clearances
	Intake manifold air leak
	Sticking valve
Engine noises	See Troubleshooting at beginning of manual

1

PART B: V6 ENGINE

47 General information

The V6 engine is a product of the PRV (Peugeot-Renault-Volvo) co-operative. It is well proven and is found in a wide selection of European cars destined for the upper end of the market.

The cylinder block, cylinder heads and crankcase are all made of aluminium alloy. The crankcase is split horizontally at the level of the crankshaft; a pressed steel oil pan is bolted onto the bottom of the lower crankcase.

A 90° V configuration is used for the two banks of cylinders. Cast iron cylinder liners of the wet type are used, as is common. (French practice: coolant circulates freely between the liners and the block.) The liners are sealed at the top by the head gasket and at the base by individually selected seals.

The crankshaft runs in four replaceable shell bearings, with endplay controlled by thrust washers at the flywheel end. Each crankpin is shared by two connecting rods. The connecting rod bearings are also of the shell type.

The cylinder heads are of the crossflow type, the common intake manifold sitting in the center of the engine and the exhaust manifolds being on the outside. Each head carries valves, a camshaft and rocker gear. The camshafts are driven by separate chains with hydraulic tensioners.

The lubrication system is conventional. A gear type pump, driven from the crankshaft by a third chain, draws oil from the oil pan. Oil under pressure passes through an external canister filter before being supplied to the crankshaft, camshafts and rocker gear. The pistons and piston pins are lubricated by splash (later models employ nozzles in the block, directed at the underside of the pistons). The timing chains are lubricated by spillage from the camshaft front bearings and the chain tensioner.

48 Routine maintenance

1   Check the engine oil level weekly, every 250 miles or before a long run. Top up if necessary (photos). See Section 2 for more details.
2   Change the oil every 6000 miles (10 000 km) or six months, also as described in Section 2. An 8 mm square drive key will be needed for the oil pan drain plug (photo).
3   At the same intervals replace the oil filter — see Sections 3, and 49.
4   Every 24 000 miles (40 000 km) or two years, or if valvegear noise becomes excessive, check the valve clearances (Section 50).
5   At the same intervals, inspect the crankcase ventilation system components (Sections 5 and 51).
6   There is no camshaft drivebelt to replace on the V6 engine. Although not specified by the makers, it would be a good idea to inspect the timing chains at roughly 48 000 mile (80 000 km) or four-year intervals. See Section 80, paragraph 2.

49 Oil filter — replacement

Proceed as in Section 3, but note that the oil filter is located on the left-hand side of the block (photo).

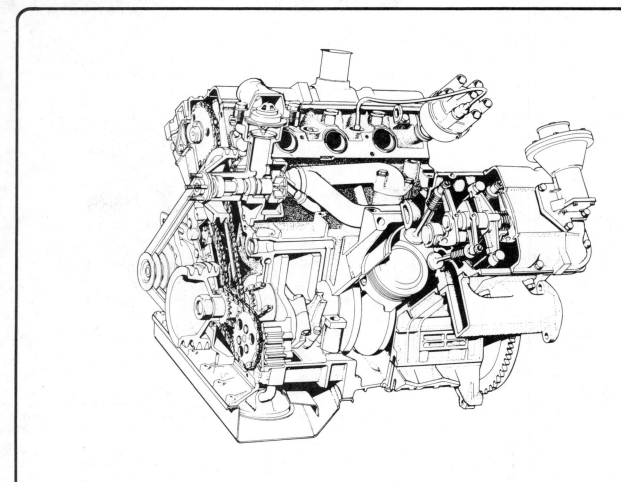

Fig. 1.22 Cutaway view of the B 28 engine (Sec 47)

48.1A Removing the engine oil dipstick

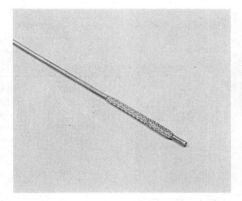

48.1B Dipstick tip — oil level should be in the hatched area

48.1C Topping-up the engine oil

48.2 Removing the oil pan drain plug

49.0 Installing a new oil filter

50.7 Removing a rocker cover bolt

50 Valve clearances — check and adjustment

1 Disconnect the battery negative lead.
2 Disconnect the ignition harness connector on the right side inner fender panel.
3 Unbolt the control pressure regulator (without disconnecting it) and place it on the intake manifold.
4 Remove the air intake ducting, the oil filler cap and the crankcase ventilation hoses.
5 Unbolt and remove the vacuum pump.
6 Remove the air conditioning compressor drivebelt (Chapter 2, Section 7). Unbolt the compressor brackets from the engine and move the compressor and brackets to one side. Do not disconnect any refrigerant hoses, nor allow the weight of the compressor to hang on them.
7 Unbolt and remove both rocker covers. Remove the gaskets (photo).
8 Using a 36 mm socket on the crankshaft pulley nut, or (manual transmission) by pushing the car along with a gear engaged, bring the engine to TDC, No 1 firing. This is achieved when the No 1 pulley notch is aligned with the O mark on the timing scale, and both rocker arms for No 1 cylinder (LH rear) have a small amount of free play, showing that the valves are closed.
9 Insert a feeler gauge of the specified thickness between the adjuster screw and valve stem on No 1 cylinder exhaust valve (the rearmost valve). The blade should be a firm sliding fit, neither tight nor loose.
10 If adjustment is required, loosen the locknut and turn the adjuster screw until the clearance is correct. Hold the adjuster screw stationary and tighten the locknut without disturbing the position of the screw. Recheck the fit of the feeler blade (photo).
11 Similarly check the clearances of the exhaust valves on cylinders No 3 and 6, and the intake valves on cylinders No 1, 2 and 4. Remember that intake and exhaust clearances are different.
Intake valves are nearest the center of the engine, exhaust valves nearest the outside.

Fig. 1.23 No 1 cylinder notch in the TDC position (Sec 50)

1 No 1 cylinder notch   2 No 6 cylinder notch

12 Turn the crankshaft 360º (one full turn) clockwise, so that the No 1 pulley notch is again aligned with the O mark, but this time No 1 cylinder rocker arms have no free play. In this position check the clearances of the exhaust valves on cylinders No 2, 4 and 5, and the intake valves on cylinders No 3, 5 and 6.
13 Recheck all clearances, turning the crankshaft as necessary.
14 Install the rocker covers, using new gaskets (photo).
15 Install the remaining components in the reverse order to removal. Tension the air conditioning compressor drivebelt (Chapter 2, Section 7).
16 Run the engine and check that there are no oil leaks from the rocker covers.

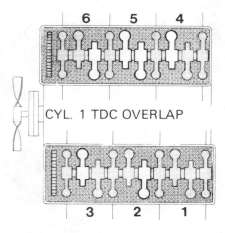

50.10   Adjusting a valve clearance — when the described clearance is obtained, tighten the locknut while holding the adjuster screw stationary with the screwdriver

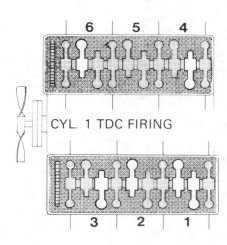

Fig. 1.24   With No 1 in firing position, adjust the valves in the light colored positions (Sec 50)

Fig. 1.25   With No 1 ending exhaust stroke (valves overlapping) adjust the other valves shown (Sec 50)

50.14   Installing a new rocker cover gasket

51   Crankcase ventilation system — general information

Refer to Section 5 for general advice, and to Fig. 1.26 for component location.

52   Major operations possible with the engine installed

1   The following components can be removed with the engine in place:
   a)   Timing chains, sprockets etc
   b)   Cylinder heads and camshafts
   c)   Crankshaft front oil seal
   d)   Oil pump
   e)   Flywheel/clutch (after removal of transmission)
   f)   Crankshaft rear oil seal (after removal of flywheel)
   g)   Engine mounts

2   The oil pan can be removed with the engine installed, but this does not give access to any major components.
3   The engine must be removed for access to the pistons, cylinder liners and crankshaft.

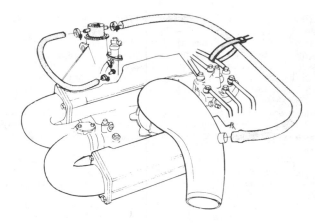

Fig. 1.26   Crankcase ventilation components (Sec 51)

53 Engine disassembly and reassembly — general information

Refer to Section 8.

54 Timing chains and sprockets — removal and installation

1 If the engine is in the vehicle, carry out the following preliminary work:
a) Disconnect the battery
b) Remove the radiator, fan shroud and fan. When installed, also remove the ATF cooler (Chapter 2)
c) Remove all accessory drivebelts (Chapter 2)
d) Unbolt and move aside the air conditioning compressor and the steering pump, both with their brackets
e) Remove the air intake ducting, the oil filler cap and the crankcase ventilation hoses

2 Unbolt and remove the vacuum pump.
3 Unbolt the control pressure regulator from the right-hand valve cover and move it aside.
4 Remove the ten bolts which secure each rocker cover, noting the locations of the various lengths of bolt.
5 Remove the rocker covers and remove the gaskets. If necessary, scrape off the old gasket with a razor blade.
6 Bring the engine to TDC, No 1 firing. See Section 50, paragraph 8.
7 Remove the blanking plate from the unused starter motor opening. Jam the starter ring gear through this opening, either by having an assistant brace a pry bar or a large screwdriver in the gear teeth, or (preferably) by bolting a suitably shaped metal segment to engage with the teeth.
8 Using a 36 mm socket, undo the crankshaft pulley center nut. This nut is very tight. Remove the ring gear jamming device.
9 Check that the keyway in the crankshaft pulley is facing up, then remove the pulley. (If the keyway was down, the key might fall into the oil pan).
10 Remove the 25 bolts which secure the timing cover (photo). Also remove the drivebelt idler pulleys, which share some of the timing cover bolts. Note the locations of the various length bolts.
11 Move aside the wiring harness which passes in front of the timing cover.
12 Pull the timing cover off its dowels and remove it. Cover the holes leading to the oil pan with paper or rag, then remove the timing cover gasket.
13 Restrain the camshaft sprockets and loosen their center bolts with a 10 mm Allen key (photo).
14 Retract each timing chain tensioner by turning the locking device anti-clockwise with a small screwdriver, at the same time pushing in the plunger (photo).
15 Unbolt the oil pump sprocket. Remove the sprocket and chain.
16 Unbolt and remove the timing chain tensioners. Identify them if they are to be re-used. Remove the oil strainer from behind each tensioner.

Fig. 1.27 Metal segment (5112) jamming the ring gear teeth (Sec 54)

17 Unbolt and remove the timing chain guides and dampers.
18 The timing marks on the sprockets are unlikely to be aligned with the marked links on the chains. Alignment only occurs once in a good many revolutions. Do not waste time trying to align the marks now.
19 Remove the camshaft sprocket center bolts, the camshaft sprockets and the timing chains. Keep the left-hand and right-hand components separate.
20 Remove the oil pump drive sprocket, the outer Woodruff key, the spacer, the twin sprocket and the inner key. A puller may be needed (photo).
21 Examine components as described in Section 80. Clean the gasket mating faces.
22 Begin reassembly by installing new oil strainers to the chain tensioner recesses in the block. Install and secure the chain tensioners, using thread locking compound on the bolts (photos).
23 Install and secure the chain guides and dampers, again using thread locking compound (photos).
24 Oil the crankshaft nose and fit the inner Woodruff key to it (photo).
25 Install the twin drive sprocket to the crankshaft. The mark on the sprocket must face outwards. Drive the sprocket home with a socket or piece of pipe if it is tight (photo). Be careful not to dislodge the Woodruff key.
26 Prepare to fit the left-hand timing chain. (Remember, left and right refer to the engine, not to the mechanic.) Temporarily install the crankshaft pulley nut and turn the crankshaft until the keyway points to the left-hand camshaft. Turn the left-hand camshaft so that the sprocket locating groove points directly upwards (Fig. 1.28).
27 Install the left-hand timing chain to the camshaft sprocket so that the two marked links on the chain are on each side of the mark on the sprocket. Install the chain on the innermost section of the crankshaft sprocket so that the single marked link is in line with the mark on the sprocket. Tension the chain on the driving side (next to the straight

54.10 Removing a timing cover bolt

54.13 Loosening a camshaft sprocket bolt — it may be necessary to insert a screwdriver through a hole in the cam sprocket to prevent it from turning

54.14 Retracting a timing chain tensioner

1

54.20   Pulling off the twin sprocket

54.22A   Installing a new oil
strainer . . .

54.22B   . . . and bolting on the
chain tensioner

54.23A   Reinstalling a chain damper

54.23B   Tightening a chain guide bolt

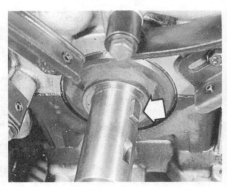

54.24   Install the inner Woodruff
key (arrowed)

54.25   Driving the inner sprocket
into place

54.27A   Single marked link aligned with
crankshaft sprocket mark . . .

54.27B   . . . and twin marked links
straddling the camshaft sprocket mark

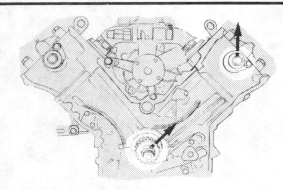

Fig. 1.28   Keyway and groove positions for installing the
left-hand timing chain (Sec 54)

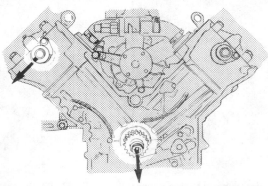

Fig. 1.29   Keyway and groove positions for installing the
right-hand timing chain (Sec 54)

guide) and install the camshaft sprocket onto the camshaft. The sprocket must line up with the groove (photos).

28 Install the bolt to the left-hand camshaft sprocket, but do not tighten it fully yet.

29 Prepare to fit the right-hand chain. Turn the crankshaft clockwise until the keyway points vertically downwards. Turn the right-hand camshaft until the sprocket locating groove is facing outwards and parallel with the head mating face (Fig. 1.29).

30 Install the right-hand chain and sprockets in the same way as the left-hand one, with the twin marked links straddling the camshaft sprocket mark and the single marked link aligned with the crankshaft sprocket mark (photos). Turn the crankshaft slightly if necessary to achieve alignment.

31 Install the bolt to the right-hand camshaft sprocket. Tighten both camshaft sprocket bolts to the specified torque, immobilizing the sprockets with a screwdriver.

32 Release the timing chain tensioners by turning the locking devices a quarter turn clockwise. Do not force the plungers out.

33 Rotate the crankshaft through two full turns clockwise to set the chain tension. (The marks will no longer align — see paragraph 18.) Turn the crankshaft a further half turn clockwise so that the keyway points upwards again.

34 Remove the crankshaft pulley nut. Install the spacer, the outer Woodruff key and the oil pump driving sprocket (photos).

35 Install the oil pump driven sprocket and chain. Use thread locking compound on the sprocket bolts.

36 Oil the chains and remove the rag or paper from the oil pan holes. Check that nothing has been overlooked.

37 Install the timing cover, using a new gasket (photo). Insert and tighten the 25 bolts, applying thread locking compound to the four bottom bolts. Remember to install the wiring harness behind the idler pulleys.

38 Install a new oil seal to the timing cover if necessary (Section 58), then install the crankshaft pulley. Be careful not to dislodge the Woodruff key.

39 Turn the starter ring gear. Install the crankshaft pulley nut and tighten it to the specified torque (photo). Remove the jamming device.

40 Install the starter motor blanking plate.

41 Trim the protruding ends of the timing cover gasket flush with the cylinder heads.

42 Install the rocker covers, using new gaskets.

43 Install the remaining components by reversing the removal procedure, referring to other Chapters as necessary.

44 Check the ignition timing (Chapter 4, Section 6) and the idle speed and mixture (Chapter 3, Section 8).

55 Oil pump — removal and installation

1   Proceed as for timing chain removal (Section 54, paragraphs 1 to 12).

2   Unbolt the oil pump sprocket. Remove the sprocket and chain (photos).

3   Remove the four bolts which secure the oil pump to the block. Withdraw the pump and remove the idler gear (photos).

4   Clean the pump and block mating faces, and clean out the pump recess in the block.

5   Begin installation by oiling all components liberally. Insert the idler gear into the recess, install the pump and secure it with the four bolts. Tighten the bolts to the specified torque.

6   Install the sprocket and chain. Use thread locking compound on the sprocket bolts.

7   Install the timing cover and associated components (Section 54).

56 Cylinder heads — removal and installation (engine installed)

Note: *Read through this procedure before starting work to understand what is involved. In particular, note that if the cylinder liners are accidentally disturbed, the engine may have to be removed and completely disassembled to properly reinstall them.*

1   Disconnect the battery negative lead.

2   Drain the cooling system (Chapter 2, Section 3).

3   Remove the intake manifold and associated components (Chap-

54.30A Right-hand chain marking at the crankshaft sprocket . . .

54.30B . . . and at the right-hand camshaft sprocket

54.34A Install the spacer . . .

54.34B . . . and the outer Woodruff key

54.37 Installing a new timing cover gasket

54.39 Tightening the crankshaft pulley nut

55.2A   Unbolt the oil pump sprocket . . .

55.2B   . . . and remove it with the chain

55.3A   Unbolt the oil pump . . .

55.3B   . . . and remove it from the block. Idler gear will stay behind

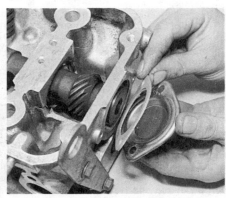

56.10   Removing the cover plate and gasket from the rear of the head

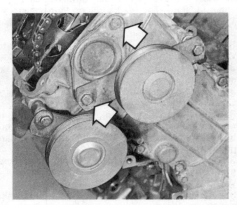

56.12A   Cover plate bolts (arrowed) for access to right-hand sprocket bolt. Idler pulley may need to be removed

56.12B   Threaded plug (arrowed) for access to left-hand sprocket bolt

56.14   Loosening a cylinder head bolt

ter 3, Section 22).

4   Disconnect the coolant hose(s) from the head(s) to be removed. Also remove the radiator top and/or bottom hoses from the water pump and thermostat housing.

5   When removing the right-hand head, disconnect or remove the following items:
   a) TDC sender and cable cable
   b) Distributor (Chapter 4, Section 4)
   c) Air conditioning compressor (without disconnecting the hoses)
   d) Engine oil dipstick and tube

6   When removing the left-hand head, disconnect or remove the following items:
   a) Vacuum pump
   b) Hot air ducting

7   Disconnect the exhaust downpipes from both manifolds. Disconnect the exhaust mounting from the transmission and move the ex-

haust system rearwards so that the downpipes are clear of the manifold studs.

8   Perform the following operations on one head at a time.

9   Unbolt and remove the rocker cover.

10   Remove the cover plate from the rear of the head (photo).

11   Remove the four timing cover bolts which enter the cylinder head.

12   Remove the cover plate (RHS) or threaded plug (LHS) which gives access to the camshaft sprocket bolt (photos).

13   Immobilize the camshaft sprocket with a screwdriver inserted through the sprocket. Loosen the sprocket center bolt with a 10 mm Allen key.

14   Loosen the cylinder head/rocker gear bolts progressively in the sequence shown in Fig. 1.30. Remove the bolts and the rocker gear; identify them if both heads are to be removed (photo).

15   Loosen the camshaft thrust plate bolt. Move the thrust plate aside.

16   It is now necessary to install a tool (Volvo tool No 5213, or equivalent) to retain the camshaft sprocket and to keep the chain taut.

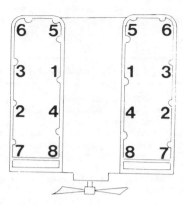

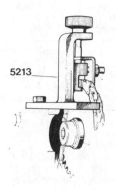

Fig. 1.30 Cylinder head bolt loosening and tightening
sequence (Sec 56)

Fig. 1.31 Volvo tool 5213 for retention of the camshaft
sprocket (Sec 56)

If the timing chain is allowed to slacken, the timing cover will have
to be removed (Section 5) to reset the tensioner. If the tool is not
available, proceed by removing the timing chains.

17 With the sprocket securely supported and the chain tension
assured, unscrew the camshaft sprocket center bolt. Remove the bolt
from the right-hand camshaft, being careful not to drop it into the timing
case. On the left-hand side there is not room to remove the bolt
completely.

18 Move the camshaft rearwards so that it is clear of the sprocket.

19 Place a wooden or plastic lever between the head and the water
outlet pipe. Lever the head away from the block with a rocking motion
and remove it. Do not try to lift the head straight off the block, or the
cylinder liners will be disturbed.

20 Remove the gasket from the cylinder head or block. Remove the
dowels if they are loose.

21 Install cylinder liner retaining clamps, using some head bolts,
spacers, and large washers or suitable pieces of scrap metal. The
precise dimensions of the retainers are not important unless the pistons
are to be removed, in which case they must not interfere with the bores
(photo).

22 If it is necessary to turn the crankshaft while the head is removed,
or if the other head is to be removed, the camshaft sprocket retaining
tool must be changed for one which will allow the sprocket to rotate.
Volvo tool No 5105 is suitable.

23 Repeat the operations from paragraph 9 to remove the other
cylinder head.

24 If the head has been removed to replace a blown gasket, check
the head for distortion (Section 36) and measure the liner protrusion
(Section 85) to establish the reason for the gasket failure.

25 Begin installation by removing the liner retaining clamps. Install
the camshaft sprocket retaining tool, if it was removed, being careful
to keep the chain taut.

26 Install the dowels in the cylinder block and keep them raised by

Fig. 1.32 Tool 5105 is needed in addition if the sprocket
must be rotated (Sec 56)

inserting a nail or twist drill (3 mm/0.12 in diameter) in the holes beneath
the dowels (photo).

27 Make sure that the exposed sections of the timing cover gasket
are in good condition. If not, repair them with fragments cut from a
new gasket. Apply RTV sealer to the gasket sections.

28 With the gasket mating face clean and dry, install a new head
gasket to the block. Make sure that it is positioned correctly (photo).

29 Lower the cylinder head and camshaft into position. Turn the camshaft until its hole lines up with the locating pin in the sprocket, then
push the camshaft forwards to engage with the sprocket. Insert the
sprocket center bolt and tighten it lightly.

30 Remove the nails or drills from below the dowels. Install the rocker

56.21 Home-made liner retaining
clamps in position

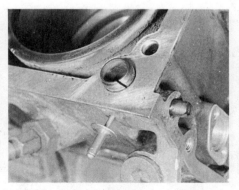

56.26 A rivet inserted below the dowel
will keep the dowel from being pushed
into the block when the head is installed

56.28 When installing a cylinder head
gasket, make sure all of the holes line
up and TOP or UP marks are
positioned correctly

gear and the cylinder head bolts. The bolts must be clean and have oiled threads.

31 Tighten the cylinder head bolts progressively, in the correct sequence (Fig. 1.30) and to the Stage 1 specified torque.

32 Loosen the first bolt, then retighten it to the Stage 2A specified torque. Tighten the bolt further through the angle specified for Stage 2B. Make up a cardboard template to indicate the angle required (photo).

33 Repeat the Stage 2 tightening process on each bolt in turn.

34 Remove the camshaft sprocket retaining tool. Move the camshaft thrust plate into position and tighten its retaining bolt.

35 Hold the camshaft sprocket from turning and tighten the sprocket center bolt to the specified torque.

36 Install the cover plate or access plug to the front of the timing cover. Use a new O-ring under the cover plate.

37 Install and tighten the four timing cover bolts.

38 Install the head rear cover plate, using a new gasket.

39 Install the other cylinder head if it was removed.

40 Check and adjust the valve clearances (Section 50).

41 Temporarily install the rocker covers, using new gaskets. Only secure them with a bolt at each corner for the time being, as they will have to come off again soon.

42 Install the exhaust downpipes to the manifolds and secure the exhaust mounting.

43 Install the items listed in paragraphs 5 and 6, with the exception of the air conditioning compressor.

44 Install the coolant hoses. Refill the cooling system (Chapter 2, Section 5).

45 Install the intake manifold and fuel injection equipment (Chapter 3, Section 22).

46 Reconnect the battery. Run the engine and bring it up to normal operating temperature.

47 Stop the engine and allow it to cool for two hours.

48 Remove the rocker covers again. Tighten each cylinder head bolt, in the correct sequence, through the angle specified for Stage 3 tightening.

49 Install the rocker covers, this time using all the bolts. Install any other disturbed components.

50 Install the air conditioning compressor.

51 Check the ignition timing (Chapter 4, Section 6) and the idle speed and mixture (Chapter 3, Section 8).

57 Camshaft — removal and installation

1   Remove the cylinder head and rocker gear (Section 56 or 70).

2   If not done during removal, unbolt the camshaft thrust plate and remove the cover plate from the rear of the head (photo).

3   Pull the camshaft through the hole in the rear of the head, being careful not to damage the bearing surfaces (or your fingers) with the sharp edges of the cam lobes (photo).

4   Install by reversing the removal operations, applying plenty of oil to the bearing journals and the cam lobes. If special lubricant is supplied with a new camshaft, use it.

5   Run in a new camshaft at moderate engine speeds (in the range 1500 to 2500 rpm) for a few minutes, or as specified by the manufacturer.

58 Crankshaft oil seal (front) — replacement

1   Disconnect the battery negative cable.

2   Remove the radiator, fan shroud and fan. If equipped, also remove the ATF auxiliary cooler (Chapter 2).

3   Remove all the accessory drivebelts (Chapter 2, Section 7).

4   Turn the crankshaft until No 1 pulley notch is aligned approximately with the 20° BTDC mark on the timing scale. This will position the keyway correctly.

5   Remove the crankshaft pulley (Section 54, paragraphs 7 to 9).

6   Carefully pry the oil seal from its location. Do not damage the seal seat.

7   Clean the seal seat in the timing cover and inspect the seal rubbing surface on the pulley. If the rubbing surface is damaged, it must be cleaned up or the pulley must be replaced, otherwise the new seal will fail prematurely.

8   Grease the lips of the new seal. Install the seal, lips inwards, and tap it in using a large socket or a seal driver or piece of pipe.

9   Install the crankshaft pulley, being careful not to dislodge the Woodruff key.

10 Jam the ring gear and tighten the crankshaft pulley nut to the specified torque. Remove the jamming device.

11 Install the other components by reversing the removal sequence.

59 Flywheel/driveplate — removal and installation

Proceed as in Section 12, but disregard the references to the ignition system. Note also that the arrangement of the driveplate washers differ (Fig. 1.33).

60 Crankshaft oil seal (rear) — replacement

Refer to Section 13, but disregard references to the installed depth of the seal.

61 Flywheel ring gear — replacement

Refer to Section 14.

62 Crankshaft pilot bearing — removal and installation

Refer to Section 15, but note that there is no bearing retaining circlip on the V6 engine.

56.32 Angle-tightening a cylinder head bolt

57.2 Removing a camshaft thrust plate

57.3 Removing a camshaft

63 Oil pan — removal and installation

Note: *The oil pan can be removed with the engine installed, but this does not give access to any major components.*

1   If the engine is in the vehicle, drain the oil. If it is on the bench, invert it.
2   Remove the 23 bolts and washers which secure the oil pan (photo).
3   Remove the oil pan, tapping or levering it gently if necessary to free it. Remove the gasket.
4   The oil baffle and oil pump pick-up strainer are now accessible. If the strainer is removed, replace its O-ring.
5   Install by reversing the removal operations, using a new gasket (photo). Tighten the oil pan bolts evenly.

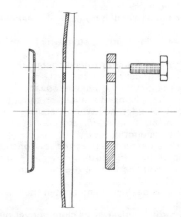

Fig. 1.33   Driveplate and washers (Sec 59)

63.2   Removing an oil pan bolt

63.5   Installing a new oil pan gasket

64 Engine mounts — removal and installation

1986 and earlier models

1   Disconnect the battery negative cable.
2   Raise and support the front of the vehicle. From below, remove the through-bolt and nut and the nuts from the lower part of the mounting to be removed.
3   Connect an engine hoist to the engine. Raise the engine slightly to unload the mounts and remove the lower part.
4   The upper part of the mount, complete with rubber block, can now be removed.
5   Install by reversing the removal operations.

1987 and later models

6   Raise and support the front of the vehicle. From below, remove the engine mount-to-crossmember nut (on the underside of the crossmember), the two remaining mount-to-crossmember nuts, (on the top side of the crossmember) and the two mount-to-engine block bolts.
7   Connect and engine hoist to the engine, raise it slightly and maneuver the mount out from its seat on the crossmember.
8   Installation is the reverse of the removal procedure.

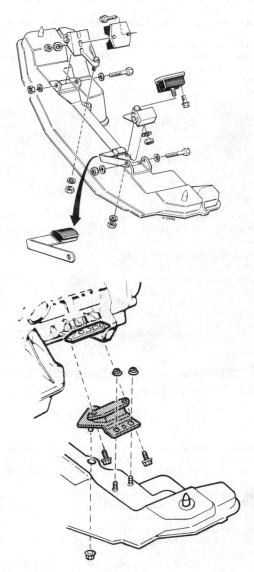

Fig. 1.34   Engine mounts (top — 1986 and earlier models; bottom — 1987 and later models)

1

65   Methods of engine removal

The makers recommend that the engine and transmission be removed together. This method is preferred if adequate lifting tackle is available.

Removal of the engine alone is easy enough on models with automatic transmission. This was done in our workshop. Installation proved quite difficult because the angle at which the engine is suspended has to be just right in order to mate with the transmission. Thought should be given to this when attaching the lifting tackle: ideally the chains should be attached to a bar running lengthways and pivoted about its center so that the angle can easily be adjusted.

Removal of the engine alone on manual transmission models is not recommended by the makers and has not been tried. This is not to say that it is impossible, but the problems mentioned above will be magnified because of the need to align the clutch with the transmission input shaft.

66   Engine — removal (alone)

1   Open the hood to the vertical position, or remove it completely.
2   Remove the battery (Chapter 12, Section 5).
3   Drain the cooling system and remove the radiator, the fan shroud and the fan clutch assmbly (Chapter 2, Sections 3, 8 and 9). Remove the radiator top and bottom hoses from the engine.
4   Remove the air intake ducting from the air cleaner and the airflow sensor, together with the oil filler cap and the crankcase ventilation hoses.

66.24   Removing the torque converter cover plate

5   Disconnect the exhaust downpipes from the manifolds. (If preferred, these can be removed from below later on.) Remove the gaskets.
6   If equipped, remove the transmission fluid auxiliary cooler (Chapter 2, Section 17).
7   Unbolt the crossmember which carries the radiator top mounting brackets. Four of the hood latch bolts pass through this crossmember. Disengage the crossmember from the hood release cable and remove it.
8   Unbolt the air conditioning condenser bottom mountings. Move the condenser forwards, being careful not to strain the refrigerant pipes. Do not disconnect the pipes.
9   Remove the air conditioning compressor drivebelt (Chapter 2, Section 7). Disconnect the wires from the compressor clutch. Unbolt the compressor and its mounting brackets; place the compressor in the

battery tray, being careful not to strain the refrigerant hoses. Do not disconnect the hoses.
10   Disconnect the engine and fuel injection wiring harness electrical connectors on top of the engine and next to the expansion tank. Unclip the impulse relay from the expansion tank so that it stays with the harness. Place the harness on the engine.
11   Unbolt the air conditioning harness ground strap from the intake manifold. Move the harness out of the way.
12   Loosen the fuel tank filler cap to release any pressure. Disconnect the fuel feed pipe from the top of the fuel filter. Be prepared for fuel spillage.
13   Disconnect the fuel return pipe from the union on the left-hand inner fender, or from the fuel distributor.
14   Disconnect the throttle, kickdown and cruise control cables (as applicable) and move them aside.
15   Remove the hot air ducting from the air cleaner and the downpipe shroud.
16   Unbolt one end of the ground strap which joins the fuel distributor to the firewall.
17   Disconnect the distributor-to-coil secondary cable and the distributor primary electrical connector.
18   Disconnect the distributor vacuum advance pipes from the control valve behind the right-hand suspension turret (if equipped). Make identifying marks for reference when installing.
19   Disconnect the brake booster/heater control vacuum feed from the T-fitting near the vacuum pump.
20   Disconnect the heater hoses at the rear of the engine.
21   Remove the oil filter (Sec 49).
22   Raise and support the vehicle. Remove the engine undertray (if not already done).
23   Drain the engine oil. Install and tighten the drain plug afterwards for safekeeping.
24   Unbolt the torque converter or clutch cover plate from the bottom of the bellhousing (photo).
25   Remove the starter motor (chapter 12, Section 11).
26   Remove the steering pump drivebelt (Chapter 2, Section 7). Unbolt the pump and its brackets — some of the mounting bolts are more easily reached from above — and support the pump below the engine.
27   Unbolt and remove the blanking plate from the unused starter motor aperture.
28   Unbolt the ground strap from behind the engine right-hand mount.
29   On automatic transmission models, make alignment marks between the torque converter and driveplate. Working through the cover plate or starter motor aperture, remove the torque converter-to-driveplate bolts, turning the crankshaft to gain access. Lever the torque converter rearwards to check that it is free from the driveplate.
30   On all modles, remove the bellhousing-to-engine bolts which are accessible from below (photo).
31   Loosen the exhaust mounting bracket at the rear of the transmission.
32   Remove the through-bolt from each engine mount, and the nut(s) from each mount which secures it to the front crossmember.
33   Lower the vehicle. Remove the alternator and its drivebelts (Chapter 12, Section 8). Remove the water pump pulley, which is now free.
34   Remove the remaining bellhousing nuts and bolts. On automatic transmission models, one of these bolts also secures the transmission dipstick/filler tube.
35   Attach a hoist to the engine, using the eyes provided.
36   Support the transmission with a floor jack under the bellhousing.
37   Check that no attachments have have been overlooked.
38   Lift the engine until the mounting studs are clear of the crossmember. Raise the jack so that the transmission is still supported, then pull the engine forwards and off the transmission. With a manual transmission, do not allow the weight to rest on the input shaft.
39   Lift the engine out of the bay (photo). As assistant should guide it out and make sure that items such as the air conditioning compressor are not snagged. Be careful not to damage the air conditioning condenser, which will be punctured by the water pump pulley studs if the engine lurches forwards.
40   If an engine stand is available, mount the engine on it (the flywheel or driveplate may have to be removed). If not, set the engine down on the bench or on blocks of wood, making sure it is securely supported.
41   On automatic transmission models, secure a bar or a block of wood across the mouth of the bellhousing to keep the torque converter in place (photo).

66.30 One of the bellhousing bolts — this one retains a fluid cooler pipe bracket as well

66.39 Lifting out the engine

66.41 Retain the torque converter with a block of wood and string

67 Engine — removal (with transmission)

1 Proceed as described in Section 66, paragraphs 1 to 4 and 6 to 20.
2 Raise and support the vehicle. Remove the engine undertray.
3 Remove the steering pump (Section 66, paragraph 26).
4 Unbolt the ground strap from behind the engine right-hand mounting.
5 On manual transmission models, disconnect the clutch cable or remove the clutch slave cylinder (without disconnecting the hydraulic hose) and remove the gear lever. See Chapter 5, Section 3 or 7, and Chapter 6, Section 21.
6 On automatic transmission models, unbolt the selector linkage from below at the shift lever end, and separate the wiring connectors.
7 On all models, disconnect the exhaust downpipe from the rest of the system.
8 Disconnect the driveshaft from the transmission flange, making alignment marks for reference when installing.
9 Support the rear of the engine from above, or use a floor jack and a piece of wood from below, then remove the transmission rear mounting crossmember and associated components.
10 Remove the through-bolt for each engine mounting, and the single nut from each mounting which secures it to the front crossmember.
11 Lower the vehicle. Support the transmission with a floor jack and a piece of wood (if not already done).
12 Attach a hoist to the four lifting eyes.
13 Take the weight of the engine/transmission unit. Check that no attachments have been overlooked, then lift the unit out of the engine bay, lowering the jack under the transmission as the lifting begins. Have an assistant guide the unit and check that nothing is still connected.
14 Set the unit down on the bench or on blocks of wood, making sure it is securely supported.

68 Engine — separation from transmission

Refer to Section 23, and note the following points:
a) It will be necessary to remove the oil filter before the starter motor can be removed
b) Remove the blanking plate from the unused starter motor aperture
c) Remove the exhaust downpipes

69 Engine — disassembly

1 With the engine removed for disassembly, remove external components as follows:
a) Engine mounts (photo)
b) Exhaust manifolds
c) Dipstick tube and dipstick (photos)
d) Clutch pressure and driven plates (Chapter 5)
e) Alternator, accessory drivebelts and pulleys
f) Intake manifold (Chapter 3)
g) Distributor (Chapter 4)
h) Water pump with hoses and distribution pipe (Chapter 2)
j) Ignition sensor and diagnostic socket
k) Vacuum pump (Chapter 9)
m) Oil level sensor (Section 94)
n) Sensors, brackets, sender units, etc

2 Complete disassembly of the engine can now proceed as described in the following Sections.
3 The oil pump should be removed at some stage after the removal of the timing chains and sprockets.

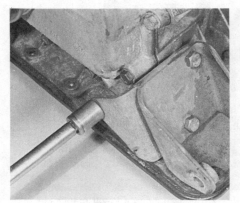

69.1A Unbolting an engine mount bracket

69.1B Unbolting the dipstick tube bracket . . .

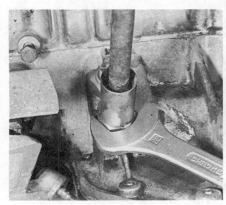

69.1C . . . and the tube base nut

70   Cylinder heads — removal (engine removed)

1   Remove the timing chains and sprockets as described in Section 54, paragraph 4 onwards.
2   Loosen the cylinder head/rocker gear bolts progressively in the sequence shown in Fig. 1.30. Remove the bolts.
3   Remove the rocker gear, Keep left-hand and right-hand components separate.
4   Remove the cylinder heads, using a couple of metal bars inserted in two bolt holes to rock them away from the center of the engine. (This is to avoid disturbing the liners. If the liners will be removed anyway, just lift the heads straight off.)
5   Remove the cylinder head gaskets.
6   If the cylinder liners are not to be disturbed, install liner retaining clamps (Section 56, paragraph 27).

71   Pistons and connecting rods — removal

1   With the engine on the stand, remove the cylinder heads and the oil pan (Sections 63 and 70).
2   Remove the oil baffle and the oil pump pick-up strainer. Remove the O-ring (photos).
3   Remove the 14 small bolts and the eight main bearing nuts which secure the lower crankcase (photo). Lift off the lower crankcase; remove the oil pick-up tube O-ring.
4   Install spacers to the main bearing cap studs and then install the main bearing nuts so that the main bearings and crankshaft are secured for subsequent operations. This is particularly important if the main bearings are not to be disturbed. In any event it is undesirable to have the crankshaft fall out unexpectedly.
5   If it is hoped to re-use the existing cylinder liners, make sure that they are securely clamped.
6   Turn the engine over on the stand so that the bottom is facing up.
7   Inspect the connecting rods and caps to see that they carry identification marks or numbers. Note that the numbering system used here by the makers does not correspond to the cylinder numbering (Fig. 1.35).
8   Check the side clearance between each pair of connecting rods (photo). If it is outside the specified limits, all six connecting rods must be replaced.
9   Remove the nuts from one connecting rod cap, tapping it with a soft-faced hammer if it is stiff. Remove the bearing shell if it came out and keep it with the cap.
10   Push the piston and rod out through the cylinder bore. Catch the piston as it emerges. Tap the rod with a hammer handle if it is stiff. Be extremely careful not to damage the cylinder walls. Remove the bearing shell if it came out and keep it with the cap.
11   Assemble the rod and cap and secure them with the nuts. Keep the bearing shells identified if they are to be re-used.
12   Repeat the process to remove the other five pistons and rods, turning the crankshaft as necessary to gain access.

Cylinder			1	4	2	5	3	6
Marking of con rod and cap	early type		A	B	C	D	E	F
	late type		1	2	3	4	5	6
Crank webs (from rear)			1		2		3	

Fig. 1.35   Relationship of cylinder and connecting rod numbering. Letter (L shown here) is arbitrary (Sec 71)

72   Crankshaft and main bearings — removal

1   Remove the pistons and connecting rods (Section 71). Also remove the flywheel or driveplate, if not already done.
2   Unbolt and remove the rear oil seal housing (photo).
3   Remove the main bearing nuts and spacers.
4   Remove the main bearing caps, making identifying marks if necessary so that they can be installed in the same position. Tap them free with a soft-faced hammer. Keep the main bearing shells with their caps; remove the thrust washers from each side of the rear cap (photo).
5   Lift out the crankshaft. If necessary, get help from an assistant; it is heavy.
6   Remove the upper half main bearing shells from their seats in the crankcase by pressing the end of the shell furthest from the locating

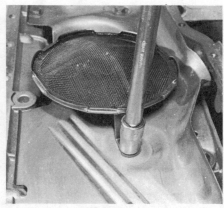

71.2A   Unbolting the oil baffle and pick-up strainer

71.2B   Removing the oil pick-up strainer

71.3   Removing a lower crankcase bolt — be sure to loosen all of them a little bit before removing any of them

71.8 Measuring the side clearance between a pair of connecting rods

72.2 Removing the rear oil seal housing

72.4 Removing the rear main bearing cap with thrust washers

75.1A Oil pump, showing relief valve

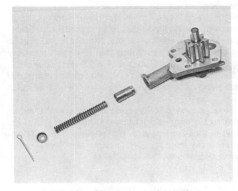

75.1B Oil pump and relief valve components

tab. Keep the shells in order if they may be re-used.
7 Remove the upper halves of the thrust washers from each side of the rear bearing seat.

73 Cylinder liners — removal

1 With the cylinder heads and pistons removed, mark the position of each liner relative to the block. Also mark the cylinder number on each liner.
2 Remove the liner retaining clamps (if installed), then lift the liners out of the block.
3 Clean the sealing lip on the outside of the liner and the sealing surface in the block.

74 Inspection and overhaul — general information

Refer to Section 27.

75 Oil pump — inspection and overhaul

1 Remove the relief valve components by depressing the cap and extracting the cotter pin. Remove the cap, spring and plunger (photos).
2 Clean the pump body and the gears and inspect them for wear and damage. If evident, the pump must be replaced as an assembly. Although clearances and wear limits are specified, they are not easy to measure because of the design of the pump. If in doubt, replace the pump.
3 Inspect the relief valve plunger for scoring. Measure the spring free length and if possible check its load/length characteristic — see Specifications. Relief valves are available separately.
4 Reassemble the pump and relief valve components. Use a new cotter pin.

76 Crankshaft and bearings — inspection

Refer to Section 29.

77 Cylinder block and liners — inspection

1 Remove the various blanking plugs from the cylinder block. Clean the block inside and out, not forgetting the oil and water passages. Blow through the passages with compressed air.
2 Inspect the block for cracks, distortion of mating faces or other

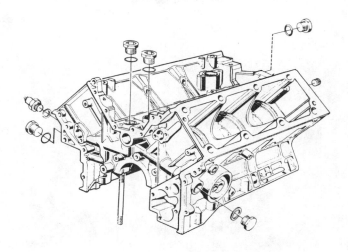

Fig. 1.36 Cylinder block blanking plugs (Sec 77)

damage. Seek professional advice if damage is found. Also check the condition of threaded holes.

3   Install the blanking plugs to the block using new seals or copper washers.

4   Inspect the liners for cracks, internal scoring or other visible damage.

5   Check the liners for wear and ovality by measuring the internal diameter at several points, using an internal micrometer. Alternatively, measure a piston ring end gap at the bottom end of the liner (where it is unworn) and towards the top (where wear is greatest). Liners cannot be rebored and must be replaced, complete with pistons and in sets of six, if excessively worn. Refer to the next Section.

78 Pistons and connecting rods — inspection and overhaul

1   Examine the pistons for scoring, burning and cracks. Replace the complete set of pistons and liners if such damage is found.

2   Measure the piston diameter. If satisfactory, remove the piston rings to clean out the grooves and to check the gaps. See Section 31, paragraphs 4 to 7, and Fig. 1.37.

3   Inspect the connecting rod bolts for evidence of stretching or damaged threads. Replace the bolts if necessary by clamping the connecting rod in a soft-jawed vise and driving out the old bolts with a plastic mallet. Support the piston when doing this. Press in the new bolt using the vise, the connecting rod cap and a 12 mm socket.

4   The piston pins are an interference fit in the connecting rod bushings. Press tools are needed to remove and install them; this must be done by specialists.

5   Accurate inspection of the connecting rods for twisting or other distortion requires them to be separated from the pistons.

6   New pistons and liners are supplied with piston pins. The old connecting rods must be removed from the old pistons and installed to the new ones by a Volvo dealer or other specialist.

79 Flywheel/driveplate — inspection

Refer to Section 34.

80 Timing chains and sprockets — inspection

1   Worn timing chains make a characteristic thrashing sound. Of itself chain wear is not serious, but if the chain stretches too far, a plunger may fall out of one of the tensioners. This will cause loss of oil pressure and possibly serious damage to the engine.

2   Chain wear may be checked without too much disassembly by removing the left-hand valve cover. The left-hand chain tensioner can now be inspected with the aid of a flashlight. If the tensioner plunger protrudes by four notches (8mm/0.32 in) or more, wear is excessive and the chains must be replaced.

3   Chains and sprockets wear together and should always be replaced together. To do otherwise is risking noise and rapid wear.

4   Inspect the chain guides and dampers. Replace them if they are badly grooved or otherwise damaged.

5   Inspect the chain tensioners, but do not disassemble them. If the plunger is removed from a tensioner, the tensioner must be replaced. Check that the tensioner oilways are not blocked.

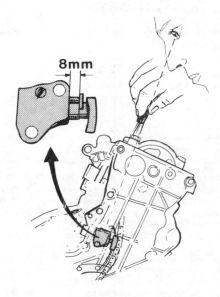

Fig. 1.38 Removing a connecting rod bolt (Sec 78)

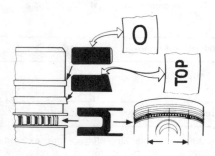

Fig. 1.37 Piston ring profiles. Stagger oil control rail gaps as shown (Sec 78)

Fig. 1.39 Installing a new connecting rod bolt (Sec 78)

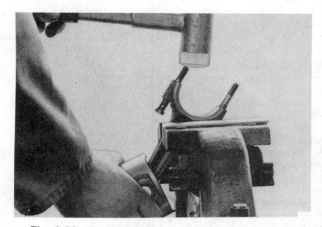

Fig. 1.40 Checking timing chain wear (Sec 80)

6   Replace the tensioner oil strainers, the timing cover gasket and the camshaft cover gaskets as a matter of course. Also replace the crankshaft front oil seal unless it is known to be in perfect condition.

81 Camshafts and rocker gear — inspection and overhaul

1   Inspect the cam lobes and the camshaft bearing journals for scoring, scuffing or other damage. Once the surface hardening of the lobes has been penetrated, wear will progress rapidly.
2   Measure the bearing journals with a micrometer and check them for ovality and taper. To establish the bearing running clearance, an internal micrometer must be used to measure the bearings in the cylinder heads. Excessive wear or damage can only be corrected by replaceing the camshaft and/or head.
3   Measure camshaft endplay with the camshaft installed in the head (photo). If endplay is excessive, replace the thrust plate.
4   Disassemble the rocker shaft for examination as follows.
5   Remove the bolt from the pedestal furthest from the circlip. Hold the pedestal against spring pressure as the bolt is removed (photo).
6   Slide the pedestals, rocker arms, springs and spacers off the shaft, being careful to keep them all in order (photo). Remove the circlip from the end of the shaft.
7   Clean all components, paying particular attention to the oil passages. Replace worn or damaged items. The camshaft rubbing faces of the rocker arms are surface hardened and must not be machined.
8   Reassemble in the reverse order of disassembly, oiling all components liberally. Note that the flat faces of the pedestals face the circlip end of the shaft, and that the shaft oil passages face downwards.

82 Cylinder head — disassembly

1   Remove the camshaft (Section 57).
2   Unbolt and remove the exhaust manifold. Remove the gasket sections.

3   Remove the spark plugs and any coolant unions, blanking plates, etc.
4   Have ready a box divided into six segments. Remove the valves as described in Section 35, paragraphs 9 to 13. Note that valve stem oil seals are installed both to intake and to exhaust valves on this engine (photos).
5   Keep the components of the left-hand and right-hand heads separate if both are being disassembled.

83 Cylinder head — overhaul

1   Refer to Section 36, and note the following additional points.
2   If decarbonising the pistons while still in the liners, stuff paper or clean rags into the water jacket around the cylinder liners to keep dirt out. Remove the paper or rags on completion.
3   Replace both the intake and the exhaust valve stem oil seals.
4   Replace the freeze plugs if they are obviously rusty or have seen much service.

84 Cylinder head — reassembly

1   Install the valves as described in Section 37, paragraphs 2 to 6, noting that stem oil seals are installed on all valves (photo).
2   Install the exhaust manifold, using new gaskets. Separate the gasket sections by cutting, not by tearing.
3   Install the camshaft (Section 57).
4   Install the spark plugs, coolant unions, etc.

85 Cylinder liners — installation

1   The protrusion of the cylinder liners above the top of the block must be accurately set to ensure good sealing of the head gaskets and liner

81.3   Measuring camshaft endplay — a dial indicator could be used in place of the feeler gauge

81.5   Removing the rocker pedestal bolt

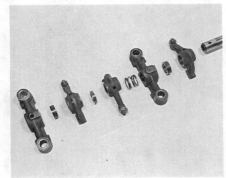

81.6   Rocker shaft components removed

82.4A   Valve spring lower seat is not dished on the V6 engine

82.4B   Removing a valve stem oil seal

84.1   Pressing a new valve stem oil seal onto a valve guide

bases. Base seals are available in various thicknesses; a selection should be obtained for this procedure.

2   Make sure that the liners and their seats are perfectly clean.

3   Install one liner in the block without a seal. Observe position and alignment marks if re-using the old liners. Clamp the liner lightly (Section 56, paragraph 21).

4   Using a straight-edge and feeler gauges, or (preferably) a dial test indicator and a suitable bracket, measure the protrusion of the top of the liner relative to the top of the block (photo). Measure in three different places and record the results.

5   The difference between the three measurements must not exceed 0.05 mm (0.002 in). If it does, remove the liner and check for dirt on the liner or seat. If the difference is within limits, use the largest of the three measurements as the basis for calculation. For example:

Measurement 1 = 0.10 mm
Measurement 2 = 0.06 mm
Measurement 3 = 0.07 mm
Maximum difference = 0.04 mm
Largest measurement = 0.10 mm

6   Select a base seal of thickness such that the final protrusion of the liner will be within the specified range. Aim for the maximum allowable protrusion. For example:

Desired protrusion = 0.23 mm (max)
Measurement 1 (above) = 0.10 mm
Difference (seal thickness required) = 0.13 mm

7   The seal closest in thickness to that required carries a red mark (see Specifications). It might prove marginally too thick, in which case a white marked seal would have to be used.

8   Remove the liner from the block.

9   Install the thickness of seal just calculated to all the liners. The colored identification tab should be positioned so that it will be visible when the liner is installed. The tongues round the inside of the seal must fit into the liner base groove (photo).

10   Install all the liners to the block, again observing position and alignment marks if applicable (photo). Clamp the liners.

11   Working on one cylinder bank at a time, measure the protrusion of each liner relative to the block and relative to the adjacent liner(s). The protrusion relative to the block must be as specified, and the difference between adjacent liners must not exceed 0.04 mm (0.0016 in).

12   Install different thickness seals to individual liners if necessary to achieve the desired result. (No more than one seal may be used per liner). New liners may be rotated or swapped around if necessary. Clamp the liners securely on completion.

86   Crankshaft and main bearings — installation

1   Wipe clean the main bearing shell locations in the cylinder block and bearing caps.

2   Install the bearing shells to their original locations if re-using the old shells. Insert the shells so that the tangs engage in the grooves. Make sure that the oil holes in the shells and block are aligned. The shells in the caps are plain (photo).

3   Install the upper half thrust washers on each side of the rear bearing seat in the block. The grooves must face outwards. Use a thin coat of grease to hold them in position (photo).

4   Oil the bearing shells in the block. Lower the crankshaft into position, being careful not to dislodge the thrust washers.

5   Inject oil into the crankshaft oil passages. Oil the shells in the main bearing caps and install the thrust washers to the rear cap, grooves outwards. Install the caps to their locations. Tap them down if necessary.

6   Secure each cap with a spacer and a nut (photo). Install two spacers to the rear cap and tighten the nuts to 40 Nm (30 ft-lbs).

7   Position a dial indicator probe against the crankshaft rear flange (photo). Lever the crankshaft back and forth and measure the endplay. If it is outside the specified limits, different thickness thrust washers will have to be installed.

8   Check that the crankshaft is free to rotate. Some stiffness is to be expected with new components, but there must be no light spots or binding.

85.4   Measuring cylinder liner protrusion

85.9   Liner with base seal installed. Identification tab is arrowed

85.10   Installing a liner to the block

86.2   Installing a main bearing shell to its cap

86.3   Rear main bearing seat and thrust washers

86.6   Main bearing caps retained with spacers and nuts

86.7   Measuring crankshaft endplay

86.9   Trimming the oil seal
housing gasket

87.2A   Installing a piston in its liner —
if any resistance is encountered, stop
and find out why

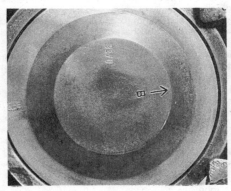

87.2B   Piston crown markings — arrow
points to front, B is grade mark

87.2C   Installing a connecting rod cap

87.3   Tightening a connecting rod
cap nut

9   Install the rear oil seal housing, using a new gasket. Make sure that the flat edge of the housing is flush with the block, then tighten the five Allen screws to secure it. Trim the gasket flush (photo).
10   Lubricate a new rear oil seal, the crankshaft and the seal seat. Install the seal, lips inwards, and seat it with a piece of tubing.
11   If the pilot bearing was removed (manual transmission only), install it now.

87   Pistons and connecting rods — installation

1   Deglaze the liner bores if new rings are being installed on old pistons and liners. See Section 18, paragraph 9.
2   Install one piston and connecting rod as described in Section 18, paragraphs 10 to 12, but do not tighten the nuts yet. Remember that the connecting rod numbers do not correspond to the cylinder numbers (photos).

3   Install the other five pistons. Tighten the bearing cap nuts to the specified torque when each pair of rods are installed on a crankpin (photo). (If the nuts are tightened when only one rod is installed, the twisting of the rod may produce a false reading.)
4   Check that the crankshaft is still free to rotate.
5   Remove the main bearing cap nuts and spacers. Make sure that the old pick-up tube is in place and install a new O-ring to it (photo).
6   Clean the upper and lower crankcase mating faces, then apply sealant to one face, including the areas around the main bearing studs (photo).
7   Install the lower crankcase. Install the main bearing nuts and the 14 small bolts, but only tighten them lightly at this stage.
8   Use a straight-edge to check that the rear edges of the crankcase halves are aligned (photo). Reposition the lower crankcase if necessary, first loosening the nuts and bolts.
9   Tighten the main bearing nuts in the sequence shown in Fig. 1.41 to the Stage 1 specified torque.

87.5   Oil pick-up tube O-ring (arrowed)

87.6   Applying sealant to the crankcase
mating face

87.8   Checking the alignment of the
crankcase halves

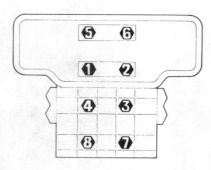

Fig. 1.41 Main bearing nut tightening sequence
(Sec 87)

10 Recheck the alignment of the crankcase halves. Loosen the nuts if necessary and start again.
11 Loosen the first nut and retighten it to the Stage 2A specified torque. Tighten the nut further through the angle specified for Stage 2B. Use a protractor or a cardboard template to indicate the angle required (photo).
12 Repeat the loosening and retightening process on each nut in turn.
13 Check that the crankshaft is still free to rotate.
14 Tighten the 14 small bolts in the lower crankcase.
15 Install the oil pump pick-up strainer, using a new O-ring, and the oil baffle.
16 Install the oil pan, cylinder heads and other components that were previously removed.

88 Cylinder heads — installation (engine removed)

1 Make sure that the head locating dowels are in position in the block. Insert a nail or similar item (approx 3 mm/0.12 in diameter) in the hole below each dowel to keep it raised.
2 Turn the crankshaft to bring No 1 cylinder to TDC.
3 Remove the liner retaining clamps from the left-hand cylinder bank. Make sure that the surface is clean, then install a new gasket. The gasket must be for the correct side (they are not identical) and the right way up.
4 Position the left-hand camshaft so that its sprocket locating groove will point upwards when the head is installed.
5 Install the left-hand head and camshaft to the block.
6 Install the left-hand rocker gear, making sure it is positioned correctly.
7 Remove the nails from below the left-hand dowels. Insert the cylinder head bolts, clean and with oiled threads. Only hand tighten the bolts at this time.
8 Similarly install the right-hand head, but position the camshaft groove so that it will point outwards and parallel with the head mating face (photo).

9 Tighten the cylinder head bolts in the correct stages and sequence (Section 56, paragraphs 31 to 33).
10 Install the timing chains, sprockets etc, as described in Section 54, paragraph 22 onwards. Remember to install the oil pump if it was removed.
11 Check the valve clearances before installing the valve covers (Section 50).
12 Only use four bolts to retain each valve cover for the time being, as they will have to be removed again after warm-up.

89 Timing scale — check and adjustment

1 To check the accuracy of the timing scales, the timing cover and crankshaft pulley must be installed, and the intake manifold must be removed. It may also be necessary to remove the water pump.
2 Bring the crankshaft to approximately 20° BTDC on No 1 cylinder.
3 Remove the blanking plug from the checking hole, using an 8 mm square drive key (the same as for the oil pan drain plug). Remove the copper washer (photo).
4 Insert a drill shank or other rod, 8 mm (0.315 in) in diameter, into the hole (photo). Slowly turn the crankshaft clockwise until the rod drops into the slot in the crankshaft. This is TDC for No 1 cylinder.
5 In this position the 0 mark on the timing scale must be aligned exactly with the No 1 notch on the pulley. Loosen the scale securing bolts if necessary and adjust the scale position. Tighten the bolts and seal them with a dab of paint.
6 Remove the drill or rod. Install the blanking plug, using a new copper washer, and tighten it.

90 Engine — reassembly after overhaul

1 Install the flywheel or driveplate, using new bolts. Tighten the bolts to the specified torque (photos).
2 Install the external components listed in Section 69. If preferred, delicate items such as the alternator can be left until after installing the engine.

91 Engine — reconnection to transmission

1 Refer to Section 41.
2 Install the exhaust downpipes.
3 Install the starter motor blanking plate.
4 Install a new oil filter.

92 Engine — installation (with transmission)

1 Installation is essentially a reversal of the procedure in Section 67, with the following additional points.
2 On automatic transmission models, adjust the gear selector mechanism (Chapter 6, Section 30).

87.11 Angle-tightening a main bearing nut

88.8 Reinstalling the right-hand head (with exhaust manifold attached)

89.3 Removing the blanking plug from the TDC checking hole

89.4 Inserting a drill shank into the hole

90.1A Installing the driveplate front washer . . .

90.1B . . . the driveplate itself . . .

90.1C . . . the thick washer and bolts

94.4 Installing the oil level sensor

94.5 Oil level warning control unit

3 Refill the engine with oil and coolant. Refill the transmission with lubricant if it was drained.
4 Refer to Section 95 before starting the engine.

93 Engine — installation (alone)

1 Refer to Section 43, paragraphs 1 to 4. Also see Section 65.
2 Once the engine and transmission are mated, proceed by reversing the removal procedure (Section 66).
3 Refer to Section 95 before starting the engine.

94 Oil level sensor — check, removal and installation

1 On models so equipped, the oil level sensor is screwed into the right-hand side of the lower crankcase. The sensor protrudes into the oil pan.
2 To test the sensor, disconnect the electrical connector from it and measure the resistance across the sensor terminals. It should be 9 ohms under all conditions.
3 To remove the sensor, unscrew it from its hole. Be careful with it, it is fragile.
4 When installing the sensor, apply some sealant to its threads. Screw the sensor into its hole, reconnect the electrical connector and check for correct operation (photo).

5 The oil level warning control unit is located under the rear console armrest/storage box (photo).

95 Initial start-up after overhaul or major repair

1 Refer to Section 44, and note the following points.
2 Check the ignition timing before adjusting the idle speed and mixture (Chapter 4, Section 6).
3 After the engine has warmed up, stop it and allow it to cool for at least two hours, then carry out the final tightening of the cylinder head bolts. Install the valve covers using all the bolts.

96 Compression check

Proceed as in Section 45, but first perform the following:
a) Remove the air intake ducting
b) Unplug the auxiliary air valve or air control valve connector
c) Disconnect the hose which joins the auxiliary air valve and the start injector

97 Troubleshooting — engine

Refer to Section 46.

Chapter 2
Cooling, heating and air conditioning systems

Contents

Specifications

General
System type .... Water-based coolant, pump-assisted circulation, thermostatically
controlled

Coolant capacity:
B23/B230 .... 10.05 quarts
B28/200 .... 10.5 quarts
Coolant type .... *See Recommended lubricants and fluids*

Pressure cap rating
Overpressure: B23 ft .... 9 to 12 psi
B230F (early type) .... 11 psi
B230F (later type) .... 14 psi
B230FT (later type) .... 21 psi
B28F (early type) .... 11 psi
B28F/B280F (later type) .... 21 psi
Underpressure .... 1 psi

Thermostat
Opens at: B23/B230 (type 1) and B280 .... 86 to 88° C (187 to 190° F)
B23/B230 (type 2) and B 28 .... 91 to 93° C (196 to 199° F)
Fully open at: B23/B230 (type 1) and B280 ..... 97° C (207° F)
B23/B230 (type 2) and B 28 .... 102° C (216° F)

Torque specifications

	Nm	Ft-lbs
Water pump bolts:		
B28/280	15 to 20	11 to 15
B23/230	Not specified	

1 General information

Engine cooling system

These vehicles employ a pressurized engine cooling system with thermostatically controlled coolant circulation. An impeller-type water pump mounted on the front of the block pumps coolant through the engine. The pump is driven by a drivebelt on all engines.

The coolant flows around each cylinder and toward the rear of the engine. Cast-in coolant passages direct coolant around the intake and exhaust ports, near the spark plug areas and in close proximity to the exhaust valve guide inserts.

A thermostat is located in the cylinder head (4-cylinder engine) or the water pump (V6 engine). During warm up, the closed thermostat prevents coolant from circulating through the radiator. When the engine reaches normal operating temperature, the thermostat opens and allows hot coolant to travel through the radiator, where it is cooled before returning to the engine.

The aluminum radiator is the crossflow type, with tanks on either side of the core.

The cooling system is pressurized, which increases the efficiency of the system by raising the boiling point of the coolant. An expansion tank accommodates variations in coolant volume with temperature.

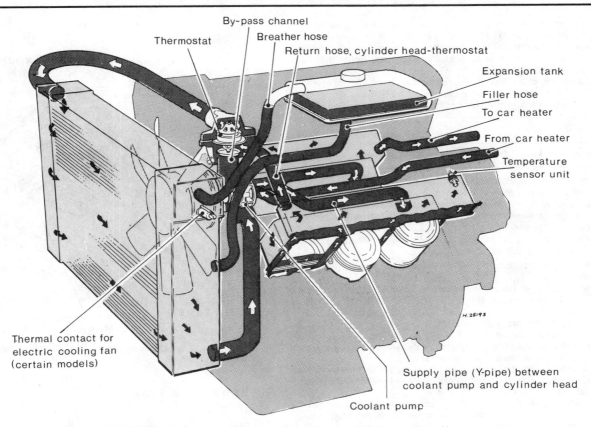

Fig. 2.1 Cooling system components and circulation — V6 shown (Sec 1)

Heating system

The heating system consists of a blower fan and heater core located under the hood and dash, the inlet and outlet hoses connecting the heater core to the engine cooling system and the heater/air conditioning through the heater core when the water valve is opened. When the heater mode is activated, a flap door opens to expose the heater box to the passenger compartment. A fan switch on the control head activates the blower motor, which forces air through the core, heating the air.

Air conditioning system

The air conditioning system consists of a condenser mounted in front of the radiator, an evaporator mounted under the hood, a compressor mounted on the engine, a filter-drier (accumulator) which contains a high pressure cycling switch and the plumbing connecting all of the above.

A blower fan forces the warmer air of the passenger compartment through the evaporator core (sort of a radiator-in-reverse), transferring the heat from the air to the refrigerant. The liquid refrigerant boils off into low pressure vapor, taking the heat with it when it leaves the evaporator.

2 Maintenance and inspection

1   Every 250 miles, weekly, or before a long journey, check the coolant level as follows.
2   Open the hood. Check the level of coolant through the translucent walls of the expansion tank (on one side of the engine bay). The level should be up to the MAX mark when the engine is cold, and may be somewhat above the mark when hot.
3   If topping-up is necessary, wait for the system to cool down if it is hot. There is a risk of scalding if the cap is removed while the system is hot. Place a thick rag over the expansion tank cap and loosen it to release any pressure. When pressure has been released, unscrew the cap and remove it.
4   Top up to the MAX mark with the specified coolant — see Section 6 (photo). In an emergency plain water is better than nothing, but remember that it is diluting the proper coolant. Do not add cold water to an overheated engine while it is still hot.
5   Install the expansion tank cap securely when the level is correct. Check for leaks if there is a frequent need for topping up — losses from this type of system are normally minimal.
6   Every 6000 miles or six months, check the antifreeze concentration using a hydrometer. (If the owner is satisfied that no water has been added to the system, and that the concentration of antifreeze was originally correct, this check may safely be omitted.)
7   Every 12,000 miles or annually, inspect the accessory drivebelt(s) for fraying, glazing or other damage. Re-tension or replace as necessary — see Section 7.

2.4 Topping-up the coolant

8   Every two years, regardless of mileage, replace the coolant. The necessary information will be found in Sections 3 to 6. At the same time inspect all the coolant hoses and hose clamps. It is worth replacing the hoses as a precautionary measure if suspect, rather than have one burst on the road.
9   Occasionally clean insects and road debris from the radiator fins, using compressed air or a soft brush.
10   For maintenance of the air conditioning system see Section 20.

3 Cooling system — draining

Warning: *Do not allow antifreeze to come in contact with your skin or painted surfaces of the vehicle. Flush contacted areas immediately with plenty of water. Antifreeze can be fatal to children and pets. Wipe up any garage floor and drip pan coolant spills immedtely. Keep antifreeze containers covered and repair leaks in your cooling system immediately. The cooling system should not be drained when the coolant is hot, as there is a risk of scalding.*

1   Remove the expansion tank filler cap. Also remove the engine undertray.
2   Move the heater temperature control to Hot. (Even though the heater is of the air mix type, the matrix water valve is closed in some conditions.)
3   Place a suitable drain pan under the engine and open the drain tap(s). V6 engines have two taps, one each side of the block; 4-cylinder engines have one tap on the right-hand side. Hoses can be installed on the taps to guide the coolant into the pan.
4   When coolant has finished flowing from the block, move the drain pan to below the radiator. Disconnect the bottom hose from the radiator and allow the rest of the coolant to drain.
5   Consult local authories regarding proper disposal procedures for antifreeze. In many areas, reclamation centers have been established to collect used oil and coolant mixtures.

4 Cooling system — flushing

Note: *Flushing should not be necessary unless regular coolant changing has been neglected, or if plain water has been used as coolant.*
1   Drain the system as previously described, and remove the thermostat (Section 13).
2   Using a garden hose, run clean water into the radiator top hose so that it flows through the radiator and out of the bottom hose stub. Do this until clean water emerges.
3   Similarly feed water into the engine via the bottom hose so that it flows out of the thermostat housing. Protect electrical components from water spillage.
4   Flushing in the reverse direction to normal flow can be beneficial in some cases. The radiator should be removed for this, inverted and shaken gently as the water flows through it to dislodge any sediment.
5   Chemical flushing compounds should only be used as a last resort. Follow the maker's instructions when using such a compound and make sure that it is suitable for mixed metal (aluminium and iron) engines.
6   When flushing is complete, install the thermostat, hoses and any other disturbed components.

5 Cooling system — filling

1   Close the drain taps and make sure that all hoses and hose clamps are securely installed and in good condition.
2   Fill the system through the expansion tank until the level in the tank is up to the MAX mark. Squeeze the large coolant hoses to disperse air pockets.
3   Install the expansion tank cap. Run the engine up to operating temperature, checking for coolant leaks. Switch off the engine and allow it to cool.
4   Check the coolant level and top up again to the MAX mark if necessary.

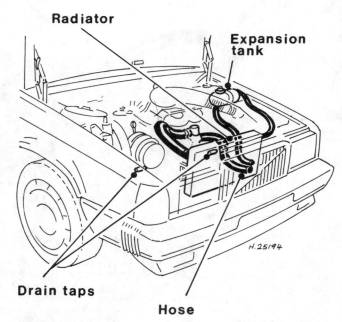

Fig. 2.2 Draining points — V6 engine (Sec 3)

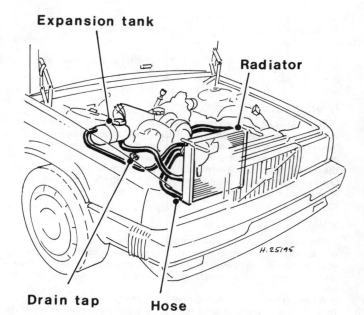

Fig. 2.3 Draining points — in-line engine (Sec 3)

6 Antifreeze mixture — general information

Warning: *Do not allow antifreeze to come in contact with your skin or painted surfaces of the vehicle. Flush contacted areas immediately with plent of water. Antifreeze can be fatal to children and pets. Wipe up any garage floor and drip pan coolant spills immediately. Keep antifreeze containers covered and repair leaks in your cooling system immediately.*

1   The antifreeze/water mixture must be replaced every two years to preserve its anti-corrosive properties. (In some owner's literature a period of three years between changes is specified. The latest recommendation is for two years, however.) Never run the engine for long periods with plain water as coolant.
2   Only use the specified antifreeze (see *Recommended lubricants*

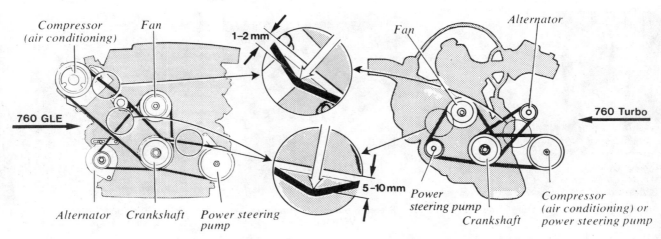

Fig. 2.4 Some typical accessory drivebelt layouts (Sec 7)

and fluids). Inferior brands may not contain the necessary corrosion inhibitors, or may break down at high temperatures. Antifreeze containing methanol is particularly to be avoided, as the methanol evaporates.

3 The specified mixture is 50% antifreeze and 50% clean soft water (by volume). Mix the required quantity in a clean container and then fill the system as described in Section 5. Save any surplus mixture for topping-up.

7 Accessory drivebelts — removal, installation and tensioning

1 The accessory drivebelts transmit power from the crankshaft pulley to the alternator, water pump/fan clutch, steering pump and air conditioning compressor (as applicable). A variety of belt arrangements and tensioning methods will be found, according to equipment and engine type. A representative selection is given here (Fig. 2.4).

2 When removing a particular drivebelt, it will obviously be necessary to remove those in front of it first.

3 Twin belts should always be replaced in pairs, even if only one is broken.

Water pump/alternator drivebelt(s)

4 Loosen the alternator pivot and adjusting strap nuts and bolts (photo).

5 Move the alternator towards the engine to release the belt tension. On some models a positive tensioning device is used; loosen the tensioner screw to move the alternator inwards (photo).

6 Slip the belts of the pulleys and remove them (photo).

7 When installing, move the alternator away from the engine until the belts can be deflected 5 to 10 mm (0.2 to 0.4 in) by firm thumb pressure in the middle of the longest run. Tighten the pivot and adjusting strap nuts and bolts in this position and recheck the tension.

8 On models with a positive tensioning device, be careful not to over-tension the belt. On models without such a device, it may be helpful to lever the alternator away from the engine to achieve the desired tension. Only use a wooden or plastic lever, and only lever at the pulley end.

Steering pump drivebelt

9 Proceed as for the water pump/alternator drivebelt, noting the location of the pivot and adjuster strap nuts and bolts (photos). On V6 models, access to the steering pump is easier from below.

Air conditioning compressor drivebelt

10 On models where the compressor mountings allow it to be pivoted, proceed as for the water pump/alternator drivebelt (photo). Note, however, that the desired deflection of the belt is only 1 to 2 mm (0.04 to 0.08 in).

11 On models where the compressor mounting is rigid, belt tension is controlled by varying the number of shims between segments of the crankshaft pulley (photo).

12 To remove the drivebelt, unbolt the pulley from its hub. Remove the pulley segments and the shims. The drivebelt can now be removed (photo).

13 When installing, experiment with the number of shims between the segments until belt tension is correct. Inserting shims decreases the tension, and vice versa. Install unused shims in front of the pulley for future use.

All drivebelts

14 Recheck the tension of a new belt after a few hundred miles.

7.4 Alternator adjusting strap nut (arrowed) — without positive tensioner

7.5 Alternator adjusting strap with positive tensioner. Adjusting screw is arrowed

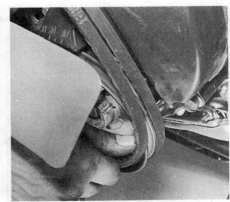

7.6 Removing a drivebelt

7.9A   Steering pump adjusting strap —
in-line engine

7.9B   Steering pump adjusting strap —
V6 engine

7.10   Air conditioning compressor
adjusting straps — V6 engine

7.11   Crankshaft pulley segments and
shims — decrease the number of shims
between the pully halves to tighten the belt

7.12   Removing the pulley front
segment

8   Radiator — removal and installation

1   Drain the cooling system (see Section 3). Take precautions against scalding if the coolant is hot.
2   Disconnect the top hose, expansion tank hose and vent hose from the radiator (photos).
3   On automatic transmission models, disconnect the fluid cooler lines from the radiator. Be prepared for fluid spillage. Plug or cap the lines to keep dirt out.
4   Disconnect the leads from any thermal switches, sensors etc, in the radiator.
5   Unbolt the power steering fluid reservoir (when located on the radiator) and move it aside.
6   Unbolt the fan shroud and move it rearwards (photo).
7   Unbolt the radiator top mounting brackets (photo).

8   Lift out the radiator. Recover the bottom mountings if they are loose (photo).
9   Install by reversing the removal operations. Refill the cooling system on completion. On automatic transmission models, check the fluid level (Chapter 6, Section 28).

9   Viscous coupled fan — removal and installation

1   Remove the nuts which secure the viscous coupling to the water pump pulley studs.
2   Pull the fan and coupling off the studs (photo). Manipulate the assembly past the fan shroud and remove it. It may be necessary to remove the shroud.
3   The fan and viscous coupling may now be separated if required.
4   Install by reversing the removal operations.

8.2A   Disconnect the radiator top
hose . . .

8.2B   . . . the expansion tank hose . . .

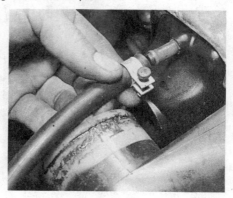

8.2C   . . . and the vent hose

8.6 Unbolting the fan shroud

8.7 Removing a radiator mounting bracket

8.8 Radiator bottom mount — check the rubber insulators for deterioration and replace them if necessary

10 Electric fan — removal and installation

1 Remove the front grille panel (Chapter 11, Section 42).
2 Remove the four screws which secure the fan mounting bars. Disconnect the electrical connector.
3 Remove the fan complete with mounting bars. The motor can be unbolted from the bars if necessary.
4 Install by reversing the removal operations.

11 Electric fan thermoswitch — removal, check and installation

1 Partially drain the cooling system to below the level of the thermoswitch (Section 3).
2 Disconnect the thermoswitch leads, unscrew it and remove it (photo).
3 To test the switch, connect a battery and test light to its terminals. Heat the switch in hot water. The switch should close (test light comes on) at approximately the temperature stamped on it, and open again (test light goes off) as it cools down. If not, replace it.
4 Install the thermoswitch, using sealant on the threads, and reconnect its leads.
5 Refill the cooling system (Section 5).

12 Water pump — removal and installation

1 Disconnect the battery negative cable.
2 Drain the cooling system (Section 3).
3 Remove the radiator and the fan shroud (Sec 8).

4 Remove the fan from the water pump (Section 9). Remove the pump drivebelt(s) and the pump pulley (photo).

In-line engine

5 Disconnect the radiator bottom hose and the heater pipe from the pump (photo).
6 Unbolt the water pump, slide it downwards and remove it (photo).
7 Before installing the pump, repace its top sealing ring and body gasket (photos). When installing, keep the pump pressed up against the cylinder head while tightening the nuts and bolts. Use a new seal on the heater pipe.

V6 engine

8 Remove the intake manifold (Chapter 3, Section 22).
9 Remove the two hoses which connect the pump to the cylinder heads. Disconnect the remaining hoses from the pump and thermostat housing. Also disconnect the sensor and switch at the sides of the pump (photos).
10 Remove the three bolts which secure the pump to the block. Lift off the pump (photo).
11 If a new pump is to be installed, transfer the rear housing, thermostat and housing, sender unit, blanking plugs etc, from the old pump to the new. Use new gaskets and seals. Also replace the pump hoses unless they are in perfect condition.
12 Install the pump to the block and secure it with the three bolts, tightened to the specified torque.

All models

13 The remainder of installation is a reversal of the removal procedure. Tighten the alternator drivebelt(s) (Section 7) and refill the cooling system (Section 5) to complete.

9.2 Removing the fan and viscous coupling — be careful not to damage the radiator with the fan blades

11.2 Fan thermoswitch in a hose adaptor. It may also be located in the radiator side tank

12.4 Removing the water pump pulley

12.5 Disconnecting the heater pipe
from the pump

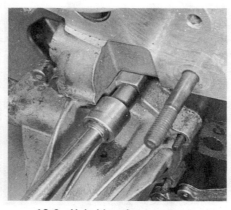

12.6 Unbolting the water pump

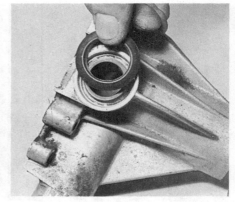

12.7A Installing a new top sealing ring

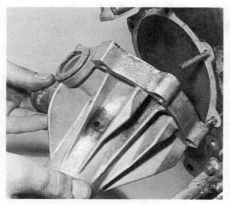

12.7B Install the pump, using a
new gasket

12.9A One of the pump-to-head hoses

12.9B Two hoses at the rear of
the pump

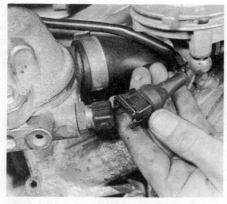

12.9C Disconnecting a temperature
sensor

12.10 Unbolting the water pump

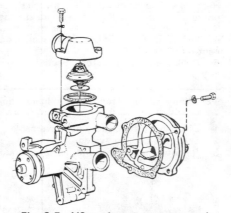

Fig. 2.5 V6 engine water pump and
peripheral components (Sec 12)

13 Thermostat — replacement

Warning: *The engine must be completely cool before beginning this procedure.*

1   Drain the cooling system (Section 3) until the coolant level is below the thermostat.
2   Unbolt the thermostat housing from the cylinder head or water pump. On some models an engine lifting eye may also be attached here; on V6 engines it will be necessary to unbolt a throttle cable bracket. Lift out the thermostat (photos).
3   Install a sealing ring to the thermostat (photo).
4   Install the thermostat and housing (and the engine lifting eye, when applicable). Install and tighten the housing nuts.
5   Refill the cooling system (Section 5).

14 Temperature gauge sender — removal and installation

Warning: *The engine must be completely cool before beginning this procedure.*

1   Unscrew the expansion tank cap to release any residual pressure within the cooling system, then tighten the cap. There is no need to drain the cooling system if a new sender unit is to be installed.
2   Disconnect the wire from the sender unit and unscrew it from the cylinder head or water pump (photo).
3   Screw in the new sender unit, using a thin coat of sealant or teflon tape on the threads. Reconnect the wire.
4   Top up the coolant level if much was lost, then tighten the expansion tank cap.

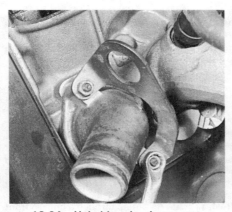

13.2A   Unbolting the thermostat housing . . .

13.2B . . . and removing the thermostat (in-line engine)

13.2C   Unbolting the thermostat housing . . .

13.2D   . . . and removing the thermostat (V6 engine)

13.3   Installing a thermostat sealing ring

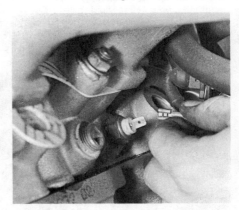

14.2   Disconnecting the temperature gauge sender unit

15   Temperature gauge — testing

Note: *If both the fuel gauge and the temperature gauge are inaccurate, the fault is probably in the instrument voltage stabilizer on the instrument panel printed circuit.*

1   Disconnect the wire from the temperature gauge sender. Connect a resistor, value approximately 68 ohms, between the wire and ground (vehicle metal). Switch on the ignition: the gauge should rise to roughly 75% of full scale deflection. If not, either the wire is broken or the gauge is defective. Switch off the ignition.
2   Measure the resistance of the temperature gauge sender with it immersed in a water bath of known temperature. The resistance should vary as follows:

Temperature	Resistance
60°C (140°F)	217 ± 35 ohm
90°C (194°F)	87 ± 15 ohm
100°C (212°F)	67 ± 11 ohm

3   If the gauge or the sender does not perform as described, replace it.
4   Reconnect the sender wire on completion.

16   Coolant level sensor — general information

1   A coolant level sensor is installed in the expansion tank on later models. It consists of a float-operated switch connected to an instrument panel warning light.
2   If the sensor malfunctions, unscrew it from the expansion tank (with the system cold and replace it.

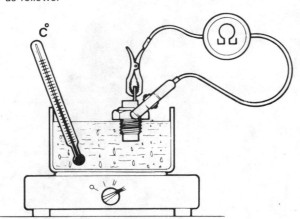

Fig. 2.6   Testing the temperature gauge sender (Sec 15)

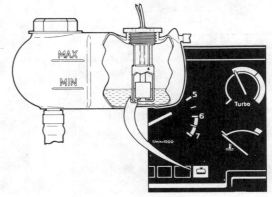

Fig. 2.7   Coolant level sensor (Sec 16)

17   Oil coolers — removal and installation

Engine oil cooler

1   If equipped, the engine oil cooler is mounted behind and to one side of the radiator.

2   Disconnect the oil cooler unions, either at the cooler itself or at the flexible hoses (photo). Be prepared for oil spillage.

3   Unbolt the oil cooler brackets and remove it (photo). The oil cooler can then be separated from the brackets if required.

4   If the oil cooler is to be re-used, flush it internally with solvent and then blow compressed air through it. Also clean it externally.

5   Install by reversing the removal operations. Run the engine and check for oil leaks, then switch off and check the oil level.

ATF auxiliary cooler

6   If equipped, the ATF auxiliary cooler is mounted between the radiator and the air conditioning condenser.

7   Disconnect the flexible hoses from the union on the radiator (photo). Be prepared for fluid spillage. Cap open unions to keep dirt out.

8   Remove the radiator (Section 8).

9   Unbolt the cooler (photo). Feed the hoses through the side panel grommets and remove the cooler and hoses together.

10   Clean the cooler fins and flush it internally with clean ATF. Replace the hoses if necessary.

11   Install by reversing the removal operations. Refill the cooling system, run the engine and check the transmission fluid level (Chapter 6, Section 28).

18   Heating and ventilation system — general information

Depending on model and options selected, the heater may be installed alone or in conjunction with an air conditioning unit. The same housings and heater components are used in all cases. The air conditioning system is described in Section 19.

The heater is of the fresh air type. Air enters through a grille in front of the windshield. On its way to the various vents a variable proportion of the air passes through the heater core, where it is warmed by engine coolant flowing through the core.

Distribution of air to the vents, and through or around the core, is controlled by flaps or shutters. These are operated by vacuum motors

17.2   Oil cooler flexible hose unions

17.3   Unbolting an oil cooler bracket

17.7   Disconnecting an ATF cooler flexible hose

17.9   An ATF cooler mounting bolt

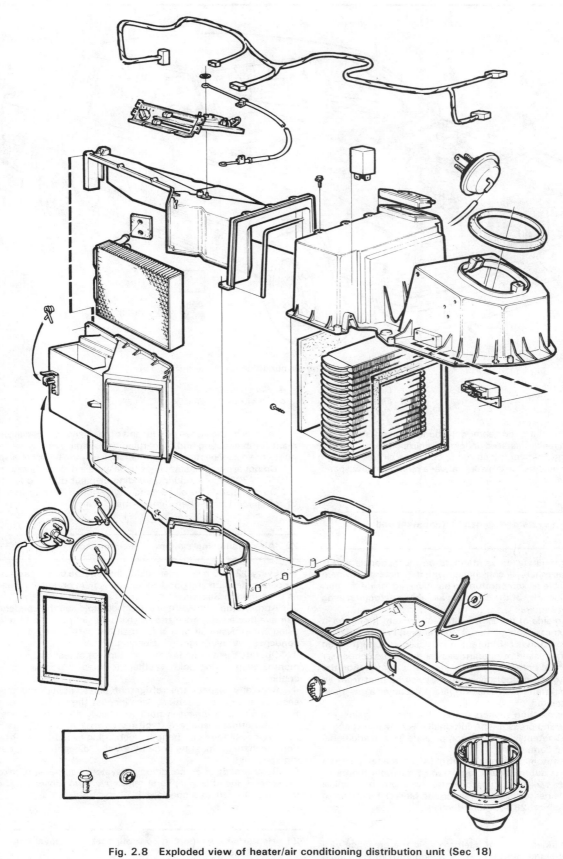

2

Fig. 2.8 Exploded view of heater/air conditioning distribution unit (Sec 18)

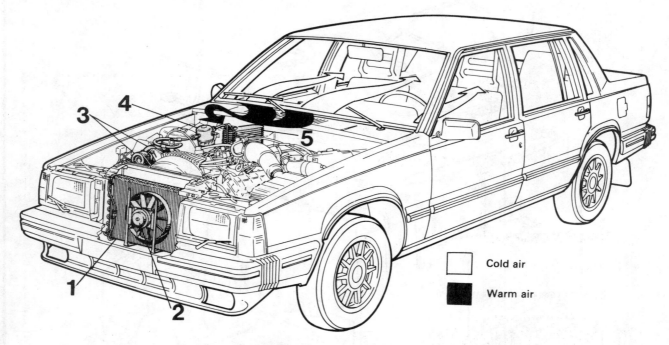

Fig. 2.9   Main components of the air conditioning system (Sec 19)

1 Condenser	4 Receiver/drier
2 Electric fan	5 Evaporator
3 Compressor	

(except for the air mix shutter on heater-only models, which is operated by cable). A vacuum tank is installed under the vehicle on some models.

A four-speed electric blower is installed to boost the airflow through the heater. On early models the blower is always running at low speed when the ignition is on.

19   Air conditioning system — general information and precautions

1   Air conditioning is installed as standard on most models and is optionally available on others. In conjunction with the heater the system enables any reasonable air temperature to be achieved inside the car. It also reduces the humidity of the incoming air, aiding defogging even when cooling is not required.

2   The refrigeration side of the air conditioning system functions in a similar way to a domestic refrigerator. A compressor, belt-driven from the crankshaft pulley, draws refrigerant in its gaseous state from an evaporator. The compressed refrigerant passes through a condenser where it loses heat and enters its liquid state. After dehydration the refrigerant returns to the evaporator where it absorbs heat from air passing over the evaporator fins. The refrigerant becomes a gas again and the cycle is repeated.

3   Various sub-controls and sensors protect the system against excessive temperature and pressures. Additionally, engine idle speed is increased when the system is in use to compensate for the additional load imposed by the compressor.

4   On models with automatic climate control (ACC), the temperature of the incoming air is automatically regulated to maintain the cabin temperature at the level selected by the operator. An electro-mechanical programmer controls heater, air conditioner and blower functions to achieve this. See Section 28 for more details.

Precautions

5   Although the refrigerant is not itself toxic, in the presence of a open flame (or a lighted cigarette) it forms a highly toxic gas. Liquid refrigerant spilled on the skin will cause frostbite. If refrigerant enters the eyes, rinse them with a diluted solution of boric acid and seek medical advice immediately.

6   In view of the above points, and of the need for specialized equipment for evacuating and recharging the system, any work which requires the disconnection of a refrigerant line must be left to a specialist.

7   Do not allow refrigerant lines to be exposed to temperatures above 110°C (230°F) — eg during welding or paint drying operations.

8   Do not operate the air conditioning system if it is known to be short of refrigerant, or further damage may result.

20   Air conditioning system — maintenance

1   Every 12,000 miles or annually, inspect the compressor drivebelt for correct tension and good condition. Adjust or replace if necessary as described in Section 7.

2   At the same intervals it is a good idea to clean the condenser fins. Remove the radiator grille and clean leaves, insects etc, from the fins, using compressed air or a soft brush. Be careful not to damage the condenser by over-vigorous cleaning.

3   Operate the air conditioning system for at least 10 minutes each month, even during cold weather, to keep the seals etc, in good condition.

4   Regularly inspect the refrigerant pipes, hoses and unions for security and good condition. Also inspect the vacuum hoses.

5   The air conditioning system will lose a proportion of its charge through normal seepage — typically up to 100 g (4 oz) per year — so it is as well to regard periodic recharging as a maintenance operation. Recharging must be done by a Volvo dealer or an air conditioning specialist.

6   Repacement of air conditioning system components, except for the sensors and other peripheral items covered in subsequent Sections, must also be left to a specialist.

21   Heater/air conditioning control panel — removal and installation

1   For best access, remove the center console side panels (Chapter 12, Section 35).

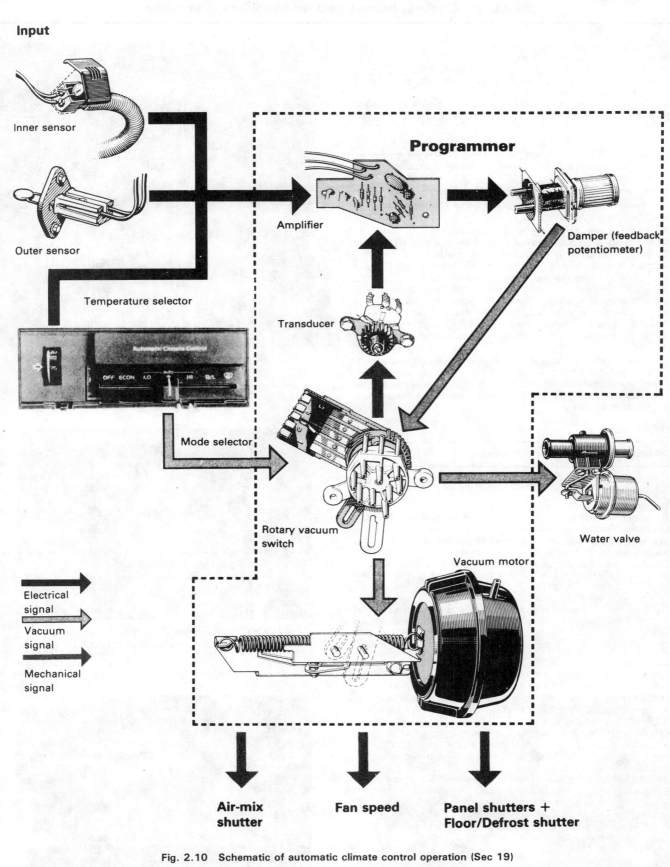

Input

Inner sensor

Outer sensor

Temperature selector

Mode selector

Programmer

Amplifier

Transducer

Damper (feedback potentiometer)

Rotary vacuum switch

Vacuum motor

Water valve

Electrical signal

Vacuum signal

Mechanical signal

Air-mix shutter

Fan speed

Panel shutters + Floor/Defrost shutter

Fig. 2.10 Schematic of automatic climate control operation (Sec 19)

2

2   Remove the trim from around the control panel, if not already done. Remove the panel securing screws (photo).
3   Withdraw the panel and disconnect the control cables, multi-plugs and vacuum unions from it. Make notes or identifying marks if necessary for reference when installing.
4   Install by reversing the removal operations. Where a mechanical temperature control cable is present, see Section 22 for adjustment.

22   Heater temperature control cable — removal, installation and adjustment

Note: *A mechanical temperature control cable is installed only on vehicles without air conditioning.*

1   Remove the glovebox (Chapter 11, Section 34).
2   With the temperature control in the WARM position, disconnect the far end of the cable from the air mix shutter lever.
3   Remove the trim from around the heater control panel. Remove the screws which hold the panel to the center console.
4   Ease the heater control panel away from the center console until the cable is accessible. Disconnect the cable from the control panel, using a screwdriver to pry the cable sleeve free.
5   The cable can now be removed.
6   Install by reversing the removal operations, noting the following points:

   a)   If the cable sleeve was damaged during removal, use a self-tapping screw to secure it (Fig. 2.13)
   b)   Adjust the position of the cable sleeve so that the air mix shutter travels over its full range of movement when the temperature control is operated

23   Heater core — removal and installation

Warning: *The engine must be completely cool before beginning this procedure.*

1   Disconnect the battery negative cable.
2   Remove the expansion tank cap to release any residual pressure, then install the cap.
3   Clamp the coolant hoses which lead to the heater core pipes on the firewall. Loosen the hose clamps and disconnect the hoses from the pipes. Be prepared for coolant spillage.
4   Remove the center console, rear console and glovebox. See Chapter 11, Sections 34 to 36.
5   Unclip the central electrical unit and move it aside.
6   Remove the center panel vent. Remove the screw from the distribution unit and disconnect all the air ducts from the unit. Also remove the rear vent distribution ducts.
7   Disconnect the vacuum hoses from the vacuum motors (photo).

21.2   Removing a control panel securing screw

Fig. 2.11   Temperature control cable connections (arrowed) at shutter lever (Sec 22)

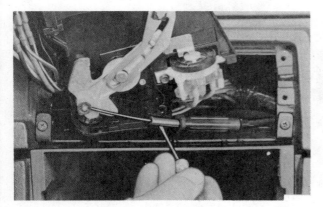

Fig. 2.12   Prying out the temperature control cable sleeve (Sec 22)

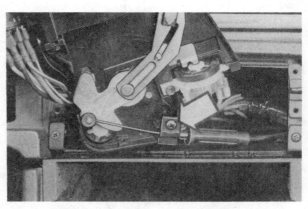

Fig. 2.13   Use a self-tapping screw (arrowed) to secure the sleeve (Sec 22)

23.7 Distribution unit vacuum motors

On models with automatic climate control, also remove the hose which leads to the inner sensor (the aspirator hose).

8   Remove the distribution unit.

9   Remove the heater core clips. Pull the core out and remove it; be prepared for coolant spillage.

10 Install by reversing the removal operations. Refer to Fig. 2.14 or 2.15 for guidance when connecting the vacuum motor hoses.

11 Top up the cooling system on completion. Run the engine and check that there are no coolant leaks, then allow it to cool and recheck the coolant level.

24   Heater vacuum motors — removal and installation

Motors in distribution unit

1   Remove the distribution unit. Refer to Section 23, but do not disconnect the coolant hoses from the heater core.

2   Remove the appropriate panel from the distribution unit for access to the motors. Remove the motors.

3   Install by reversing the removal operations.

Recirculation shutter motor

4   Remove the glovebox (Chapter 11, Section 34). Also remove the outer panel vent and air duct.

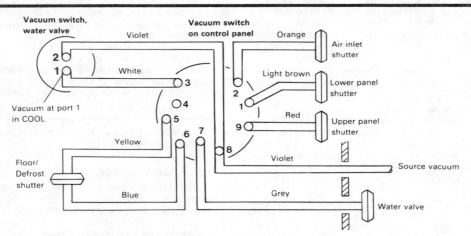

Fig. 2.14 Vacuum hose connections — models without climate control (Sec 23)

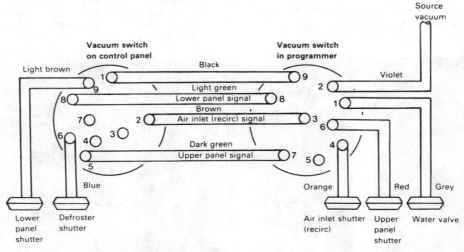

Fig. 2.15 Vacuum hose connections — models with climate control (Sec 23)

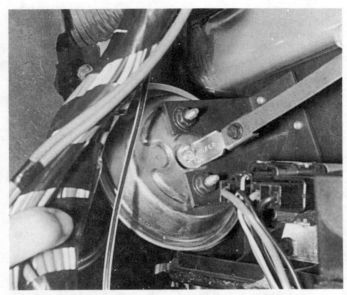

24.5   Recirculation shutter vacuum motor

5   Unbolt the control rod from the motor. Remove the two securing nuts, withdraw the motor and disconnect the vacuum hose (photo).
6   When installing, make sure that both the shutter and the vacuum motor are in the resting position before tightening the control rod bolt.
7   The remainder of installation is a reversal of the removal procedure.

25   Heater blower motor — removal and installation

1   Remove the trim panel from below the glovebox.
2   Remove the screws which secure the motor to the housing.
3   Lower the motor and disconnect the cooling hose. Disconnect the wiring and remove the motor complete with centrifugal fan (photo).
4   Do not disturb any steel clips on the fan blades. They have been installed for balancing purposes.
5   When installing, apply sealant between the motor flange and housing. Connect the wiring and secure the motor.
6   Install the motor cooling hose — this is important if premature failure is to be avoided.
7   Check for correct operation of the motor, then install the trim panel.

26   Heater blower motor resistor — removal and installation

1   Remove the glovebox (Chapter 11, Section 34).
2   Disconnect the electrical connector from the resistor.

3   Remove the two screws from the resistor and withdraw it (photo). Be careful not to damage the coils of resistance wire.
4   Install by reversing the removal operations, but check the operation of the blower on all four speeds before installing the glovebox.

27   Heater water valve — removal and installation

Warning: *The engine must be completely cool before beginning this procedure.*

1   Release any residual pressure in the cooling system by removing the expansion tank cap. Reinstall the cap.
2   Clamp the coolant hoses on each side of the valve.
3   Disconnect the vacuum and coolant hoses from the valve and remove it (photo).
4   Install by reversing the removal operations. Top up the coolant if much was lost.

28   Automatic climate control sensors — general information

The four sensors associated with the ACC are the control panel sensor, the coolant thermal switch, the inner sensor and the outer sensor.
The control panel sensor operates in conjunction with the coolant thermal switch. If cabin temperature is below 18°C (64°F) and coolant temperature is below 35°C (95°F), the blower is prevented from operating (unless 'defrost' is selected). This prevents the ACC from blowing cold air into the cabin while the coolant warms up.
The inner sensor is located above the glovebox. It senses cabin air temperature.
The outer sensor is located in the blower housing and senses the temperature of the incoming air.
Acting on information received from the inner and outer sensors, the programmer applies the appropriate heating/cooling and blower speed settings to achieve the selected temperature.

29   Automatic climate control sensors — testing, removal and installation

Control panel sensor

1   Remove the trim from around the control panel. Remove the control panel securing screws and pull the panel out.
2   Disconnect the sensor electrical connector. Use an ohmmeter to check the sensor for continuity. Continuity should be displayed above 18°C (64°F), and no continuity (open-circuit) at lower temperatures. Cool the sensor with some ice cubes, or warm it in the hands, to check that it performs as described.
3   To remove the sensor, insert a thin screwdriver or a stiff wire into the electrical connector and pry out the sensor terminals.
4   Install the new sensor by pressing its terminals into the electrical connector. Install the control panel and trim.

25.3   Removing the heater blower motor

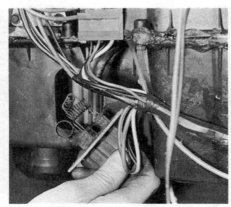

26.3   Removing the motor resistor

27.3   Disconnecting the heater water valve

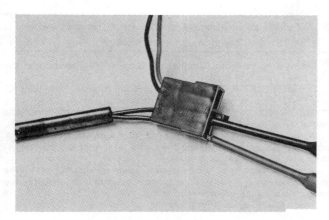

Fig. 2.16   Checking the control panel sensor for continuity (Sec 29)

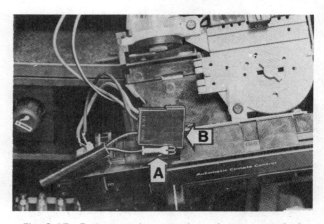

Fig. 2.17   Prying out the control panel sensor terminals (A) by inserting a stiff wire (B) (Sec 29)

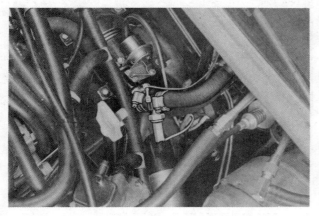

Fig. 2.18   The coolant thermal switch (Sec 29)

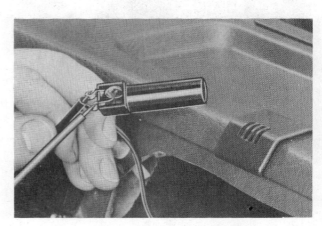

Fig. 2.19   Checking the inner sensor for continuity (Sec 29)

Coolant thermal switch

5   The coolant thermal switch is located under the hood. It is screwed into a T-piece inserted in the heater supply hose.
6   Unplug the electrical connector and unscrew the thermal switch from the T-piece.
7   Test the thermal switch using an ohmmeter, or a battery and test lamp, immersing the switch in a heated water bath. The switch should show continuity at temperatures of 30 to 40°C (86 to 104°F) upwards. As the water cools, continuity should be broken before the temperature reaches 10°C (50°F).
8   Note that if the wire to the thermal switch is accidentally disconnected, the heater blower will not work at cabin temperatures below 18°C (64°F), regardless of coolant temperature.
9   Install by reversing the removal operations.

Inner sensor

10   Remove the glovebox (Chapter 11, Section 34).
11   Pull the air hose off the sensor, unclip the sensor and remove it.
12   The only test specified for this sensor is that it should display continuity. No resistance values are given.
13   Install by reversing the removal operations.

Outer sensor

14   Access to the sensor for testing can be gained by removing the windshield wiper arms, the cowl panel and the air intake cover.
15   Measure the resistance of the sensor. At 20 to 23°C (68 to 73°F) the resistance should be 30 to 40 ohms. The higher the temperature, the lower the resistance.
16   For removal and installation of the sensor, proceed by removing

Fig. 2.20   The outer sensor location on pre-1985 models (Sec 29)

the air recirculation shutter motor (Section 24). The sensor can then be removed and a new one installed.
17   On 1985 and later models, the sensor is mounted lower down in the fan housing. Access for testing and removal should therefore be possible without much disassembling.

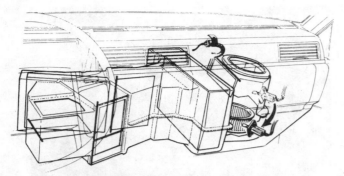

Fig. 2.21 Outer sensor location (arrowed) on later models (Sec 29)

30 Automatic climate control programmer — removal and installation

1   Remove the glovebox (Chapter 11, Section 34). Also remove the outer panel vent and duct.
2   Disconnect the air mix shutter control rod, the electrical connector and the vacuum pipe cluster from the programmer.
3   Remove the three screws which secure the programmer and remove it.
4   When installing, secure the programmer with the three screws. Connect the vacuum cluster and the electrical connector, then adjust the shutter control rod as follows.
5   Run the engine to provide vacuum. Select maximum heat on the temperature control dial. Pull the control rod until it reaches its stop and secure it to the programmer arm.
6   Install the duct, vent and glovebox.

Fig. 2.22 ACC programmer disconnection points (arrowed) (Sec 30)

Fig. 2.23 ACC programmer securing screws (arrowed) (Sec 30)

31 Troubleshooting — cooling system

System	Reason(s)
Overheating	Coolant level low
	Drivebelt slipping or broken
	Radiator blocked
	Coolant hose collapsed
	Thermostat stuck shut
	Viscous-coupled fan not working
	Electric fan not working
	Ignition timing incorrect
	Fuel system fault (weak mixture)
	Exhaust system restricted
	Engine oil level low
	Cylinder head gasket blown
	Brakes binding
	New engine not yet broken-in
Overcooling	Thermostat missing, jammed open or incorrect rating
Loss of coolant*	External leakage
	Overheating
	Radiator cap defective
	Cylinder head gasket blown
	Cylinder head or block cracked
Oil and/or combustion gases in coolant	Cylinder head gasket blown
	Cylinder head or block cracked
	Cylinder liner base seal(s), failed (V6 only)

*If the reason for loss of coolant is not obvious, have the cooling system pressure tested

32 Troubleshooting — heating and air conditioning systems

System	Reason(s)
Heater output insufficient	Overcooling (see Section 31) Water valve shut Control cable broken or out of adjustment Vacuum motor broken or disconnected Heater core blocked
Air conditioner does not work	Compressor drivebelt loose or broken Fuse blown Loss of refrigerant
ACC gives full hot or cold with maximum fan speed	Sensor(s) disconnected or defective Programmer disconnected
ACC fan delay malfunction	Control panel sensor or coolant thermal switch defective Fan relay defective
ACC fan speed does not change	Vacuum supply failure Programmer power supply failure

2

Chapter 3 Fuel and exhaust systems

Contents

Specifications

General
System type:
   B280F .... Continuous injection (CI), normally aspirated
   B230F, B280F .... LH-Jetronic, normally aspirated
   B23FT, B230FT .... LH-Jetronic, turbocharged
Fuel tank capacity .... 13.2 or 18.0 gallons depending on model year
Fuel octane rating .... 90 RON

Continuous injection system (B230 and B28)
Idle adjustments
Idle speed .... 900 rpm (adjust to 850 rpm on B28 with constant idle system)
CO level at idle:
   B230* .... $1 \begin{array}{l} + 1.0 \\ - 0.5 \end{array}$ %

   B28 .... $2 \pm 1\%$

Automatic transmission only — measure CO level at 800 rpm

Fuel pressure
Line pressure:
   B230F, B280F .... 36 psi
   B230FT, B23FT .... 43 psi
   B28F .... 67 to 78 psi
Rest pressure: B28F .... 34 to 45 psi
Control pressure (warm regulator) .... 43 to 48 psi

Control pressure regulator
Resistance: B28F .... 20 to 24 ohms

Fuel injectors
Opening pressure .... 51 to 60 psi
No leakage below .... 42 psi

Thermal time switch
Injection time ($\pm$ 2 sec):
   At $-20°C$ ($-4°F$) .... 7.5 sec
   At 20°C (68°F) .... 2.0 sec
   At 35°C (95°F) and above .... Zero

Auxiliary air valve (not constant idle speed system)
Resistance .... 40 to 60 ohm
Fully open at .... −30°C (−22°F)
Fully closed at .... 70°C (158°F)
Time to close from +20°C (68°F) .... 5 minutes

Air control valve (constant idle speed system)
Resistance (between terminals 3 and 4, and 4 and 5(...... 20 ohm approx

Coolant temperature sensor (constant idle speed system)
Resistance at:
  −10°C (14°F) .... 32,000 to 53,000 ohm
  20°C (68°F) .... 8500 to 11,500 ohm
  80°C (178°F) .... 770 to 1320 ohm

Torque specifications	**Nm**	**Ft-lbs**
Intake manifold bolts (B28F)	10 to 15	7 to 11

1 General information

All of the vehicles covered by this manual are equipped with fuel injection. The B28F engine uses a continuous injection system, while all other engines (normally aspirated and turbocharged) use the Bosch LH-Jetronic system. All U.S. models are equipped with catalytic converters to further reduce exhaust emissions. Due to this fact, they must use unleaded fuel, as leaded fuel will damage the catalyst in the converter.

This Chapter deals with descriptions, checking and repair procedures of these fuel injection and exhaust systems. Due to the variations in some systems to comply with certain regional or national emission control standards, not all of the information contained in this Chapter may be applicable to your particular vehicle.

2 Maintenance and inspection

1   Keep an adequate supply of fuel in the tank at all times. A full tank is less likely to suffer from rust and condensation, both of which can cause problems by contaminating the fuel.
2   Every 6000 miles (10,000 km) or six months, whichever comes first, check the idle speed and mixture (CO level). See Section 8.
3   Every 12,000 miles (20,000 km) or annually, check the condition and security of the exhaust system (Section 19). Also inspect the fuel lines and hoses.
4   At the same interval on Turbo models, check the integrity of the tamperproof seals, and check the boost pressure switches (Sec 45).
5   Every 24,000 miles (40,000 km) or two years, replace the fuel filter (Section 7) and the air cleaner element (Section 5). More frequent replacement of the air cleaner element may be necessary in dusty conditions.

6   Lubricate the throttle linkage occasionally and check that the cable is not frayed or kinked.

3 Tamperproof adjustment screws — caution

1   Certain adjustment points in the fuel system (and elsewhere) are protected by tamperproof caps, plugs or seals. The purpose of such tamperproofing is to discourage, and to detect, adjustment by unqualified operators.
2   In some areas, it is unlawful to drive a vehicle with missing or broken tamperproof seals.
3   Before removing a tamperproof seal, check to see that you will not be breaking local or national anti-pollution regulations by doing so. Install a new seal when adjustment is complete when this is required by law.
4   Do not break tamperproof seals on a vehicle which is still under warranty.

4 Air filter — replacement

1   Release the clips (or hose clamp) which secure the air mass sensor (four-cylinder engines) or the air intake duct (V6 engines) to the air cleaner housing.
2   Release the clips securing the air cleaner housing lid to the housing (photo), then lift the lid off.
3   Remove the air filter element from the housing (photo).
4   Wipe the inside of the housing to remove any dirt that may be present. Be careful not to push any dirt into the air mass sensor or air intake duct.
5   Install the new filter element, making sure the rubber bead around

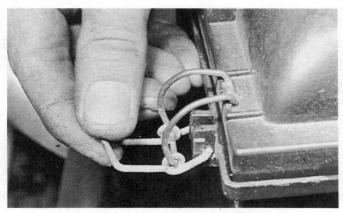

4.2 Releasing an air cleaner lid clip

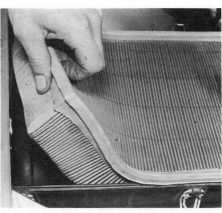

4.3 Removing the air cleaner element

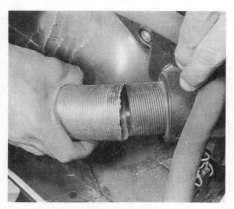

5.2A   Disconnecting the hot air duct

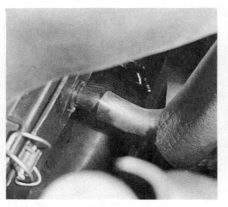

5.2B   An air cleaner crankcase ventilation hose

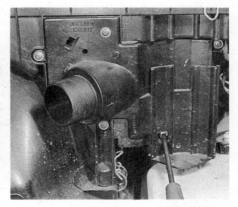

5.3A   Removing the air cleaner preheating thermostat assembly

the outside of the element seats in the housing groove.
6   Install the lid and secure the clips.
7   Connect the air mass sensor or the air intake duct to the air cleaner lid, then secure the clips or tighten the hose clamp.

5   Air cleaner unit — removal and installation

1   Remove the air cleaner element (Section 4).
2   Disconnect the hot air inlet duct from the housing. Also disconnect the crankcase ventilation hose (photos).
3   The preheating thermostat and shutter may now be removed if necessary. The operation of the thermostat may be checked using a refrigerator or a hair dryer. The marking on the thermostat gives the approximate temperature at which it will be in the half-way position (photos).
4   To remove the complete air cleaner housing, release the securing bolt or clip (photo). Lift out the housing, disengaging the cold air intake from the grommet in the fender wall.
5   Install by reversing the removal operations.

6   Fuel filter — replacement

Warning: *Gasoline is extremely flammable, so extra precautions must be taken when working on any part of the fuel system. Do not smoke or allow open flames or bare light bulbs near the work area. Also, do not work in a garage if a natural gas type appliance with a pilot light is present.*

1   Disconnect the cable from the negative battery terminal.
2   The fuel filter on B28F models is located in the engine compartment along the left side inner fender panel, just behind the suspen-

sion turret. On all other models it is located underneath the vehicle next to the fuel pump.
3   Have some rags handy to catch any spilling fuel. Hold the filter canister with a wrench to prevent it from turning. Loosen the banjo fitting bolt at the rear of the filter (it's a good idea to place a rag over the filter while loosening this bolt to prevent fuel from spraying the surrounding area). Remove the bolt and sealing washers (these washers should be replaced upon installation).

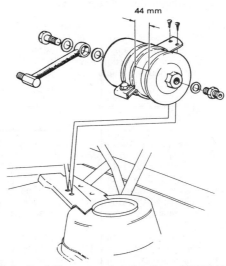

44 mm

Fig. 3.1   Fuel filter mounting details — B28F V6 engine (Sec 6)

5.3B   Preheating thermostat assembly set to take in hot air. Thermostat itself is arrowed

5.4   An air cleaner securing bolt

6.6   Fuel filter (on right) and pump — LH-Jetronic models. Arrows show direction of flow

4   Unscrew the fitting at the other end of the filter, again holding the filter canister with a wrench to prevent it from turning. Wipe up any spilled fuel immediately.

5   Loosen the canister bracket clamp bolt, then remove the bracket mounting bolts. Slide the filter canister out of the bracket.

6   Install the bracket to the new filter (don't tighten the clamp bolt yet) attach it to its mounting point and tighten the bolts securely. Make sure the arrow on the canister points in the direction of fuel flow (photo).

7   On B28F models, adjust the position of the filter canister in the bracket. There should be a space of 44 mm between the front of the filter and the bracket (see the accompanying illustration).

8   Using new sealing washers, install the fuel line fitting to the rear of the filter and tighten the banjo bolt securely.

9   Connect the fuel line to the outlet side of the filter, tightening the fitting securely.

10 Reconnect the negative battery terminal, start the engine and check for leaks.

11 Dispose of the old filter safely.

---

7   Idle speed and mixture — adjustment

Note: *An accurate tachometer and an exhaust gas analyzer (CO meter) will be needed for this procedure. Otherwise, have the job done by a Volvo dealer.*

1   Refer to Section 3.

2   The engine valve clearances must be correct, the crankcase ventilation system hoses connected, the air cleaner element and the ignition system in good condition. Air conditioning and major electrical loads must be switched off. The throttle cable must be correctly adjusted (Section 12).

3   Bring the engine to normal operating temperature. Connect the tachometer and exhaust gas analyzer as instructed by the manufacturers. Allow the engine to idle.

4   On models with a constant idle speed system (all US model B28F engines), disable the system by grounding the black and white test wire near the right-hand suspension turret (Fig. 3.2). The idle speed is then adjusted to a lower value than that normally maintained (see Specifications).

Continuous injection (CI) system (B28F engine)

5   Disconnect the Lambda sensor electrical connector.

6   Check the idle speed, comparing it to the specifications. Make sure the air conditioner is turned off.

7   If the idle speed is not to specification, unhook the link rod from the cable pulley (Fig. 3.3). Check to see that the pulley moves freely without binding, and that the throttle cable operates smoothly.

8   Check to see that the idle speed screw is turned in completely (Fig. 3.4). This screw is for adjusting the idle speed on engines not equipped with a continuous idle speed (CIS) system.

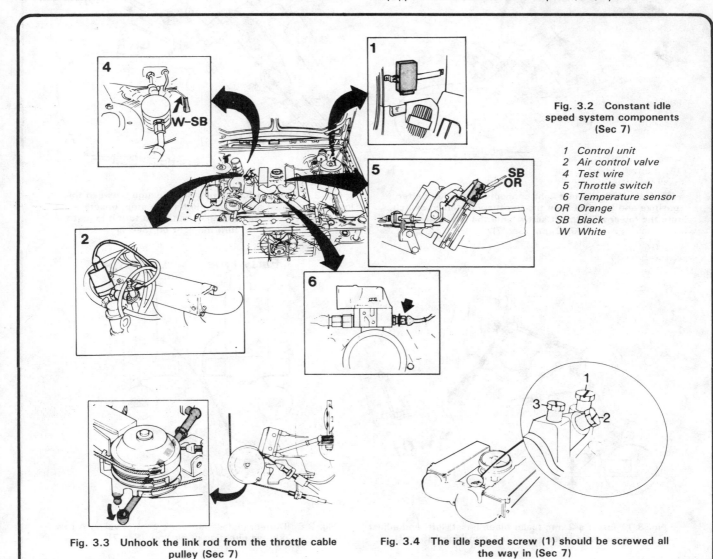

Fig. 3.2 Constant idle speed system components (Sec 7)

1 Control unit
2 Air control valve
4 Test wire
5 Throttle switch
6 Temperature sensor
OR Orange
SB Black
W White

Fig. 3.3 Unhook the link rod from the throttle cable pulley (Sec 7)

Fig. 3.4 The idle speed screw (1) should be screwed all the way in (Sec 7)

9   Connect a test light from the battery positive terminal to terminal 4 (orange wire) on the throttle valve micro switch (Fig. 3.5). The light should come on — if it doesn't, turn the upper adjustment screw until it does.

10 Turn the lower (throttle position) adjustment screw until an engine speed of 700 RPM is attained (Fig. 3.5). The test light must be on throughout the entire procedure, or the adjustment will not be accurate.

11 Disconnect the ground wire and and check to see that the idle stabilizes at 750 RPM. When the air conditioner is turned on, the engine speed should increase to 900 RPM.

12 To adjust the throttle micro switch, insert a 0.012-in feeler gauge between the lower (throttle position) adjustment screw and the throttle stop (Fig. 3.6). Unscrew the upper adjustment screw until the test light goes out, then turn the screw in until it just lights.

13 Substitute feeler gauges of 0.20 mm (0.008 in) and 0.60 mm (0.024 in) thickness. The test light should stay on with the thinner gauge, and go out with the thicker one. Disconnect the test light.

14 Check the adjustment of the throttle cable (and cruise control cable, if applicable). The cable should be just tight at idle, without holding the throttle drum off its stop.

15 Have the assistant hold the throttle pedal down. Check that the throttle drum contacts the full throttle stop. Also check the adjustment of the kickdown cable (when applicable) in this position — see Chapter 6. Release the throttle.

16 Insert a feeler gauge 2 mm (0.080 in) thick between the throttle drum and the idle stop. Reconnect the throttle link rod, adjusting its length if necessary to achieve a clearance of 0.10 mm (0.004 in) between the lower adjustment screw and the stop (Fig. 3.7). Remove the feeler gauge. If the correct idle speed can't be attained, check all related wire harness connections, vacuum hoses and the air valve (Fig. 3.8).

17 Read the CO level and adjust if necessary by turning the mixture adjustment screw next to the fuel distributor (photo). If the hole is tamperproofed, remove the air/fuel metering assembly and knock the plug (or the steel ball) out of the adjustment hole. A long Allen key

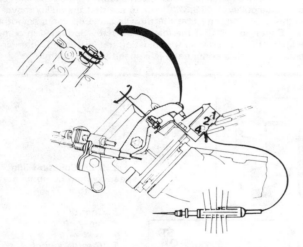

Fig. 3.5 With the test light connected between battery positive and terminal 4 on the throttle valve microswitch, turn the lower adjustment screw until the idle speed reads 700 rpm (Sec 7)

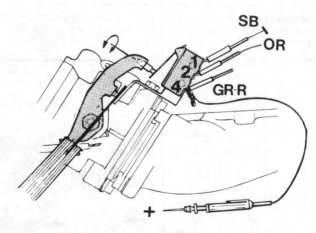

Fig. 3.6 Place a 0.012-inch feeler gauge between the lower adjustment screw and the throttle stop, unscrew the upper screw until the light goes out, then turn it in just far enough to turn the light on (Sec 7)

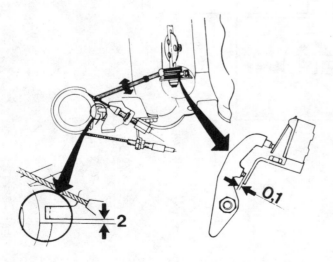

Fig. 3.7 Insert a 2 mm feeler blade (inset, left) and adjust the rod for a lever gap of 0.1 mm (right) (Sec 7)

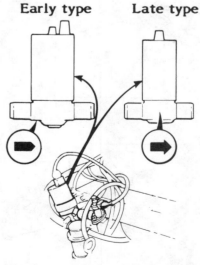

Fig. 3.8 Correct installation of air control valve. Arrow shows direction of air flow (Sec 7)

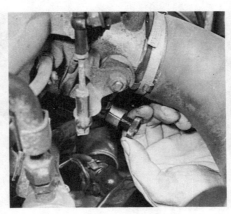

7.17 Idle mixture adjustment using a long Allen key. The hole may be tamperproofed

7.19 Idle speed adjustment — LH-Jetronic

8.3 Fuel filler pipe cover plate — Sedan

will be needed. After each adjustment, remove the Allen key, rev the engine briefly and allow the CO reading to stabilize before re-checking.

18 Readjust the idle speed if necessary.

LH-Jetronic system

19 Adjust the idle speed if necessary by turning the knurled adjustment screw next to the throttle housing (photo).

20 Disconnect the Lambda sensor connector. Read the CO meter value and, if necessary, turn the mixture screw on the air mass sensor to obtain the desired setting (Fig. 3.9). If the hole is tamperproofed, carefully drill two small holes in the plug and pull it out with a pair of snapring pliers.

21 Readjust the idle speed if necessary.

All models

22 If the CO reading is initially too high, but falls substantially when the crankcase ventilation hose is disconnected from the oil trap (in-line engines) or when the oil filler cap is removed (V6 engines), this suggests that fuel contamination of the oil is affecting the readings. Change the engine oil before proceeding.

23 When the idle speed and mixture are within the specified limits, stop the engine and disconnect the test gear.

24 Remove any jumper wires and reattach the disconnected wire harness connectors.

25 Install new tamperproof seals when required.

---

8 Fuel tank — removal and installation

Warning: *Gasoline is extremely flammable, so extra precautions must be taken when working on any part of the fuel system. DO NOT smoke or allow open flames or bare light bulbs near the work area. Also, do not work in a garage if a natural gas type appliance with a pilot light is present. Don't begin this procedure until the fuel gauge indicates that the tank is empty or nearly empty. If the tank must be removed when it's full (for example, if the fuel pump malfunctions), siphon any remaining fuel from the tank (using a siphon pump, not your mouth) into an approved fuel container prior to removal.*

1 Disconnect the cable from the negative battery terminal.

2 Unless the vehicle has been driven far enough to completely empty the tank, it's a good idea to siphon the residual fuel out before removing the tank from the vehicle. Siphon pumps are available at most auto parts stores and aren't very expensive.

3 Remove the access hatch from the trunk floor (see Section 9). Remove the fuel filler pipe cover plate (photo).

4 Loosen the clamps and pull off the hoses from the sending unit. Disconnect the tank pump electrical connector.

5 Raise the rear of the vehicle and support it securely on jackstands. Place a floor jack under the tank and position a block of wood between the jack pad and the tank. Remove the heat shield if equipped.

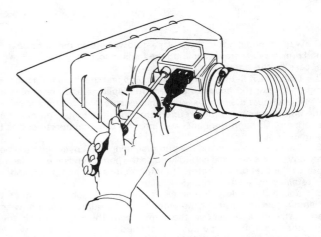

Fig. 3.9 Turn the adjustment screw on the air mass sensor to obtain the desired CO-meter reading (Sec 7)

6 Support the fuel tank and remove the securing straps and reinforcing plate nuts and bolts and carefully lower the tank from the vehicle. On some later models, the rear driveshaft must be removed (Chapter 7).

7 Repairs to the fuel tank or filler neck MUST be performed by a professional with the proper training to carry out this critical and potentially dangerous work. Even after cleaning and flushing, explosive fumes can remain and could explode during repair of the tank. "Cold" repair compounds are available and are acceptable for use by the home mechanic.

8 After removal of the fuel tank, place it in a safe area far away from open flames or sparks, as gasoline fumes spread out and settle near the floor. Once again, do not perform this job in a garage where a natural gas appliance is present.

9 Installation is the reverse of the removal procedure. Use new hoses and clamps where necessary.

---

9 Fuel tank pump and sending unit — removal, inspection and installation

Note: *The fuel tank should be no more than half full when performing this procedure.*

Warning: *Gasoline is extremely flammable, so extra precautions must be taken when working on any part of the fuel system. DO NOT smoke or allow open flames or bare light bulbs in or near the work area. Also, don't work in a garage if a natural gas appliance is present.*

Pump/sending unit removal and installation

1 Disconnect the cable from the negative battery terminal.

2 Open the trunk and lift up the trunk mat. Remove the access hatch.

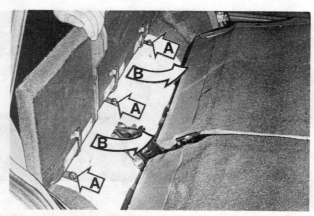

Fig. 3.10   Access to fuel tank hatch on Wagon models: remove screws (A) and pull floor forward and up (B) (Sec 9)

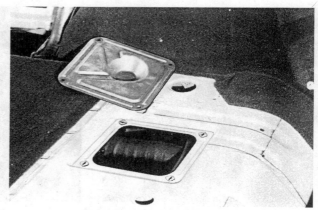

Fig. 3.11   Fuel tank access hatch removed — Station wagon (Sec 9)

On wagon models, fold the rear seat down, lift up the floor covering and remove the screws securing the folding portion of the floor to gain access to the hatch.

3   Disconnect the fuel supply, return and breather lines from the sending unit. Plug the hoses to prevent fuel spillage and contamination.

4   Disconnect the pump/sending unit electrical connector and remove the bolt that secures the ground wire. Push the rubber grommet and connector through the panel and into the same compartment as the sending unit.

5   Clean the area around the pump/sending unit cover plate. Remove the cover plate nuts and carefully guide the pump/sending unit assembly out of the fuel tank (photo). On later models the pump/sending unit is retained by a large threaded collar.

6   Unclip the pickup screen and tube from the pump. Remove the clamp screw, disconnect the wires from the pump (noting how they are installed) and remove the pump from the sending unit frame (photos). Later model pumps are retained by a clip on the lower end which can be pried up to release it. Loosen the hose clamp at the upper end of the pump then unhook the pump from its upper mounting point.

7   If the fuel pump is defective it must be replaced.

8   Install a new O-ring to the top of the pump (photo) and place the pump in the sending unit frame. Install the clamp screw. On later models, insert the pump outlet into the hose and tighten the clamp. Hook the pump onto its upper mounting point and then connect it to its lower mounting clip.

9   The remainder of installation is the reverse of the removal procedure. On pump/sending units secured by a threaded retaining ring, align the marks stamped on top of the sending unit with the fuel tank seams. Be sure to replace the sealing ring if it shows any signs of deterioration.

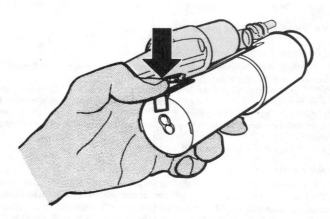

Fig. 3.12   Some later model fuel pumps attach to the sending unit assembly with a clip (Sec 9)

Sending unit check

10   To check the operation of the sending unit, connect the leads of an ohmmeter between the black and the grey/white wires. Move the float up and down and verify that the resistance changes with float position as shown in Fig. 3.13. If the sending unit resistance does not fluctuate, it must be replaced.

9.5   Removing the tank pump

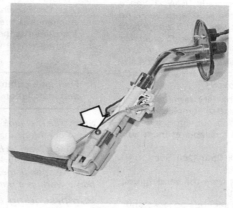

9.6A   The tank pump and sender unit. Pump clamp screw arrowed.

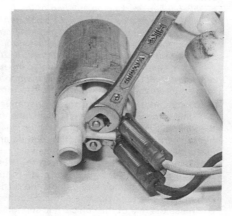

9.6B   Disconnecting a lead from the pump

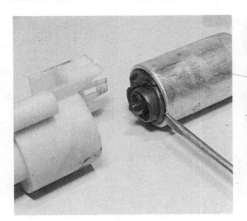

9.8 The screwdriver shows the pump O-ring

10.3 Unbolting the fuel pump cradle

10.4 Disconnecting a fuel pump lead

10 Main fuel pump — removal and installation

1   Raise the rear of the vehicle and support it securely on jackstands.
2   Disconnect the battery negative cable.
3   Unbolt the fuel pump cradle from the underside of the vehicle (photo). Pull the cradle off the grommets.
4   Disconnect the electrical leads from the pump, noting the colors of the wires and the corresponding terminals (photo).
5   Disconnect the fuel supply and outlet pipes from the pump. Be prepared for fuel spillage. Plug or cap the open pipe unions.
6   Unbolt the pump brackets and remove the pump.
7   Install by reversing the removal operations, using new sealing washers. Run the engine and check for leakage before lowering the vehicle.

11 Fuel gauge — check

1   If both the fuel gauge and the temperature gauge are malfunctioning, the fault is probably in the instrument voltage stabilizer on the instrument panel printed circuit.
2   Connect a 68 ohm resistor between the fuel gauge connector near the tank and ground (Fig. 3.14). (The wire leading to this connector is colored white and green.) Switch on the ignition: the gauge should show approximately three-quarters full. If not, the fault lies in the gauge, its power supply or the wiring.
3   Testing of the sender unit is covered in Section 9.

12 Throttle cable — removal, installation and adjustment

1   Release the housing by extracting the spring clip and unhook the cable from the drum (photos).
2   Inside the vehicle, remove the trim from below the steering column. Pull the cable through the end of the pedal and slide the split bushing off the end of the cable (photo).
3   Release the cable grommet from the bulkhead and pull the cable into the engine bay. Note the routing of the cable, release it from any clips or ties and remove it.
4   Install by reversing the removal operations, then adjust the cable as follows.
5   Disconnect the link rod which joins the cable down to the throttle valve(s) by levering off a balljoint (photo).
6   With the throttle pedal released, the cable should be just taut, and the cable drum must be resting against the idle stop. With the pedal fully depressed the drum must contact the full throttle stop. Adjust if necessary by means of the threaded sleeve.
7   On automatic transmission models, check the adjustment of the

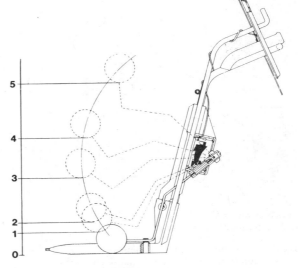

Fig. 3.13 Fuel gauge sender position/resistance characteristic (Sec 9)

Position	Resistance (approx)
0	296 ohm
1	196 ohm
2	145 ohm
3	98 ohm
4	68 ohm
5	36 ohm

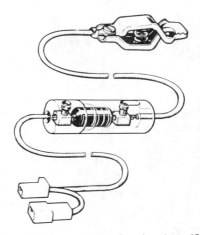

Fig. 3.14 Fuel gauge test lead and resistor (Sec 11)

12.1A Remove the spring clip . . .

12.1B . . . and unhook the cable from the drum

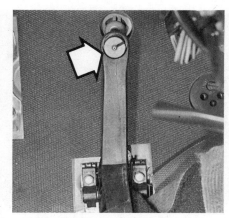

12.2 Split bush (arrowed) secures cable at pedal end

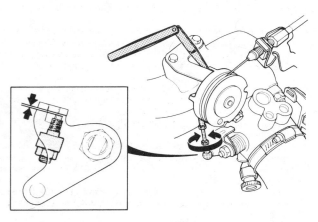

Fig. 3.15 Throttle link rod adjustment — B23/230 F/FT. For lever-to-screw clearance (inset) see text (Sec 12)

kickdown cable (Chapter 6).

8   Reconnect the link rod, adjusting its length if necessary as follows.

B28F

9   The length of the link rod should be such that neither the cable drum nor the throttle valves are disturbed from their idle positions.

B23/230F/FT

10   Reconnect the link rod and place a 1 mm (0.040 in) feeler blade between the cable drum and the idle stop (Fig. 3.15). In this position the clearance between the throttle lever and the adjustment screw must be 0.1 mm (0.004 in). Adjust the link rod (not the adjustment screw) if necessary to achieve this.

---

13   Throttle pedal — removal and installation

---

1   Remove the trim from below the steering column.
2   Depress the pedal fully. Grip the cable with pliers and release the pedal. Separate the cable from the split bush.
3   Remove the pedal bracket bolts and remove the pedal and bracket.
4   Install by reversing the removal operations. Check the cable adjustment on completion (Section 12).

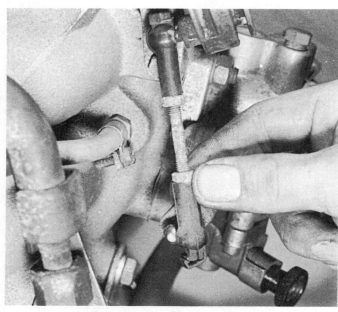

12.5 Disconnecting the throttle link rod

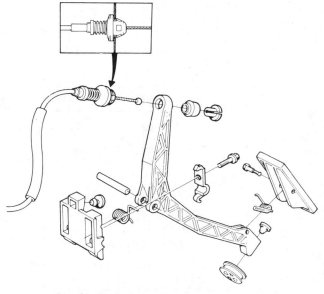

Fig. 3.16 Throttle pedal and associated components (Sec 13)

14.2   An exhaust system rubber
          mounting

15.4   Exhaust flanged joint

15.5   Exhaust U-pipe clamp

14   Exhaust system — inspection and repair

1   Periodically inspect the exhaust system for freedom from corrosion and security of mountings. Large holes will be obvious; small holes may be found more easily by letting the engine idle and partly obstructing the tailpipe with a wad of cloth.
2   Check the condition of the rubber mounts by applying downward pressure on the exhaust system and observing the mounts for splits or cracks. Replace deteriorated mountings (photo).
3   Small holes or splits in the exhaust system may be repaired temporarily using muffler tape or exhaust system compound; however, such repairs are often short-lived. For best results the section in question should be replaced.

15   Exhaust system — removal and installation

1   Details of exhaust system routing and mounting will vary with model and year, but the principles of removal and installation remain the same.
2   In many cases it will be found easier to remove the complete system from the downpipe(s) rearwards and then to replace individual sections on the bench. One exception is on models where the system passes over the rear axle; here it is better to separate the joints, or to cut the pipe if it is rusty anyway.
3   To remove the complete system, raise and support the vehicle at a convenient working height. Apply penetrating oil to the nuts, bolts and clamps which will have to be undone.
4   Unbolt the flanged joint at the union of the exhaust system with the downpipe(s) (photo).
5   If the system passes over the rear axle, remove one of the U-pipe clamps and separate the system there (photo).
6   With the aid of an assistant, unhook the system from its mountings and remove it.
7   To remove the downpipe(s), release the mounting clamp from the bellhousing and separate the joints from the manifold(s) or turbocharger.

3

Fig. 3.17   Exhaust system mountings — B 28 F. On most models the system passes above the rear axle (Sec 15)

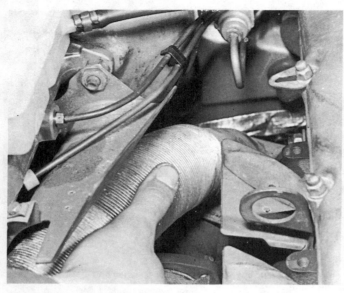

15.7 Disconnecting the hot air duct — Turbo shown

Also disconnect the hot air duct and, if necessary, unbolt the hot air shroud (photo).

8   Begin installation with the downpipe(s), using new gaskets. Apply anti-seize compound to the threads. Install the bellhousing mounting clamp bolt but do not tighten it yet.

9   Sling the rest of the system on its mountings and bolt it together, using a new sealing ring at the flanged joint. Apply exhaust jointing compound to the sliding joints and anti-seize compound to all threads.

10 Tighten all the joints from the front rearwards, but leave the bellhousing clamp loose until everything else has been tightened. (On models with the B23FT engine, follow the tightening sequence shown in Fig. 3.18). Twist the sliding joints slightly if necessary so that the system hangs easily and without touching the body.

11 Run the engine for a few minutes and check the system for leaks. Allow it to cool and retighten the joints.

12 Lower the vehicle.

16 Cruise control — general information

If equipped, the cruise control allows the vehicle to maintain a steady speed selected by the driver, regardless of gradients or prevailing winds.

The main components of the system are a control unit, a control switch, a vacuum servo and a vacuum pump. Brake and (when applicable) clutch pedal switches protect the engine against excessive

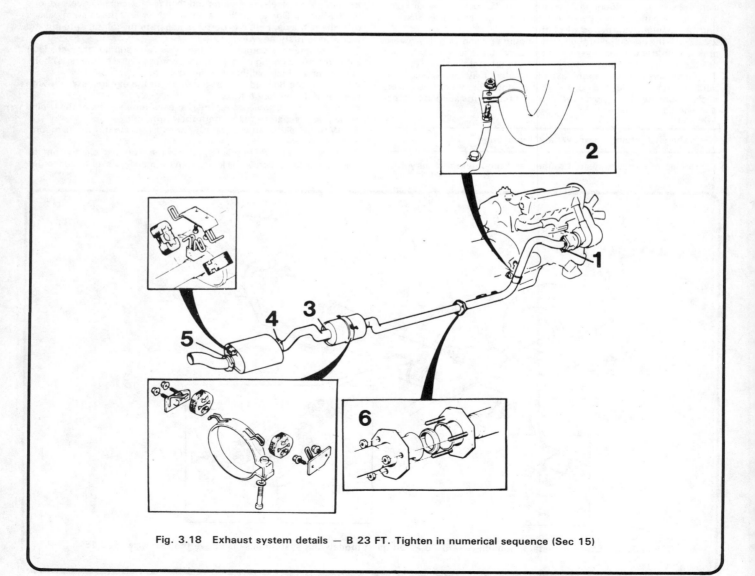

Fig. 3.18 Exhaust system details — B 23 FT. Tighten in numerical sequence (Sec 15)

speeds or loads should a pedal be depressed while the system is in use.

In operation, the driver accelerates to the desired speed and then brings the system into use by means of the switch. The control unit then monitors vehicle speed (from the speedometer pulses) and opens or closes the throttle by means of the servo to maintain the set speed. If the switch is moved to OFF, or the brake or clutch pedal is depressed, the servo immediately closes the throttle. The set speed is stored in the control unit memory and the system can be reactivated by moving the switch to RESUME, provided that vehicle speed has not dropped below 25 mph (40 km/h).

The driver can override the cruise control for passing simply by depressing the throttle pedal. When the pedal is released, the set speed will be resumed.

The cruise control cannot be engaged at speeds below 25 mph (40 km/h), and should not be used in slippery or congested conditions.

No specific removal, installation or adjustment procedures were available at the time of writing. Problems should be referred to a Volvo dealer or other specialist.

17 Intake manifold — removal and installation

1   Disconnect the battery negative cable.

Four cylinder engine

2   If the manifold is coolant-heated, drain the cooling system.
3   Disconnect the air intake duct from the throttle housing.
4   Disconnect the control cable(s) from the throttle drum.
5   Disconnect the injector electrical connectors (Turbo models) and

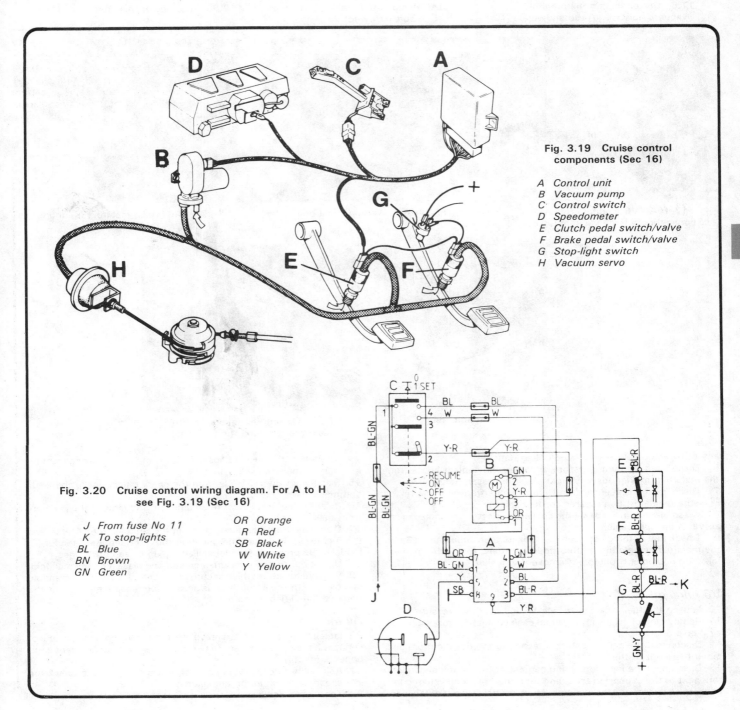

Fig. 3.19 Cruise control components (Sec 16)

A Control unit
B Vacuum pump
C Control switch
D Speedometer
E Clutch pedal switch/valve
F Brake pedal switch/valve
G Stop-light switch
H Vacuum servo

Fig. 3.20 Cruise control wiring diagram. For A to H see Fig. 3.19 (Sec 16)

J   From fuse No 11
K   To stop-lights
BL Blue
BN Brown
GN Green
OR Orange
R   Red
SB Black
W   White
Y   Yellow

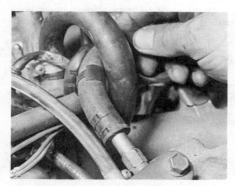

17.6 Disconnecting the manifold vacuum hoses — Turbo shown

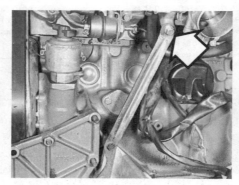

17.9A Remove the bracing strut top bolt (arrowed) . . .

17.9B . . . and the manifold-to-head nuts

17.14A V6 manifold removal: disconnecting a large vacuum hose . . .

17.14B . . . and a small one

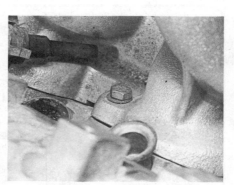

17.19A An intake manifold mounting bolt . . .

17.19B . . . and an O-ring

17.20 Cutting the intake manifold gasket to clear the thermal timer

any other electrical services obstructing removal.

6   Disconnect vacuum, pressure, breather and coolant hoses from the manifold, making identifying marks if necessary (photo).

7   Disconnect the fuel feed and return pipes from the fuel rail or pressure regulator. Be prepared for fuel spillage.

8   Disconnect or move aside the cold start injector and the auxiliary air valve (as applicable).

9   Check that nothing has been overlooked, then unbolt and remove the manifold complete with throttle housing and (on Turbo models) injection equipment (photos). Remove the gasket.

V6 engine

10 Loosen the fuel tank cap to release any residual pressure.

11 Remove the oil filler cap, the crankcase ventilation hoses and the air intake duct.

12 Disconnect the control cables attached to the throttle drum and move them out of the way.

13 Disconnect the injection wiring harness at the electrical connectors next to the expansion tank, and from the injection system components on and around the manifold. Move the harness out of the way.

14 Disconnect the vacuum hoses from the manifold, making identifying marks if necessary (photos).

15 Disconnect the HT leads from the spark plugs, unclip the leads and move them aside.

16 Release the fuel injector retaining clips and remove the injectors from their bores.

17 Disconnect the fuel feed line from the top of the fuel filter, and the fuel return line from the union on the left-hand inner fender (CI models). Be prepared for fuel spillage; plug or cap open lines.

18 Unbolt the control pressure regulator and place it on the manifold.

19 Remove the bolts which secure the manifold. Lift off the manifold complete with the throttle housing and fuel injection components. Remove the O-rings (photos).

All models

20 Install by reversing the removal operations, using new gaskets or O-rings. It may be necessary to cut the gasket to clear adjacent components (photo).

21 Adjust the throttle drum cable(s), run the engine and check the idle speed and mixture on completion.

22 Top up the cooling system if necessary.

18.10 An exhaust manifold-to-downpipe flanged joint

18.15 Exhaust manifold gaskets (head removed)

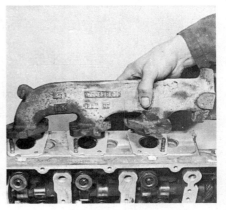

18.16 Installing an exhaust manifold (head removed)

18 Exhaust manifold(s) — removal and installation

Four cylinder engines (except Turbo)

1 Remove the hot air duct (when so equipped).
2 Disconnect the exhaust downpipe from the manifold.
3 Unbolt the manifold from the cylinder head and remove it. Remove the gaskets.
4 When installing, use new gaskets. The marking UT must face away from the cylinder head.
5 Apply anti-seize compound to the threads. Install the manifold to the head and tighten the nuts evenly.
6 Reconnect the exhaust downpipe and the hot air duct.
7 Run the engine and check for leaks.

Four cylinder engines (Turbo)

8 See Section 27.

V6 engines

9 Raise and support the front of the vehicle. Disconnect the battery negative cable.
10 Disconnect the exhaust downpipes from the manifold flanges (photo). (Both must be disconnected even if only one manifold is to be removed.)
11 Disconnect the hot air duct if it is in the way.
12 Disconnect the exhaust system front mounting from the transmission. Move the exhaust system rearwards until the pipes are clear of the manifolds. Support the exhaust system if necessary so that it is not strained.
13 Remove the securing nuts and take off the manifolds. Remove the gaskets; obtain new ones for use when installing.
14 Manifold gaskets are supplied in packets of three. Separate the gasket sections by cutting, not by folding or tearing.
15 Install the gasket sections over the cylinder head studs, with the reinforced metallic edge facing the head (photo).
16 Install the manifolds over the studs (photo). Secure them with the nuts; use a little anti-seize compound on the threads. Tighten the nuts evenly.
17 Install the exhaust pipes to the manifold, using new gaskets, metallic edges facing the manifolds. Install and tighten the nuts, again using anti-seize compound.
18 Install the exhaust system front mounting.
19 Install the hot air duct.
20 Lower the vehicle and reconnect the battery.
21 Run the engine and check for leaks.

19 Troubleshooting — fuel system (general)

Excessive fuel consumption, poor performance or difficult starting are not necessarily caused by fuel system faults. Ignition system faults and engine maladjustment or wear may also cause such symptoms. Simple causes of high consumption are under-inflated tires, binding brakes, a harsh driving style or unfavorable conditions of use. A clogged air cleaner element or fuel filter can also adversely affect performance and consumption.

The specific Troubleshooting sections later in this chapter assume that the above points have been checked and that the fuel used is of good quality and of the specified octane rating.

20 Continuous injection system — general information

The continuous fuel injection system is found on B28F engines. It is a well-proven system, with little to go wrong and no black boxes to worry about. As the name implies, fuel injection takes place continuously while the engine is running. The rate of injection is varied to suit the prevailing speed and load.

Fuel is drawn from the tank by the tank pump. It passes to the main fuel pump where the line pressure of around 73 psi is established. An accumulator next to the pump provides a reservoir of pressure to improve hot starting. From the accumulator the fuel passes through a filter and then to the fuel distributor on top of the intake manifold.

The fuel distributor looks a little like an ignition distributor, but it has fuel lines instead of HT leads. There is one fuel line per injector, with additional lines for the start injector and the control pressure regulator. The fuel distributors main function is to regulate the fuel supply to the injectors in proportion to the incoming airflow. Incoming air deflects the airflow sensor plate, which moves the control plunger in the fuel distributor and so varies the supply to the injectors. The airflow sensor and the fuel distributor together are sometimes called the fuel control unit.

The control pressure regulator reduces the control pressure during warm-up and under condition of low manifold vacuum, and so enriches the mixture. (A lower control pressure means that the airflow sensor plate is deflected further, and the quantity of fuel injected is increased.)

An electrically-controlled start injector provides extra fuel during engine starting. A thermal time switch controls the duration of start injector operation when the engine is cold; on a hot engine an impulse relay provides a smaller quantity of extra fuel to be injected. An auxiliary air valve provides the extra air needed to maintain idle speed when the engine is cold. On models with the constant idle speed system, an air control valve takes the place of the auxiliary air valve.

21 Continuous injection system — check

Warning: *Gasoline is extremely flammable, so extra precautions must be taken when working on any part of the fuel system. Do not smoke or allow open flames or bare light bulbs near the work area. Also, do not work in a garage if a natural gas type appliance with a pilot light is present.*

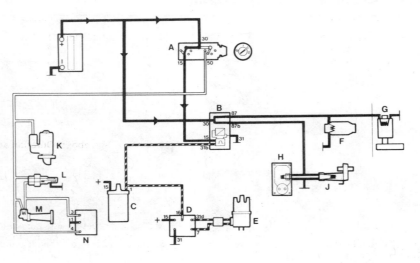

Fig. 3.21 Schematic wiring diagram for
continuous injection system (Sec 20)

A Ignition/starter switch
B Fuel pump relay
C Ignition coil
D Ignition control unit
E Ignition distributor
F Main fuel pump
G Tank pump
H Control pressure regulator
J Auxiliary air valve
K Starter motor
L Thermal timer
M Start injector
N Impulse relay

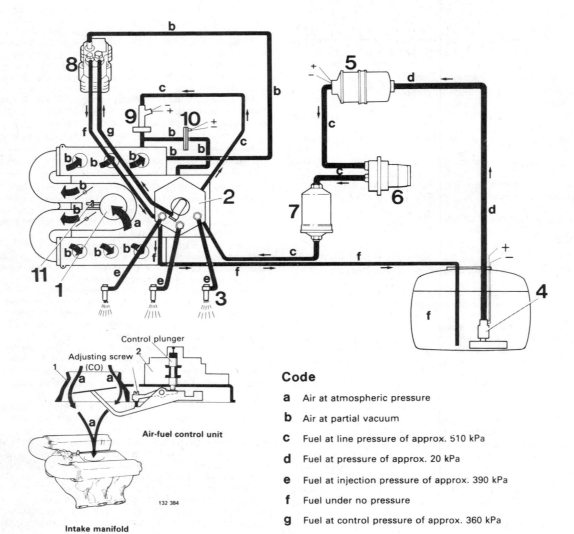

Air-fuel control unit

Intake manifold

132 384

Code

a Air at atmospheric pressure

b Air at partial vacuum

c Fuel at line pressure of approx. 510 kPa

d Fuel at pressure of approx. 20 kPa

e Fuel at injection pressure of approx. 390 kPa

f Fuel under no pressure

g Fuel at control pressure of approx. 360 kPa

Fig 3.22 Continuous injection system components (Sec 20)

1 Airflow sensor   5 Main fuel pump   9 Start injector
2 Fuel distributor   6 Accumulator   10 Auxiliary air valve
3 Injector   7 Filter   11 Mixture adjustment screw
4 Tank pump   8 Control pressure regulator

1 All the tests described in this Section are within the capability of the competent home mechanic. Some extra equipment, such as a pressure gauge and a multi-meter, may have to be purchased or rented for some of the tests.

2 Some tests result in fuel being sprayed from unions or injectors. Take stringent safety precautions, not only against fire but also against fume intoxication. Dispose of ejected fuel safely — only return it to the tank if its cleanliness is certain.

3 It is emphasized that it is no use attempting to diagnose faults in the injection system until all other engine-related systems are in good order. In particular, the battery must be fully charged when making electrical tests.

4 Disconnect the plug from the ignition control unit before starting the tests. Also disconnect the control pressure regulator and auxiliary air valve wiring plugs until they are to be tested, otherwise they will heat up during preliminary tests and give false results.

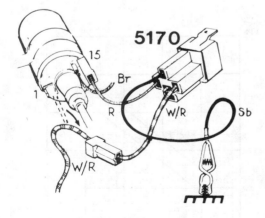

21.7 Disconnecting the impulse relay

Start injector and associated components

5 The engine must be cold for this test.

6 Remove the two Allen screws which secure the start injector. Withdraw the injector and position it with its nozzle in a clean glass jar.

7 Unclip the impulse relay (next to the expansion tank) and disconnect it (photo).

8 Have a stop-watch ready. Time the duration of fuel injection from the start injector while an assistant cranks the engine on the starter motor. Duration will vary from 7.5 seconds at coolant temperatures of −20ºC (−4ºF) to zero at 35ºC (95ºF) and above. Duration at 20ºC (68ºF) should be about two seconds.

9 If no injection occurs at all, disconnect the start injector wiring plug. Connect a 12 volt test lamp or voltmeter across the plug terminals and repeat the cranking test. If voltage is present during cranking, but the injector did not operate, the injector is defective. No voltage suggests a fault in the thermal timer or wiring.

10 If injection occurs continuously, disconnect the injector wiring plug and repeat the test. Fuel spraying without the plug connected means that the injector is defective. If no fuel sprays where it did before, the fault is probably in the thermal timer.

11 When satisfied with the results, reconnect the injector plug, then test the impulse relay as follows.

12 Reconnect the impulse relay plug. Again have an assistant crank the engine. After the initial period of continuous injection controlled by the thermal timer, the impulse relay should cause the injector to chatter and deliver 0.1 sec bursts of fuel, with intervals of 0.3 sec between them. If this is not the case, test the relay by substitution.

13 Run the fuel pump by switching on the ignition and connecting Volvo test relay 5170. Feel the fuel filter to check that the pump is running — it will vibrate slightly. Leakage from the start injector must not exceed one drop per minute — if it does, replace it.

14 Switch off the ignition and install the start injector and other components that were removed.

Air-fuel control unit

15 Remove the air intake ducting from the top of the airflow sensor.

16 Inspect the airflow sensor plate. Pass a slip of paper around its edge to check that it does not touch anywhere (Fig. 3.24). Center the plate if necessary by loosening its central screw, repositioning the plate and tightening the screw.

17 Run the fuel pump (paragraph 13). Depress the airflow sensor plate to simulate airflow into the manifold, at the same time listening to the injectors. The injectors should buzz when the plate is moved, and stop buzzing when it is released. If the injectors buzz with the plate at rest, the fuel distributor control plunger has jammed. If the injectors do not buzz at all, the line pressure is incorrect (perhaps because the fuel pump is not working). If the sensor plate jams, the airflow sensor needs to be rebuilt or replaced. Some resistance to motion is normal — do not mistake this for jamming.

18 Check the line and control pressures as described later in the test procedures, then measure the resting height of the airflow sensor plate. The fuel pump must be running and control pressure must be at its

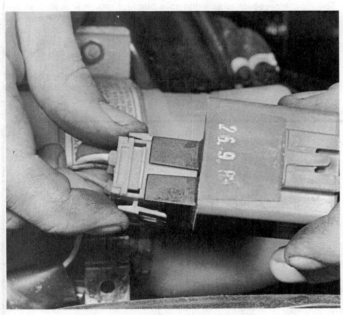

Fig. 3.23 Starting the fuel pumps with test relay 5170 (Sec 21)

Br	Brown	1	Ignition coil (distributor side)
R	Red	15	Ignition coil (battery side)
Sb	Black		
W	White		

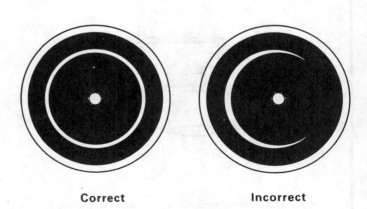

Correct   **Incorrect**

Fig. 3.24 Check the centralization of the airflow sensor plate (Sec 21)

maximum value, so the control pressure regulator must have been energised for at least five minutes.

19 Measure the height of the sensor plate relative to the venturi waist. The plate should be flush with, or no more than 0.3 mm (0.012 in) above, the waist. Adjustment is made by tapping the pin to the left of the mixture screw hole up or down (Fig. 3.25). To tap the pin upwards, the airflow sensor will have to be removed.

20 It is emphasized that the resting height of the sensor plate depends on the control pressure. If the control pressure is incorrect, it is no use trying to adjust the sensor plate.

21 Install the components that were removed and plug in the electrical connectors.

Line, control and resting pressures

22 A pressure gauge of adequate range will be needed for these tests (0-100 psi), together with a switchable T-piece and the appropriate pipes and unions. If these are not available, it will probably be quicker and cheaper to have a Volvo dealer or fuel injection specialist perform the tests.

23 With the ignition off, connect the gauge and T-piece between the control pressure regulator and the fuel distributor (Fig. 3.26). Switch the T-piece so that the gauge is connected to the fuel distributor, and the control pressure regulator is isolated.

24 Run the fuel pump (paragraph 13).

25 Wait for the pressure gauge reading to stabilize, then record it and compare it with the specified line pressure. If the pressure is too high, either the fuel return line is blocked or the line pressure regulator is defective. Too low a pressure can be caused by leakage on the pressure side of the main pump; a defective accumulator; a defective tank pump or a clogged pick-up filter or main fuel filter.

26 With the line pressure correct, switch the T-piece to connect the control pressure regulator and the fuel distributor (Fig. 3.27). When the pump is running, the gauge will show control pressure. Desired pressure from a cold regulator (ie the wrong plug is not connected) varies with ambient temperature as shown in the graph (Fig. 3.28). Too high a pressure can only be due to a blocked return line. If the pressure is too low, the test should be repeated with a new control pressure regulator.

27 Having achieved the correct cold control pressure, connect the wiring plug to the control pressure regulator. Leave the ignition on for five minutes to allow the regulator to warm up, then read the control pressure again. Desired warm pressure is given in the Specifications. Too high a pressure is still due to a blocked return line, and should have shown up in the cold test. Too low a pressure may mean that the regulator is not heating up — check for battery voltage at the wiring plug, and measure the resistance across the regulator terminals. If voltage is present at the regulator but it is not heating up, it should be replaced.

28 With line pressure and control pressure correct, finally check the resting pressure. With the gauge still connected to read control

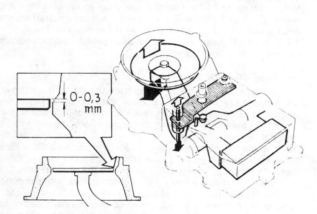

Fig. 3.25 Sensor plate height is adjusted by moving pin (small arrows) (Sec 21)

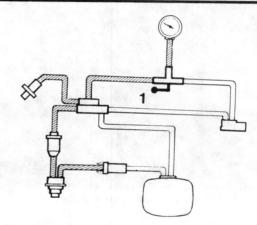

Fig. 3.26 Measuring line pressure — T-piece in position 1 (Sec 21)

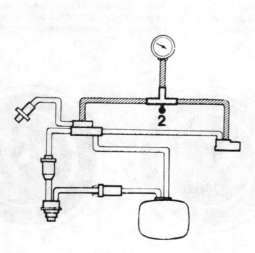

Fig. 3.27 Measuring control pressure — T-piece in position 2 (Sec 21)

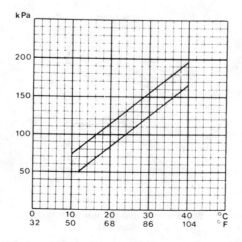

Fig. 3.28 Control pressure versus temperature (Sec 21)

pressure, switch off the ignition. Pressure should stabilize at 35 to 46 psi and after 20 minutes should still be above 35 psi. Pressure drop denotes external leakage, a leaking line pressure regulator, or a defective fuel pump non-return valve. Loss of resting pressure is a cause of hot start difficulties.

29 When all pressures are correct, disconnect the gauge and restore the original connections.

Auxiliary air valve (without constant idle system)

30 With the auxiliary air valve cold (at room temperature), disconnect the air hoses from it. Shine a flashlight through the valve to establish that it is at least partly open. If it is not, and refuses to open when tapped or shaken, replace it (Fig. 3.29).

31 Connect the wiring plug to the valve and switch on the ignition. The valve should close completely within five minutes. If it does not, tap it lightly (engine vibrations will normally cause the valve to close). If it still does not close, and there is battery voltage at the wiring plug, replace the valve.

Air control valve (with constant idle system)

32 With the ignition off, disconnect the electrical connectors from the constant idle system control unit (behind the side trim in the front passenger footwell).

33 Start the engine and allow it to idle. Using two pieces of wire, connect electrical connector terminals Nos 5 and 2, and 4 and 1. Engine speed should rise to between 1600 and 2400 rpm — if not, the valve (or its power supply) is at fault.

Injectors and fuel distributor

34 Release the injector securing clips and pull the injectors from their recesses. Place them on clean rags.

35 Run the fuel pump (paragraph 13). Observe the injectors: if they drip, the fuel distributor is leaking internally and should be replaced. (The injector tips may become moist with fuel — this is acceptable.)

36 Depress the airflow sensor plate slowly, observing the injectors. They should all start to discharge fuel at the same time. If one or more start to discharge before the others, have the suspect injector(s) cleaned and tested or replaced.

37 Injector delivery can be checked by leading each injector into an identical measuring tube or glass. (Since the object is to detect difference in delivery, it does not matter if the receptacles are not calibrated, so long as they are all the same). Depress the airflow sensor plate through half its travel, hold it in this position until the tubes are nearly full, then release it. All injectors should have delivered the same quantity of fuel, to within 20%.

38 If a difference in delivery greater than 20% is found, exchange good and bad injectors and repeat the test. If the difference follows the injector, the injector is defective. If the difference stays with the same line regardless of injector, the fault is in the fuel distributor.

39 Install the injectors and other components when the test is complete.

40 Further testing and cleaning of fuel injectors should be left to a Volvo dealer or fuel injection specialist, since a special test rig is required.

41 A rough assessment of injector spray pattern can be made when performing the delivery test. Examples of good and bad spray patterns are given in Fig. 3.33.

Line pressure regulator — adjustment

42 Line pressure is adjusted by adding or removing shims at the pressure regulator spring. The pressure regulator is located in the fuel distributor. It is not recommended that any attempt be made at adjust-

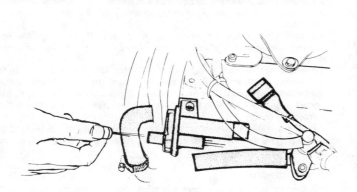

Fig. 3.29 Shining a flashlight through the auxiliary air valve (Sec 21)

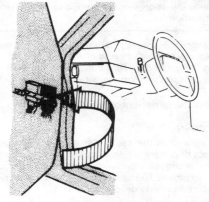

Fig. 3.30 Constant idle system control unit (arrowed) (Sec 21)

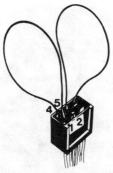

Fig. 3.31 Bridge terminals 5 and 2, and 4 and 1 (Sec 21)

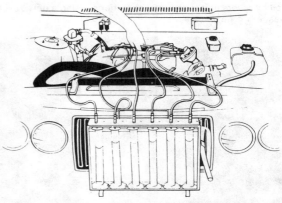

Fig. 3.32 Checking injector delivery with measuring cylinders (Sec 21)

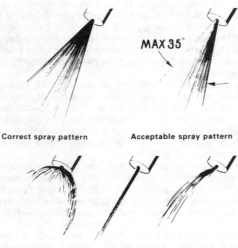

Correct spray pattern　　Acceptable spray pattern

Examples of poor spray patterns (injector should be replaced)

Fig. 3.33 Injector spray patterns (Sec 21)

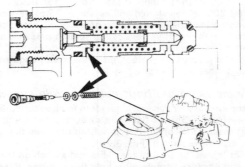

Fig. 3.34 Line pressure regulator — adjusting shims arrowed (Sec 21)

ment unless the necessary seals, shims and pressure gauges are available. Scrupulous cleanliness must be observed.

43 For every 0.1 mm (0.004 in) increase in shim thickness, line pressure will be increased by 2.2 psi. Various shim thicknesses are available

---

22 Continuous injection system components — removal and installation

---

Warning: *Gasoline is extremely flammable, so extra precautions must be taken when working on any part of the fuel system. Do not smoke or allow open flames or bare light bulbs near the work area. Also, do not work in a garage if a natural gas type appliance with a pilot light is present.*

1 Disconnect the battery negative cable.

Fuel accumulator

2 This is removed in the same way as the main fuel pump (Section 10), except that there are no electrical connections to disconnect.

3 In reality it is probably easier to remove the pump, accumulator and cradle all together. The accumulator can then be removed under relatively clean conditions on the bench.

Injectors

4 Release the spring clip and pull the injector from its recess (photos).

5 Disconnect the fuel line union from the injector.

6 Install by reversing the removal operations, using a new seal and union washers if necessary.

7 Note that new injectors are filled with a preservative wax before storage. This wax must be flushed out of the injector before it is fitted. Take advice from the seller of the injectors.

Fuel control unit

8 Loosen the fuel filler cap to release residual pressure.

9 Disconnect the various fuel unions from the fuel distributor, making notes or identifying marks if necessary (photos). Be prepared for fuel spillage.

10 Remove the air intake ducting from the top of the airflow sensor.

11 Disconnect the electrical connectors from the constant idle system throttle switch (when so equipped).

12 Remove the twelve Allen screws which secure the upper half of the control unit. Note the location of the ground wire (photo).

13 Lift off the upper half of the control unit and recover the gasket.

14 Further disassembly is described in Section 23. Note that the fuel distributor can be removed independently of the airflow sensor if required.

15 When installing, use a new gasket (photo). If necessary use new sealing washers on the fuel unions. Leave one of the injector unions disconnected.

16 Perform the basic setting of the control unit as follows. Run the fuel pump (Section 21, paragraph 13). Turn the mixture adjustment screw clockwise until fuel just starts to drip from the open union, then back the screw off half a turn. Stop the fuel pump and reconnect the remaining union.

17 Check the line, control and testing pressures, and the resting height of the airflow sensor plate (Section 21). Adjust the idle speed and mixture on completion (Section 7).

Start injector

18 Disconnect the fuel and electrical feeds from the injector. Be prepared for fuel spillage.

19 Remove the two Allen screws and withdraw the injector.

20 Install by reversing the removal operations.

Air control/auxiliary air valve

21 Disconnect the electrical plug from the valve.

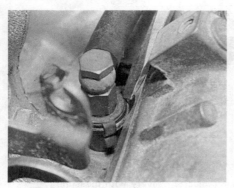

22.4A Pry up the injector spring clip . . .

22.4B . . . and pull out the injector

22.9A Disconnecting an injector union — sealing washers should be replaced upon reassembly

22.9B Disconnecting the fuel supply union from the distributor

22.12 Control unit showing some of the securing screws. Note ground wire (arrow)

22.15 Always use a new gasket when reassembling the control unit

22 Disconnect the air hoses from the valve.
23 Remove the valve securing screws and remove the valve.
24 Install by reversing the removal operations.

Control pressure regulator

25 Disconnect the electrical connectors and vacuum hoses from the regulator (photo). Mark the hoses with pieces of numbered tape to ease installation.
26 Disconnect the fuel unions from the regulator. They are different sizes so they cannot be confused. Be prepared for fuel spillage.
27 Unbolt the regulator and remove it.
28 Install by reversing the removal operations. Use new union sealing washers if necessary.

Thermal timer

Note: *the engine must be cool before beginning this procedure.*

29 Unscrew the expansion tank filler cap to release any pressure in the cooling system. Take precautions against scalding if the coolant is hot.
30 Disconnect the electrical plug from the thermal timer (photo).
31 Unscrew the thermal timer and remove it. Plug the hole with a tapered wooden plug to minimize coolant loss.
32 When installing, apply sealant to the timer threads and screw it into position. Reconnect the electrical connector.
33 Top up the cooling system if necessary.

Fuel pump relay

34 This relay is located in position E of the central electrical unit. See Chapter 12.

---

23 Continuous injection system control unit — overhaul

Warning: *Gasoline is extremely flammable, so extra precautions must*

be taken when working on any part of the fuel system. Do not smoke or allow open flames or bare light bulbs near the work area. Also, do not work in a garage if a natural gas type appliance with a pilot light is present.

1 Remove the upper half of the control unit (Section 22).
2 Remove the three plain screws which secure the fuel distributor (photo). Lift off the fuel distributor, being careful not to drop the control plunger. Recover the O-ring.
3 Remove the control plunger (photo). Clean it with clean solvent and a soft brush or the fingers only — do not use any tools on it. Also clean the metering slots in the fuel distributor.
4 Unscrew the pressure regulator plug and withdraw the pressure regulator components, keeping them in order. Clean the plungers and replace the O-rings and sealing washers. Install the components and tighten the plug (photos).
5 If any plungers are scored or otherwise damaged, or if the control plunger sticks in the distributor, the complete fuel distributor must be replaced. Do not attempt to disassemble it further.
6 To disassemble the airflow sensor, remove the two circlips which secure the pivot shaft end plugs. Remove the plugs, O-rings, spring and balls. Note which side the spring is installed (photos).
7 Loosen the clamp screws on the sensor plate lever and tap out the pivot shaft. Lift out the lever, plate and arm (photo).
8 Examine all parts and replace as necessary. Make sure that the spring and pin which determine the resting height of the plate are not loose (photo).
9 Reassemble the airflow sensor, lightly greasing the shaft and balls. Align the lever so that the mixture adjustment screw is in line with its hole before tightening the clamp screws.
10 Center the sensor plate in the venturi and tighten its clamp screw. Adjust the height of the plate by tapping the pin up or down so that the plate rests just above the venturi waist. After installing, the plate can only be adjusted downwards (Section 21).
11 Install the fuel distributor and control plunger, using a new O-ring, and tighten the securing screws (photo).

22.25 Control pressure regulator electrical and vacuum connections

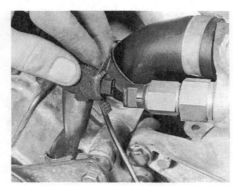

22.30 Disconnecting the thermal timer multi-plug

23.2 Removing a fuel distributor securing screw. The other two are arrowed

23.3   Removing the fuel distributor control plunger

23.4A   Installing the pressure regulator outer plunger . . .

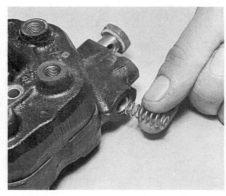

23.4B   . . . pressure regulator spring . . .

23.4C   . . . the inner plunger and plug. Shims control pressure

23.6A   Remove the pivot shaft circlip . . .

23.6B   . . . the end cover . . .

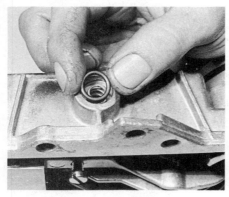

23.6C   . . . the O-ring . . .

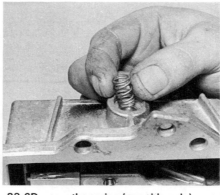

23.6D   . . . the spring (one side only) . . .

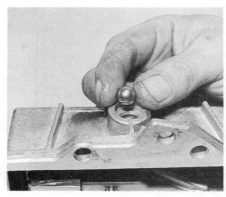

23.6E   . . . and the ball

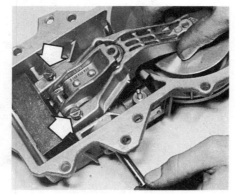

23.7   Loosen the clamp screws (arrowed) and withdraw the pivot shaft

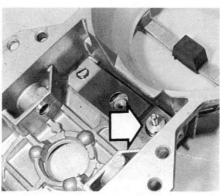

23.8   Spring and pin (arrowed) must not be loose

23.11   Distributor with control plunger and O-ring in place

24 Troubleshooting — continuous injection system

Symptom	Reason(s)
Engine will not start	Tank empty
	Fuel pump or relay defective
	Induction air leak
	Fuel distributor control plunger seized
	Fuel pressure incorrect
	Airflow sensor plate height incorrect
Difficult starting when cold	Start injector defective
	Thermal timer defective
	Auxiliary air valve defective
	Constant idle system fault
Difficult starting when hot	Start injector leaking
	Impulse relay defective
	Fuel pressure lost at rest
Erratic running when cold and during warm-up	Cold control pressure incorrect
Erratic running when hot	Warm control pressure incorrect
	Line pressure incorrect
Erratic running, hot and cold	Induction air leak
	Control pressure incorrect
	Mixture adjustment incorrect
	Throttle valve(s) loose or worn
Excessive fuel consumption	External leakage
	Start injector leaking
	Control pressure incorrect
	Mixture adjustment incorrect
Poor performance	Throttle valve(s) not opening fully
	Control pressure incorrect
	Tank pump defective
	Main pump defective
	Fuel filter blocked
	Mixture adjustment incorrect
Erratic idle	Misfiring (ignition fault)
	Induction air leak
	Fuel distributor control plunger sticking
	Throttle valve(s) loose or worn
	Injector(s) leaking or poor spray pattern

25 Turbocharger — general information

The turbocharger increases the efficiency of the engine by raising the pressure in the intake manifold above atmospheric pressure. Instead of the air/fuel mixture being simply sucked into the cylinders it is actively forced in.

Energy for the operation of the turbocharger comes from the exhaust gas. The gas flows through a specially-shaped housing (the turbine housing) and in so doing spins the turbine wheel. The turbine wheel is attached to a shaft, at the other end of which is another vaned wheel known as the compressor wheel. The compressor wheel spins in its own housing and compresses the inducted air on the way to the intake manifold.

After leaving the turbocharger, the compressed air passes through an intercooler, which is an air-to-air heat exchanger mounted in front of the radiator. Here the air gives up heat which it acquired when being compressed. This temperature reduction improves engine efficiency and reduces the risk of detonation.

Boost pressure (the pressure in the intake manifold) is limited by a wastegate, which diverts the exhaust gas away from the turbine wheel in response to a pressure-sensitive actuator. As a further precaution, a pressure-sensitive switch cuts out the fuel pump if boost pressure becomes excessive. Boost pressure is displayed to the driver by a gauge on the instrument panel.

The turbo shaft is pressure-lubricated by means of a feed pipe from

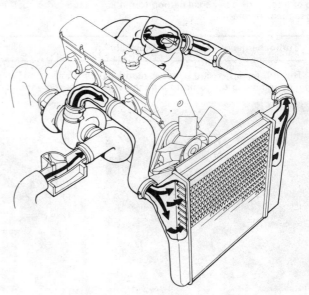

Fig. 3.35 Air flow through turbocharger and intercooler to intake manifold (Sec 25)

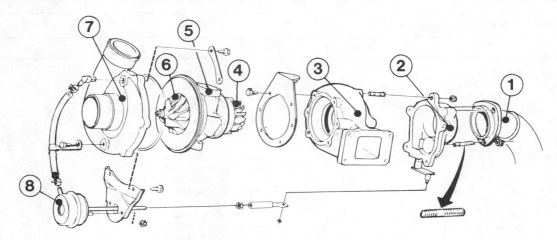

Fig. 3.36 Turbocharger and associated components (Sec 25)

1 *Exhaust downpipe*	4 *Turbine wheel*	7 *Compressor housing*
2 *Wastegate housing*	5 *Shaft housing*	8 *Wastegate actuator*
3 *Turbine housing*	6 *Compressor wheel*	

the engine's main oil gallery. The shaft 'floats' on a cushion of oil. A drain pipe returns the oil to the oil pan.

26 Turbocharger — precautions

1   The turbocharger operates at extremely high speeds and temperatures. Certain precautions must be observed to avoid premature failure of the turbo or injury to the operator.
2   Do not operate the turbo with any parts exposed. Foreign objects falling onto the rotating vanes could cause extensive damage and (if ejected) personal injury.
3   Do not race the engine immediately after start-up, especially if it is cold. Give the oil a few seconds to circulate.
4   Always allow the engine to return to idle speed before switching it off — do not blip the throttle and switch off, as this will leave the turbo spinning without lubrication.
5   Allow the engine to idle for several minutes before switching off after a high-speed run.
6   Observe the recommended intervals for oil and filter changing, and use a reputable oil of the specified quality. Neglect of oil changing or use of inferior oil can cause carbon formation on the turbo shaft and subsequent failure.

27 Turbocharger — removal and installation

1   The turbocharger and exhaust manifold are removed together. Begin by removing the turbo-to-intercooler and the airflow meter-to-

turbo hoses. The airflow meter hose is also connected to the bypass valve (photo).
2   Remove the air cleaner hot air duct.
3   Disconnect the exhaust downpipe from the turbo outlet. Remove the heat shield (photo).
4   Disconnect the oil drain pipe from the turbo. Be prepared for some oil spillage (photo).
5   Unbolt and remove the stiffener plate from below the manifold (photo).
6   Unbolt the oil feed pipe from the block (photo).
7   Remove the eight nuts which secure the exhaust manifold to the cylinder head. Note that one of the nuts secures a lifting eye (photo).
8   Lift off the manifold and turbocharger. Remove the exhaust port gaskets (photo).
9   Remove the oil feed pipe and remove the gasket.
10 Remove the locking plates from the four bolts which secure the turbocharger to the manifold. Bend up the plate tabs with a chisel and pry or drive them off the bolts. New plates will be needed for reassembly.
11 Clamp the manifold in a vise and remove the four bolts. Lift the turbo off the manifold. Remove the other halves of the locking plates.
12 Measure the length of the bolts and replace them if they have stretched to longer than 89 mm (3.50 in).
13 Install the turbo to the manifold and secure it with the four bolts, applying anti-seize compound to their threads. Remember to install the new locking plate sections.
14 Tighten the bolts to the specified torque, following the sequence in Fig. 3.37. Make up a template for the final angular tightening (photo).
15 Install the outer halves of the locking plates. Drive them over the bolt heads with a hammer and a tube, crimp the tabs with pliers and

27.1 Turbo connecting hoses

27.3 Turbo-to-downpipe bolts — two arrowed, third is hidden

27.4 Turbo oil drain pipe connection

27.5 Exhaust manifold stiffener plate

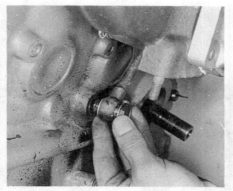

27.6 Turbo oil feed connection — note sealing washers

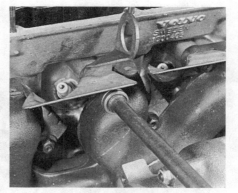

27.7 Removing an exhaust manifold nut

27.8 An exhaust port gasket

27.14 Angle-tightening the bolts

27.15A Install the lockplate outer half . . .

27.15B . . . drive it over the bolt heads . . .

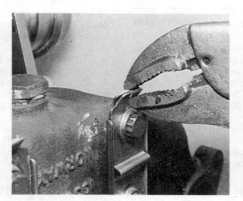

27.15C . . . crimp over the tabs . . .

27.15D . . . and knock the tabs down

finally knock the tabs down with a mallet (photos).

16 The remainder of installation is a reversal of the removal procedure. Use new gaskets, oil pipe sealing washers, etc.

17 Before starting the engine, disconnect the ignition coil LT wire and crank the engine with the starter for six 10-second bursts. This will prime the turbocharger with oil.

18 Reconnect the ignition coil, run the engine and check that there are no oil leaks.

28 Turbocharger — inspection and overhaul

1 With the turbo removed from the manifold, inspect the housings for cracks or other visible damage.

2 Spin the turbine or compressor wheel to verify that the shaft is

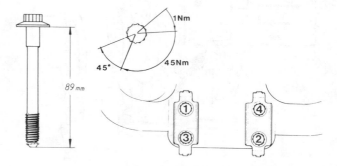

Fig. 3.37 Turbo bolt tightening sequence and stages. Replace bolts if they are longer than shown (Sec 27)

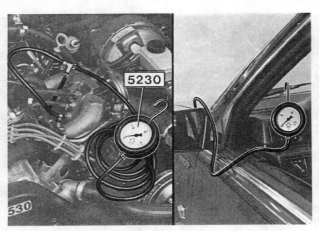
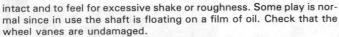

Fig. 3.38 Boost pressure gauge (5230) connected (left)
and positioned for the road (right) (Sec 29)

29.3 Wastegate actuator rod and seal

intact and to feel for excessive shake or roughness. Some play is normal since in use the shaft is floating on a film of oil. Check that the
wheel vanes are undamaged.
3   Inspect the wastegate actuator (see Section 30) and check that
the seal and locking wire are intact.
4   If the exhaust or induction passages are obviously oil-contaminated,
the shaft oil seals have probably failed. Oil on the induction side will
collect in the intercooler, which should at least be drained and preferably
flushed out before fitting a new turbo.
5   No DIY repair of the turbo is possible. The old unit may be accepted
in part exchange for a new one.

29 Turbo boost pressure — check and adjustment

Caution: *Unskilled or improper adjustment can cause serious engine
damage.*

1   Using a T-piece, connect a pressure gauge (range approximately
0 to 15 psi) into the boost pressure hose at the manifold. Position the
gauge so that it can be read from inside the vehicle.
2   With the engine warmed up, have an assistant read the gauge.
Accelerate at full throttle from 1500 rpm in 3rd gear, applying the
brakes at the same time for a few seconds at 3500 rpm. (Do not apply
the brakes for more than five seconds, or damage may result.) The
assistant must note the highest pressure recorded.
3   If the boost pressure is not as specified, allow the engine to cool,
then remove the seal from the wastegate actuator rod (photo). Unclip
the rod from the wastegate lever and screw the threaded sleeve in or

out after releasing the locknut. Lengthening the rod decreases the
pressure, and vice versa; one complete turn of the sleeve will raise
or lower pressure by approximately 0.4 psi.
4   Secure the actuator rod with a new retaining clip and repeat the
test.
5   When adjustment is correct, install a new locking wire and seal
if required. Tighten the actuator rod locknut.

30 Turbo wastegate actuator — check and replacement

1   If the boost pressure is incorrect and cannot be adjusted, the
wastegate actuator may be defective. Check as follows.
2   Break the seal and unclip the actuator rod from the wastegate lever.
The rod should retract into the actuator a little way. Mark the position
of the rod where it enters the actuator, then reconnect the rod to the
wastegate and measure the distance moved by the mark. It must be 2
to 6 mm (0.08 to 0.24 in); if not, replace the actuator.
3   To remove the actuator, unclip the link rod, remove the connecting hose and unscrew the two retaining nuts.
4   Begin installation by securing the actuator to its bracket using two
new nuts, then perform a preliminary adjustment as follows.
5   Connect a pump and pressure gauge to the actuator. Apply 7 psi
pressure.
6   With the pressure applied, adjust the link rod so that it fits onto
the wastegate lever (in the closed position) without being tight or slack.
Tighten the adjuster locknut.
7   Secure the link rod to the wastegate lever using a new clip.

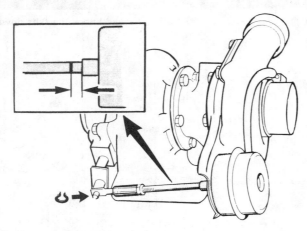

Fig. 3.39 Measuring wastegate actuator retraction
(inset) (Sec 30)

31.2 Disconnecting an intercooler hose

8 Remove the pump and gauge. Connect the actuator hose to the compressor housing.
9 Check the boost pressure (Section 29).

31 Intercooler — removal and installation

1 Remove the radiator top mounts and carefully move the radiator rearwards.
2 Disconnect the hoses from the intercooler and lift it out (photo).

3 If turbocharger failure has occurred, the intercooler may contain a substantial quantity of oil. A drain plug is provided.
4 Install by reversing the removal operations.

32 LH-Jetronic fuel injection system — general information

The Bosch LH-Jetronic fuel injection is used on all four cylinder engines, whether they are turbocharged or normally aspirated, and the B280F six-cylinder engine. It is an electronically controlled fuel injec-

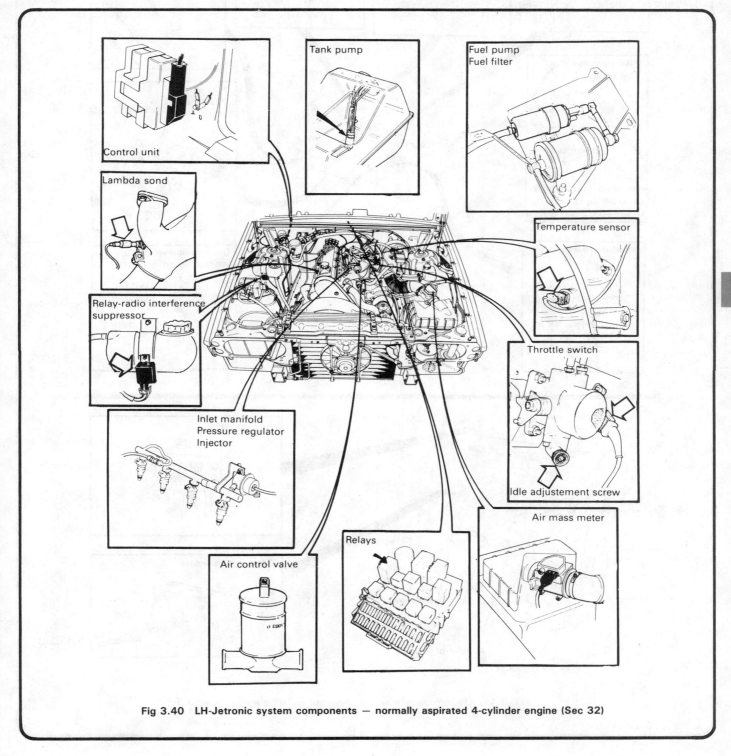

Fig 3.40 LH-Jetronic system components — normally aspirated 4-cylinder engine (Sec 32)

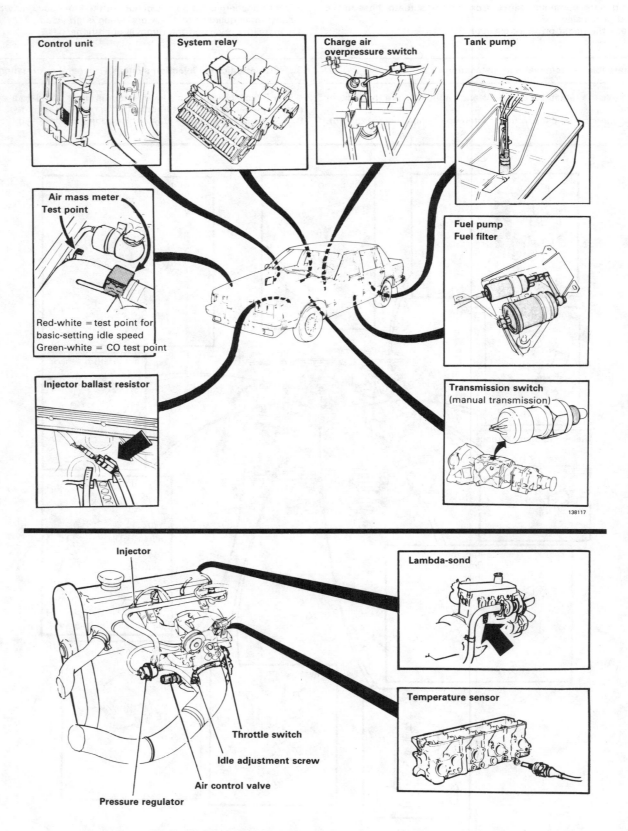

Control unit

System relay

Charge air overpressure switch

Tank pump

Air mass meter
Test point

Red-white = test point for
basic-setting idle speed
Green-white = CO test point

Fuel pump
Fuel filter

Injector ballast resistor

Transmission switch
(manual transmission)

138117

Injector

Lambda-sond

Throttle switch

Idle adjustment screw

Air control valve

Pressure regulator

Temperature sensor

Fig. 3.41 LH-Jetronic system components — Turbo models (Sec 32)

system that utilizes one solenoid operated fuel injector per cylinder. The system is governed by an electronic control unit (ECU) which processes information sent by various sensors, and in turn precisely meters the fuel to the cylinders by adjusting the amount of time that the injectors are open.

An electric fuel pump in the fuel tank feeds fuel to the main fuel pump, which delivers fuel under high pressure to the to the injectors through the fuel feed line and an in-line filter. A pressure regulator keeps fuel available at an optimum pressure, allowing pressure to rise or fall de-

pending on engine speed and load. Fuel in excess of injector needs is returned to the fuel tank by a separate line.

A sensor in the air intake duct constantly measures the mass of the incoming air, and through the ECU adjusts the fuel mixture to provide an optimum air/fuel ratio.

Another device, called the Lambda sensor, is mounted on the exhaust manifold and continually reads the oxygen content of the exhaust gas. This information is also used by the ECU to adjust the duration of injection, making it possible to meter the fuel very accurately to comply

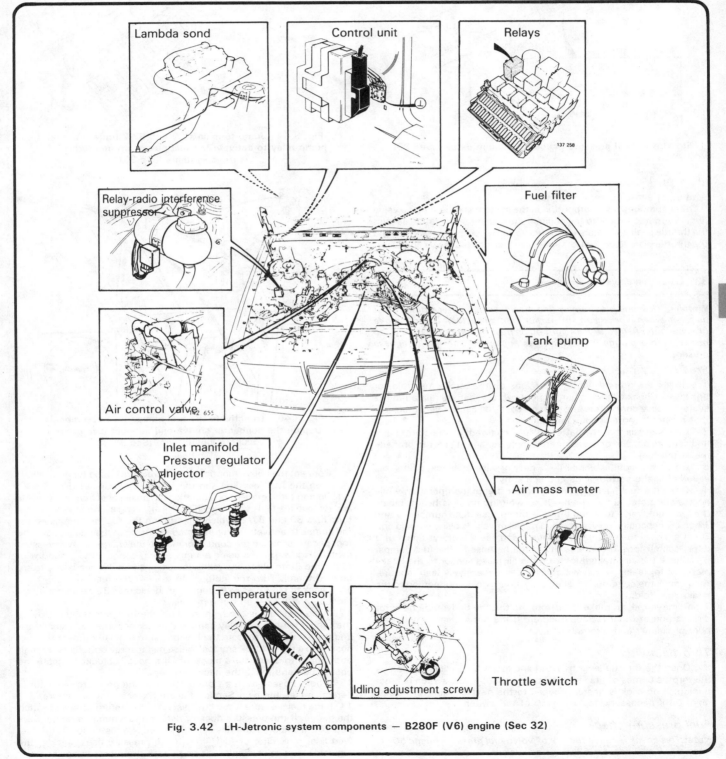

Fig. 3.42 LH-Jetronic system components — B280F (V6) engine (Sec 32)

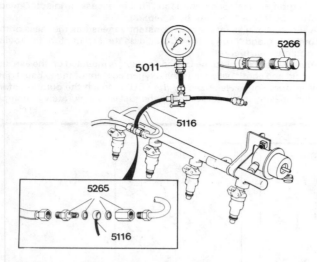

Fig. 3.43   Fuel pressure gauge installation details (Sec 33)

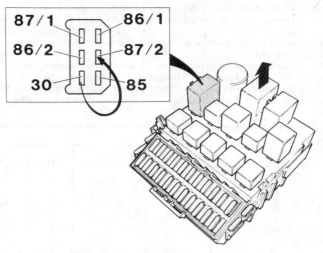

Fig. 3.44   Jump terminals 30 and 87/2 under the fuel pump relay to activate the fuel pumps on non-turbo LH-Jetronic systems (Sec 33)

with strict emission control standards.

Other components incorporated in the system are the throttle valve (which controls airflow to the engine), the coolant temperature sensor, the throttle position switch, air control valve (which bypasses air around the throttle plate to control idle speed) and associated relays and fuses.

33   LH-Jetronic system — check

Warning: *Gasoline is extremely flammable, so extra precautions must be taken when working on any part of the fuel system. Do not smoke or allow open flames or bare light bulbs near the work area. Also, do not work in a garage if a natural gas appliance with a pilot light is present.*

Preliminary checks

1   Check the ground wire connections on the intake manifold for tightness. Check all wiring harness connectors that are related to the system. Loose connectors and poor grounds can cause many problems that resemble more serious malfunctions.
2   Check to see that the battery is fully charged, as the control unit and sensors depend on an accurate supply voltage in order to properly meter the fuel.
3   Check the air filter element — a dirty or partially blocked filter will severly impede performance and economy.
4   Open the fuel filler cap and listen for fuel pump operation while an assistant cranks the engine. If no whirring noise is heard, check the fuel pump relay fuse and the tank pump fuse (fuse numbers 1 and 11 or 15, depending on the year and model of vehicle being worked on).
5   If a blown fuse is found, replace it and see if it blows again. If it does, search for a grounded wire in the harness to the fuel pumps.
6   Check the air intake duct from the air mass sensor to the intake manifold for leaks, which will result in an excessively lean mixture. Also check the condition of all of the vacuum hoses connected to the intake manifold.
7   Remove the air intake duct from the throttle body and check for dirt, carbon or other residue build-up. If it's dirty, clean it with carburetor cleaner and a toothbrush.

Throttle switch

8   Open the throttle lever by hand and listen for a click as soon as the throttle comes off its stop, indicating that the idle switch is functioning. If no click is heard, proceed to the next Section for adjustment (or if necessary, replacement) of the switch.

Fuel pressure check

Note: *This check requires the use of Volvo fuel pressure guage 5011, hose 5116 and adapter 5266, or equivalent.*

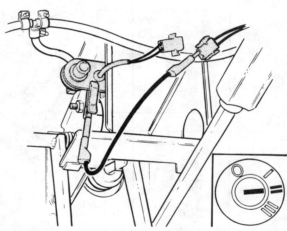

Fig. 3.45   To activate the fuel pumps on turbo models, unplug the connector shown and connect it to ground, using a jumper wire (Sec 33)

9   Connect the above mentioned fuel pressure gauge (or equivalent) between the fuel feed line and the fuel distribution rail (Fig. 3.43).
10   On non-turbo models, pull out the relay/fuse panel from the console and remove the fuel pump relay (Fig. 3.44). Using a jumper wire, bridge terminals 30 and 87/2, which will turn on the fuel pumps (listen for the pumps to activate). On turbo models, Remove the panel above the foot pedals, separate the connector next to the charge air overpressure switch (Fig. 3.45) and using a jumper wire, connect the ground wire to ground (both wires are yellow/black — it may be necessary to try both of them). Turn the ignition On to start the fuel pumps.
11   Check the fuel pressure gauge — it should read 36 psi on non-turbo models, and 42 psi on turbo models.
12   If the pressure is too high, turn off the fuel pumps by removing the jumper wire on the relay panel and disconnect the fuel return hose and the vacuum hose from the fuel pressure regulator (cover the fuel hose with a rag to block any fuel which might spray out). Blow through both hoses to check for a blockage. If a hose is blocked, locate the obstruction and make the necessary repairs.
13   If both hoses are free from blockages, the pressure regulator is defective (see the next Section for the replacement procedure).
14   If the fuel pressure is too low, pinch the fuel return hose and watch the gauge. If the pressure doesn't rise, the fuel pump is faulty (Section 10). If the pressure rises slowly, there is a restriction in the fuel feed line, tank filter or fuel filter. If the pressure rises quickly, the regulator is at fault. Replace it and check the pressure again.

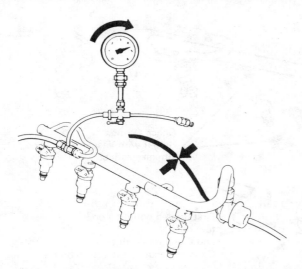

Fig. 3.46 Pinch the fuel return line and pressure should rise (Sec 33)

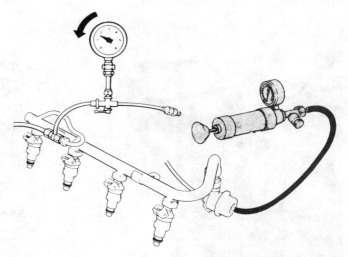

Fig. 3.47 Apply vacuum to the regulator and pressure should fall (Sec 33)

15 To check operation of the regulator, reconnect the return hose and connect a vacuum pump to the nipple on the regulator. Energize the fuel pump (Step 10) and apply vacuum to the regulator. The fuel pressure should drop. Release the vacuum and the pressure should return to its normal static value (36 psi).

16 Reconnect the vacuum hose to the regulator, disconnect the jumper wire and remove the fuel pressure gauge. Connect the fuel feed line to the pressure regulator, tightening the fitting securely.

Injectors

17 With the engine running, place a screwdriver against each injector, one at a time, and listen through the handle for a clicking sound, indicating operation.

18 Unplug the injector connectors (one at a time) and measure the resistance across the terminals with an ohmmeter. The meter should read 16 ohms — replace any injector that fails this test (Section 34). The remainder of the system checks should be left to a Volvo service department or other qualified repair shop, as there is a chance that the control unit may be damaged if not performed properly.

34 LH-Jetronic system components — removal and installation

Warning: *Gasoline is extremely flammable, so extra precautions must be taken when working on any part of the fuel system. Do not smoke or allow open flames or bare light bulbs near the work area. Also, do not work in a garage if a natural gas appliance with a pilot light is present.*

Air mass sensor

1 Disconnect the cable from the negative terminal of the battery. Unplug the electrical connector from the air mass sensor.

2 On turbo models, loosen the hose clamps on either side of the sensor. On normally aspirated models, loosen the hose clamp and unclip the sensor from the air cleaner housing.

3 Carefully remove the sensor from the air intake duct. Inspect the platinum filament inside the sensor — if it is severed, the sensor will have to be replaced.

4 Installation is the reverse of the removal procedure. Be sure to install the sensor with the arrow on the housing pointing in the direction of airflow.

Throttle body

5 Unplug the electrical connector from the throttle switch. Carefully pry the link rod from the throttle lever. Loosen the air intake duct hose clamp and slide the duct off the throttle body.

6 Remove the throttle body-to-intake manifold nuts. Lift the throttle

body off the manifold, tapping it gently with a soft faced hammer if it is stuck.

7 Clean all traces of old gasket material from the throttle body and manifold mating surfaces. Install a new gasket over the studs on the intake manifold.

8 Place the throttle body onto the manifold, install the nuts and tighten them to the specified torque.

9 The remainder of installation is the reverse of the removal procedure.

Throttle switch

10 Unplug the throttle switch electrical connector, remove the two securing screws and pull the switch from the throttle body.

11 Position the switch on the throttle body, making sure that the locating slots or tab engages with the tang inside the throttle body. Install the screws but don't tighten them completely yet.

12 Turn the switch clockwise slightly then turn the switch back until a click is heard. Tighten the screws securely, being careful not to change the setting of the switch.

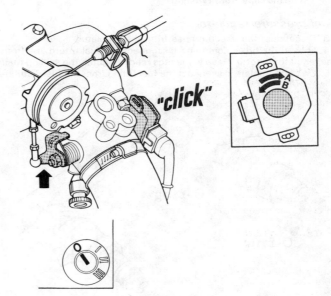

Fig. 3.48 To adjust the throttle switch, loosen the screws, turn the switch clockwise a little bit then turn it back slowly until a click is heard (Sec 34)

34.14   Disconnecting the regulator return pipe

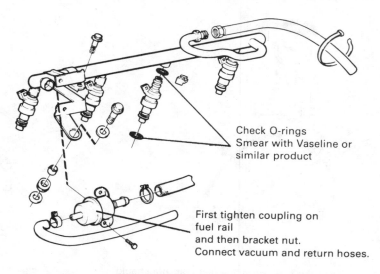

Check O-rings
Smear with Vaseline or
similar product

First tighten coupling on
fuel rail
and then bracket nut.
Connect vacuum and return hoses.

Fig. 3.49   Fuel pressure regulator installation details — 4-cylinder normally aspirated model shown (Sec 34)

34.15   When loosening the fuel pressure regulator-to-fuel distribution rail union, use a backup wrench to prevent the pipe from twisting

34.18   Pry out the wire clip, then pull upward on the injector electrical connector to unplug it

34.19   Separate the feed line from the distribution rail

Fuel pressure regulator

13 Disconnect the vacuum hose from the regulator.
14 Loosen the hose clamp and disconnect the fuel return line from the regulator (photo). Have some rags ready to catch the spilling fuel.
15 On turbo models, disconnect the fuel fitting from the fuel distribu-

Clamp

O-ring

O-ring

Fig. 3.50   Fuel injector installation details — always use new O-rings on all injectors whenever any injectors are removed (Sec 34)

tion rail to the regulator (photo).
16 Remove the regulator securing nut or bolt and remove the regulator (Fig. 3.49).
17 Installation is the reverse of the removal procedure.

Fuel distribution rail and fuel injectors

18 Pry out the fuel injector connector securing clips and disconnect the connectors from the injectors (photo).
19 Disconnect the fuel feed line from the fuel distribution rail (photo), using a backup wrench to prevent the rail from twisting. Cover the fitting with a rag when loosening to catch any fuel spray.
20 Disconnect the return and vacuum hoses from the fuel pressure regulator.
21 Unbolt the fuel distribution rail from the manifold, noting the position of any ground straps. Carefully lift the fuel rail, complete with injectors, from the manifold.
22 Set the fuel rail and injector assembly on a clean working surface. Pry the injector retaining clips (Fig. 3.50) from the rail with a small screwdriver.
23 Pull the injectors straight out of the fuel rail, using a gentle side-to-side wiggling motion, if necessary. Use care not to damage the electrical connector pins or the injector nozzles.
24 Using a small screwdriver, pry the injector O-ring seals off each end of each injector. Even if only one injector is being replaced or the same injectors will be reused, replace these O-rings as a matter of course. If you don't replace them, you are just asking for fuel leaks to occur in the near future. Lubricate the O-rings with petroleum jelly

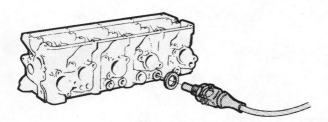

Fig. 3.51 The coolant temperature sensor is located on the side of the cylinder head (Sec 34)

prior to installing them.

25 Before installing the injectors and fuel distribution rail on the manifold, clean each injector port in the manifold with a cotton swab dipped in solvent.

26 Installation is the reverse of the removal sequence.

Air control valve

27 Disconnect the electrical connector from the end of the valve.
28 Loosen the hose clamps and disconnect the hoses from the valve.
29 Unbolt the valve and carefully guide it out from under the manifold.
30 Installation is the reverse of the removal procedure.

Coolant temperature sensor

Warning: *The engine must be completely cool before starting this procedure.*

31 With the engine cool, open the expansion tank cap to release any residual pressure. Squeeze the upper radiator hose and reinstall the cap (this will create a slight vacuum within the cooling system and minimize coolant loss when the sensor is removed).

32 If the sensor is being replaced with a new one, prepare the new sensor by wrapping the threads of the sensor with teflon tape or by coating it with a sealing compound.

33 Disconnect the sensor electrical connector.

34 Unscrew the sensor from the cylinder head (Fig. 3.51). Install the new sensor as quickly as possible and tighten it securely.

35 Plug in the electrical connector. Top up the cooling system if necessary.

Lambda sensor

Warning: *To prevent burning yourself, wait until the engine is cool before starting this procedure.*

36 Unplug the Lambda sensor connector.
37 Unscrew the sensor from the exhaust pipe.
38 Before installing the sensor, coat the threads with an anti-seize compound.
39 Install the sensor, tightening it securely. Reconnect the electrical connector.

35 Troubleshooting — LH-Jetronic system

Symptom	Reason(s)
Difficult starting (hot or cold)	Blown fuse Loose or dirty connections Induction air leak Fuel pump defective Fuel pressure incorrect Overpressure switch defective (turbo only)
Difficult starting when cold	Auxiliary air valve not opening Start injector or thermal timer defective Coolant temperature sensor defective (turbo only)
Irregular idle	Induction air leak Throttle linkage incorrectly adjusted Throttle switch incorrectly adjusted Coolant temperature sensor defective Idle mixture adjustment incorrect
Irregular running	Induction air leak Injector(s) defective Fuel pressure incorrect Control unit defective
Surge on overrun	Bypass valve not opening
Fuel consumption excessive	External leakage Fuel pressure incorrect Idle mixture adjustment incorrect
Poor performance	Throttle linkage incorrectly adjusted Air cleaner element clogged Induction air leak Tank pump not operating Fuel pressure incorrect Boost pressure incorrect (turbo only) Charge air temperature sensor defective (turbo only) Air mass sensor defective

3

Chapter 4 Ignition system

Contents

Specifications

General

System type	Electronic (breakerless); computerized control on all except B28F

Maker's designation:

B23FT	EZ102K
B230F and B230FT	EZ117K
B28F	T5Z-4
B280F	EZ115K

Firing order:

4-cylinder	1-3-4-2 (No 1 at front)
6-cylinder	1-6-3-5-2-4 (No 1 LH rear)

Spark plugs

Make and type:

B23FT and B230FT	Bosch W7DC, Champion N7YC, or equivalent
B230F	Bosch W6DC, Champion N7YC, or equivalent
B28F	Bosch HR6DC, Champion S9YC, or equivalent
Electrode gap	0.7 mm (0.028 in)

Spark plug wires

Resistance (typical)	5.6 ± 1 k ohm/meter

Ballast resistor

Resistance (total)	1.0 ± 0.1 ohm

Ignition timing*

B23FT	12° BTDC @ 750 rpm
B230F	12° BTDC @ 750 rpm
B230FT	12° BTDC @ 750 rpm
B28F	23° BTDC @ 2500 rpm
B280F	16° BTDC @ 750 rpm

Vacuum unit disconnected (when applicable)

Ignition coil

Primary resistance (typical)	0.5 to 0.9 ohm
Secondary resistance (typical)	6.0 to 9.5 ohms

Distributor (B28F)

Direction of rotation	Clockwise
Impulse sender coil resistance	540 to 660 ohms
Rotor air gap	0.3 mm (0.012 in)
Rotor track resistance	4 to 6 k ohms

Torque specifications

	Nm	Ft-lbs
Spark plugs (dry threads):		
4-cylinder	25 ± 5	18 ± 4
6-cylinder	12 ± 2	9 ± 1.5
Knock sensor bolt	11	8

1   General information

The ignition system is responsible for igniting the compressed fuel/air charge in each cylinder in turn. This must be done at precisely the right moment for the prevailing engine speed and load. The various engines have slightly different systems, but the principles of operation are the same.

Low tension primary pulses are no longer produced by a contact breaker, but by the rotation of a toothed wheel in a magnetic field. These pulses are received by a control unit where they are amplified to the level necessary to drive the ignition coil. The ignition coil converts the primary pulses into the high tension secondary pulses needed to fire the spark plugs. Secondary pulses are sent to the appropriate spark plugs via the secondary spark plug wires, distributor cap and rotor.

Ignition timing (the moment when the spark occurs) is varied according to engine speed and load. The faster the engine is turning, the earlier the spark must occur (more advance) in order to allow enough time for combustion. On B28F V6 engines, ignition advance is controlled mechanically by centrifugal weights and springs in the distributor. A vacuum unit provides additional advance under conditions of high intake manifold vacuum. On the other engines, the ignition advance is determined by the control unit, which receives information on engine temperature, throttle position and (on Turbo models) charge air temperature, as well as engine speed.

The EZ-K systems incorporate an anti-knock sensor mounted under the intake manifold. (The B280F engine uses two of them.) This sensor causes the control unit to retard ignition timing if pre-ignition occurs, protecting the engine from damage caused by over-advanced timing or poor quality fuel.

Take care to avoid receiving electric shocks from the HT side of the ignition system. Do not handle spark plug wires or touch the distributor or coil when the engine is running. When tracing faults in the HT system, use well insulated tools to handle live wires. Electronic ignition secondary voltage can kill!

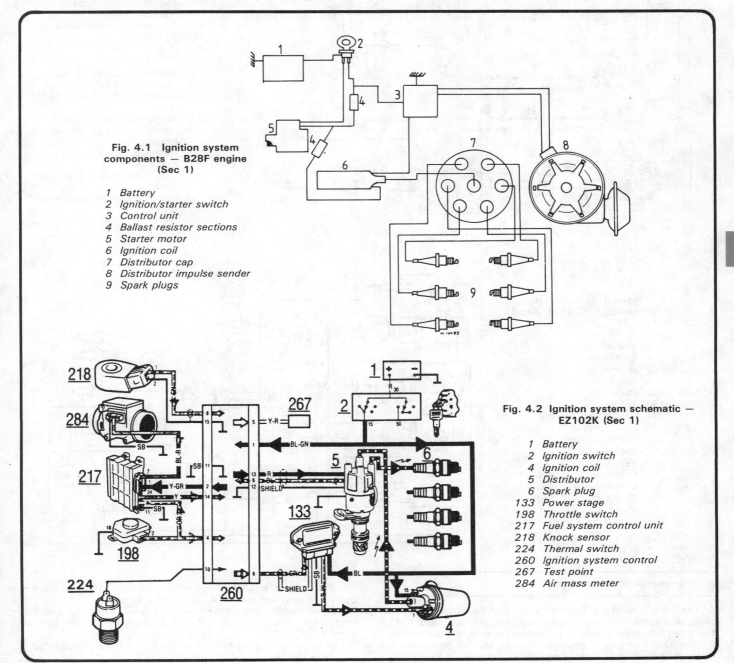

Fig. 4.1 Ignition system components — B28F engine (Sec 1)

1 Battery
2 Ignition/starter switch
3 Control unit
4 Ballast resistor sections
5 Starter motor
6 Ignition coil
7 Distributor cap
8 Distributor impulse sender
9 Spark plugs

Fig. 4.2 Ignition system schematic — EZ102K (Sec 1)

1 Battery
2 Ignition switch
4 Ignition coil
5 Distributor
6 Spark plug
133 Power stage
198 Throttle switch
217 Fuel system control unit
218 Knock sensor
224 Thermal switch
260 Ignition system control
267 Test point
284 Air mass meter

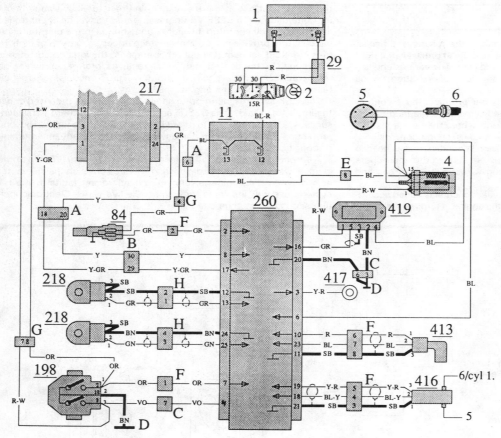

Fig. 4.3 Ignition system schematic — EZ115K (Sec 1)

1 Battery
2 Ignition switch
4 Ignition coil
5 Distributor
6 Spark plug
11 Fuse box
29 Positive terminal
84 Temperature sensor
198 Throttle switch
217 Fuel system control unit
218 Knock sensor
260 Control unit
413 Engine rpm/crankshaft position sensor
416 Cylinder 1 position sensor
417 Test socket
419 Power stage

A Connector at right A-post
B Connector at left A-post
C Connector at left suspension tower
D Intake manifold ground
E Connector at right suspension tower
F Connector at left suspension tower
G Connector at right suspension tower
H Connector at left suspension tower

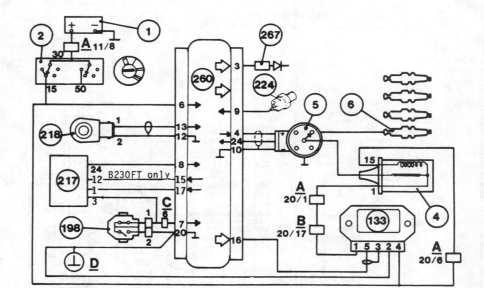

Fig. 4.4 Ignition system schematic — EZ117K (Sec 1)

1 Battery
2 Ignition switch
4 Ignition coil
5 Distributor
6 Spark plug
133 Power stage
198 Throttle switch
217 Fuel system control unit
218 Knock sensor
224 Thermal switch
260 Control unit
267 Test point
A = Connector, right A-post
B = Connector, left A-post
C = Connector, left suspension tower
D = Connector, intake manifold

2 Maintenance and inspection

1   Every 6000 miles (10 000 km) or six months, inspect the spark plugs as described in Section 3. Replace them or clean, regap and install them (The makers specify replacement at every service interval.)
2   On B23FT and B28F engines, lubricate the felt pad under the distributor rotor with a couple of drops of engine oil every 12 000 miles

(20 000 km) or annually. Do not over-lubricate. (To remove the distributor cap, see Section 4, paragraphs 19 to 21).
3   On all models, inspect the spark plug wires, distributor cap and rotor every 12 000 miles (20 000 Km). Replace cracked, damaged or burnt items.
4   At all times keep the coil tower, spark plug wires and distributor cap clean and dry.

3.3   Pulling a spark plug wire boot off a spark plug

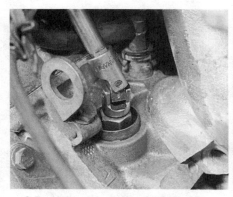

3.5   Unscrewing a spark plug with a socket and a universal joint

4.2   Timing marks on the in-line engine — pulley notch is at 0° (TDC)

4.4   Removing the distributor (B 23FT)

4.5   Rotor tip aligned with notch in distributor rim (B 23FT) — dust shield removed

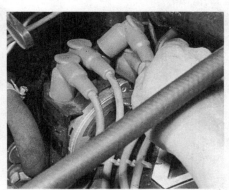

4.7   Disconnecting a spark plug wire (B 230F/FT)

3   Spark plugs — removal, inspection and installation

Note: *Spark plugs should not be removed when the engine is hot.*

1   Open the hood. Make sure that the ignition is switched off. Remove any air cleaner ducting or similar items obstructing access to the spark plugs.

2   Inspect the spark plug wires to see if they carry their cylinder numbers — if not, mark each wire, using pieces of numbered tape.

3   Pull the spark plug wires off the plugs. Pull on the boots, not on the wires (photo).

4   Blow away any dirt from around the spark plug recesses in the cylinder head(s), using compressed air.

5   Unscrew and remove the plugs, using a spark plug socket, extension and ratchet. (For the V6 engine a universal joint between the socket and extension will be helpful — photo).

6   Inspect the plugs and compare them with those illustrated by the colored photographs in this Chapter. The condition of the plugs will tell much about the overall condition of the engine.

7   If the plugs are to be re-used, they should be cleaned with an abrasive blasting machine. Many repair shops have such a machine, or smaller versions can be purchased for home use. Do not use plugs for more than 12 000 miles, even if they still appear to be in good condition.

8   Before installing spark plugs, whether new or used, check the electrode gap with a feeler gauge. Adjust if necessary by careful bending of the side electrode. Do not attempt to bend the centre electrode, or lever against it when bending the side electrode.

9   Make sure that the plug insulators are clean and that the screwed HT cable adaptors are tight. Pay particular attention to the plug seating surfaces on V6 engines, since these plugs have no sealing washers (taper seat type) and any dirt will cause a bad seal.

10   Screw each plug into its hole by hand. If a plug is reluctant to go in, do not force it with a socket, but unscrew it and try again. If the plug is cross-threaded, it is the cylinder head which will be damaged.

11   Final tightening of the spark plugs should ideally be carried out using a torque wrench. The tightening torques are given in the Specifications. If a torque wrench is not available, tighten the plugs beyond the point where they contact the head as follows:

Taper seat plugs — 1/16-turn maximum

Plugs with washers — 1/4-turn maximum

12   If the taper seat type of plug is overtightened, the sealing faces will bite together and removal will be very difficult.

13   Install the spark plug wires to the plugs, paying attention to the cylinder numbers. Push each connector firmly onto its plug.

14   Run the engine to verify that the spark plug wires have been installed correctly.

4   Distributor — removal and installation

B23FT

1   Unclip the distributor cap, or remove its securing screws, and move it aside.

2   Bring the engine to TDC, No 1 firing. Turn the engine with a wrench on the crankshaft pulley bolt until the notch on the pulley is aligned with the D (TDC) mark on the timing scale, and the distributor rotor tip is pointing to the quarter corresponding to No 1 spark plug tower (photo).

3   Make alignment marks between the rotor tip and the rim of the distributor body, and between the base of the distributor body and the engine block.

4   Unbolt the clamp plate and lift out the distributor (photo). Notice how the rotor turns as the distributor is withdrawn.

5   When installing, set the rotor in roughly the same position as it assumed after removal. Insert the distributor so that the distributor-to-block marks are aligned. As the distributor is pushed in, the rotor will turn and should end up in the previously marked position for No 1 firing (photo). If not, remove the distributor and try again.

6   Install and secure the distributor clamp plate.

4.8   Distributor cap securing screws (arrowed) — distributor removed

4.14   Removing the distributor (B 230F/FT)

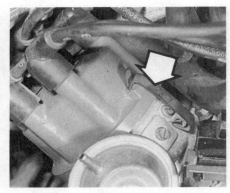

4.21   One of the distributor cap clips (arrowed) — B 28F

4.22   Timing marks on the V6 engine. Pulley notch is at 0° (TDC), but there are two notches

4.23A   Pry up the spring clip . . .

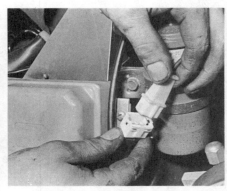

4.23B   . . . and unplug the primary harness connector

B230F/FT and B280F

7   Using pieces of numbered tape, mark the spark plug wires and disconnect them from the cap (photo).

8   Loosen the three screws which secure the distributor cap. Access is restricted on 4-cylinder models. The screws are captive, so do not attempt to remove them from the cap (photo).

9   Lift off the distributor cap.

10   Pull off the rotor and remove the dust shield.

11   Make alignment marks between the distributor flange and the cylinder head.

12   Remove the two bolts which secure the distributor.

13   Disconnect the primary harness connector from the distributor (when applicable).

14   Remove the distributor from the cylinder head (photo).

15   Replace the distributor O-rings if necessary.

16   When installing, insert the distributor into the head, aligning the marks, and turn the shaft to align the drive dogs with the slots in the camshaft. The drive is offset, so there is no possibility of incorrect installation.

17   The remainder of installation is a reversal of the removal procedure.

18   Check the ignition timing and adjust if necessary (Section 6).

B28F

19   Remove the air intake duct from the airflow sensor.

20   Remove the twelve Allen screws which secure the fuel control unit top section. (If only the distributor cap and rotor will be removed, it is not necessary to remove the fuel control unit. Some of the spark plug wires will have to be disconnected from the cap.)

21   Using pieces of numbered tape, mark the spark plug wires. Unclip the distributor cap and remove it, disconnecting spark plug wires as necessary (photo). Lift the fuel control unit up, without straining the fuel lines, to provide clearance for the cap.

22   Bring the engine to TDC, No 1 firing (photo). (See paragraph 2 and Fig. 4.11).

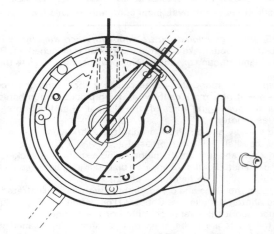

Fig. 4.5   Rotor position before installation (shown solid) and after installation (dotted) (Sec 4)

23   Disconnect the primary harness connector between the distributor and the ignition control unit. Also disconnect the vacuum advance hose (photos).

24   Make alignment marks between the distributor flange and the cylinder head. Remove the clamp nut and lift out the distributor, again lifting the fuel control unit to provide clearance.

25   Begin installation by positioning the rotor approximately 30° clockwise of the No 1 reference notch in the rim of the distributor (Fig. 4.5).

26   Insert the distributor, observing the previously made alignment marks. The rotor should turn to align with the reference notch as the

4.26 Rotor tip aligned with No 1 cylinder notch in distributor rim (B 28F) — dust shield removed

distributor is pushed in (photo). Install the clamp nut and tighten it lightly.

27 Reconnect the primary wiring connector.

28 Install the distributor cap and spark plug wires.

29 Secure the fuel control unit and install the air duct.

30 Check the ignition timing and adjust if necessary (Section 6), then fully tighten the clamp nut.

5 Distributor — overhaul

1 Check the availability and cost of replacement parts before deciding to overhaul the distributor.

T5Z-4 system (B28F)

2 Pull off the rotor and remove the dust shield (photo).

3 Remove the circlip from the shaft. Carefully pull or pry off the rotor wheel. Recover the locating pin (photos).

4 Remove the primary wiring connector securing screw. Pull out the connector (photo).

5 Remove the two screws which secure the vacuum unit. Unhook the vacuum unit from the baseplate and remove it (photos).

6 Loosen the screws which secure the cap clips. There is no need to remove the clips unless they are to be replaced.

7 Remove the three screws which secure the baseplate to the distributor body. Remove the remaining circlip from the shaft. Lift out the baseplate complete with coil and magnet (photo).

8 The centrifugal advance weights and springs are now accessible (photo).

9 To remove the distributor shaft itself, drive out the roll pin which secures the gear to the shaft. Remove the gear and lift out the shaft.

10 Examine all parts and replace as necessary. Measure the resistance of the impulse sender coil (see Specifications for the correct value). Apply vacuum to the vacuum unit to verify that the arm moves and that the diaphragm is intact. Replace the rotor and distributor cap unless they are known to be in perfect condition.

11 Reassemble by reversing the disassembly procedure. Lubricate the shaft bearing and the centrifugal mechanism with a little light oil. Tap the rotor wheel pin in with a punch or similar tool (photos).

12 After installing the rotor wheel, check that the gaps between the rotor and station teeth are as specified. Bend the stator teeth carefully if necessary.

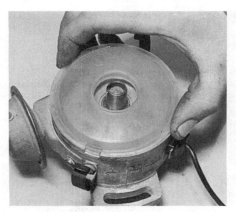

5.2 Removing the dust shield

5.3A Removing the upper circlip. Note locating pin (arrowed) in groove

5.3B Pulling off the rotor wheel

5.4 Loosening the primary harness connector screw

5.5A Remove the vacuum unit screws ...

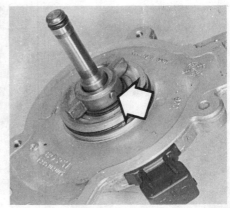

5.11A   Align the grooves and insert the rotor wheel pin . . .

5.11B   . . . and tap it into position

5.13   Drive out the dog securing pin (arrowed) to release the shaft components

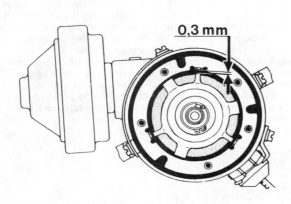

0,3 mm

Fig. 4.7   Gap between rotor and stator teeth must be as shown (Sec 5)

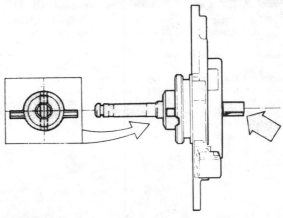

Fig. 4.8   Relationship between dog offset (left) and shaft cutaway (right) on EZ 115-117K distributor (Sec 5)

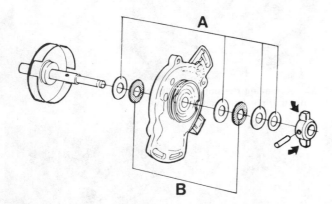

A

B

Fig. 4.9   EZ 115-117K distributor shaft components (Sec 5)

A   Steel washers   B   Fibre washers

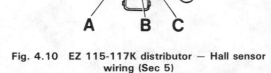

A   B   C

Fig. 4.10   EZ 115-117K distributor — Hall sensor wiring (Sec 5)

A   Black
B   Green
C   Red

EZ115-117K systems (B230F/FT, B280F)

13   If parts are available, the Hall sensor on the distributor baseplate can be replaced. The shaft and associated components must be removed first; they are released by driving out the dog securing pin (photo). Note the relationship of the dog offset to the shaft.

14   Drill out the rivets which secure the old sensor. Remove the sensor and connector; transfer the connector and wiring to the new sensor.
15   Secure the sensor with new rivets. Reassemble the shaft components and secure them with a new pin.

CARBON DEPOSITS

Symptoms: Dry sooty deposits indicate a rich mixture or weak ignition. Causes misfiring, hard starting and hesitation.

Recommendation: Check for a clogged air cleaner, high float level, sticky choke and worn ignition points. Use a spark plug with a longer core nose for greater anti-fouling protection.

OIL DEPOSITS

Symptoms: Oily coating caused by poor oil control. Oil is leaking past worn valve guides or piston rings into the combustion chamber. Causes hard starting, misfiring and hesition.

Recommendation: Correct the mechanical condition with necessary repairs and install new plugs.

TOO HOT

Symptoms: Blistered, white insulator, eroded electrode and absence of deposits. Results in shortened plug life.

Recommendation: Check for the correct plug heat range, over-advanced ignition timing, lean fuel mixture, intake manifold vacuum leaks and sticking valves. Check the coolant level and make sure the radiator is not clogged.

PREIGNITION

Symptoms: Melted electrodes. Insulators are white, but may be dirty due to misfiring or flying debris in the combustion chamber. Can lead to engine damage.

Recommendation: Check for the correct plug heat range, over-advanced ignition timing, lean fuel mixture, clogged cooling system and lack of lubrication.

HIGH SPEED GLAZING

Symptoms: Insulator has yellowish, glazed appearance. Indicates that combustion chamber temperatures have risen suddenly during hard acceleration. Normal deposits melt to form a conductive coating. Causes misfiring at high speeds.

Recommendation: Install new plugs. Consider using a colder plug if driving habits warrant.

GAP BRIDGING

Symptoms: Combustion deposits lodge between the electrodes. Heavy deposits accumulate and bridge the electrode gap. The plug ceases to fire, resulting in a dead cylinder.

Recommendation: Locate the faulty plug and remove the deposits from between the electrodes.

NORMAL

Symptoms: Brown to grayish-tan color and slight electrode wear. Correct heat range for engine and operating conditions.

Recommendation: When new spark plugs are installed, replace with plugs of the same heat range.

ASH DEPOSITS

Symptoms: Light brown deposits encrusted on the side or center electrodes or both. Derived from oil and/or fuel additives. Excessive amounts may mask the spark, causing misfiring and hesitation during acceleration.

Recommendation: If excessive deposits accumulate over a short time or low mileage, install new valve guide seals to prevent seepage of oil into the combustion chambers. Also try changing gasoline brands.

WORN

Symptoms: Rounded electrodes with a small amount of deposits on the firing end. Normal color. Causes hard starting in damp or cold weather and poor fuel economy.

Recommendation: Replace with new plugs of the same heat range.

DETONATION

Symptoms: Insulators may be cracked or chipped. Improper gap setting techniques can also result in a fractured insulator tip. Can lead to piston damage.

Recommendation: Make sure the fuel anti-knock values meet engine requirements. Use care when setting the gaps on new plugs. Avoid lugging the engine.

SPLASHED DEPOSITS

Symptoms: After long periods of misfiring, deposits can loosen when normal combustion temperature is restored by an overdue tune-up. At high speeds, deposits flake off the piston and are thrown against the hot insulator, causing misfiring.

Recommendation: Replace the plugs with new ones or clean and reinstall the originals.

MECHANICAL DAMAGE

Symptoms: May be caused by a foreign object in the combustion chamber or the piston striking an incorrect reach (too long) plug. Causes a dead cylinder and could result in piston damage.

Recommendation: Remove the foreign object from the engine and/or install the correct reach plug.

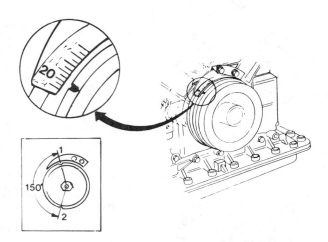

Fig. 4.11   Timing marks for B28F — 20° BTDC highlighted. Note the two pulley notches (Sec 6)

1 No 1 cylinder notch
2 No 6 cylinder notch

6   Ignition timing — checking and adjustment

This is not a routine operation, since there is normally no reason why the timing should vary. On EZ115K systems (B280F engines) the timing cannot be adjusted; although it can be checked if wished.

1   Bring the engine to operating temperature with the air conditioning switched off. With the engine stopped, connect a timing light (stroboscope) and a tacometer as instructed by the manfacturers.

2   Highlight the notch on the crankshaft pulley and the desired marks on the timing scale with white paint or typist's correction fluid. (See Specifications for the desired values). Be sure to use the correct pulley notch on the B28F engine (Fig. 4.11).

3   On B28F engines, disconnect and plug the distributor or control unit vacuum advance hose (photo).

4   Run the engine at the specified idle speed and shine the timing light on the timing scale. **Caution:** *Do not get wires, clothing, long hair etc, caught in the drivebelts or the fan. The pulley notch will appear stationary and (if the timing is correct) in alignment with the appropriate mark on the timing scale.*

5   If adjustment is necessary, stop the engine. Loosen the distributor mounting bolts and turn the distributor a small amount. Turning the distributor against the direction of shaft rotation advances the timing, and vice versa. Tighten the distributor mounting bolt(s) after each adjustment, restart the engine and recheck the timing.

6   When the timing at idle is correct, check the advance on non-Turbo models by observing the timing at the higher specified speed. If this is incorrect on B28F engines, it is caused by a defective mechanical advance mechanism; on other models it must be due to a fault in the control unit or its inputs. (Normal operation of the knock sensor, when applicable, will also retard the timing.)

7   If a vacuum pump is available, apply vacuum to the advance unit (when so equipped) and verify that the timing advances.

8   Stop the engine, disconnect the test gear and connect the original electrical and vacuum connections.

7   Ignition advance systems — description and check

1   Beside the speed, load and knock-related controls regulating the ignition timing, some models are subject to ignition advance applied for the purpose of raising or maintaining engine speed. The advance may be controlled electrically (within the control unit) or mechanically (by switching a vacuum feed).

Temperature-related advance (overheating)

2   This system is installed to certain vehicles with air conditioning

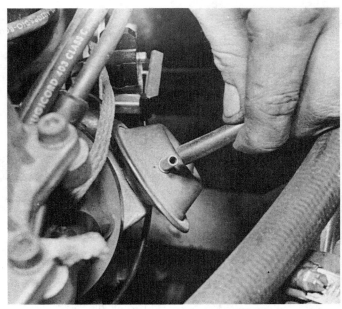

6.3   Disconnecting the distributor vacuum hose

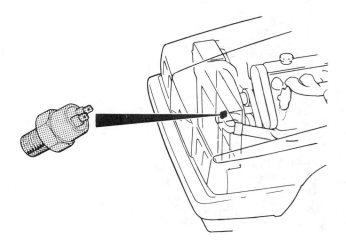

Fig. 4.12   Radiator thermoswitch for some temperature-related advance systems (Sec 7)

and the EZ-K ignition systems. By means of a radiator-mounted thermoswitch, ignition timing is advanced by 8 to 13° if the coolant temperature exceeds 103° C (217° F). The throttle switch must be closed (indicating that the throttle pedal is released).

3   The system may be checked by bridging the thermoswitch terminals with the engine idling: the timing advance will be evidenced by a raised idle speed and may be verified accurately using a timing light.

4   The thermoswitch may be tested as described in Chapter 2, but using oil instead of water to heat the switch.

Temperature-related advance (warm-up)

5   This system is installed on some engines to maintain idle speed and promote rapid warm-up. Acting on information received from the coolant temperature sensor, the control unit advances the timing by 15° below 5°C (41°F), and by 5 to 6° between 5 and 12°C (41 and 54°F).

6   The system may be checked by watching the ignition timing during warm-up after a cold start in winter. Alternatively, the sensor may be fooled by immersing it in iced water. (A spare sensor, or a blanking plug, would have to be installed in the cylinder head).

5.5B . . . and unhook the vacuum unit

5.7 Removing the baseplate with coil and magnet

5.8 Distributor body showing centrifugal advance weights and springs

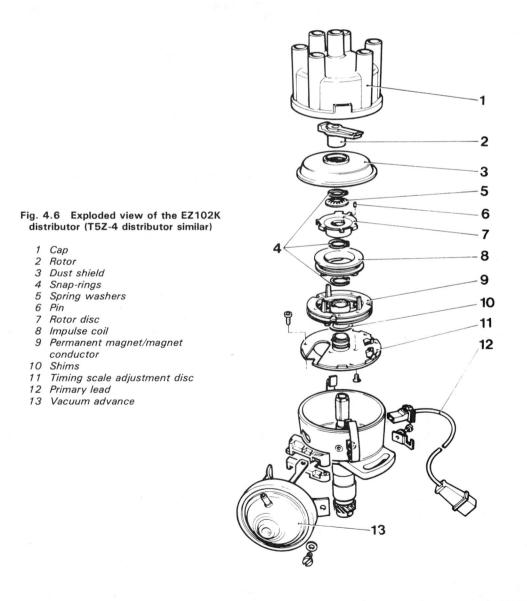

Fig. 4.6 Exploded view of the EZ102K distributor (T5Z-4 distributor similar)

1 Cap
2 Rotor
3 Dust shield
4 Snap-rings
5 Spring washers
6 Pin
7 Rotor disc
8 Impulse coil
9 Permanent magnet/magnet conductor
10 Shims
11 Timing scale adjustment disc
12 Primary lead
13 Vacuum advance

4

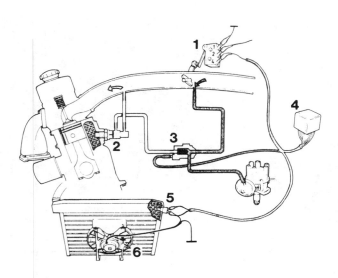

Fig. 4.13 Components of switched vacuum advance system (Sec 7)

1　Throttle switch
2　Thermal vacuum valve
3　Solenoid valve

4　Relay
5　Thermoswitch
6　Electric fan

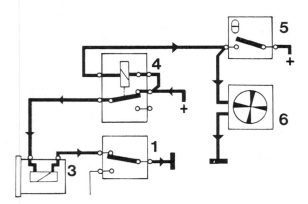

Fig. 4.14　Circuit diagram of switched vacuum advance system. For key see Fig. 4.13 (Sec 7)

7.9　Solenoid vacuum valve on B 28 engine

Switched vacuum advance (temperature-related)

7　This system is installed to some B28F engines. It is linked with the throttle microswitch (part of the constant idle system). Not all the features of the system described here are installed to all models. The main components of the system are shown in Fig. 4.14.

8　At coolant temperature below 55° C (131° F), the thermal vacuum valve is closed and no vacuum is applied.

9　Between 55 and 100° C (137 and 212° F) the thermal vacuum valve is open. The throttle microswitch controls the solenoid valve so that manifold vacuum is applied above idle (photo). At idle the solenoid valve changes to a vacuum tapping above the throttle valve. The ignition is thus retarded, which makes for smooth idling.

10　Above 100° C (212° F) the radiator thermoswitch closes. This operates the electric cooling fan and also de-energises the relay. The solenoid valve is thus de-energised, regardless of throttle position, and manifold vacuum is applied all the time. This raises the idle speed and improves engine cooling.

11　Testing of the warm-up and normal running phases may be carried out by observing the shift in timing while an assistant operates the throttle microswitch. The overheating mode may be simulated by

disconnecting the thermoswitch and bridging the connector terminals. The thermoswitch itself can be tested by immersing it in boiling water.

8　Engine RPM/crankshaft position sensor (EZ115K) — removal and installation

1　Disconnect the sensor connector near the firewall.
2　Remove the Allen screw which secures the sensor to the bracket. Access is restricted .
3　Withdraw the sensor from the bracket and remove it.
4　Install by reversing the removal operations.

9　Knock sensor (EZ-K systems) — removal and installation

1　Disconnect the electrical connector from the knock sensor.
2　Remove the sensor securing bolt and the sensor itself (photo). It is located under the intake manifold.
3　Install by reversing the removal operations. Apply thread locking compound to the bolt and tighten it to the specified torque.

10　Ignition control unit — removal and installation

1　Disconnect the battery negative cable.

T5Z-4 (B28F)

2　The control unit is located on the right-hand inner fender panel, next to the coil. Disconnect the connector from the base of the unit (photo).
3　Remove the securing screws and lift out the control unit.
4　Install by reversing the removal operations.

EZ-K systems

5　Remove the trim from below the steering column.
6　Remove the four screws which secure the control unit to the right-hand end of the pedal bracket. Depress the throttle pedal for access to two of the screws (photo).

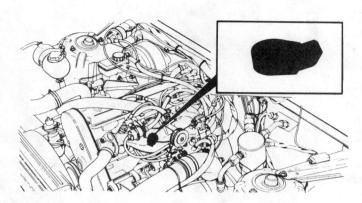

Fig. 4.15 Knock sensor location (Sec 9)

9.2 Knock sensor securing bolt (arrowed)

10.2 Ignition control unit — T5Z-4

10.6 Removing an ignition control unit screw — EZ-K systems

10.7 Disconnecting the control unit electrical connector. Vacuum hose fitting is arrowed

4

7 Disconnect the electrical connector and the vacuum hose. Remove the control unit (photo).

8 Install by reversing the removal operations.

11 Ballast resistor — checking, removal and installation

1 A ballast resistor is only installed on B28F engines. Its function is to assist starting. During normal running the resistor is in series with the coil primary windings, and approximately 6 volts are dropped across both resistor and coil. During start-up a section of the resistor is by-passed to compensate for the drop in battery voltage caused by the starter motor.

2 To test the ballast resistor, first disconnect the wiring from it. Use a suitable multi-meter to measure the resistances across the two upper-most terminals. The desired value is given in the Specifications.

3 To remove the ballast resistor, disconnect the wiring from it, remove the securing screw and remove the resistor complete with bracket (photo).

4 Install by reversing the removal procedure.

12 Coil — checking, removal and installation

1 Inspect the coil visually for cracks, leakage of insulating oil or other obvious damage. Replace it if such damage is evident.

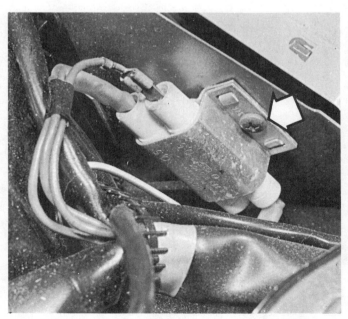

11.3 Ignition ballast resistor — securing screw (arrowed)

2   Disconnect the primary and secondary wires from the coil (photo).
Use an ohmmeter to measure the primary resistance (between the
primary terminals). The desired value is given in the Specifications.
3   Measure the secondary resistance (between one of the primary
terminals and the secondary terminal) and compare it with that
specified.
4   Replace the coil if the resistance of either winding differs widely
from the correct value.
5   To remove the coil, disconnect the wires from it and release the
clamp bracket. Slide the coil out of the bracket.
6   Install by reversing the removal operations.

---

13   Troubleshooting — ignition system

Electronic ignition systems are normally very reliable. Faults are most
likely to be due to loose or dirty connections, or tracking of secondary
voltage due to dirt, dampness or damaged insulation.
The old practice of checking for a spark by holding the live end of
a spark plug wire a short distance away from the block is not recommended, since there is a risk of damaging the coil insulation. For the
same reason, diagnosing misfires by pulling off one plug wire at a time
from the distributor cap is also forbidden. In either case there is the
risk of a powerful electric shock.

12.2   **Disconnecting the coil wire**

Engine will not start

1   If the ignition system seems completely dead, check the appropriate
fuse (see Chapter 12   Specifications — on early models the ignition
system is not fused).
2   Inspect the coil, the distributor and the control unit for loose
connections.
3   Make sure that the coil tower, the distributor cap and the spark
plug wires are clean and dry. Measure the resistance of the wire lead
from the coil to the distributor cap (see Specifications).
4   Inspect the inside of the distributor cap and the rotor for visible
damage, tracking (thin black lines) and burning. Check that the center
brush in the cap is intact and free to move. Test the rotor by substitution if possible.
5   On the B28F engine, measure the resistance of the distributor impulse sender coil. This can be done at the terminals of the electrical
connector which connects the distributor with the control unit.
6   Further testing should be left to a Volvo dealer or other specialist.

Engine misfires

7   An irregular misfire suggest a loose connection or an intermittent
fault on the primary side of the system, or a high voltage fault on the
coil side of the rotor.
8   Regular misfiring is almost certainly due to a fault in the distributor
cap, spark plug wires or spark plugs. Since disconnecting plug wires
with the engine running is forbidden, the use of a timing light (strobe)
on each plug wire in turn to verify the presence of secondary voltage
is suggested.
9   If spark is not presentng on one particular wire, the fault is in the
wire or the distributor cap. If spark is present on all wires, the fault
is in a spark plug. Remove the plugs and replace them, or clean and
re-gap them (Section 3).
10 Again, further testing should be done by a specialist.

Chapter 5   Clutch

Contents

Specifications

General

Clutch type . . . .   Single dry plate, diaphragm spring
Actuation . . . .   Hydraulic or cable, according to model and market
Plate diameter (nominal):
 B230F . . . .   216 mm (8.5 in)
 All other models . . . .   229 mm (9.0 in)

Adjustment

Hydraulic actuation . . . .   Automatic in use
Cable actuation — free play at release fork . . . .   1 to 3 mm (0.04 to 0.12 in)

Driven plate

Lining wear limit . . . .   Not specified

Pressure plate

Warp limit . . . .   0.2 mm (0.008 in)

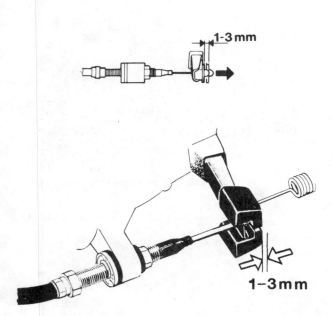

Fig. 5.1 Clutch cable adjustment at release fork — with
return spring (bottom) or without (top) (Sec 3)

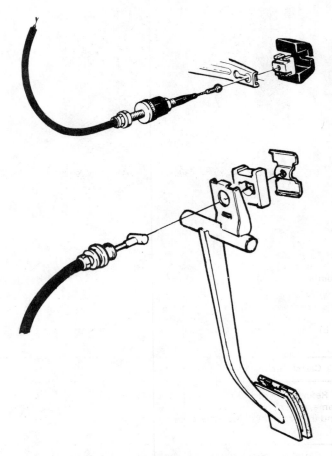

Fig. 5.2 Clutch cable attachment details (Sec 3)

1 General information

A single dry plate diaphragm spring clutch is used. Operation may
be hydraulic or mechanical, according to model and market.

The main components of the clutch are the pressure plate, the driven
plate (sometimes called the friction plate or disc) and the release bearing. The pressure plate is bolted to the flywheel, with the driven plate
sandwiched between them. The center of the driven plate carries female
splines which mate with the splines on the transmission input shaft.
The release bearing is attached to the release fork and acts on the
diaphragm spring fingers of the pressure plate.

When the engine is running and the clutch pedal is released, the
diaphragm spring clamps the pressure plate, driven plate and flywheel
firmly together. Power is transmitted through the friction surfaces of
the flywheel and pressure plate to the linings of the driven plate and
the transmission input shaft.

When the clutch pedal is depressed, the pedal movement is transmitted (hydraulically or by cable) to the release fork. The fork moves
the release bearing to press on the diaphragm spring fingers. Spring
pressure on the pressure plate is relieved, and the flywheel and pressure
plate spin without moving the driven plate. As the pedal is released,
spring pressure is restored and power is routed to the transmission.

The clutch hydraulic system consists of a master cylinder, a slave
cylinder and the associated pipes and hoses. The fluid reservoir is
shared with the brake master cylinder.

Wear in the drive plate linings is compensated for automatically by
the hydraulic system components. The cable needs periodic adjustment to compensate for wear and stretch.

2 Maintenance and inspection

1   Every 12,000 miles (20,000 km nominal) or annually, check the
clutch adjustment on models with cable actuation — see Section 3.
2   Periodically check the clutch hydraulic components for leakage,
and check the condition of the flexible hose.
3   When replacing the brake fluid, also replace the fluid in the clutch
system by bleeding (Section 9).
4   Prompt investigation of clutch slip, screeching etc, may prevent
further damage from occurring.

3 Clutch cable — adjustment, removal and installation

1   Cable adjustment is correct when the free play at the release fork
is as given in the Specifications. Adjust if necessary by means of the
locknuts and threaded adjuster at the end of the cable casing.
2   To remove the cable, loosen the adjuster as far as possible. Disconnect the return spring (if equipped) from the release fork and unhook
the cable. If a rubber insulator is installed at the end of the cable, note
which way it faces.
3   Remove the trim panel below the steering column for access to
the pedals. Remove the retainer which secures the cable to the pedal.
4   Pull the cable into the engine bay and remove it.
5   Install by reversing the removal operations, making sure the cable
is correctly routed. Adjust the cable on completion.

4 Clutch master cylinder — removal and installation

1   Disconnect the fluid supply hose from the master cylinder. Have
a container ready to catch the fluid which will spill. Wash spilled fluid
off paint immediately.
2   Disconnect the pressure pipe union from the end of the cylinder.
Be prepared for further fluid spillage. Cover the open pipe union with
a plastic bag and a rubber band to keep dirt out.
3   Remove the trim panel below the steering column.
4   Remove the clevis pin which secures the clutch pedal to the master
cylinder pushrod (photo).
5   Remove the two nuts which secure the master cylinder to the
firewall.
6   Remove the master cylinder, being careful not to drip fluid onto
the paint.

4.4 Clutch pedal clevis pin (arrowed)

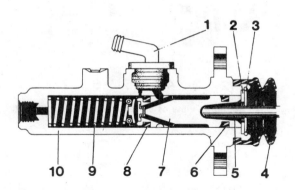

Fig. 5.3 Sectional view of clutch master cylinder (Sec 5)

1	Fluid inlet	6	Outer seal
2	Washer	7	Piston
3	Circlip	8	Inner seal
4	Dust boot	9	Spring
5	Pushrod	10	Cylinder body

7   Install by reversing the removal operations, noting the following points:

  a) With the pedal released there should be 1 mm (0.04 in) clearance between the pushrod and the piston. Adjust if necessary by screwing the clevis up or down the pushrod

  b) Bleed the hydraulic system when finished (Section 8)

5 Clutch master cylinder — overhaul

Refer to Section 7. Overhaul of the master cylinder is basically the same, except that there is a washer under the piston retaining circlip, and the piston has two seals (note which way the seals are installed).

6 Clutch slave cylinder — removal and installation

1   Raise the vehicle and support it securely on jackstands.
2   Loosen the flexible hose union on the slave cylinder (photo).
3   Unbolt the slave cylinder or remove its securing circlip, according to type (photo).
4   Withdraw the slave cylinder with pushrod. Unscrew the cylinder

from the flexible hose. Plug or cap the open end of the hose to minimize fluid loss. Recover the sealing washer.
5   Install by reversing the removal operations. Check the set of the flexible hose after tightening making sure it isn't twisted (correct it if necessary by repositioning the hose-to-pipe union in the bracket).
6   Bleed the clutch hydraulic system (Section 8).

7 Clutch slave cylinder — overhaul

1   Remove the slave cylinder (Section 6). Empty the fluid out of the cylinder and clean it externally.
2   Remove the dust boot and pushrod.
3   Remove the circlip (if present) from the mouth of the cylinder.
4   Shake or tap out the piston and spring. If the piston is stuck, carefully blow it out with low air pressure (point the cylinder in a safe direction while doing this — the piston may shoot out like a bullet).
5   Remove the seal from the piston.

5

6.2 Undoing the clutch slave cylinder hydraulic union

6.3 Removing the slave cylinder circlip

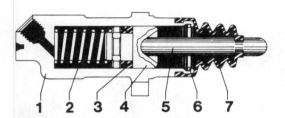

Fig. 5.4　Sectional view of clutch slave cylinder (Sec 7)

1 *Cylinder body*	5 *Pushrod*
2 *Spring*	6 *Circlip*
3 *Seal*	7 *Dust boot*
4 *Piston*	

6　Clean the piston and bore with steel wool and denatured alcohol or brake system cleaner. If either is badly rusted or scored, replace the complete cylinder. Otherwise, obtain a repair kit containing a new seal and dust boot.

7　Dip the new seal in clean brake fluid and install it onto the piston, using the fingers only. Make sure the seal lips face the right direction.

8　Lubricate the piston and bore with clean brake fluid. Insert the spring and the piston into the bore (photos).

9　When applicable, install the circlip in the open end.

10　Install the new dust boot over the pushrod. Place the pushrod in the cup of the piston and seat the dust boot on the cylinder (photo).

8　Clutch hydraulic system — bleeding

1　Top up the hydraulic fluid reservoir with fresh brake fluid of the specified type.

2　Loosen the bleed screw on the slave cylinder (photo). Install a length of clear hose over the screw. Place the other end of the hose

in a jar containing an inch or so of hydraulic fluid.

3　Have an assistant depress the clutch pedal. Tighten the bleed screw when the pedal is depressed. Have the assistant release the pedal, then loosen the bleed screw again.

4　Repeat the process until clean fluid, free of air bubbles, emerges from the bleed screw. Tighten the screw at the end of a pedal downstroke and remove the hose and jar.

5　Top up the hydraulic fluid reservoir.

9　Clutch — removal and installation

Warning: *Dust produced by clutch wear and deposited on clutch components may contain asbestos, which is hazardous to your health. DO NOT blow it out with compressed air and DO NOT inhale it. DO NOT use gasoline or petroleum-based solvents to remove the dust. Brake system cleaner should be used to flush the dust into a drain pan. After the clutch components are wiped clean with a rag, dispose of the contaminated rags and cleaner in a covered container.*

Removal

1　Access to the clutch components is normally accomplished by removing the transmission, leaving the engine in the vehicle. If, of course, the engine is being removed for overhaul, then the opportunity should always be taken to check the clutch for wear and replace worn components as necessary. The following procedures will assume that the engine will stay in place.

2　Make alignment marks between the pressure plate and the flywheel.

3　Loosen the pressure plate bolts a couple of turns at a time until the spring pressure is released. Remove the bolts, the pressure plate and the driven (clutch) plate (photo). Note which way the clutch plate is installed.

4　Begin installation by cleaning the friction surfaces of the flywheel and pressure plate with brake system cleaner. Clean oil or grease off the hands before handling the clutch.

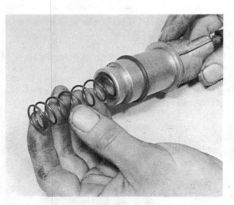

7.8A　Insert the spring . . .

7.8B　. . . followed by the piston. Make sure it's facing the right way

7.10　Installing the dust boot and pushrod

8.2　Clutch slave cylinder bleed screw (arrowed)

9.3　Removing the clutch pressure plate

9.5　Installing the clutch driven plate

9.7 Clutch centering tool in position

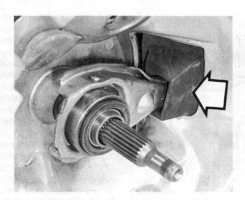

10.2 Clutch release components in position. Dust boot arrowed

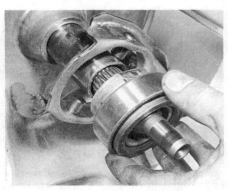

10.4 Removing the release bearing and fork

5 Position the clutch plate on the flywheel, making sure it is installed correctly (photo). It is probably marked SCHWUNGRAD or FLYWHEEL SIDE. If not, install it with the damper springs toward the transmission.

6 Hold the driven plate in position with a clutch alignment tool and install the pressure plate over it. Observe the alignment marks if the original plate is being reinstalled.

7 Install the pressure plate bolts and tighten them evenly until the driven plate is being gripped but can still be moved. Insert the alignment tool, if it is not already in position, and tighten the pressure plate bolts progressively in a criss-cross pattern, to the specified torque (photo).

8 Remove the alignment tool and check to see that the driven plate is central relative to the crankshaft pilot bearing. If the plate is not central, it will be impossible for the transmission input shaft to enter it. Apply a light coat of high-temperature grease to the input shaft splines.

9 Install the transmission.

10 Clutch release bearing — removal and installation

Warning: *Dust produced by clutch wear and deposited on clutch components may contain asbestos, which is hazardous to your health.*

DO NOT blow it out with compressed air and DO NOT inhale it. DO NOT use gasoline or petroleum-based solvents to remove the dust. Brake system cleaner should be used to flush the dust into a drain pan. After the clutch components are wiped clean with a rag, dispose of the contaminated rags and cleaner in a covered container.

1 Remove the transmission (Chapter 6).

2 Free the release fork dust boot from the bellhousing (photo).

3 Disconnect the release fork from the pivot ball-stud. There may be a spring clip securing the fork to the stud, or there may be nothing.

4 Slide the bearing and fork off the guide sleeve and separate them (photo).

5 Clean the guide sleeve and smear a little grease on it. Lightly grease the fork pivot and tips too.

6 Install by reversing the removal operations. When the release fork is secured by a spring clip, note that the clip should pass below the groove in the ball-stud.

11 Clutch components — inspection

Warning: *Dust produced by clutch wear and deposited on clutch components may contain asbestos, which is hazardous to your health. DO NOT blow it out with compressed air and DO NOT inhale it. DO NOT use gasoline or petroleum-based solvents to remove the dust. Brake system cleaner should be used to flush the dust into a drain pan. After the clutch components are wiped clean with a rag, dispose of the contaminated rags and cleaner in a covered container.*

1 Clean the flywheel, driven plate and pressure plate with brake system cleaner or denatured alcohol.

2 Examine the friction surfaces of the flywheel and the pressure plate for scoring or cracks (photo). Light scoring may be ignored. Excessive

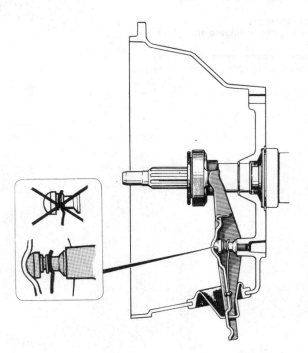

Fig. 5.5 Correct installation of release fork clip below ball-stud groove (Sec 10)

11.2 Flywheel friction surface, showing light scoring and a small crack

5

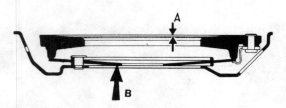

Fig. 5.6 Check the pressure plate for warping (A) and inspect the spring finger tips (B) (Sec 11)

scoring or cracks can sometimes be machined off the flywheel face by an automotive machine shop. The pressure plate must be replaced if it is badly scored or warped.

3   Inspect the pressure plate cover and the diaphragm spring for damage, or blue discoloration indicating overheating. Pay attention to the tips of the spring fingers where the release bearing operates. Replace the pressure plate if in doubt.

4   Replace the driven plate if the friction linings are worn down to, or approaching, the rivets. If the linings are oil-soaked or have a hard black glaze, the source of oil contamination — the crankshaft rear oil seal or transmission input shaft oil seal — must be repaired before the plate is replaced. Also inspect the driven plate springs, hub and splines.

5   Note that if the driven plate only is replaced, problems may be experienced related to the bedding-in of the driven plate and old pressure plate. It is a good idea to replace the driven plate and pressure plate together, if possible.

6   Try the fit of the driven plate (whether new or used) on the transmission input shaft splines. It must neither bind nor be slack.

7   Spin the release bearing in the clutch bellhousing and feel for roughness or shake. The bearing should be replaced as a matter of course unless it is known to be in perfect condition. For the replacement procedure see Section 10.

8   Replacement of the crankshaft pilot bearing should also be considered at this stage. See Chapter 1.

12   Troubleshooting — clutch

Symptom	Reason(s)
Shudder when engaging clutch	Clutch friction surfaces worn Oil contamination of clutch Splines on driven plate or input shaft worn Pressure plate defective Engine/gearbox mountings worn
Clutch drag (failure to release)	Air in hydraulic system Driven plate sticking on splines Driven plate rusted to flywheel (after long periods of non-use) Cable free play excessive Input shaft seized in crankshaft pilot bearing
Clutch slip (engine speed increases without increasing vehicle speed)	Friction surfaces worn or oil contaminated Pressure plate defective Insufficient free play in cable
Noise when depressing clutch pedal (engine stopped)	Pedal shaft dry Clutch cable or release fork pivot dry
Noise when clutch pedal held depressed (engine running)	Release bearing dry or worn Pressure plate spring fingers damaged

Chapter 6 Manual transmission, overdrive and automatic transmission

6

Contents

Specifications

Manual transmission and overdrive
General
Transmission type:

M46	4 forward gears, overdrive and one reverse. Synchro on all forward gears
M47	5 forward gears and one reverse. Synchro on all forward gears
Overdrive type	Laycock J or P
Lubricant type	See *Recommended lubricants and fluids*

Lubricant capacity:

M46	2.4 qts
M47	1.7 qts

Overhaul data

Reverse gear-to-selector clearance	0.1 to 1.0 mm (0.004 to 0.039 in)

Shaft endplay:

Input shaft	0.01 to 0.20 mm (0.0004 to 0.0079 in)
Countershaft — M46	0.03 mm (0.0012 in) endplay to 0.05 mm (0.0020 in) preload
Countershaft — M47	0.01 to 0.10 mm (0.0004 to 0.0039 in)
Mainshaft	0.01 to 0.20 mm (0.0004 to 0.0079 in)
5th gear synchro hub-to-circlip clearance (M47)	0.01 to 0.20 mm (0.0004 to 0.0079 in)

Torque specifications

	Nm	Ft-lbs
Bellhousing nuts and bolts	35 to 50	26 to 37
Gear lever mounting bracket bolts	35 to 50	26 to 37
Gearcase cover bolts	15 to 25	11 to 18
Countershaft bolt (M47)	35 to 45	26 to 33
Drive flange nut:		
M46	175	129
M47, size M16	70 to 90	52 to 66
M47, size M20	90 to 110	66 to 87
Rear cover bolts:		
M46	12 to 18	9 to 13
M47	35 to 50	26 to 37
Bearing retaining plate bolts (M47)	15 to 25	11 to 18
Overdrive-to-intermediate case nuts	12	9
Overdrive main-to-rear case nuts	12	9
Overdrive bridge piece nuts	10	7
Overdrive solenoid	50	37

Automatic transmission
General

Type	4 forward speeds and one reverse. Torque converter, with high-speed lock-up on some models
Designation	AW71 or ZF4HP22
Lubricant type	See *Recommended lubricants and fluids*

Lubricant capacity — drain and refill*:

AW71	7.9 qts
ZF4HP22	7.9 qts

Lubricant capacity — from dry:

AW71	10.5 qts
ZF4HP22	10.5 qts

* A greater quantity will be needed for fluid replacement (See Section 29)

Throttle cable setting
Stop-to-sleeve distance:

Idling	0.25 to 1.00 mm (0.01 to 0.04 in)
Kickdown	51.0 ± 1.6 mm (2.01 ± 0.07 in)

Torque specifications
AW71

	Nm	Ft-lbs
Converter housing to engine:		
M10	35 to 50	26 to 37
M12	55 to 90	41 to 66

Driveplate to torque converter	41 to 50	30 to 37
Center support to gearcase (in steps of 5 Nm/4 ft-lbs)	24 to 28	18 to 21
Oil pan.	4 to 5	3 to 4
Drain plug	18 to 23	13 to 17
Drive flange nut	45	33

ZF4HP22

Converter housing to engine:		
M10	35 to 50	26 to 37
M12	55 to 90	41 to 66
Driveplate to torque converter:		
M8	17 to 27	13 to 20
M10	41 to 50	30 to 37
Oil pan.	7 to 9	5 to 7
Drive flange nut	100	74

PART A: MANUAL TRANSMISSION AND OVERDRIVE

1   General information

Depending on model and year, the manual transmission will be four-speed with overdrive (type M46) or five-speed (type M47 or M4711). The three transmissions are very similar. They are conventional in design and very sturdy.

Drive from the engine is transmitted to the input shaft by the clutch. The gear on the input shaft is permanently meshed with the front gear on the countershaft; the remaining countershaft gears (except reverse) are permanently meshed with their counterparts on the mainshaft. Only one mainshaft gear at a time is actually locked to the shaft, the others are freewheeling. The selection of gears is by sliding synchro units: movement of the gear lever is transmitted to selector forks, which slide the appropriate synchro unit towards the gear to be engaged and lock it to the mainshaft. In 4th gear the input shaft is locked to the mainshaft. In neutral, none of the mainshaft gears are locked.

Reverse gear is obtained by sliding an idler gear into mesh with the countershaft and mainshaft reverse gears. The introduction of the idler gear reverses the direction of rotation of the mainshaft.

A gear ratio higher than 4th is provided by the overdrive (described in Section 16) or by 5th gear. On M47 models, the 5th gear components are mounted at the rear of the transmission, in a housing separate from the main transmission.

The M4711 transmission is essentially the same as the M47, but the 5th gear synchronizer and gear wheel are located on the counter-shaft.

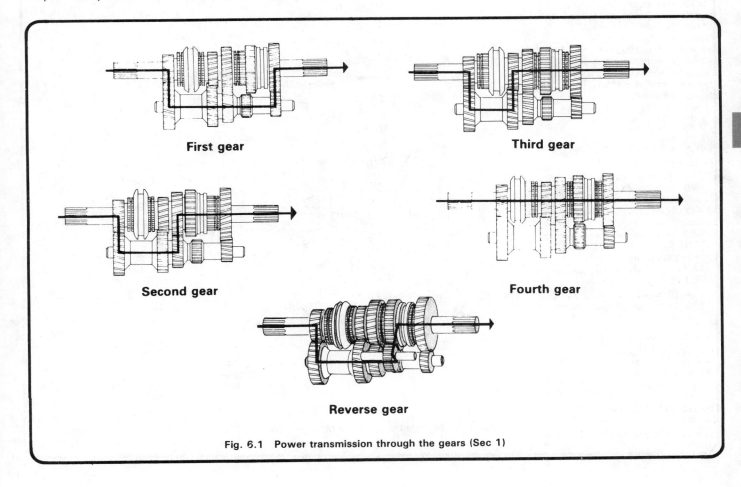

First gear

Third gear

Second gear

Fourth gear

Reverse gear

Fig. 6.1   Power transmission through the gears (Sec 1)

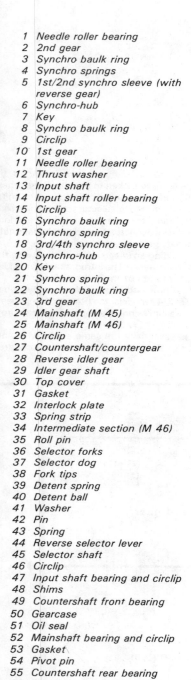

1 Needle roller bearing
2 2nd gear
3 Synchro baulk ring
4 Synchro springs
5 1st/2nd synchro sleeve (with reverse gear)
6 Synchro-hub
7 Key
8 Synchro baulk ring
9 Circlip
10 1st gear
11 Needle roller bearing
12 Thrust washer
13 Input shaft
14 Input shaft roller bearing
15 Circlip
16 Synchro baulk ring
17 Synchro spring
18 3rd/4th synchro sleeve
19 Synchro-hub
20 Key
21 Synchro spring
22 Synchro baulk ring
23 3rd gear
24 Mainshaft (M 45)
25 Mainshaft (M 46)
26 Circlip
27 Countershaft/countergear
28 Reverse idler gear
29 Idler gear shaft
30 Top cover
31 Gasket
32 Interlock plate
33 Spring strip
34 Intermediate section (M 46)
35 Roll pin
36 Selector forks
37 Selector dog
38 Fork tips
39 Detent spring
40 Detent ball
41 Washer
42 Pin
43 Spring
44 Reverse selector lever
45 Selector shaft
46 Circlip
47 Input shaft bearing and circlip
48 Shims
49 Countershaft front bearing
50 Gearcase
51 Oil seal
52 Mainshaft bearing and circlip
53 Gasket
54 Pivot pin
55 Countershaft rear bearing
56 Shim

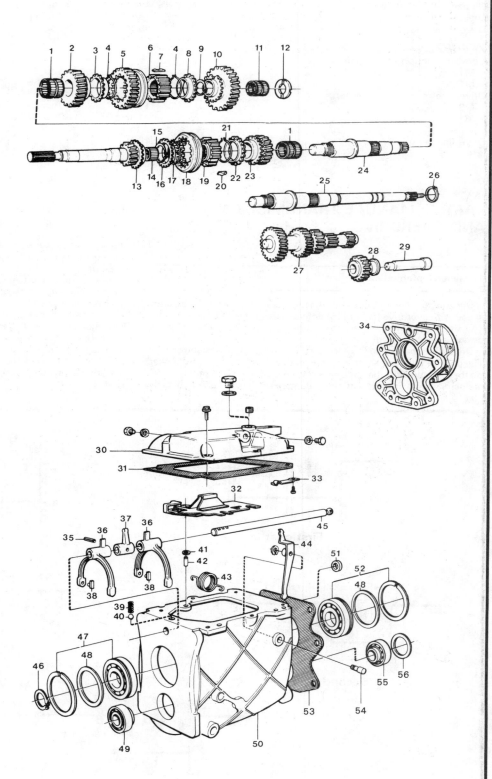

Fig. 6.2 Exploded view of the M 46 transmission.

Fig. 6.3 Exploded view of M 47 transmission (Sec 1)

1 Gear end casing
2 Oil seal
3 Top cover
4 Gasket
5 Spring strip
6 Interlock plate
7 5th gear housing
8 Gasket
9 Bearing race
10 Bearing track
11 Speedometer worm (no longer applicable)
12 Bearing track
13 Bearing race
14 Shim
15 Bearing retainer
16 Selector dog
17 Roll pins
18 Selector shaft
19 5th gear selector fork
20 Reverse selector lever
21 Pivot pin
22 Selector forks
23 Selector dog
24 Fork tips
25 Detent spring
26 Detent ball
27 Selector shaft
28 Washer
29 Pin
30 Circlip
31 Shims
32 Input shaft bearing and circlip
33 Countershaft front bearing
34 Gearcase
35 Gasket
36 Oil seal
37 Mainshaft bearing and circlip
38 Spacer
39 Bearing retaining plate
40 Countershaft 5th gear
41 Countershaft rear bearing
42 Countershaft/countergear
43 Reverse idler gear
44 Idler gear shaft
45 5th synchro-hub
46 Collar
47 Spring
48 Key
49 5th synchro sleeve
50 Spring
51 Synchro baulk ring
52 Circlip
53 Spacer
54 Needle roller bearing
55 Mainshaft 5th gear
56 Spacer
57 Pilot bearing
58 Input shaft
59 Input shaft roller bearing
60 Circlip
61 Synchro baulk ring
62 Springs
63 3rd/4th synchro sleeve
64 Synchro-hub
65 Synchro baulk ring
66 3rd gear
67 Key
68 Mainshaft
69 2nd gear
70 Synchro baulk ring
71 1st/2nd synchro sleeve (with reverse gear)
72 Springs
73 Synchro-hub
74 Key
75 Synchro baulk ring
76 Circlip
77 Washer
78 1st gear
79 Vibration damper ring
80 Damper spring
81 Damper washer
82 Thrust washer

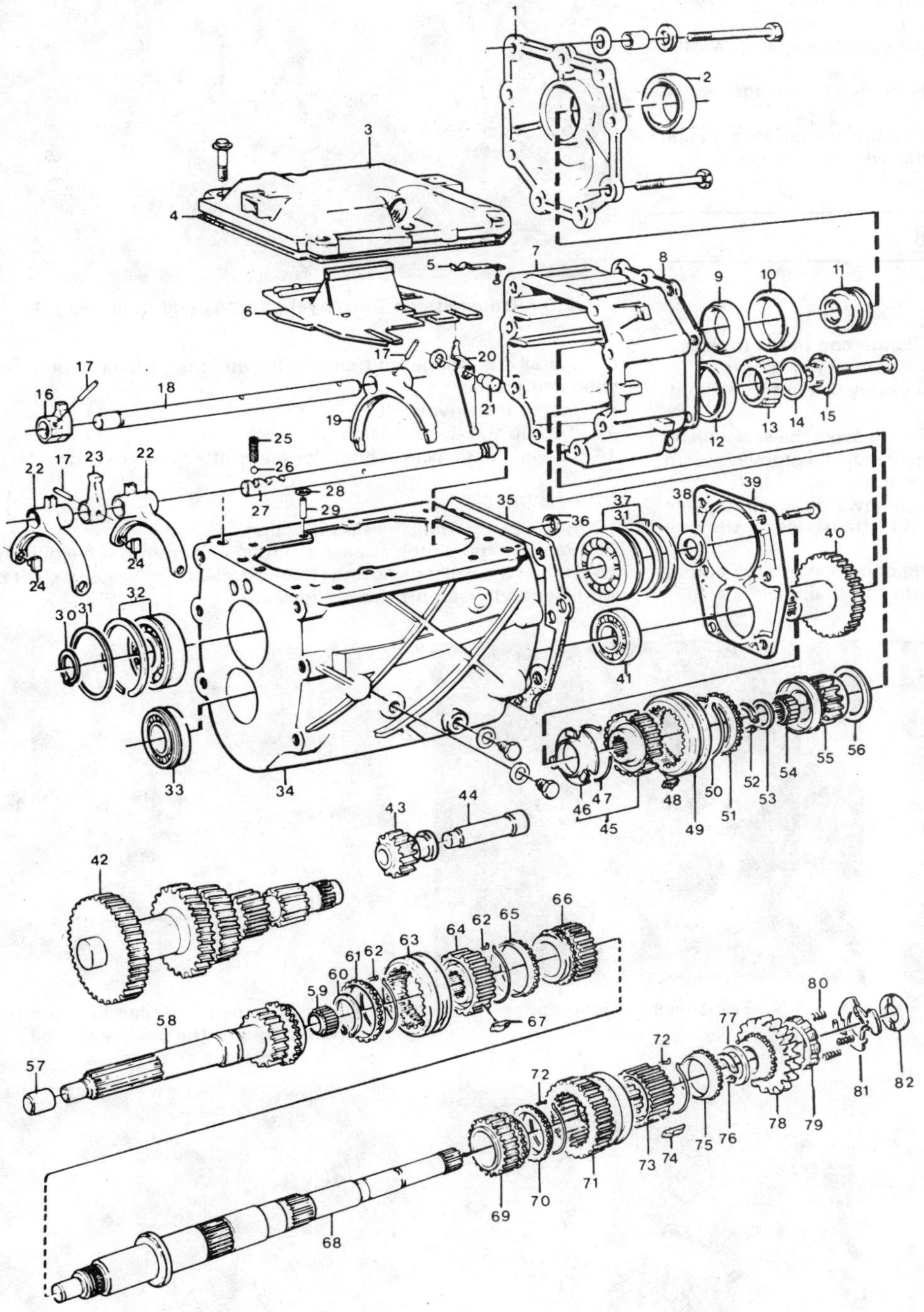

6

2 Maintenance and inspection

1   Every 12,000 miles or annually, or if prompted by unusual noises or evidence of leakage, check the transmission oil level as follows.
2   Raise the vehicle and support it on jackstands so that it is still level.
3   Clean the area round the filler/level plug on the side of the transmission. Unscrew and remove the plug (photo).
4   Oil should be up to the level of the bottom of the plug hole. Insert a clean piece of stiff wire if necessary to check.
5   Top up if necessary with the specified oil (photo). Do not overfill: allow any surplus to drip out of the plug hole.
6   Install and tighten the filler/level plug, using a new sealing washer if necessary.
7   Frequent need for topping-up can only be due to leakage, which should be found and corrected.
8   Oil changing is no longer specified as a routine operation, although a drain plug is provided for the owner who wishes to do so.

3 Transmission oil seals — replacement

Drive flange

1   Raise and support the vehicle.
2   Unbolt the driveshaft from the drive flange and move it aside.
3   Counterhold the flange and remove its central nut (photo).
4   Remove the flange, using a puller if necessary. Do not try to hammer it off. Be prepared for oil spillage.
5   Pry out the old oil seal and clean up its seat. Inspect the seal rubbing surface on the flange: clean it, or replace the flange if a groove is worn in it, to avoid premature failure of the new seal.
6   Lubricate the new seal and install it, lips inwards, using a piece of pipe or seal driver to tap it in. On the M47 transmission the seal should be recessed by 2.5 mm (0.1 in).
7   On the M46 transmission, apply locking compound to the output shaft splines. Be careful not to contaminate the seal.

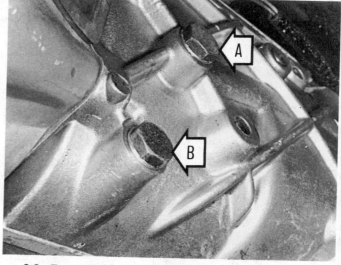

2.3   Transmission filler/level plug (A) and drain plug (B)

8   Install the flange and secure it with the nut, tightened to the specified torque.
9   Install the driveshaft.
10   Top up the transmission oil.
11   Lower the vehicle. Check for leaks after the next run.

Input shaft

12   Remove the transmission (Section 4).
13   Remove the clutch release components from the bellhousing.
14   Unbolt the bellhousing and remove it. Recover the input shaft bearing shim and clean off the old gasket.

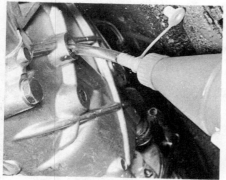

2.5   Topping-up the transmission oil

3.3   Transmission drive flange

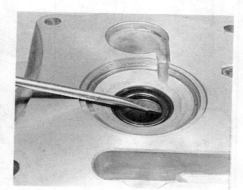

3.15   A screwdriver can be used to carefully pry the input shaft oil seal out of the case

3.17   Seating the input shaft oil seal

3.18   Installing the bellhousing gasket

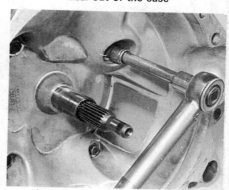

3.19   Tighten the bellhousing bolts in a criss-cross pattern

15 Lever the old oil seal out of the bellhousing and clean out its seat (photo).
16 Inspect the seal rubbing face of the input shaft. If it is damaged, a new shaft may be required.
17 Lubricate the new seal and install it to the bellhousing, lips pointing to the transmission side. Use a piece of tube to seat it (photo).
18 Install the bellhousing to the transmission, using a new gasket (photo). Remember to install the input shaft bearing shim; use a thin coat of grease to hold it in position if necessary.
19 Install the bellhousing bolts and tighten them to the specified torque (photo).
20 Install the clutch release components.
21 Install the transmission.

4 Manual transmission — removal and installation

1 On overdrive transmissions, if the overdrive is to be disassembled the pressure should first be relieved as described in Section 17, paragraph 1.
2 Disconnect the battery negative cable.
3 On B230 engines, arrangements must be made to support the engine from above to prevent damage to the distributor due to engine movement. The best way to support the engine is with a bar resting

Fig. 6.4 Engine support bar (5006) resting in the hood channels (Sec 4)

in the hood channels with an adjustable hook appropriately placed.
4 Raise the vehicle and support it securely on jackstands.
5 Unbolt the driveshaft from the transmission output flange.
6 Remove the Allen screw which secures the gear lever to the selector rod. Push out the pin and separate the rod from the lever.
7 Loosen the exhaust downpipe-to-muffler joint so that some movement of the pipe is possible.
8 Unbolt the transmission mounting crossmember from the transmission and from the side rails. Remove the crossmember.
9 On B230 engines, adjust the engine support so that the distributor cap is 10 mm (0.4 in) from the firewall.
10 Disconnect the transmission wiring harness electical connectors.
11 Remove the gear lever (Section 21). Alternatively, the gear lever carrier can be unbolted now and left on the vehicle.
12 Remove the starter motor (Chapter 12). On B28 engines, also remove the cover plate from the unused starter motor mounting.
13 Remove the clutch slave cylinder without disconnecting the hydraulic pipe, or disconnect the clutch cable, as applicable. See Chapter 5.
14 Remove all but two of the engine-to-transmission nuts and bolts. Note the position of cable clips, exhaust brackets, etc.
15 Support the transmission, preferably with a floor jack and transmission adapter, or else with the aid of an assistant. It is too heavy for one person to remove alone.
16 Remove the remaining engine-to-transmission nuts and bolts. Pull the transmission from the engine. Do not allow the weight of the transmission to hang on the input shaft.
17 Remove the transmission from under the vehicle.
18 Install by reversing the removal operations, noting the following points:

   a) Apply a thin coat of high-temperature molybdenum-based grease to the input shaft splines
   b) Make sure that the clutch driven plate is properly centered, and that the clutch release components have been installed in the bellhousing
   c) Adjust the clutch cable (when applicable)
   d) Refill or top up the transmission oil

19 Check for correct operation on completion.

5 Transmission (M46) — disassembly

1 Clean the transmission and drain the oil. Unbolt the gear lever carrier if this was removed with the transmission, disconnecting the associated wiring (photo).

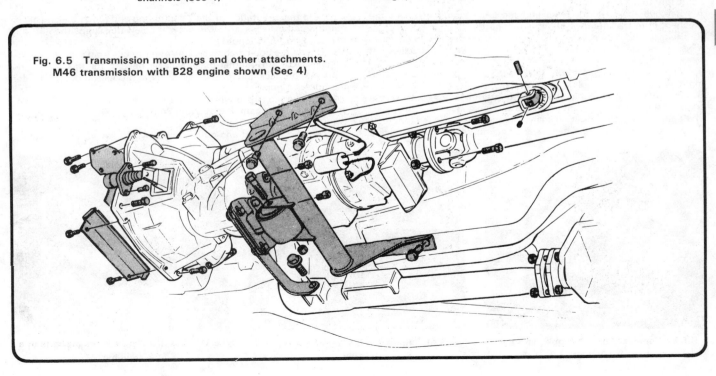

Fig. 6.5 Transmission mountings and other attachments. M46 transmission with B28 engine shown (Sec 4)

6

5.1   Three of the gear lever carrier bolts (arrowed)

5.2A   Remove the coupling pin . . .

5.2B   . . . and remove the selector rod

5.3   Unbolting the transmission top cover

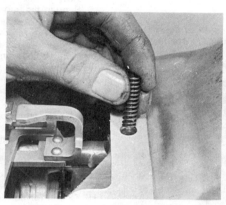

5.4A   Remove the detent spring . . .

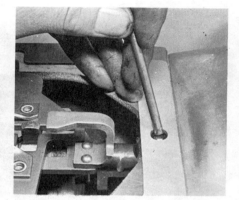

5.4B   . . . and extract the ball with a magnet

2   Separate the selector rod coupling by sliding back the coupling sleeve and pressing out the rear pin. Remove the selector rod (photos).
3   Unbolt and remove the top cover (photo). Peel off the gasket.
4   Remove the detent spring and ball from the hole above the selector shaft (photos).
5   Remove the interlock plate and the large spring. Recover the washers from the interlock plate pegs (photos).
6   Remove the eight nuts which secure the overdrive unit to the intermediate section. Pull off the overdrive; if it is stuck, use a puller, not hammer blows.
7   Turn the selector shaft 90°. Remove the other pin from the coupling and pull off the coupling (photo).
8   Remove the bolts which secure the intermediate section to the transmission. Remove the intermediate section and remove the mainshaft and countershaft bearing shims which will be released (photos).
9   Remove the clutch release fork and bearing, referring if necessary

to Chapter 5.
10   Remove the four bolts which secure the bellhousing. Lift off the bellhousing and recover the input shaft bearing shim.
11   Knock out the roll pin which secures the selector dog to the selector shaft.
12   Note the orientation of the selector dog and forks, making alignment marks if necessary. Withdraw the selector shaft, then lift out the dog and forks (photos).
13   Extract the countershaft bearing outer tracks from each end of the transmission. An internal puller will be needed for this. Drive the countershaft back and forth if necessary to produce enough slack for the puller to grip.
14   Remove the circlip which secures the oil pump cam to the mainshaft. Pull off the cam. Recover the Woodruff key if it is loose, otherwise leave it in place (photos).
15   Remove the inner and outer circlips which secure the mainshaft

5.5A   Removing the interlock plate and spring

5.5B   Removing an interlock plate washer

5.7   Removing the other pin from the coupling

5.8A Unbolting the intermediate section

5.8B Removing the countershaft shim

5.12A Removing the selector dog . . .

5.12B . . . and a selector fork

5.14A Remove the circlip . . .

5.14B . . . and slide off the cam

5.15A Removing the mainshaft bearing inner circlip . . .

5.15B . . . and outer circlip

5.15C Pulling off the mainshaft bearing

5.16A Levering out the input shaft bearing

5.16B Removing the input shaft

5.16C Recover 4th synchro baulk ring

6

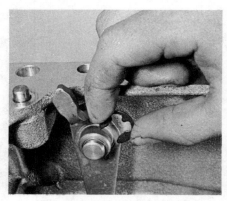

5.17   Removing the mainshaft from the gearcase

5.19   Driving out the reverse idler shaft

5.20   Reverse selector lever E-clip

ball-bearing. Lever the bearing out of the case using a couple of screwdrivers in the outer circlip groove. The shaft will come out with the bearing until a gear meets the transmission; at this point a long-legged puller will have to be used to pull the bearing off the shaft (photos).

16   Remove the input shaft and bearing by levering under the bearing outer circlip. Pull the shaft out of the transmission. Recover the roller bearing and 4th synchro baulk ring (photos).

17   Work the mainshaft out of the top of the transmission. It is a tight install (photo).

18   Lift out the countershaft/countergear assembly.

19   Note the orientation of reverse idler gear. Drive the idler shaft rearwards and remove the shaft and gear (photo).

20   Remove the reverse selector lever, which is secured by an E-clip (photo).

21   The transmission is now disassembled into its major component groups for inspection or replacement.

---

6   Transmission (M47 and M4711) — disassembly

Remove the gear lever carrier, the selector rod and coupling, the top cover and the interlock plate. See Section 5, paragraphs 1 to 5 and 7.

2   Remove the clutch release components. Unbolt and remove the bellhousing; recover the input shaft shim.

3   Counterhold the drive flange and remove the flange nut. Pull the flange off the splines.

4   Unbolt and remove the rear end casing. Remove the gasket.

5   Remove the bolt from the rear end of the countershaft. Put aside the bearing retainer and shim which were secured by the bolt. Reinstall the bolt, screwing it in five or six turns only.

6   Pull off 5th gear housing, using a two-legged puller acting on the countershaft bolt as shown (Fig. 6.7). Remove the gasket.

7   Remove the washers and the roller bearing from the end of the mainshaft.

Pre-1986 models

8   Pull 5th gear off the countershaft, using a two-legged puller acting on the countershaft bolt.

9   From the mainshaft remove 5th gear, the two needle roller bearings, the spacer and 5th synchro baulk ring.

10   Remove the countershaft bolt.

11   Note the position of the selector dogs and forks. Drive out the roll pins and remove the selector shafts, dogs and forks.

12   Remove the circlip which secures 5th synchro-hub to the mainshaft. Unhook the synchro spring, pull off the sleeve and remove the sliding keys.

13   Pull 5th synchro-hub off the mainshaft. It may be necessary to remove some bolts from the rear bearing retainer plate to provide clearance for the puller. Remove the spacer.

14   Remove the remaining bolts from the bearing retaining plate. Remove the plate and remove the mainshaft shim.

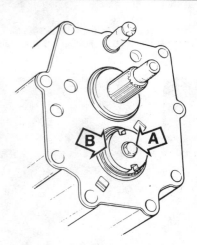

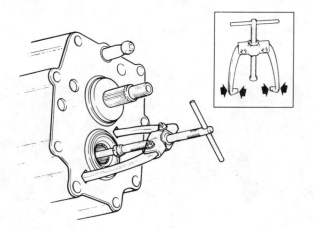

Fig. 6.6   Countershaft bolt (A) and bearing retainer (B) (Sec 6)

Fig. 6.7   Pulling off 5th gear housing. Puller feet may need to be ground down (inset) (Sec 6)

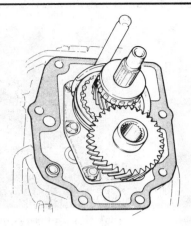

Fig. 6.8   5th gear components — pre-1986 models (Sec 6)

1986 and later models

15 Proceed as above, but making allowance for the fact that 5th gear synchro components are now on the countershaft instead of the mainshaft.

All models

16 Further disassembly is now as described in Section 5, paragraph 13 onwards.

7   Mainshaft — disassembly

1   Clamp the mainshaft in a soft-jawed vice, front end of the shaft pointing up.
2   Remove the circlip which secures 3rd/4th synchro unit (photo).
3   Pull off 3rd/4th synchro and 3rd gear together.
4   Remove 3rd gear needle roller bearing (photo).
5   Invert the shaft. If a vibration damper is fitted to 1st gear, lever off the washer and remove the springs (photos).
6   Remove 1st gear, with the vibration damper ring if applicable. Use a puller if it is tight.
7   Remove 1st gear needle roller bearing and baulk ring (photos).
8   Remove the circlip which secures 1st/2nd synchro unit.

Fig. 6.9   Selector components — M 47 transmission (Sec 6)

1 Roll pins	4 5th selector fork
2 Main selector shaft	5 1st/2nd selector fork
3 5th selector shaft	6 3rd/4th selector fork

9   Pull off 1st/2nd synchro unit (which includes reverse gear) and 2nd gear together.
10   Remove 2nd gear needle roller bearing (photo).
11   The synchro units and gears which were removed together may be disassembled for examination, but take care not to get the parts mixed up.

8   Countershaft — disassembly

If the countershaft bearings are to be replaced, pull the races off the ends of the shaft (photo).

9   Input shaft — disassembly

1   If the input shaft bearing is to be replaced, remove its securing circlip (photo).
2   Press or drive the shaft out of the bearing.

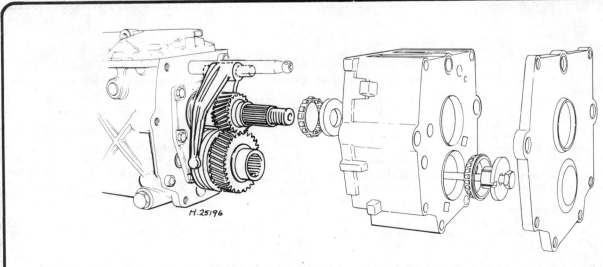

H.25196

Fig. 6.10   5th gear components — 1986 models (Sec 6)

7.2   Removing 3rd/4th synchro circlip

7.4   Removing 3rd gear needle roller bearing

7.5A   Pry off the vibration damper washer . . .

7.5B   . . . and remove the springs

7.7A   Removing 1st gear needle roller bearing . . .

7.7B   . . . and 1st gear baulk ring

7.10   Removing 2nd gear needle roller bearing

8.1   Countershaft and bearing

9.1   Removing the input shaft bearing circlip

10   Transmission components — inspection and overhaul

1   Before beginning a comprehensive overhaul, check the availability and price of spare parts. Also check the price of a new or reconditioned unit.

2   Oil seals, gaskets, roll pins and similar items must be replaced as a matter of course (photo).

3   Bearings should be replaced unless they are known to be in perfect condition. A selection of bearing preload shims will then also be required: read through the reassembly procedure.

4   Synchro baulk rings should be replaced if they have seen much service. Examine the other synchro components, particularly the springs and sliding keys, and replace as necessary.

5   Inspect the gear teeth for chips or other damage. If such damage is found, check the mating gear also. Mainshaft gears can be replaced individually, but damage to a countershaft gear means that the complete countershaft must be replaced.

6   Examine the selector forks for wear, especially at the tips. The tips may be replaceable separately (photo).

11   Input shaft — reassembly

1   If the input shaft bearing has been replaced, press the bearing onto the shaft, applying pressure only to the inner race. Install the bearing circlips.

10.2 Prying out the selector shaft oil seal (M 46 transmission)

10.6 Selector fork with separate tips

11.2A Installing the input shaft roller bearing . . .

11.2B . . . and 4th synchro baulk ring

13.2A Installing the mainshaft 2nd gear . . .

13.2B . . . and 2nd gear baulk ring

13.3 End of synchro spring (arrowed) in cut-out

13.4A Installing 1st/2nd synchro-hub

13.4B . . . and its circlip

2 Install the roller bearing and 4th synchro baulk ring to the shaft (photos), then put it aside until needed for reassembly.

12 Countershaft — reassembly

Install the bearing races to the countershaft and tap them into place, using a tube resting on the inner part of the bearing only.

13 Mainshaft — reassembly

1 Lubricate all components as they are installed to the mainshaft.
2 With the mainshaft in the vice rear end upwards, start by installing 2nd gear needle roller bearing, 2nd gear and its synchro baulk ring (photos).

3 If the synchro unit has been disassembled, it may either be reassembled on the bench, or on the shaft as shown here. Start by inserting the spring into the 2nd gear side of the synchro-hub, with the spring end in one of the cut-outs (photo). The tail of the spring should curve away from the hub center rather than towards it.
4 Install the synchro-hub to the mainshaft and drive it into place with a piece of tube. Secure it with the circlip (photos).
5 Install the circlip keys in the cut-outs (photo). Have an assistant hold the keys in place and install 1st/2nd synchro sleeve, with the reverse gear teeth towards 2nd gear. If there are three bevelled teeth inside the sleeve, they must line up with the three cut-outs in the hub.
6 Install the other synchro spring, engaging its free end in the same key as the lower one (photo). Again pay attention to the direction in which the tail curves (Fig. 6.12).
7 Install 1st gear needle roller bearing, 1st gear baulk ring and 1st gear itself (photo).
8 When a vibration damper is installed, insert the damper ring into

13.5   Inserting a sliding key

13.6   Installing the other synchro spring

13.7   Installing the mainshaft 1st gear

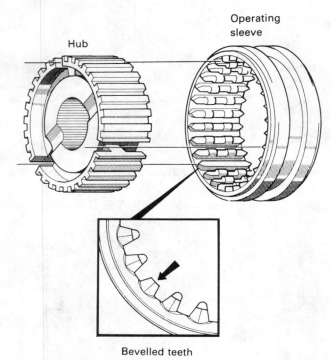

Hub

Operating sleeve

Bevelled teeth

Fig. 6.11   Relationship of synchro-hub to sleeve (Sec 13)

Fig. 6.12   Synchro spring hooked into key (1). Tail (2) must curve away from hub (Sec 13)

1st gear (photo). Install the springs and tap the washer into place. The tangs in the washer go into the recesses in the ring.
9   Invert the shaft. Install 3rd gear needle roller bearing, 3rd gear and 3rd gear baulk ring (photos).
10   Install 3rd/4th synchro unit complete, or build it up on the shaft as was done for the other unit. Use a piece of tube to seat the hub (photos).
11   Install the 3rd/4th synchro circlip.

13.8   Installing the vibration damper ring

13.9A   Installing the mainshaft 3rd gear . . .

13.9B   . . . and 3rd gear baulk ring

13.10A Installing the assembled 3rd/4th synchro unit . . .

13.10B . . . and driving it into position

14 Transmission (M47 and M4711) — reassembly

1 The first stages of reassembly, and calculation of the input shaft bearing shim, are carried out as described for the M46 transmission (Section 15, paragraphs 8 to 24).
2 Mainshaft bearing shim calculation is also similar (Section 15, paragraphs 25 to 27), but the bearing seat is located in the bearing retaining plate.
3 Install the bearing retaining plate with the selected mainshaft bearing shim. Tighten the bolts to the specified torque. Tap the plate while tightening the bolts to settle the bearings.

Pre-1986 models

4 Install the spacer and 5th synchro-hub to the mainshaft. Tap the hub home and install the circlip.
5 Measure the clearance between the hub and the circlip. If it is not as specified, remove the hub again and change the spacer for one of the required thickness.
6 Install 5th synchro sliding keys, sleeve and spring. The three bevelled teeth in the sleeve must align with the keys.
7 Install the selector shafts, dogs and forks, making sure that they are facing the right direction. Secure them with new roll pins. The 5th selector fork roll pin should be driven in flush; support the shaft when doing this.
8 Lubricate the roller bearings for mainshaft 5th gear. Place them in the gear with the spacer.
9 Install 5th synchro baulk ring to the synchro-hub.
10 Install mainshaft and countershaft 5th gears together. Pull the countershaft 5th gear into position using the countershaft bolt and bearing retainer. Remove the bolt and retainer.
11 Install the roller bearing and washers to the mainshaft; bearing taper facing rearwards.
12 Install the bearing outer races and a new selector shaft oil seal to the 5th gear housing.
13 Install the 5th gear housing, using a new gasket smeared with grease.
14 If the countershaft, its bearings or 5th gear housing have been replaced, calculate the shim thickness as follows.

Countershaft bearing shim calculation

15 Secure 5th gear housing with four bolts and spacers. Tighten the bolts to the specified torque.
16 Temporarily install the countershaft bearing retainer and bolt, without the shim. Tighten the bolt to the specified torque. Measure the countershaft endplay using a dial test indicator. Push the countershaft up and down, rotating it at the same time to settle the bearings.

Fig. 6.13 Pressing countershaft 5th gear into position (Sec 14)

Fig. 6.14 Measuring countershaft endplay (Sec 14)

17 Subtract the specified endplay from the measured endplay to give the shim thickness required. For example:

  Measured endplay = 0.72 mm
  Specified endplay = 0.01 to 0.10 mm
  Difference = 0.62 to 0.71 mm

Shims are available in thicknesses from 0.10 to 0.75 mm.

18 Remove the dial indicator, the countershaft bolt and the bearing retainer, the housing bolts and spacers.

Final reassembly

19 Install the selected countershaft bearing shim, the bearing retainer and the bolt. Use thread locking compound on the bolt threads and tighten it to the specified torque.

20 Check that the vent hole in the end casing is not blocked. Install a new oil seal and a new gasket to the end casing, smearing them with grease.

21 Secure the end casing with two lower bolts.

22 Install the gear selector coupling and selector rod.

23 Install the gear lever carrier and the remaining end casing/carrier bolts with washers and spacers. Tighten the bolts to the specified torque.

24 Install the interlock plate and top cover (Section 15, paragraphs 34 to 38).

25 Install the clutch release components.

26 Install the drive flange. Counterhold the flange and tighten the nut to the specified torque.

1986 and later models

27 The operations are similar to those just described, making allowance for the different position of 5th gear synchro components.

---

15 Transmission (M46) — reassembly

Countershaft bearing shim calculation

1 After replacement of the countershaft, countershaft bearings or the transmission casing, the required shim thickness must be determined as follows.

2 Place the countershaft in the casing. Install the front bearing race and drive it in from the outside of the casing, using a piece of tube. Leave the race protruding by a small amount (1 mm/0.04 in approx) — it will adopt its correct position in the next step.

3 Install the bellhousing and its gasket. Secure it with the four bolts, tightened to the specified torque.

4 Invert the transmission so that it stands on the bellhousing. Install the countershaft rear bearing outer race and drive it into position. Rotate the countershaft while driving in the race; it is correctly installed when a slight resistance to turning is felt.

5 Use a depth gauge, or a straight-edge and feeler gauges, to measure the distance from the rear end face of the casing (with gasket in place) to the rear bearing outer race (photo). Select shims from the thicknesses available to make up a total thickness equal to the distance measured, or close enough to it to fall within the specified tolerance. For example:

  Distance measured = 1.52 mm
  Allowed tolerance = 0.03 mm endplay to 0.05 mm preload
  Acceptable shim thickness = (1.52 − 0.03) to (1.52 + 0.05)
                    = 1.49 to 1.57 mm

6 Shims are available in the following thicknesses:

  0.5 mm   0.50 mm
  0.10 mm   0.70 mm
  0.15 mm   1.00 mm
  0.35 mm

Therefore in the above example, shim packs of 1.50 or 1.55 mm could be made up, both of which fall within tolerance.

7 Remove the bellhousing and gasket, the countershaft and its races.

Installing shafts and bearings (part 1)

8 Install the reverse selector lever and secure it with the E-clip (photo).

9 Install reverse idler gear and shaft, engaging the groove on the gear with the end of the selector lever (photo).

10 Tap the idler gear shaft in completely until it is flush with the end casing, or protruding no more than 0.05 mm (0.002 in) (photo).

11 Check that clearance exists between the reverse idler gear groove and the tip of the lever (Fig. 6.15). Adjust if necessary by tapping the lever pivot pin.

12 Install the countershaft (photo).

13 Install the mainshaft into the transmission. Install the thrust washer to the rear of the mainshaft (models without a 1st gear vibration damper).

14 Install the mainshaft rear bearing, with the outer circlip in the bear-

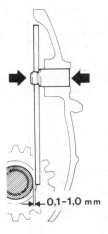

0,1–1,0 mm

Fig. 6.15 Reverse gear-to-selector lever clearance. Adjust by tapping shaft in or out (arrows) (Sec 15)

15.5 Measuring the depth of the countershaft bearing race

15.8 Installing the reverse selector lever

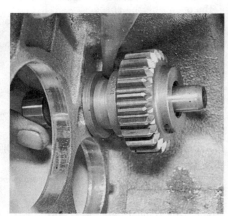

15.9 Installing reverse idler gear and shaft

ing groove. Do not try to drive the bearing home yet.

15 Install the input shaft and bearing, remembering to insert 4th synchro baulk ring and the roller bearing between the input shaft and the mainshaft. Tap the outer race of the input shaft bearing into the case until the outer circlip contacts the case.

16 Install the countershaft bearing races (photo). Tap them in gently.

17 If a new input shaft bearing or bellhousing has been installed, determine the shim thickness as follows.

Input shaft bearing shim calculation

18 Measure the protrusion of the input shaft bearing from the front of the transmission (photo).

19 Install a new gasket to the bellhousing. Measure the depth of the bearing seat, including the thickness of the gasket (photo).

20 Subtract the bearing protrusion of the seat depth, then subtract the specified endplay from the result, to determine shim thickness. For example:

Depth = 5.32 mm
Protrusion = 4.65 mm
Difference = 0.67 mm
Specified endplay = 0.01 to 0.20 mm
Difference minus endplay = 0.47 to 0.66 mm

The range of shims available is from 0.25 to 1.00 mm. Select the correct thickness from the range.

Installing shafts and bearings (part 2)

21 Install the selected input shaft shim to the bellhousing, using a thin coat of grease to hold it in position (photo).

22 Install the bellhousing, using a new gasket. Insert the securing bolts and tighten them to the specified torque.

23 Stand the transmission on the bellhousing. Drive the mainshaft bearing into place and install the inner circlip (photo). (It may be necessary temporarily to remove the outer circlip to enable the bearing

to sit slightly deeper while the inner circlip is installed. The bearing can then be levered up and the outer circlip installed.)

24 If the mainshaft bearing or the intermediate case section has been replaced, the bearing shim thickness must be calculated as follows.

Mainshaft bearing shim calculation

25 Install a new gasket to the rear of the transmission. Measure the protrusion of the mainshaft bearing above the transmission.

26 Measure the depth of the bearing seat in the intermediate use section.

27 Calculate the shim thickness required as described in paragraph 20. The range of shims available is from 0.60 to 1.00 mm.

Final reassembly

28 Install the overdrive oil pump cam and circlip. Make sure that the Woodruff key is secure.

29 Install the selector forks, dog and shaft, making sure they are facing the right direction. Secure the dog with a new roll pin (photo).

30 Install the selected countershaft bearing shim to the countershaft rear bearing, and the mainshaft bearing shim to the intermediate case (photo). Use a thin coat of grease to hold them in position.

31 Install the intermediate case to the rear of the transmission, using a new gasket. Secure it with the lower bolts. (The upper bolts also secure the gear lever carrier.)

32 Install the selector shaft-to-rod coupling and the selector rod.

33 Install the overdrive unit. Tighten the nuts to the specified torque.

34 Install the washers to the interlock plate pegs. Install the interlock plate and the large spring.

35 Install a new top cover gasket.

36 Install the detent ball and spring (photo).

37 Install the top cover (photo). Install and tighten its securing bolts.

38 Check the engagement of all gears, at the same time rotating the input shaft.

39 Install the clutch release components.

40 Install the gear lever carrier if it was removed with the transmission.

15.10   Checking the protrusion of the reverse idler shaft

15.12   Countershaft installed in the gearcase

15.16   Installing a countershaft bearing race

15.18   Measuring the protrusion of the input shaft bearing

15.19   Measuring the depth of the input shaft bearing seat

15.21   Installing the input shaft bearing shim

15.23   Mainshaft bearing with circlips installed

15.29   Driving in the selector dog roll pin

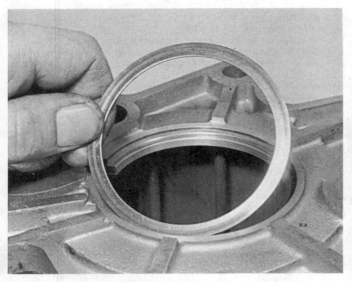

15.30   Installing the mainshaft bearing shim

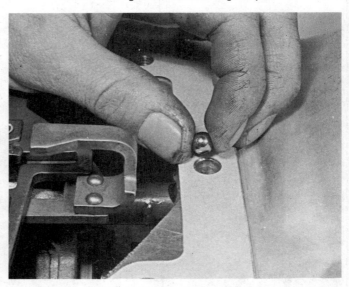

15.36   Installing the detent ball

15.37   Installing the top cover

16 Overdrive — general information

The overdrive is essentially an extra transmission, driven by the output shaft of the main transmission and producing on its own output shaft a step-up ratio of 0.797 : 1. The gear change is controlled hydraulically, the hydraulic control valve being operated by a solenoid. The electrical connections to the solenoid are taken through a switch on the cover of the main transmission which ensures that overdrive can only be brought into operation when the car is in top gear. The activating switch for the whole system is mounted in the top of the gear lever knob.

A cutaway illustration of the overdrive and an exploded view are shown in Figs. 6.16 and 6.17.

The heart of the overdrive is the planetary gear system, whose components are shown in Fig. 6.17. These parts are assembled on the elongated mainshaft which extends from the main transmission. Two of these parts, the planet carrier and the unidirectional clutch, are splined to the mainshaft and always revolve at mainshaft speed. The unidirectional clutch sits inside the output shaft and ensures that if nothing else is driving the output shaft, it will be driven by the transmission mainshaft. In this manner the 1 : 1 ratio is obtained. When this occurs, the planet carrier and the annulus on the output shaft are revolving at the same speed, so the planet gears within the planet carrier are not being driven forwards or backwards and remain stationary on their splines. This means that the sun wheel must also be revolving at the same speed as the planet carrier and the annulus. The sun wheel is splined to the sliding clutch member and this too is revolving at the mainshaft speed. In practice the sliding clutch member is held against the tapered extension of the mainshaft when the 1 : 1 ratio is required and the whole gear system is locked together (Fig. 6.18).

To obtain the step-up ratio, the sliding clutch member is pulled away from the output shaft annulus and comes up against the outer casing of the transmission which holds it stationary. It is still splined to the sun wheel, so this, too, is prevented from turning.

The planet carrier continues to revolve at mainshaft speed, but because the sun wheel is stationary the planet wheels turn around their spindles in the planet carrier. This means that the outer teeth of the planet wheel (which mesh with the annulus) are moving relative to the planet carrier, and this makes the annulus move faster than the planet carrier.

The sliding member is bolted to bridge pieces. Behind these bridge pieces are hydraulically operated pistons which are able to push the bridge pieces away from the case against the action of the clutch return springs when the hydraulic pressure is great enough. This means that changing gear is simply a matter of raising the oil pressure applied to the pistons. The oil pressure is generated in the first instance by a piston

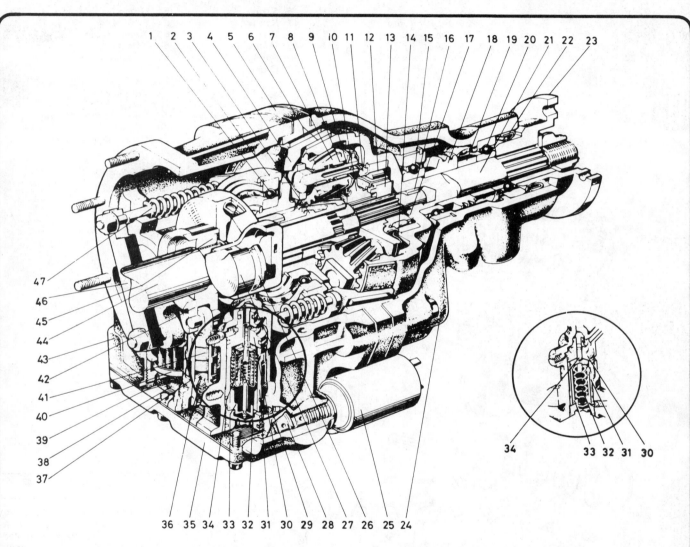

Fig. 6.16 Cutaway view of Type J overdrive. Inset shows later type pressure relief valve (Sec 16)

1 Thrust bearing	13 Uni-directional clutch	25 Solenoid	37 Pump cylinder
2 Thrust bearing retainer	14 Oil trap	26 Piston seal	38 Magnet
3 Sun wheel	15 Ball-bearing	27 Piston	39 Pick-up strainer
4 Clutch sliding member	16 Bush	28 Operating valve	40 Pressure filter
5 Brake ring	17 Thrust washer	29 Orifice nozzle	41 Pump plunger
6 Clutch member linings	18 Speedometer worm (no longer	30 Cylinder top	42 Connecting rod
7 Planet gear	applicable)	31 Cylinder	43 Front casing
8 Needle bearing	19 Spacer	32 Spring	44 Input shaft
9 Shaft	20 Ball-bearing	33 Large piston	(transmission mainshaft)
10 Planet carrier	21 Output shaft	34 Small piston	45 Cam
11 Oil thrower	22 Oil seal	35 Baseplate	46 Bridge piece
12 Uni-directional clutch	23 Coupling flange	36 Check valve for oil pump	47 Spring
rollers	24 Rear casing		

6

168

Fig. 6.17   Exploded view of Type J overdrive (Sec 16)

1 Nut	18 Circlip	36 Stud	52 Plug
2 Lockwasher	19 Circlip	37 Orifice nozzle	53 Nut
3 Bridge piece	20 Circlip	38 Seal	54 Piston
5 Breather	21 Stud	39 Plug	57 O-ring
6 Front casing	22 Piston seal	40 O-ring	58 Cylinder
7 Gasket	23 Piston	41 End piece	59 O-ring
8 Brake ring	24 Connecting rod	42 Piston	60 Plug
9 O-ring	25 Non-return ball	43 Washer	61 Spring
10 O-ring	26 Non-return valve spring	44 Spring	62 Ball
11 Seal	27 Plug	45 Retainer	63 Non-return body
12 Gasket	28 Key	46 Spring	64 O-ring
13 Solenoid	29 Resilient ring	47 Screw	65 Pump body
14 Bolt	30 Circlip	48 Screw	66 Pump plunger
15 Thrust bearing retainer	31 Cam	49 Holder	67 Washer
16 Spring	32 Piston pin	50 Spring	68 Pressure filter
17 Thrust bearing	33 Gasket	51 O-ring	69 Seal

70 Plug
71 Data plate
72 Screw
73 Planet gear and carrier
74 Sun wheel
75 Clutch sliding member
76 Pick-up strainer
77 Gasket
78 Magnet
79 Baseplate
80 Bolt
81 Resilient washer
84 Bush
85 Thrust washer
86 Oil thrower
87 Circlip
88 Uni-directional clutch
89 Stud
90 Resilient washer
91 Nut
95 Speedometer pinion*
96 O-ring*
97 Bush*
99 Bolt*
100 Retainer*
101 Oil seal*
102 Stud
106 Speedometer worm*
110 Output shaft
111 Ball bearing
112 Spacer
113 Rear casing
114 Ball bearing
115 Oil seal
116 Flange
117 Washer
118 Nut

* No longer applicable

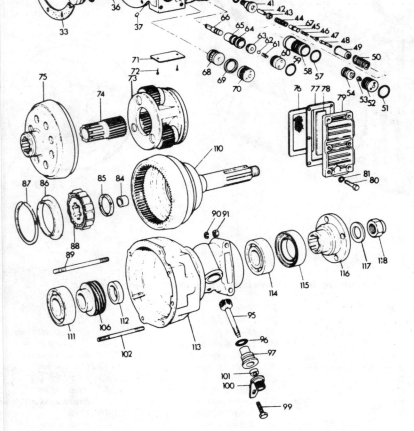

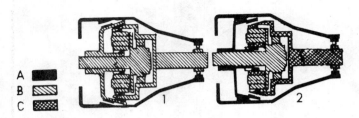

Fig. 6.18 Operating principle of overdrive (Sec 16)

1 *Direct drive*	B *Parts rotating at speed of*
2 *Overdrive*	*input shaft*
A *Non-rotating parts*	C *Parts rotating faster than*
	input shaft

pump which is driven by a cam on the mainshaft extension. A solenoid valve controls the application of oil pressure to the pistons.

The overdrive hydraulic system incorporates a pressure relief valve, a pick-up strainer and a pressure filter.

From 1986 a type P overdrive is installed on some models instead of the type J previously installed. The main difference between the two types is that the P can handle a greater torque without slipping, due to the increased dimensions of the friction linings and some other components. This renders the torque limiting system (Chapter 4, Section 13) unnecessary.

17 Overdrive — removal and installation

Note: *It is only necessary to remove the overdrive for overhaul or replacement. Work on the hydraulic system components can be carried out on the vehicle provided that scrupulous cleanliness is observed.*

1   Relieve the pressure in the overdrive by driving the vehicle with overdrive engaged, then disengaging the overdrive with the clutch pedal depressed.
2   Raise and support the vehicle.
3   Unbolt the driveshaft from the drive flange.
4   Support the transmission and remove the crossmember. Lower the rear of the transmission, being careful not to damage the distributor on the B230 engine.
5   Disconnect the wiring from the overdrive solenoid and (when applicable) the pressure switch (photo).
6   Remove the eight nuts which secure the overdrive to the transmission intermediate section. Lift off the overdrive (photos); be prepared for oil spillage. If the overdrive will not come off, use a slide hammer on the drive flange; do not lever between the transmission and overdrive casings.

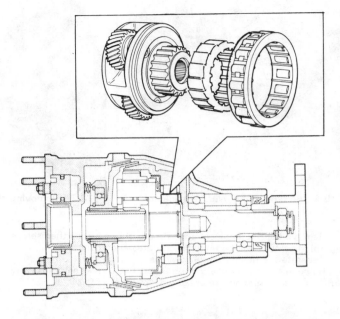

Fig. 6.19 Sectional view of Type P overdrive. Inset shows later type unidirectional clutch and gear carrier (Sec 16)

7   Install by reversing the removal operations, noting the following points:

   a) Use a new gasket between the transmission and the overdrive
   b) Tighten the nuts progressively to the specified torque
   c) Top up the transmission oil, road test the vehicle, then check the oil level again

18 Overdrive — disassembly

1   With the overdrive removed from the transmission, clean it externally and clamp it in a soft-jawed vise.
2   Disconnect the ground wire fom the solenoid. Unscrew and remove the solenoid, using a 1 inch open-end wrench with thin jaws (photo).
3   Remove the overdrive pressure switch (Turbo models only) (photo).
4   Loosen the six nuts which secure the main and rear casings (photo). Remove four of the nuts, leaving two (opposite and on long studs) which should be loosened alternately a little at a time until the spring pressure separating the casings is relieved. Note the location of the solenoid ground wire under one of the nuts. Remove the special washers.

6

17.5   Disconnecting the overdrive solenoid

17.6A   Four of the overdrive securing nuts

17.6B   Lifting off the overdrive (transmission on bench)

18.2   Removing the overdrive solenoid

18.3   Removing the pressure switch

18.4   Loosening an overdrive casing nut

5   Remove the bridge piece nuts and the bridge pieces themselves (photo). The nuts will be under spring pressure at first.

6   Separate the main and rear casings.

7   Remove the planet gears and carrier, the sun wheel with cone clutch and springs, and the brake ring (photos).

8   Clamp the main casing in the vise. Unbolt and remove the valve cover and the oil pick-up strainer (photo).

9   Remove the two pistons, using long-nosed pliers if necessary (photo).

10   Using a pin spanner or (if unavailable) a pair of circlip pliers,

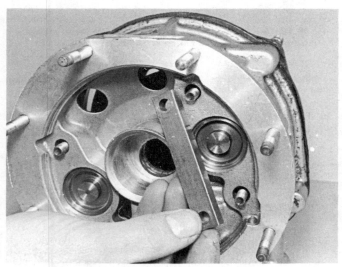

18.5   Removing a bridge piece

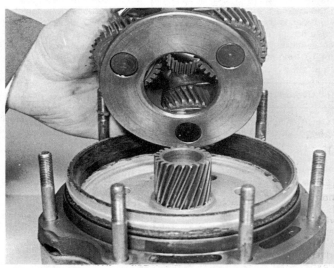

18.7A   Removing the planet gear set . . .

18.7B   . . . and the sun wheels, cone clutch and springs

18.8   Removing the overdrive valve cover

18.9   Removing a piston

18.10   Removing the pressure filter

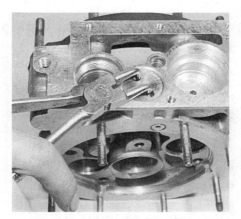

18.11A   Unscrewing the non-return valve plug

18.11B   Remove the non-return valve spring . . .

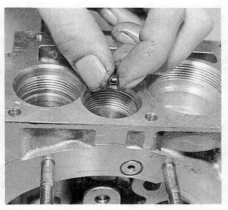

18.11C   . . . the ball . . .

18.11D   . . . and the valve seat

unscrew the pressure filter (large) plug. Remove the washer and filter (photo).

11   Similarly remove the non-return valve (small) plug. Remove the spring, ball and valve seat (photos). The sleeve and pump plunger can then be removed if desired.

12   Finally unscrew the relief valve plug. Remove the piston, springs and plunger, being careful not to lose any shims. The valve sleeve may be extracted if necessary (photos).

13   Further disassembly depends on the work to be undertaken. The thrust bearing can be removed from its cage after removing the two circlips and separating the cage from the sun wheel and cone clutch (photo).

14   The unidirectional clutch can be removed from the rear casing after removing the circlip and the oil thrower. Remove the thrust washer.

15   To remove the output shaft bearings, the flange must be removed and the shaft pressed out of the rear casing. The front bearing can then be pulled off the shaft and the rear bearing driven out of the casing. There is a spacer between the two bearings.

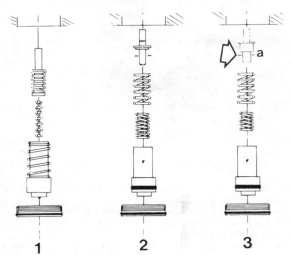

Fig. 6.20   Relief valve components. Types 1 and 2 are obsolete, type 3 is current (Sec 18)

a Shims

1   2   3

18.12A   Removing the relief valve piston . . .

18.12B   ... the small spring ...

18.12C   ... the large spring ...

18.12D   ... and the plunger with shims

18.12E   Removing the relief valve sleeve

18.13   The thrust bearing in its cage

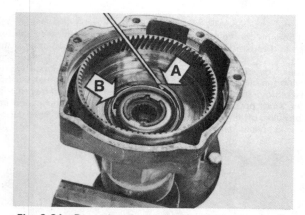

Fig. 6.21   Removing the circlip (A) which secures the unidirectional clutch (Sec 18)

B Oil thrower

Fig. 6.22   Pulling off the output shaft front bearing (Sec 18)

19 Overdrive — overhaul

1   See Section 10, paragraphs 1 and 2.
2   Flush oilways and control orifices with solvent and blow them dry.
3   Examine hydraulic system components such as pistons, valves and valve seats for wear and damage. Replace as necessary.
4   Wash the bearings and the one-way clutch in solvent. Check for roughness and visible damage.
5   Clean out the groove in front of the annulus (ring gear). Dirt will collect here as a result of centrifugal force.
6   Examine the gears for wear and damage. Do not try to diassemble the planet gear set.
7   Check the brake ring for cracks, and the clutch linings for burning or abrasion.
8   Check the condition of the clutch springs. They should be 55.5 ± 1.5 mm (2.185 ± 0.059 in) long.
9   Check the solenoid using a 12 volt battery and an ammeter. Current draw should be approximately 2A and the solenoid plunger should move in and out without sticking.
10 Install the oil pick-up strainer and the pressure filter unless they are in perfect condition.
11 All parts must be perfectly clean, and reassembly must take place under clean conditions, to avoid subsequent trouble with the hydraulic system.

20.7 Installing the oil pump sleeve and plunger

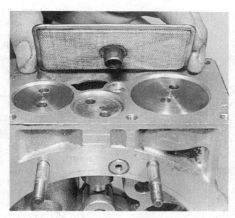

20.11 Installing the oil pick-up strainer

20.13 Installing a casing gasket

20.16 Installing a casing stud nylon washer

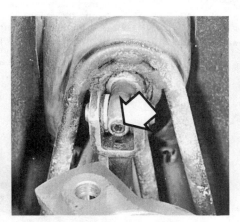

21.2 Allen screw (arrowed) securing gear lever pin

21.3 Circlip (arrowed) at base of gear lever on later models

20 Overdrive — reassembly

1 Press the output shaft bearings into the rear casing and onto the shaft. Do not forget the spacer. Press the output shaft into the casing and install a new flange oil seal.

2 Install the thrust washer, the one-way clutch inner race and the roller cage. Install the oil thrower and circlip, then check the operation of the one-way clutch.

3 Install the drive flange, using locking compound on the splines. Do not contaminate the oil seal. Counterhold the flange and tighten the nut to the specified torque.

4 Install the planet gear set to the output shaft, lining up the splines.

5 Install the thrust bearing to its cage. Assemble the cage, sun wheel and cone clutch. Make sure the clutch linings are clean and dry, then lubricate them with ATF.

6 Install the relief valve components and secure them with the plug, using a new O-ring.

7 Install the oil pump sleeve and plunger, lubricating them with ATF (photo). The groove and bevel on the sleeve must align with the pressure filter recess, and the chamfer on the plunger ring must face forwards.

8 Install the non-return valve seat and ball. Install the spring into the plug and install the plug, using a new O-ring.

9 Install the pressure filter, washer and plug.

10 Tighten all the plugs with a peg wrench.

11 Install the oil pick-up strainer, a new cover gasket and the valve cover (photo). Tighten the cover bolts.

12 Lubricate the two pistons and insert them into their bores. Make sure they are facing the right direction.

13 Install the brake ring to the rear casing, using a new gasket. Install another new gasket on the main casing side of the brake ring (photo).

14 Install the sun wheel/cone clutch assembly. Install the clutch springs over the bearing cage studs.

15 Install the main and rear casings together, being careful not to displace the gasket. Install the piston bridge pieces and the nuts, tightening the nuts against spring pressure.

16 Install the main-to-rear casing nuts, using new nylon washers (photo). Remember the solenoid earth tag. Tighten the nuts progressively to the specified torque, then recheck the tightness of the bridge piece nuts.

17 Install and tighten the solenoid. Also install the pressure switch, when applicable.

21 Gear lever — removal and installation

1 Raise and support the vehicle for access to the underside of the gear lever.

2 Remove the Allen screw which secures the pin at the end of the gear lever (photo). Press out the pin from the gear lever and the selector rod.

3 On 1986 and later models, remove the large circlip from the base of the gear lever (photo).

4 Inside the vehicle, remove the console section from around the gear lever.

5 Remove the outer gaiter. Remove the four screws which secure the inner gaiter clamp plate. Remove the clamp plate, noting which way it is positioned, and peel the inner gaiter up the gear lever.

6 On pre-1986 models, remove the large circlip from the base of the gear lever (photo).

7 Pull the gear lever upwards and withdraw it. Disconnect the overdrive switch wires (when applicable). Do not disturb the reverse detent plate bolts.

6

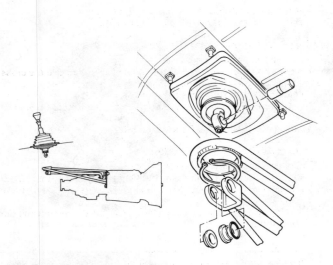

Fig. 6.23   Base fixings of later type gear lever (Sec 21)

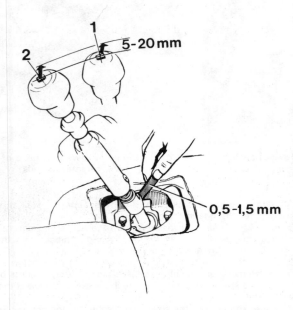

Fig. 6.24   Gear lever adjustment in 1st or 2nd gear positions (1 and 2) (Sec 21)

8   Install by reversing the removal operations. Check the clearance between the reverse detent plate and finger with 1st gear engaged: it should be between 0.5 and 1.5 mm (0.02 to 0.06 in). Adjust if necessary by loosening the detent plate bolts. When adjustment is correct, side-to-side play of the gear lever knob in 1st or 2nd gear should be 5 to 20 mm (0.2 to 0.8 in).

22   Gear lever pullrod — replacement

1   The gear lever pullrod transmits the motion from the collar under the gear knob to the interlock sleeve at the base of the gear lever. If it breaks, it will not be possible to engage reverse gear. Proceed as follows.

2   On models with overdrive, remove the trim panel from the right-hand side of the center console. Separate the overdrive wiring connector there and tie a piece of string to the wire leading to the gear lever.

3   On all models, remove the gear lever boot. Drive out the roll pin which secures the lever to the stub. Lift off the gear lever, at the same time pulling the overdrive wire and string through, when applicable. Untie the string.

4   Remove the overdrive switch, when applicable. Remove the gear lever knob by gripping the lever in a soft-jawed vise and tapping the knob with a soft hammer and an open-ended wrench (photo). The knob is glued onto splines and may not come off undamaged. Clean off the old glue.

5   Remove the old pullrod. It may be plastic or metal. The metal rod is removed by loosening the grub screw at the top of the lever, then

21.6   Removing the gear lever circlip — earlier models

22.4   Removing the gear lever knob

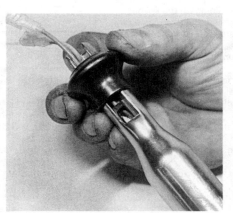

22.5A   Lift up the collar . . .

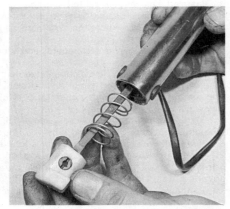

22.5B   . . . and remove the pullrod with the spring and interlock sleeve

withdrawing the pullrod, spring and interlock sleeve downwards. To remove the plastic rod, release the catch at the base and (on overdrive models) lift up the collar slightly to free the top of the rod (photos).

6 Soak the new pullrod in water for one hour before installing it. Install the new rod from below on overdrive models, being careful not to displace the rubber bushes and wiring. Make sure it engages with the collar. On models without overdrive, install the pullrod to the collar and then insert them both from above. On all models, position the pullrod bottom lug to receive the interlock sleeve.

7 Install the spring and interlock sleeve, engaging the pullrod lug in the catch on the sleeve.

8 Install the gear lever over the splines, using a little glue if wished. Do not use powerful glue, or there will be a problem with any subsequent removal.

9 Install the gear lever to the stub and secure it with the roll pin. On overdrive models, reattach the string to the wiring and draw the wire back to the center console. Reconnect the wires and install the trim panel.

10 Check the selection of all gears, including reverse. If adjustment is necessary, see Section 21, paragraph 8.

11 When adjustment is satisfactory, install the gear lever boot, the overdrive switch and any other items that were removed.

23 Overdrive switches — removal and installation

Control switch

1 Pry off the trim plate from the top of the gear lever knob (photo).

2 Pry out the switch and disconnect it (photos).

3 Install by reversing the removal operations.

Inhibitor (transmission) switch

4 Raise and support the vehicle.

5 Except on V6 models, support the transmission, remove the crossmember and loosen the exhaust flanged joint. Lower the rear of the transmission slightly for access to the top cover.

6 Clean around the switch, disconnect the wires and unscrew it (photos).

7 Install by reversing the removal operations.

Pressure switch (Turbo only)

8 Raise and support the vehicle.

9 The switch is located in front of the overdrive solenoid. Clean around the switch, disconnect the wiring and unscrew it. Be prepared for oil spillage.

10 Install by reversing the removal operations. Top up the transmission oil if necessary.

24 Reversing light switch — removal and installation

1 Gain access to the transmission top cover (Section 23, paragraphs 4 and 5).

2 Clean around the switch, disconnect the wires and unscrew it (photo).

3 Install by reversing the removal operations.

23.1 Removing the gear lever knob trim plate

23.2A Pry out the overdrive switch . . .

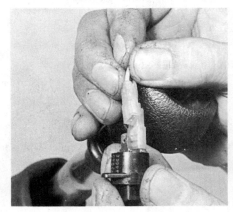

23.2B . . . and disconnect it

23.6A Disconnect the inhibitor switch . . .

23.6B . . . and unscrew it from the cover

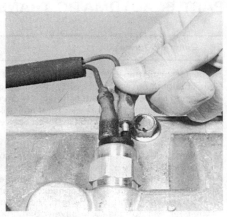

24.2 Disconnecting the reversing light switch

25 Troubleshooting — manual transmission and overdrive

Note: *It is not necessarily a good idea to disassemble the transmission in an attempt to correct a minor fault. A transmission which is noisy, or on which the synchro can be beaten by a quick change, may last for a long time in this state. Part-by-part replacement of components can actually increase noise by presenting different wear surfaces to each other*

Symptom	Reason(s)
Excessive noise	Oil level low or incorrect grade Gear lever boot torn or out of place Worn bearings or shafts Worn gear teeth
Difficult engagement of gears	Clutch problem Gear lever adjustment incorrect Synchro units worn or damaged Selector components worn or damaged
Jumps out of gear	Synchro units worn or damaged Selector components worn
Overdrive will not engage	Oil level low Solenoid or wiring defective Gear lever switch defective Inhibitor switch defective Relay defective Oil pump non-return valve stuck open Oil filter blocked
Overdrive will not release. (**Caution:** *Do not reverse the vehicle or damage will result)*	Control valve sticking Solenoid sticking Electrical fault (solenoid permanently energized) Cone clutch stuck (tap brake ring to release) Relief valve stuck
Overdrive slips when engaging	Oil level low Oil filter blocked Oil pump non-return valve leaking Relief valve piston sticking Clutch linings worn or glazed Torque limiter system malfunction (see Chapter 4)
Overdrive noisy in direct drive, quiet in overdrive	Thrust (cone clutch) bearing worn
Overdrive noisy except during engagement	Output shaft bearings worn

PART B: AUTOMATIC TRANSMISSION

26 General information

The automatic transmission has four forward speeds and one reverse. Gear changing between forward speeds is normally fully automatic, responding to speed and load, although the driver can prevent the selection of higher ratios. On the AW71 transmission the highest (4th) gear is provided by an overdrive unit installed between the torque converter and the rest of the transmission. The ZF4HP transmission is an integrated four-speed unit.

Power is taken from the engine to the transmission by a torque converter. This is a type of fluid coupling which under certain conditions has a torque multiplying effect. On later models the torque converter is mechanically locked at high speeds in 3rd and 4th gear, eliminating losses due to slip and improving fuel economy.

The gear selector has six or seven positions: P, R, N, D, 3 (on some models), 2 and 1. The engine can only be started in positions P and N. In position P the transmission is mechanically locked: this position must

only be engaged when the vehicle is stationary. In position R reverse is engaged, in N neutral. in position D gear changing is automatic throughout the range; positions 3, 2 and 1 prevent the selection of higher ratios when this is desired. These lower positions must not be selected at speeds so high as to cause engine overrevving.

When position 3 is missing from the selector, a button on the side of the selector knob serves to inhibit the engagement of 4th (overdrive) gear. A dashboard warning light reminds the driver when this has been done.

A kickdown mode causes the transmission to shift down a gear (subject to engine speed) when the throttle is fully depressed. This is useful when extra acceleration is required. Kickdown is controlled by a cable linkage from the throttle cable drum.

The transmission fluid is cooled by a heat exchanger built into one of the radiator side tanks, and (on some models) by an auxiliary cooler mounted in front of the radiator. See also Chapter 2.

The automatic transmission is a complex unit, but if it is not abused it is reliable and long-lasting. Repair or overhaul operations are beyond the scope of many dealers, let alone the home mechanic; specialist advice should be sought if problems arise which cannot be solved by the procedures given in this Chapter.

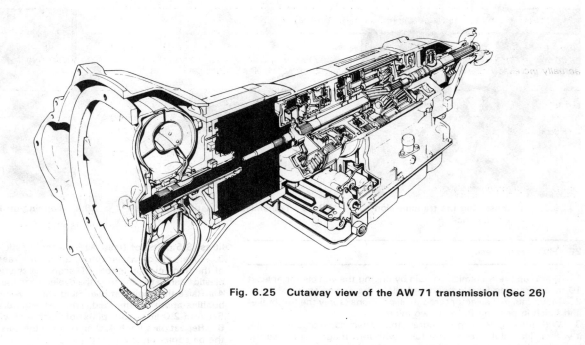

Fig. 6.25   Cutaway view of the AW 71 transmission (Sec 26)

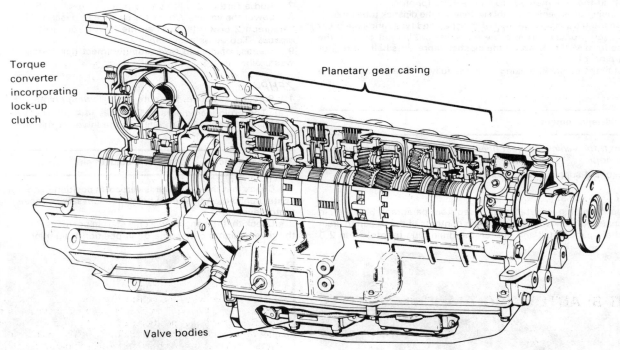

Torque converter incorporating lock-up clutch

Planetary gear casing

Valve bodies

Fig. 6.26   Cutaway view of the ZF 4HP transmission (Sec 26)

27   Maintenance and inspection

1   Every 12,000 miles or annually, or at the first sign of any malfunction, check the transmission fluid level (Section 28). Investigate the cause of persistent fluid loss.

2   At the same intervals check the adjustment of the selector mechanism (Section 30) and the kickdown cable (Section 31).

3   Every 24,000 miles or two years replace the transmission fluid as described in Section 29.

4   If contamination of the fluid occurs, or the transmission overheats and the fluid smells burnt, flush the cooling system by following the procedure in Section 29; also flush the auxiliary cooler (when installed) using a hand pump. The auxiliary cooler is thermostatically controlled and will not be flushed during the fluid replacement procedure.

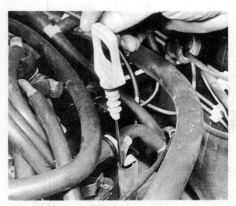

28.3A Withdrawing the transmission dipstick

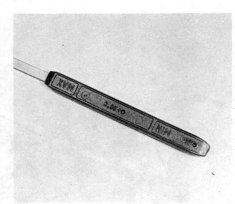

28.3B Transmission dipstick markings

28.4 Topping-up the transmission fluid

28 Fluid level check

1   Warm up the transmission fluid by driving the vehicle for at least 10 miles. Park on level ground and allow the engine to idle.
2   Move the gear selector through all positions (apply the footbrake) and finish in position P. Wait two minutes.
3   With the engine iding, withdraw the transmission dipstick. Wipe it with a clean cloth, re-insert it fully, withdraw it again and read the level. Read the side marked HOT or +90ºC (photos).
4   If topping-up is necessary, this is done via the dipstick tube (photo). Only use fresh transmission fluid of the specified type, and take great care not to introduce dirt into the transmission. Do not overfill: the distance from MIN to MAX on the dipstick represents half a litre (not quite a pint) of fluid.
5   Install the dipstick, making sure it is fully inserted, and stop the engine.

29 Fluid replacement

Caution: *If the vehicle has just been run, the transmission fluid may be very hot.*

1   Raise and support the vehicle.

AW71

2   If no drain plug is installed, proceed from paragraph 3. If a drain plug is installed, remove it and allow the contents of the oil pan to drain into a drain pan. Install and tighten the drain plug (photo). Add 2.0

litres (3.5 pints) of fresh ATF via the dipstick tube.
3   Clean the oil cooler return union (the rearmost one) on the side of the transmission (photo). Disconnect the union and attach a clear plastic hose to the line from the cooler. Lead the hose into the drain pan.
4   Raise the engine at idle. Fluid will flow into the drain pan. When bubbles appear in the fluid, stop the engine.
5   Add 2.0 litres (3.5 pints) of fresh ATF via the dipstick tube.
6   Repeat paragraph 4, then remove the plastic hose and reconnect the oil cooler union.
7   Add a further 2.0 litres (3.5 pints) of fresh ATF.
8   Lower the vehicle. Check the oil level as described in Section 28, paragraph 2 onwards, but use the 'COLD' or ' +40°C' side of the dipstick. Top up as necessary.
9   Dispose of the old fluid properly (most gas stations will accept waste oil).

ZFHP422

10 Proceed as above, but note the following points:
   a) Top up in increments of 2.5 litres (4.4 pints)
   b) The oil cooler return union is the lower of the two

30 Gear selector — check and adjustment

1   Check that the gear lever is vertical in position P (not touching the center console). Adjust from below if necessary by loosening the actuator lever nut.
2   Check that the engine will only start in positions P and N, and that the reverse lights only come on in position R (ignition on).

29.2 Transmission drain plug

29.3 Oil cooler return union (arrowed)

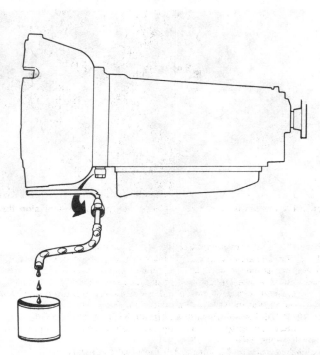

Fig. 6.27 Oil cooler return union disconnected from ZF
transmission for fluid changing (Sec 29)

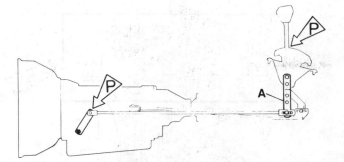

Fig. 6.28 Automatic transmission selector linkage in
position P (Sec 30)

A Actuator lever

30.4 Gear selector reaction lever nut (arrowed, under cable)

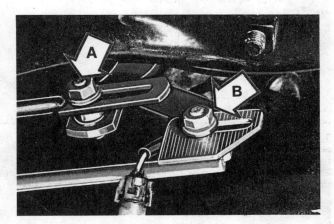

Fig. 6.29 Automatic transmission selector linkage
adjustment nuts (Sec 30)

A Actuator lever   B Reaction lever

31.2 Checking kickdown cable adjustment at full throttle

3   Check that the free play from D to N is the same as, or less than,
the play from 2 to 1 (AW71) or from 3 to 2 (ZFHP422).
4   If there is insufficient play in D, loosen the reaction lever nut
(beneath the vehicle) and move the lever approximately 2 mm (0.08
in) rearwards (photo).
5   If there is insufficient play in 3 or 2, loosen the nut and move the
lever approximately 3 mm (0.12 in) forwards.
6   Tighten the nut and recheck the adjustment.

31 Kickdown cable — adjustment

1   With the throttle linkage in the idle position, the distance from the
crimped stop on the kickdown cable to the adjuster sleeve should be
0.25 to 1.0 mm (0.01 to 0.04 in). The cable should be taut.

2   Have an assistant depress the throttle pedal fully. Measure the
distance from the stop to the adjuster again (photo). It should be 50.4
to 52.6 mm (1.99 to 2.07 in). From this position it should be possible
to pull the cable out by 2 mm (0.08 in).

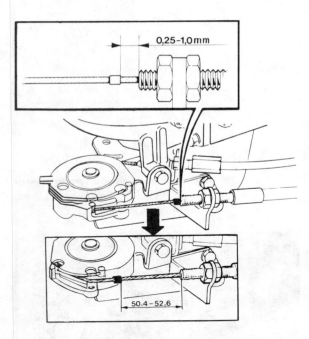

Fig. 6.30 Kickdown cable adjustment at idle (inset, top)
and at full throttle (below) (Sec 31)

3   Adjust if necessary by loosening the locknuts, turning the adjuster
sleeve and tightening the locknuts.
4   If correct adjustment cannot be achieved, either the throttle linkage
adjustment is incorrect (Chapter 3) or the cable crimped stop is incorrectly positioned (Section 32).

32   Kickdown cable — replacement

1   Loosen the cable adjuster at the throttle end. Disconnect the cable
from the drum and the cable casing from the bracket (photo).
2   Raise and support the vehicle. Drain the transmission oil pan by
removing the drain plug (where applicable) and make the dipstick/filler
tube nut (photo). **Caution:** *The fluid may be very hot.*
3   Clean the oil pan, then unbolt and remove it. Be prepared for fluid
spillage. Remove the gasket.
4   Clean around the cable casing where it enters the transmission.
Unhook the cable from the cam, using a screwdriver to turn the cam.
Cut the cable below the stop at the throttle end if there is not enough
slack. Release the cable casing and remove the cable.
5   Install the new cable to the transmission, attaching it to the cam
and securing the casing to the transmission case. Use a new O-ring
and grease the cable casing where it enters the transmission.
6   Attach the cable casing at the throttle end. Pull the cable until light
resistance is felt, and in this position crimp the inner stop 0.25 to 1.0
mm (0.01 to 0.04 in) from the adjuster.
7   Reconnect the cable to the throttle drum. Adjust the cable as
described in Section 31.
8   Clean the inside of the oil pan, including the magnets when present.
9   Install the oil pan, using a new gasket. Reconnect the dipstick/filler
tube.
10 Top up the transmission fluid.
11 Lower the vehicle. Road test the transmission, then recheck the
fluid level and inspect the oil pan for leaks.

33   Kickdown marker — adjustment

Early models (marker in floor)

1   Release the retainer and screw the marker in towards the floor as
far as possible.

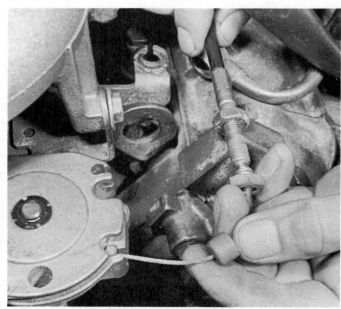

32.1   Disconnecting the kickdown cable at the throttle end

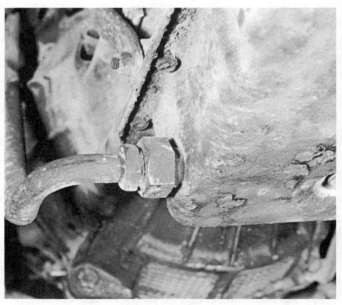

32.2   Transmission dipstick/filler tube nut

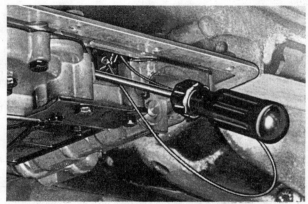

Fig. 6.31   Removing the kickdown cable — AW
transmission (Sec 32)

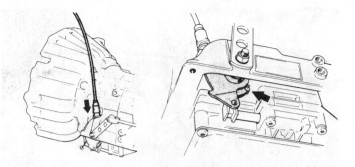

Fig. 6.32   Kickdown cable attachments — ZF transmission
(Sec 32)

2   Depress the throttle pedal by hand to the start of the kickdown position (beginning of resistance). Hold the pedal in this position and screw the marker upwards to meet it.
3   Install the retainer.

Later models (marker in pedal)

4   Screw the marker into the pedal as far as possible.
5   Depress the throttle pedal by hand to the start of the kickdown position. Hold the pedal in this position and screw the marker down to meet the floor.

34   Starter inhibitor/reversing light switch — removal and installation

1   Remove the ashtray and the center console panel in front of the selector.

Models up to 1984

2   Remove the two screws which secure the left-hand half of the selector cover — one screw at each end of the brush (photo). Lift off the half of the cover.
3   Remove the switch securing screws, disconnect the electical connector and remove it (photo).
4   If a new switch is being installed, transfer the lens to it.
5   Install by reversing the removal operations. Make sure that the stud on the lever enters the slot in the switch.

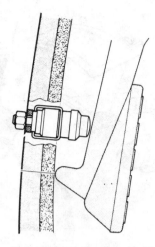

Fig. 6.33   Kickdown marker in floor (Sec 33)

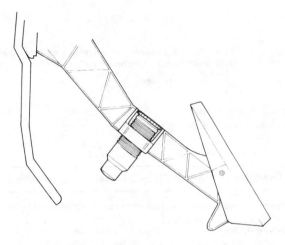

Fig. 6.34   Kickdown marker in throttle pedal (Sec 33)

6

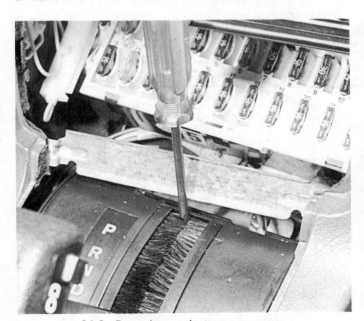

34.2   Removing a selector cover screw

34.3   Two screws (arrowed) which secure the starter inhibitor switch

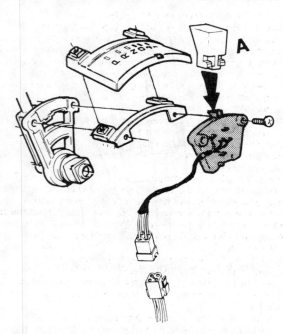

35.1   Removing the overdrive switch

Fig. 6.35   Later type automatic transmission selector cover
and associated components (Sec 34)

A Lens

Models from 1985

6   Proceed as above, but note the different selector cover installings (Fig. 6.35).

35 Overdrive switch (AW71) — removal and installation

1   Pry the switch out of the side of the selector lever and disconnect it (photo).
2   Install by reversing the removal operations.

36 Transmission oil seals — replacement

Note: *It is important not to allow dirt to enter the transmission when working on it.*

Drive flange

1   Proceed as described in Section 3. The flange central nut may be secured by a lockwasher.

Input shaft/torque converter

2   Remove the transmission (Section 37).
3   Lift the torque converter out of its housing. Be careful, it is full of fluid.
4   Pull or lever out the old seal. Clean the seat and inspect the seal rubbing surface on the torque converter.
5   Lubricate the new seal with ATF and install it, lips inwards. Seat it with a piece of tube.
6   Install the torque converter and the transmission.

Selector shaft

7   Remove the selector arm nut and pull the arm off the shaft (photo).
8   Pry the seal out with a small screwdriver. Clean the seat.
9   Grease the new seal and install it, lips inwards. Seat the seal with a tube or socket.
10   Install the selector arm and tighten the nut.

All seals

11   Check the transmission fluid level on completion.

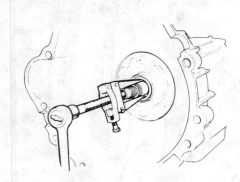

Fig. 6.36   Pulling out the input shaft oil seal (Sec 36)

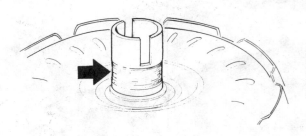

Fig. 6.37   Inspect the seal rubbing surface (arrowed) on
the torque converter (Sec 36)

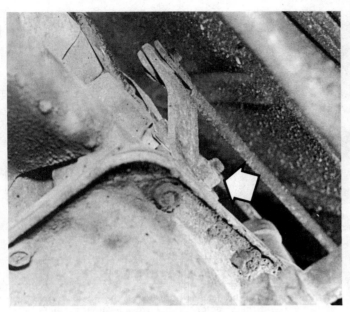

36.7   Remove the selector arm nut (arrowed)

2   Disconnect the battery negative cable.
3   Disconnect the kickdown cable at the throttle end.
4   Raise and support the vehicle. Drain the transmission fluid by removing the dipstick/filler tube nut. **Caution:** *The fluid may be very hot.*
5   Disconnect the selector linkage and (when applicable) the overdrive wiring connector from the side of the transmission.
6   Remove the starter motor (Chapter 12). On B28 engines, also remove the other starter motor aperture blanking plate.
7   Remove the dipstick/filler tube.
8   Disconnect the fluid cooler unions at the transmission. Be prepared for spillage. Cap the open unions to keep dirt out.
9   Disconnect the exhaust downpipe and unbolt the exhaust support bracket from the transmission crossmember (photo). Support the exhaust system if necessary.
10   Unbolt the driveshaft flange.
11   If equipped, remove the cover plate from the bottom of the torque converter housing. Also remove the cooling grilles (photo).
12   Jam the driveplate and remove the bolts which hold the torque converter to the driveplate (photo). Turn the crankshaft to bring the bolts into view. It is possible to work through the starter motor aperture on some models.
13   Support the transmission, preferably with a properly designed cradle. Unbolt and remove the transmission crossmember.
14   Lower the transmission until it takes up a stable position. On the B230 engine, make sure that the distributor is not crushed against the firewall .
15   Remove the converter housing-to-engine nuts and bolts.
16   With the aid of an assistant, pull the transmission off the engine, at the same time levering the torque converter away from the driveplate. Keep the transmission tilted rearwards and lower it from the vehicle. It is heavy.
17   Install by reversing the removal operations, noting the following points:
   a)   Put a thin coat of grease on the torque converter hub
   b)   Tighten the torque converter-to-driveplate bolts progressively to the specified torque

37   Automatic transmission — removal and installation

Note: *If the transmission is being removed for repair, check first that the repairer does not need to test it in the vehicle.*
1   Select P (AW71) or N (ZF).

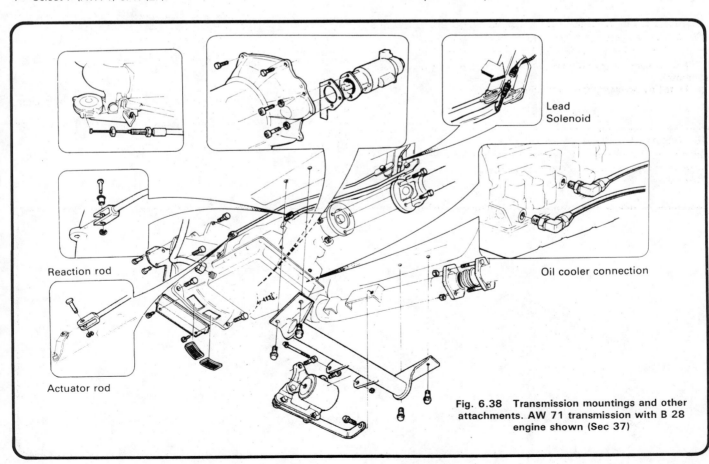

Reaction rod

Actuator rod

Lead Solenoid

Oil cooler connection

Fig. 6.38   Transmission mountings and other attachments. AW 71 transmission with B 28 engine shown (Sec 37)

6

37.9   **Exhaust bracket and transmission crossmember**

37.11   **Removing a torque converter housing grille**

37.12   **Removing a torque converter-to-driveplate bolt**

c) Do not fully tighten the dipstick tube nut until the tube bracket has been secured

d) Adjust the selector mechanism (Section 30) and the kickdown cable (Section 31)

e) Refill the transmission with fluid. If a new transmission has been installed, flush the oil cooler(s) — see Section 29, paragraph 3 onwards, and Section 27, paragraph 4

38   Troubleshooting — automatic transmission

In the event of a fault, check the fluid level, the kickdown cable adjustment and the selector mechanism adjustment. Faults which persist when these three items are correct should be referred to a Volvo dealer or transmission specialist.

Chapter 7 Driveshaft

Contents

7

Specifications

General

Shaft type..................................... Tubular, two-section, with center support bearing
Number of universal joints....................... Two or three (plus rubber coupling on some models)

1 General information

A two-section tubular driveshaft is utilized. Two or three universal joints are used, and on some models a rubber coupling is utilized between the transmission output flange and the driveshaft flange. A center bearing supports the shaft at the junction of the two sections.

The universal joints are secured with circlips instead of by staking, which makes them relatively easy to overhaul. .

2 Maintenance and inspection

1   Every 12,000 miles or annually, or if unusual noises or vibrations are noticed, inspect the driveshaft as follows.
2   Raise the vehicle and support it securely on jackstands.

3   Check the flange bolts and the center bearing bracket bolts for tightness.
4   Visually check the condition of the rubber coupling, if installed. Replace it if it is damaged (Section 3).
5   Check for play in the universal joints and center bearing by attempting to lift, shake and twist the sections of the shaft relative to each other and to the flanges. Repair or replace as necessary (Section 5 or 6).
6   Check that the center bearing rubber boot is intact. To replace it, the two halves of the shaft must be separated (Section 6).
7   No routine lubrication is required. Occasional oiling of the universal joint circlips is recommended to stop them rusting solid.
8   None of the above checks will detect a seized universal joint, which can cause heavy vibration — the shaft must be removed, or the flanges separated, so that the freedom of movement of the joint may be tested.
9   An out-of-balance or out-of-true shaft can also cause vibration, but these conditions are unlikely to arise spontaneously. Consult a Volvo dealer or a repair shop.

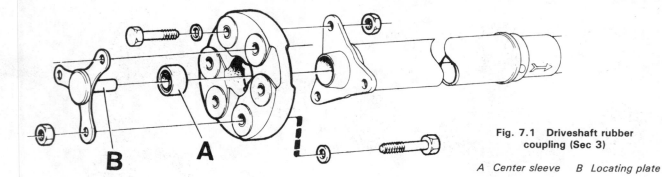

Fig. 7.1 Driveshaft rubber coupling (Sec 3)

A Center sleeve   B Locating plate

3 Rubber coupling — removal and installation

1   Raise the vehicle and support it securely on jackstands.
2   Make alignment marks between the shaft and the transmission output flange.
3   Remove the six nuts and bolts which hold the flanges to the coupling (photo). (It may not be possible actually to remove the forward-facing bolts, which will stay on the flange).
4   Pull the shaft rearwards and lower the front section. Remove the rubber coupling, the center sleeve and the locating plate (photo).
5   Install by reversing the removal operations, observing the alignment marks. Apply a little anti-seize compound to the locating plate pin.

4 Driveshaft — removal and installation

1   Raise the vehicle and support it securely on jackstands.
2   Make alignment marks between the shaft flanges and the transmission and axle flanges, and between the two sections of the shaft.

3   Remove all the flange nuts and bolts except one at each end (photo). Leave these last ones loose.
4   Have an assistant support the shaft. Remove the bolts which secure the center bearing carrier (photo).
5   With the aid of the assistant, remove the remaining flange bolts. Remove the shaft and bearing from under the vehicle. Recover the rubber coupling (if equipped).
6   In the absence of an assistant, the shaft may be removed in two sections (rear section first). The two sections simply pull apart. Release the rubber boot from the rear of the center bearing carrier as this is done (photo).
7   Install by reversing the removal operations, observing the flange alignment marks. Do not tighten the bearing carrier bolts until the flange bolts have been tightened; the carrier mountings are slotted to allow the bearing to take up an unstrained position.

5 Universal joints — replacement

1   The joints may need to be replaced because of excess play; a joint which is stiff will cause vibration and must also be replaced.

3.3 Rubber coupling nuts and bolts

3.4 Rubber coupling locating plate

4.3 Driveshaft rear flange — note alignment marks (arrowed)

4.4 Driveshaft center bearing bolts

4.6 Withdrawing the rear section from the center bearing

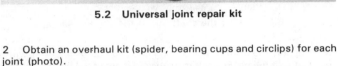

5.2   Universal joint repair kit

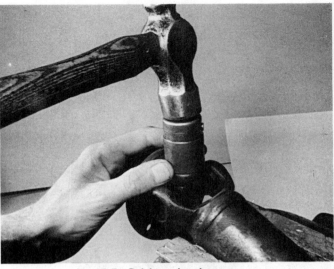

5.5   Raising a bearing cup

2   Obtain an overhaul kit (spider, bearing cups and circlips) for each joint (photo).

3   Clean the joint and apply penetrating oil or releasing fluid to the circlips.

4   Remove the circlips. If they are stuck, tap them with a punch.

5   Rest the yoke of the joint on the open jaws of a vise. Tap the flange with a plastic or copper hammer, or place a piece of tube over the bearing cup and strike that, until the cup protrudes a little way (photo). Do not hit too hard, or clamp the shaft too firmly in the vise — if it is distorted it will be scrap.

6   Grasp the bearing cup with self-locking pliers and withdraw it (photo). Recover any loose rollers.

7   Repeat this process until the spider can be removed from the yoke and all the bearing cups have been removed.

8   Clean the cup seats in the shaft and flange.

9   Carefully remove the cups from the new spider. Check that each cup contains all of its rollers and that the seals are securely attached. The roller should already be packed with grease. If not, pack them with wheel bearing or chassis grease.

10   Install the spider in the yoke. Install a cup on the spider, making sure that the rollers are not displaced (photo).

11   Tap the cup lightly to seat it, then press it in using the vise and a tube or socket (photo). The cup should be recessed by 3 to 4 mm (0.12 to 0.16 in).

5.6   Removing a bearing cup

7

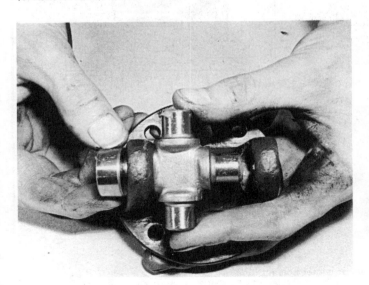

5.10   Installing a cup to the spider

5.11   Pressing in the cup

5.12   Installing a circlip

6.2   Driving the shaft out of the center bearing

12 Install the circlip to secure the cup (photo).
13 Similarly install and secure the opposite cup, then assemble the rest of the joint in the same way.
14 Check the joint for freedom of movement. If it is stiff, tap it lightly with a plastic or copper hammer.
15 If vibration persists after overhauling the joints, it may be that the shaft needs to be balanced. This must be done by a specialist.

6 Center bearing — replacement

Note: *Several different patterns of center bearing and rubber boot have been used (Figs. 7.2 and 7.3). If buying new components in advance, be careful to obtain the correct ones.*
1   Remove the driveshaft (Section 4) and separate the two sections.

2   Support the front of the bearing and cage on V-blocks or with a piece of split tubing. Press or drive the shaft out of the bearing (photo). Recover the protective rings from both sides of the bearing.
3   If the bearing cage is undamaged, the old bearing can be driven out and a new one pressed in. Otherwise, replace the bearing and cage complete.
4   Install a new front protective ring to the shaft and tap it into place with a wooden or plastic mallet.
5   Install the new bearing and cage. Seat them with a piece of tube pressing on the bearing inner race.
6   Install the rear protective ring, keeping it square as it is tapped into place.
7   Check that the bearing spins freely, then reassemble the two sections of the shaft, observing the previously made alignment marks. Use a new rubber boot and/or retaining rings if necessary.
8   Install the shaft to the vehicle.

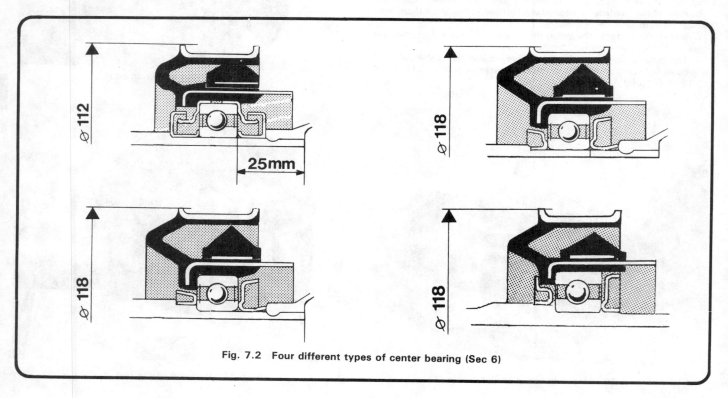

Fig. 7.2   Four different types of center bearing (Sec 6)

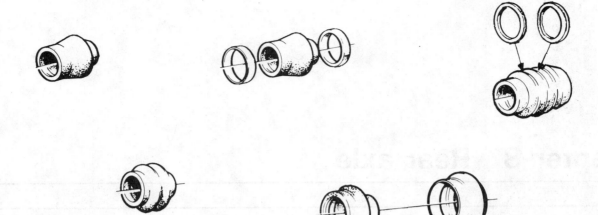

Fig. 7.3 Five different types of rubber boot (Sec 6)

7 Troubleshooting — driveshaft

Symptom	Reason(s)
Noise when accelerating from a standstill	Universal joint worn or seized Flange bolts loose Splined coupling worn Rubber coupling worn Center bearing worn
Noise or vibration when running	Universal joint worn or seized Center bearing worn Shaft distorted or out of balance

7

Chapter 8 Rear axle

Contents

Specifications

General
Axle type.. Hypoid final drive gears; limited slip differential on some models
Ratio (depending on model and year)................. 3.31, 3.54, 3.73 or 3.91:1

Lubrication
Lubricant type....................................... See *Recommended lubricants and fluids*
Lubricant capacity.................................. Approximately 1.7 qts

Pinion bearing preload
Turning torque at pinion (wheels free):
  New bearing..................................... 2.5 to 3.5 Nm (1.8 to 2.6 Ft-lbs)
  Used bearing.................................... 1.5 to 2.5 Nm (1.1 to 1.8 Ft-lbs)

Torque specifications

	Nm	Ft-lbs
Pinion flange nut:		
Solid spacer............................	200 to 250	148 to 185
Collapsible spacer (see text)...........	180 to 280	133 to 207
Multi-link differential...................	120 to 280	89 to 207
Speedometer sensor locknut...............	30 to 50	22 to 37
Axleshaft retaining plate bolts.............	40	30
Trailing arm bracket bolts.................	45	33
Trailing arm bracket nuts.................	85	63
Trailing arm to axle.....................	45	33
Panhard rod..........................	85	63
Shock absorber lower mountings...........	85	63
Torque rods...........................	140	103

---

1 General information

Pre-1988 models use a conventional rear axle design. A rigid casing encloses the final drive unit and two axleshafts. The casing is located by two torque rods bolted to a central subframe, by the two trailing arms and the Panhard rod.

Beginning in 1988, four-door 760 models employ an independent rear suspension design. With this "Multi-link" rear suspension, each rear wheel is free to move up and down without affecting the other.

Power is transmitted to the rear wheels through two driveaxles, each of which is equipped with two constant velocity joints. The differential is mounted to a subframe-type assembly which is bolted to the underside of the vehicle. The outer ends of the driveaxles are splined to the hubs, which run in bearings and are supported by the wheel bearing housings. The components that suspend the housings will be covered in Chapter 10.

The final drive unit is mounted centrally in the casing (or subframe on Multi-link rear ends). It consists of the differential unit, the crownwheel and pinion. Drive from the driveshaft is transmitted to the crownwheel by the pinion. The differential unit is bolted to the crownwheel and transmits the drive to the axleshafts or driveaxles. The differential gears and pinions allow the axleshafts to turn at different speeds when necessary, for example when cornering.

On some models the differential is of the limited slip type. Here the difference in speed between the two axles is limited by means of friction clutches. This improves traction on slippery surfaces.

Work on the rear axle should be limited to the operations described in this Chapter. If overhaul of the final drive unit is necessary, consult a Volvo dealer or other specialist.

---

2 Maintenance and inspection

1 Every 12 000 miles or annually, or if noise or leakage is evident, check the oil level as described in Section 3. Rectify any leakage.
2 Routine oil changing is not specified by the makers, although a drain plug is provided.

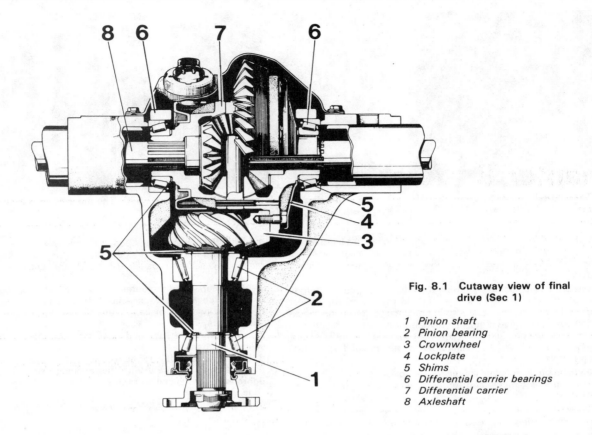

Fig. 8.1 Cutaway view of final
drive (Sec 1)

1 *Pinion shaft*
2 *Pinion bearing*
3 *Crownwheel*
4 *Lockplate*
5 *Shims*
6 *Differential carrier bearings*
7 *Differential carrier*
8 *Axleshaft*

3 Oil level — check

1 Park the vehicle on level ground. Raise the vehicle if necessary
to improve access to the rear axle, but keep it level.
2 Wipe the area around the filler/level plug and unscrew it (photo).
3 Oil should be up to the bottom of the plug hole. Check if necessary
by inserting an angled piece of wire to serve as a dipstick.
4 Top up if necessary, using fresh gear oil of the specified type,
via the plug hole (photo). Do not overfill: allow any excess to drip out
of the hole.
5 Install and tighten the plug.

4 Pinion oil seal — replacement

Caution: *If the axle has a collapsible spacer in front of the pinion bearing (denoted by the letter S preceding the serial number), care must*

be taken not to overtighten the pinion flange nut. If the nut is overtightened, it may be necessary to take the axle to a Volvo dealer for
a new spacer to be installed.

1 Raise and support the rear of the vehicle on jackstands.
2 Unbolt the driveshaft flange from the pinion flange. Make alignment marks between the flanges.
3 Paint or scribe alignment marks between the pinion flange and the
flange nut.
4 Restrain the pinion flange with a bar and a couple of bolts. Unscrew
the flange nut, counting the number of turns needed to remove it
(photo).
5 Pull off the pinion flange (photo). If it is tight, strike it from behind
with a copper mallet. Be prepared for oil spillage.
6 Lever out the old oil seal. Clean the seal seat and tap in the new
seal, lips facing inwards.
7 Inspect the seal rubbing surface of the pinion flange. Clean it,
or replace the flange, as necessary.
8 Oil the seal lips, then install the flange.

8

3.2 Removing the oil filler/level plug

3.4 Topping-up the axle oil

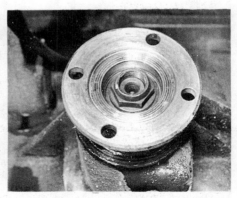

4.4 Pinion flange nut partly unscrewed

4.5 The oil seal exposed by removal of
the flange

5.2 Undoing an axleshaft retaining
plate bolt

5.4 The inner oil seal in the axle tube

9   Install the flange nut. If the original flange and nut are being used, tighten the nut through the number of turns noted and align the marks that were made before disassembly. With new components, proceed as follows:

a) Axle with solid spacer — tighten the nut to the specified torque
b) Axle with collapsible spacer — tighten the nut to the lowest specified torque, then use a spring balance to determine the pinion bearing preload (wheels free, handbrake off). If the preload is lower than specified, carry on tightening the nut until it is correct. Do not exceed the maximum specified preload or tightening torque

10 Install the driveshaft and lower the vehicle.
11 Check the axle oil level and top up if necessary.

5 Axleshaft, bearing and seals — removal and installation

1   Remove the handbrake shoes (Chapter 9, Section 26).
2   Remove the four bolts which secure the axleshaft retaining plate (photo). Recover the handbrake shoe clips.
3   Install the brake disc backwards (drum facing outwards) and secure it with the wheel nuts, flat faces inwards. Pull on the brake disc to withdraw the axleshaft. Be prepared for oil spillage.

4   With the axleshaft removed, the inner (axle oil) seal may be removed by prying it out of the axle tube (photo). Clean the seal seat and tap the new seal into position using a hammer and a seal driver or piece of pipe.
5   Replacement of the outer (grease) seal and bearing should be left to a Volvo dealer or other specialist, as press tools are required (photo).
6   Before installing, make sure that the bearing and seal lips are packed with grease.
7   Clean the axle tube and retaining plate mating faces and apply sealant to them.
8   Fit the axleshaft into the axle tube, being careful not to damage the inner seal. Secure it with the retaining plate and the four bolts, tightened to the specified torque. Remember to install the handbrake shoe clips.
9   Remove the brake disc (if not already done) and install the handbrake shoes.
10 Check the rear axle oil level and top up if necessary.

6 Rear axle housing — removal and installation

1   Loosen the rear wheel nuts. Raise and support the vehicle with the rear wheels free. **Caution:** *If raising the front of the vehicle as well,*

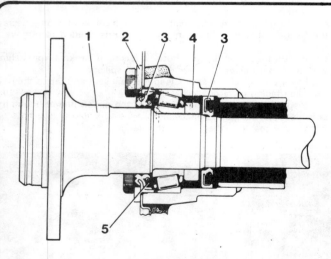

Fig. 8.2 Sectional view of axleshaft, bearing and
seals (Sec 5)

1 Axleshaft   4 Bearing retainer
2 Lockplate   5 Grease space
3 Seals

5.5 The outer oil seal is below the bearing

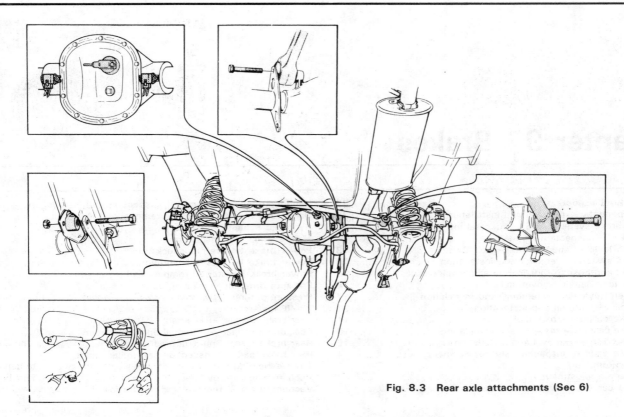

Fig. 8.3   Rear axle attachments (Sec 6)

place the supports under the front control arm brackets, not under the jacking points. If the front jacking points are used, the vehicle may become nose-heavy.

2   Remove the rear wheels.

3   Remove the rear brake calipers (without disconnecting them), the brake discs and the handbrake shoes. Refer to Chapter 9 for full details.

4   Disconnect the handbrake cables from the brake backplates and from the brackets on the axle.

5   Unbolt the axle torque rods from the subframe, and the lower torque rod from the axle.

6   Support the axle with a cradle and a jack. Take the weight of the axle on the jack.

7   If the exhaust system runs below the axle, remove it.

8   Remove the Panhard rod.

9   Disconnect the speedometer sender/ETC electrical connector(s) (as applicable). The speedometer sender connector may be secured by a locking wire and seal, which must be broken.

10   Unbolt the driveshaft/axle flanged joint.

11   Unbolt the upper torque rod from the axle.

12   Unbolt the rear shock absorber lower mountings.

13   Remove the trailing arm front mounting bracket nuts and bolts.

14   Lower the axle, at the same time freeing the trailing arm front moun-

tings, and remove it from under the vehicle.

15   The stabilizer bar (if equipped) and the trailing arms may now be removed if desired. The trailing arms are different for each side of the vehicle — do not mix them up.

16   Install by reversing the removal operations, noting the following points:

a)   When installing the trailing arms to the axle, tighten the nuts progressively and in diagonal sequence to the specified torque

b)   Do not finally tighten the torque rods until the weight of the vehicle is back on the wheels (or jack the axle up to simulate this condition)

c)   Check the axle oil level on completion

---

7   Driveaxles — general information

Consult your local Volvo dealer for any service or repair procedures pertaining to the driveaxles, constant velocity joints and/or boots, as no information on these components was available at the time of writing.

---

8   Troubleshooting — rear axle

Symptom	Reason(s)
Noise on drive or coasting	Oil level low or incorrect grade Bearings worn or dmaaged Gear teeth worn or damaged
Noise when turning (either way)	Differential worn or damaged
Noise when turning left only	Right-hand axleshaft bearing worn (and *vice versa*)
Knock when accelerating from stop	Driveshaft flange bolts loose Wheel nuts loose Pinion flange loose Axleshaft splines worn Final drive worn or damaged

8

Chapter 9 Brakes

Contents

Specifications

General

System type:

Footbrake .... Discs all round. Hydraulic operation with servo assistance. Anti-lock braking (ABS) on some models

Handbrake .... Mechanical to drums on rear wheels

Hydraulic system split:

Without ABS .... Double triangular

With ABS .... Front-rear

Hydraulic fluid type .... See *Recommended lubricants and fluids*

Brake pads

Lining minimum thickness:

Front pads .... 3.0 mm (0.12 in)

Rear pads .... 2.0 mm (0.08 in)

Front brake discs

Diameter

Solid .... 280 mm (11.02 in)

Ventilated .... 262 or 287 mm (10.32 or 11.30 in)

Thickness — solid:

New .... 14.0 mm (0.55 in)

Wear limit .... 11.0 mm (0.43 in)

Thickness — ventilated:

New .... 22.0 mm (0.87 in)

Wear limit .... 20.0 mm (0.79 in)

Runout .... 0.08 mm (0.003 in) maximum

Rear brake discs

Thickness:

Standard

New .... 9.6 mm (0.38 in)

Wear limit .... 8.4 mm (0.33 in)

Multi-link

New .... 10.0 mm (0.394 in)

Wear limit .... 8.0 mm (0.252 in)

Runout .... 0.10 mm (0.004 in) maximum

Handbrake

Lever travel:
  After adjustment............................... 2 to 8 clicks
  In service.................................... 11 clicks maximum
Drum diameter................................... 160.45 mm (6.317 in) maximum
Drum run-out.................................... 0.15 mm (0.006 in) maximum
Drum out-of-round............................... 0.20 mm (0.008 in) maximum

Torque specifications

	Nm	Ft-lbs
Front caliper bracket screws.., ...	100	74
Rear caliper mounting bolts*	58	43
Upper guide pin to caliper bracket.................	25	18
Caliper guide pin bolts..........................	34	25
Front dust shield...............................	24	18
Rear dust shield................................	40	30
Master cylinder nuts............................	30	22
Rigid pipe unions..............................	14	10
Flexible hose unions............................	17	13

*Use new bolts every time

1 General information

The brake pedal operates disc brakes on all four wheels by means of a dual circuit hydraulic system with servo assistance. The handbrake operates separate drum brakes on the rear wheels only by means of cables. An anti-lock braking system (ABS) is installed on some models, and is described in detail in Section 30.

The hydraulic system is split into two circuits, so that in the event of failure of one circuit, the other will still provide adequate braking power (although pedal travel and effort may increase). Except on models with ABS, the split is triangular, ie each circuit serves one rear caliper and half of both front ones.

The power brake booster is of the direct-acting type, mounted between the brake pedal and the master cylinder. The booster magnifies the effort applied by the driver. It is vacuum-operated, the vacuum being derived from the intake manifold or (on some models) a mechanical vacuum pump.

Instrument panel warning lights alert the driver to hydraulic circuit failure (by means of a pressure differential valve) and on some models

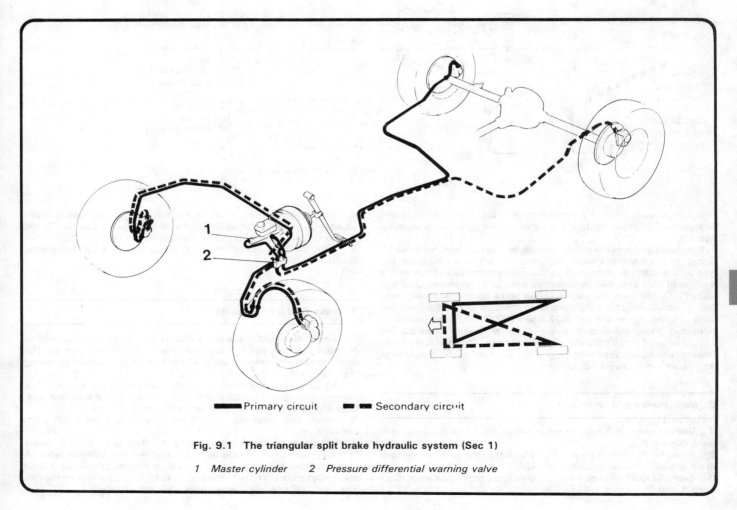

——— Primary circuit   ■■ ■■ Secondary circuit

Fig. 9.1 The triangular split brake hydraulic system (Sec 1)

1 Master cylinder   2 Pressure differential warning valve

9

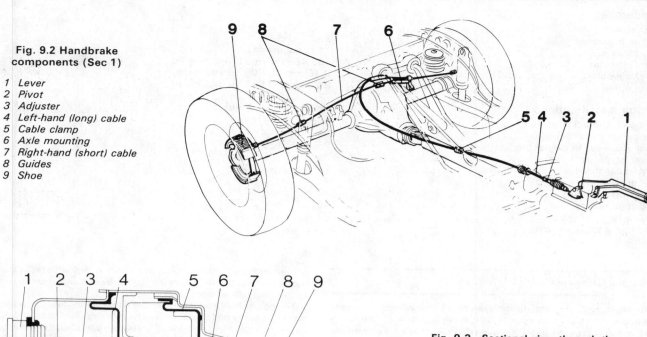

Fig. 9.2 Handbrake components (Sec 1)

1 *Lever*
2 *Pivot*
3 *Adjuster*
4 *Left-hand (long) cable*
5 *Cable clamp*
6 *Axle mounting*
7 *Right-hand (short) cable*
8 *Guides*
9 *Shoe*

Fig. 9.3 Sectional view through the brake booster (Sec 7)

1   *Check valve*
2   *Front pushrod*
3   *Spring for diaphragms*
4   *Front diaphragm*
5   *Rear diaphragm*
6   *Housing*
7   *Valve seat*
8   *Seal*
9   *Pushrod spring*
10 *Rear pushrod*
11 *Air filter*
12 *Air filter*
13 *Spring*
14 *Reaction disc*

to low fluid level. Another warning light reminds when the handbrake is applied. The brake lights are covered by the bulb failure warning system.

Work on the brake system should be careful and methodical. Scrupulous cleanliness must be observed when working on the hydraulic system. Replacement parts should preferably be the maker's own, or at least of known manufacture and quality. **Warning:** *Dust produced by brake wear and deposited on brake components may contain asbestos, which is hazardous to your health. DO NOT blow it out with compressed air and DO NOT inhale it. DO NOT use gasoline or petroleum-based solvents to remove the dust. Brake system cleaner should be used to flush the dust into a drain pan. After the brake components are wiped clean with a rag, dispose of the contaminated rags and cleaner in a covered container.*

2 Maintenance and inspection

1   Weekly, every 250 miles or before a long trip, check the brake fluid level (Secion 3).
2   Every 6000 miles or six months, check that the spare wheel well drain is clear (only on models with ABS).
3   Every 12 000 miles or annually, check the brake pad wear (Sections 4 and 5).

4   At the same intervals check the operation of the power brake booster (Section 6), the adjustment of the handbrake (Section 7) and the condition of the hydraulic pipes and hoses (Section 8).
5   Every 24 000 miles or two years, replace the brake fluid by bleeding (Section 9).

3 Brake fluid level — check

1   The level of fluid in the brake master cylinder reservoir should be between the MAX and MIN marks on the outside of the reservoir. The reservoir is translucent, so the level can be checked without removing the cap.
2   If topping-up is necessary, wipe the area around the reservoir cap. Remove the cap and top up with fresh brake fluid of the specified type. Only top up to the MAX mark; do not overfill (photo).
3   Install the reservoir cap. Wash any spilled fluid off paint immediately.
4   Regular need for more fluid shows that there is a leak somewhere in the system which should be found and rectified without delay. A slow fall in fluid level, as the pads wear, is normal; provided the level stays above the MIN mark, there is no need to top up for this reason. The level will rise again when new pads are installed.

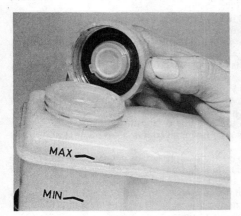

3.2 Removing the brake fluid reservoir cap. Note MAX and MIN marks

4.2 Removing a front caliper lower guide pin bolt

4.3 Pivot the caliper upwards

4.4 Slide the brake pads out of the caliper mounting bracket

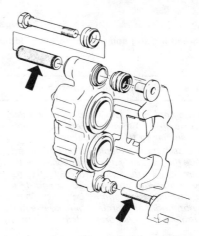

Fig. 9.4 Apply anti-seize compound to the caliper guide pins (arrowed) (Sec 4)

4 Front brake pads — inspection and replacement

Warning: *Disc brake pads must be replaced on both front wheels at the same time — never replace pads only on one wheel. Dust produced by brake wear and deposited on brake components may contain asbestos, which is hazardous to your health. DO NOT blow it out with compressed air and DO NOT inhale it. DO NOT use gasoline or petroleum-based solvents to remove the dust. Brake system cleaner should be used to flush the dust into a drain pan. After the brake components are wiped clean with a rag, dispose of the contaminated rags and cleaner in a covered container.*

1 Remove a front wheel. The brake pad lining thickness can now be seen through the inspection hole in the caliper. However, for a thorough inspection it is preferable to remove the pads as follows.
2 Remove the caliper lower guide pin bolt, if necessary counterholding the guide pin with an open-ended wrench (photo). On Girling calipers, also loosen the upper guide pin bolt.
3 Pivot the caliper upwards, free the bellows and slide it off the guide pin (photo). Support the caliper so that the hose(s) are not strained. Do not press the brake pedal while the caliper is removed.
4 Remove the pads from the caliper bracket, noting their positions if they are to be re-used (photo). Remove the anti-squeal shims (if equipped) from the backs of the pads.
5 Measure the thickness of the pad friction linings. If any one pad lining has worn down to the specified minimum, all four front pads must be replaced. Do not interchange pads in an attempt to even out wear. (Uneven pad wear may be due to the caliper sticking on the guide pins).

6 Clean the caliper and bracket with brake cleaner. Inspect the caliper piston and dust boots for signs of fluid leakage. Also inspect the rubber bellows which cover the guide pins. Repair or replace as necessary (Section 11).
7 Remove any scale or rust from the outer rim of the brake disc with a wire brush or file. Inspect the disc visually; if grabbing brakes have been a problem, carry out a more thorough inspection (Section 14).
8 If new pads are to be installed, press the caliper pistons back into their bores with a pair of pliers, being careful not to damage the dust boots. As the pistons are pressed back, the fluid level in the master cylinder reservoir wil rise. Remove some fluid if necessary, using a syringe or an old poultry baster. Do not syphon the fluid by mouth: it is poisonous.
9 Apply anti-seize compound or disc brake lubricant to the backs of the pads and to the caliper guide pins. Do not allow lubricant to contact the disc or pad friction surfaces. Also lubricate both sides of the anti-squeal shims (if equipped) and install them to the pads.
10 Slide the caliper onto the upper guide pin and engage the bellows. Position the pads with the friction surfaces towards the disc and swing the caliper down over the pads. Make sure that the anti-rattle spring in the caliper is sitting correctly on the pads.
11 Apply thread locking compound to the guide pin bolt, insert it and tighten it to the specified torque (photo). On Girling calipers, also tighten the upper guide pin bolt.
12 Press the brake pedal several times to bring the pads up to the disc.
13 Repeat the operations on the other front brake.
14 Install the wheels, lower the vehicle and tighten the wheel lug nuts.
15 Check the brake fluid level and top up if necessary.
16 If new pads have been installed, avoid hard braking as far as possible for the first few hundred miles to allow the linings to bed in.

9

4.11   Use thread locking compound on the guide pin bolt

5   Rear brake pads — inspection and replacement

Note: *This procedure applies to 1987 and earlier models only. If you are replacing rear pads on a 1988 model, refer to Section 4 as the new design calipers are similar to the front calipers.*

Warning: *Disc brake pads must be replaced on both wheels at the same time — never replace the pads only on one wheel. Also, the dust created by the brake system may contain asbestos, which is harmful to your health. Never blow it out with compressed air and do not inhale any of it. An approved filtering mask should be worn when servicing the brake system. Do not, under any circumstances, use petroleum-based solvents to clean brake parts. Use brake cleaner or denatured alcohol only.*

1   Loosen the rear wheel nuts, raise and support the rear of the vehicle and remove the rear wheel.
2   The pad lining thickness can now be seen through the jaws of the caliper. For a more thorough inspection, or to replace the pads, proceed as follows.
3   Drive the two retaining pins out of the caliper using a hammer and punch (photo). Remove the anti-rattle spring. Obtain a new spring for reassembly.
4   Press each pad away from the disc, using pliers. Do not lever between the pads and the disc.
5   Pull the pads out of the caliper, along with the anti-squeal shims (if equipped). Identify their position if they are to be re-used. Do not press the brake pedal with the pads removed.

6   Measure the thickness of the pad friction linings. If any one pad lining has worn down to the specified minimum, all four rear pads must be replaced. Do not interchange pads in an attempt to even out wear.
7   Clean the caliper with brake cleaner. Inspect the caliper pistons and dust boots for signs of fluid leakage. Repair or replace as necessary (Section 13).
8   Inspect the visible surface of the brake disc. If deep scoring, cracks or grooves are evident, or if grabbing brakes have been a problem, carry out a more thorough inspection (Section 14). Remove the caliper if necessary for access to the inboard face of the disc.
9   Anti-squeal shims may be installed if wished, even if none were installed before.
10 If new pads are to be installed, press the caliper pistons back into their bores. Remove a little fluid from the master cylinder reservoir if necessary to prevent overflow.
11 Smear the backs of the pads and both sides of the anti-squeal shims (if used) with anti-seize compound or disc brake lubricant. Keep this off the friction surfaces of the pads.
12 Install the pads and shims into the jaws of the caliper with the friction surfaces towards the disc (photo).
13 Insert one of the pad retaining pins and tap it into place. Install a new anti-rattle spring and the other pad retaining pin, making sure that the pins pass over the tongues of the spring (photo).
14 Repeat the operations on the other rear brake.
15 Install the wheels, lower the vehicle and tighten the wheel nuts.
16 Pump the brake pedal several times to being the new pads up to the discs.
17 Check the brake fluid level and top up if necessary.
18 If new pads have been installed, avoid harsh braking as far as possible for the first few hundred miles to allow the linings to bed in.

6   Power brake booster — check

1   Normally, brake booster malfunction will be evident to the driver by the increased effort needed at the pedal. A quick check may be made as follows.
2   With the engine stopped, apply the footbrake several times to equalize the pressure in the booster.
3   Hold the brake pedal depressed and start the engine. If the brake booster is working, the pedal will be felt to move downwards slightly. If not, there is a fault in the brake booster, the non-return valve or hose, or (if equipped) the vacuum pump.

7   Handbrake — adjustment

1   The handbrake should be fully applied within the specified number of clicks of the lever ratchet. Adjustment will be necessary periodically to compensate for lining wear and cable stretch.
2   Remove the rear ashtray and the cigarette lighter/seat belt warning light panel for access to the cable adjuster (photo).
3   Release the locking sleeve from the front of the adjuster, either by driving the sleeve forwards or by pulling the adjuster back. Turn

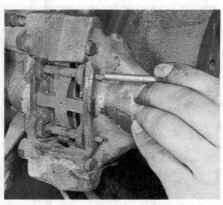

5.3   Driving out a pad retaining pin

5.12   Installing a rear pad and anti-squeal shim

5.13   Installing the pad retaining pin over the spring tongue

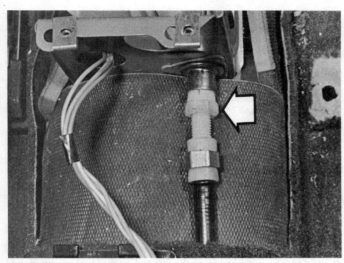

7.2 Handbrake cable adjuster (arrowed) with surrounding trim removed

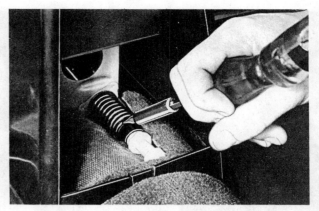

Fig. 9.5 Driving forwards the handbrake cable adjuster locking sleeve (Sec 7)

the adjuster nut until handbrake operation occurs within the specified number of clicks. Check that the brake is not binding when the lever is released.
4   Re-engage the locking sleeve and install the panel and rear ashtray.

8   Brake lines and hoses — inspection and replacement

1   Inspect the rigid lines for security in their mounts. The lines must be free from rust or impact damage.
2   Inspect the flexible hoses for cracks, splits and bulges. Bend the hoses between finger and thumb to expose small cracks. Replace any hoses whose condition is at all questionable.
3   Details of brake line and hose replacement will vary according to the location of the item in question, but the basic steps are the same.
4   Minimize hydraulic fluid loss by removing the master cylinder reservoir cap, placing a piece of plastic film over the reservoir and tightening the cap over it.
5   Clean around the unions which are to be disconnected. Unscrew the unions, preferably with a flare-nut wrench — with a flexible hose, release it at the metal line first, then from the caliper. Free the line or hose from any mounting clips and remove (photos).
6   Before installing, blow through the new line or hose with dry compressed air. Any bending needed for a rigid line should take place before the unions are connected. If genuine Volvo parts are used, the lines should install without bending.
7   When satisfied that the line or hose is correctly routed and will not touch adjacent components, install and tighten the unions.
8   Bleed the hydraulic system as described in Section 9.

9   Hydraulic system — bleeding

1   Whenever the hydraulic system has been overhauled, a part replaced or the level in the reservoir has become too low, air will have entered the system. This will cause some or all of the pedal travel to be used up in compressing air rather than pushing fluid against brake pistons. If only a little air is present, the pedal will have a spongy feel, but if an appreciable amount has entered, the pedal will not offer any appreciable resistance and the brakes will hardly work at all.
2   To overcome this, brake fluid must be pumped through the hydraulic system until all the air has been passed out in the form of bubbles in the fluid.
3   If only one hydraulic circuit has been disconnected, only that circuit need be bled. If both circuits have been disconnected, or at time of fluid replacement, the whole system must be bled.
4   Bleed the system in the following order:

Without ABS	With ABS
RH rear	LH front
LH rear	RH front
RH front	LH rear
LH front	RH rear

5   There are two bleed screws on each front caliper, and one on each rear caliper (photo).

Bleeding with an assistant

6   Gather together two clear plastic tubes to install over the bleed screws, a glass jar and a supply of fresh brake fluid.
7   Top up the master cylinder reservoir. Keep it topped up throughout the operation.
8   Attach the tube(s) to the bleed screw(s) of the first caliper to be bled (paragraph 4). Pour a little brake fluid into the jar and place the open ends of the tube(s) in the jar, submerging them into the fluid.
9   Loosen the bleed screw(s). Have the assistant depress and release

8.5A   Releasing a hose-to-line union . . .

8.5B   . . . and removing the securing clip

9.5   Bleed screw (arrowed) on a rear caliper

9

9.16   One-way valve bleeder connected to a front bleed screw

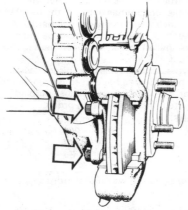

Fig. 9.6   Two Allen screws (arrowed) which secure the front caliper bracket (Sec 10)

11.3   Removing the caliper anti-rattle spring

the brake pedal five times, stopping on the fifth downstroke. Tighten the bleed screw(s) and have the assistant release the pedal.

10 Top up the master cylinder reservoir.

11 Repeat paragraphs 9 and 10 until clean fluid, free from air bubbles, emerges from the bleed screw(s).

12 Repeat the process on the remaining calipers in the order given.

13 On completion, check that the brake pedal feels hard. Top up the master cylinder reservoir and install the cap.

14 Discard the fluid bled from the system as it is not install for reuse. Dispose of it in a sealed container.

Bleeding using a one-way valve kit

15 There are a number of one-man brake bleeding kits available from most auto parts stores. These devices simplify the bleeding process and reduce the risk of expelled air or fluid being drawn back again into the system.

16 To use this type of kit, connect the outlet tube to the bleed screw and then open the screw half a turn. If possible, position the tube so that it can be viewed from inside the car. Depress the brake pedal as far as possible and slowly release it. The one-way valve in the bleed kit will prevent expelled air or fluid from returning to the system at the end of each pedal return stroke (photo). Repeat this operation until clean hydraulic fluid, free from air bubbles, can be seen coming through the bleed tube. Tighten the bleed screw and remove the tube.

17 Repeat the operations on the remaining bleed screws in the correct sequence. Make sure that throughout the process the fluid reservoir level never falls so low that air can be drawn into the master cylinder, otherwise the work up to this point will have been wasted.

---

10   Front brake caliper — removal and installation

Warning: *Dust produced by brake wear and deposited on brake components may contain asbestos, which is hazardous to your health. DO NOT blow it out with compressed air and DO NOT inhale it. DO NOT use gasoline or petroleum-based solvents to remove the dust. Brake system cleaner should be used to flush the dust into a drain pan. After the brake components are wiped clean with a rag, dispose of the contaminated rags and cleaner in a covered container.*

Conventional system

1 Proceed as for brake pad removal (Section 4), but additionally disconnect the caliper hoses from the hydraulic lines at the bracket on the inner fender panel. Identify the hoses so that they can be reinstalled on the same lines; be prepared for hydraulic fluid spillage. Keep dirt out of the open unions.

2 If it is desired to remove the caliper bracket, remove the two Allen screws which secure it to the steering knuckle. Obtain new screws for reassembly.

3 When installing the caliper bracket, apply thread locking compound to the Allen screws and tighten them to the specified torque.

4 Install the caliper as described in Section 4 and reconnect the hydraulic hoses.

5 Bleed the hydraulic system on completion (Section 9).

ABS

6 Proceed as above, but note that as there is only one hydraulic hose per caliper, the hose-to-line union can be left undisturbed. Loosen the hose union at the caliper, remove the caliper from the guide pins and unscrew it from the hose. Check the set of the hose when installing. Make sure it isn't twisted.

---

11   Front brake caliper — overhaul

Warning: *Dust produced by brake wear and deposited on brake components may contain asbestos, which is hazardous to your health. DO NOT blow it out with compressed air and DO NOT inhale it. DO NOT use gasoline or petroleum-based solvents to remove the dust. Brake system cleaner should be used to flush the dust into a drain pan. After the brake components are wiped clean with a rag, dispose of the contaminated rags and cleaner in a covered container.*

11.4A   Remove a piston dust boot ...   11.4B   ... and the piston itself   11.10   Install a new piston seal into
                                                                                                the groove

1   With the brake caliper removed (Section 10), clean it externally with brake cleaner or denatured alcohol and a soft brush.
2   Remove the hydraulic hose(s) and the bleed screws. Empty any remaining brake fluid out of the caliper.
3   Remove the anti-rattle spring (photo).
4   Remove one of the piston dust boots and pull the piston out of its bore (photos). If it is reluctant to move, install the bleed screws and apply low air pressure to the fluid inlet. Place a wood block between the pistons and the caliper frame. **Caution:** *The piston may be ejected with some force. Keep your fingers clear and don't attempt to catch the piston.*
5   Remove the piston seal from the bore using a blunt instrument.
6   Repeat the above operations on the other piston. Identify the pistons if they are to be re-used.
7   Clean the pistons and bores with a clean rag and some clean brake fluid or denatured alcohol. Slight imperfections may be polished out with steel wool. Pitting, scoring or wear ridging of bores or pistons mean that the whole caliper must be replaced.
8   Replace all rubber components (seals, dust boots and bellows) as a matter of course. Blow through the fluid inlet and bleed screw holes with compressed air.
9   Check that the guide pins slide easily in their housings. Clean or replace them as necessary, and lubricate them with a copper-based anti-seize compound.
10 Lubricate a new piston seal with clean brake fluid. Insert the seal into the groove in the bore, using the fingers only to seat it (photo).
11 Install a new dust boot to the piston at the end furthest from the piston groove. Extend the dust boot for installation.
12 Lubricate the piston and bore with clean brake fluid, or with

assembly lubricant if this is supplied with the repair kit.
13 Insert the piston and dust boot into the caliper. Engage the dust boot with the groove in the piston housing, then push the piston through the dust boot into the caliper bore. Engage the dust boot with the groove on the piston.
14 Repeat the above operations on the other piston and bore.
15 Install the bleed screws, hydraulic hoses and other components that were removed.
16 Install the caliper to the vehicle.

12 Rear brake caliper — removal and installation

Warning: *Dust produced by brake wear and deposited on brake components may contain asbestos, which is hazardous to your health. DO NOT blow it out with compressed air and DO NOT inhale it. DO NOT use gasoline or petroleum-based solvents to remove the dust. Brake system cleaner should be used to flush the dust into a drain pan. After the brake components are wiped clean with a rag, dispose of the contaminated rags and cleaner in a covered container.*

1   Remove the rear brake pads (Section 5).
2   Clean around the hydraulic union on the caliper. Loosen the union half a turn.
3   Remove the two bolts which secure the caliper. Of the four bolts on the caliper, these are the two nearest the hub. Do not remove the other two bolts, which hold the caliper halves togther. Obtain new bolts for installation.

Fig. 9.7   Caliper dust boot and piston. Install the boot to the end furthest from the groove (arrowed) (Sec 11)

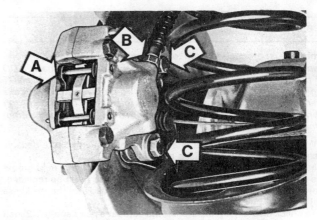

Fig. 9.8   Rear brake caliper removal (Sec 12)

A Rear pads   C Caliper securing bolts
B Hydraulic union

9

12.4   Removing a rear caliper

13.3   Pay attention to the position of the piston step (shaded)

4   Remove the caliper from the disc and unscrew it from the hydraulic hose (photo). Be prepared for fluid spillage. Plug or cap the hose end to prevent contamination and excessive fluid loss.
5   Begin installation by screwing the caliper onto the flexible hose. Do not tighten the union fully yet.
6   Install the caliper over the disc and secure it to the axle bracket with two new bolts. Tighten the bolts to the specified torque.
7   Tighten the flexible hose union at the caliper. Check that the routing and set of the hose are such that it does not contact adjacent components. Correct if necessary by releasing the hose union at the brake line bracket, repositioning the hose and tightening the union.
8   Install the brake pads (Section 5).
9   Bleed the appropriate hydraulic circuit (Section 9).

13   Rear brake caliper — overhaul

1   This is essentially the same procedure as that described for the front caliper (Section 11). In addition, to the following points.
2   Do not attempt to separate the caliper halves.
3   Pay attention to the position of the step on the piston (photo). It should be at a 20 degree angle to the lower surface of the caliper (see Fig. 9.9).

14   Brake discs — inspection

Warning: *Dust produced by brake wear and deposited on brake components may contain asbestos, which is hazardous to your health. DO NOT blow it out with compressed air and DO NOT inhale it. DO NOT use gasoline or petroleum-based solvents to remove the dust. Brake system cleaner should be used to flush the dust into a drain pan. After the brake components are wiped clean with a rag, dispose of the contaminated rags and cleaner in a covered container.*

1   Whenever new pads are installed, or if a pulsating brake pedal is noticed, inspect the brake discs as follows.
2   Inspect the friction surfaces for cracks or deep scoring (light grooving is normal and may be ignored). A cracked disc must be replaced; a scored disc can be repaired by machining provided that the thickness is not reduced below the specified minimum.
3   To check disc runout, place a dial indicator at a point about 1/2-inch from the outer edge of the disc. Set the indicator to zero and turn the disc. The indicator reading should not exceed the specified allowable runout limit. If it does, the disc should be refinished by an automotive machine shop. **Note:** *Professionals recommend resurfacing of brake discs regardless of the dial indicator reading to produce a smooth, flat*

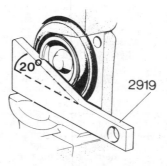

Fig. 9.9   Using a template (Volvo tool 2919) to determine the correct position of the rear caliper piston stop (Sec 13)

surface that will eliminate brake pedal pulsations and other undesirable symptoms related to discs. At the very least, if you elect not to have the discs resurfaced, deglaze the brake pad surface with medium grit emery cloth. Use a swirling motion to ensure a non-directional finish.
4   Disc thickness variation in excess of 0.015 mm (0.0006 in) can also cause pulsations. Check this using a micrometer, measuring at several points around the disc.
5   Whenever the rear discs are removed, check the condition of the handbrake drums. Refinishing, run-out and out-of-round limits are given in the Specifications. The drums are unlikely to wear unless the handbrake is habitually used to stop the vehicle.

15   Front brake disc — removal and installation

Warning: *Dust produced by brake wear and deposited on brake components may contain asbestos, which is hazardous to your health. DO NOT blow it out with compressed air and DO NOT inhale it. DO NOT use gasoline or petroleum-based solvents to remove the dust. Brake system cleaner should be used to flush the dust into a drain pan. After the brake components are wiped clean with a rag, dispose of the contaminated rags and cleaner in a covered container.*

1   Remove the brake caliper and bracket (Section 10), but do not disconnect the hydraulic hoses. Tie the caliper up so that the hoses are not strained. On 1988 models, unscrew the wheel locating stud, then pull the disc from the hub.
2   Pry or tap off the hub nut grease cap. Obtain a new cap if the old one is damaged during removal.
3   Remove the cotter pin from the spindle. Unscrew and remove the nut.

16.2 **Removing a wheel locating pin**

4   Pull the brake disc out to displace the outer bearing. Remove the bearing, then pull the disc off the spindle.
5   If the inner bearing has stayed on the spindle, pull or lever it off.
6   Clean the spindle and the oil seal mating face.
7   If a new disc is to be installed, replace the bearing races. Replace the oil seal in any case (Chapter 10, Section 15).
8   Clean rustproofing compound off a new disc with denatured alcohol or brake cleaner and a rag.
9   Grease the spindle and the oil seal lips. Place the disc and bearing assembly onto the spindle and push it into position. Install the outer bearing.
10 Install the castellated nut. Adjust the bearings (Chapter 10, Section 4) and secure the nut with a new cotter pin.
11 Position the grease cap on the hub and gently tap it into place.
12 Install the brake caliper and bracket (Section 10).

16 Rear brake disc — removal and installation

Warning: *Dust produced by brake wear and deposited on brake components may contain asbestos, which is hazardous to your health. DO NOT blow it out with compressed air and DO NOT inhale it. DO NOT use gasoline or petroleum-based solvents to remove the dust. Brake system cleaner should be used to flush the dust into a drain pan. After the brake components are wiped clean with a rag, dispose of the contaminated rags and cleaner in a covered container.*

1   Remove the rear brake caliper without disconnecting the brake hose (Section 12). Tie the caliper up out of the way.

Fig. 9.10 Removing a rear brake disc (Sec 16)

2   If a wheel locating pin is installed, unscrew it from the disc (photo).
3   Make sure that the handbrake is released, then pull off the disc. Tap it with a soft-faced mallet if necessary to free it.
4   Install by reversing the removal procedure. If a new disc is being installed, remove the traces of rustproofing compound from it.

17 Brake master cylinder — removal and installation

1   Syphon as much fluid as possible from the master cylinder reservoir, using a hydrometer or old poultry baster. Do not syphon the fluid by mouth, it is poisonous.
2   Unbolt the heat shield (if equipped) from around the master cylinder.
3   Disconnect the clutch master cylinder feed hose from the side of the reservoir (when applicable). Be prepard for fluid spillage. Plug the open end of the line (photo).
4   Disconnect the hydraulic unions from the master cylinder. Be prepared for fluid spillage. Cap the open unions to keep dirt out (photo).
5   Remove the nuts which secure the master cylinder to the power brake booster. Pull the master cylinder off the booster studs and remove it (photo). Be careful not to spill any brake fluid on the paint.
6   Install by reversing the removal operations. Bleed the complete brake hydraulic system, and if necessary the clutch hydraulic system, on completion.

18 Brake master cylinder — overhaul

1   Empty the fluid out of the master cylinder by pumping the pistons with a screwdriver. Clean the cylinder externally.
2   Pull the reservoir off the master cylinder and recover the seals (photo).

17.3 **Disconnecting the clutch feed hose**

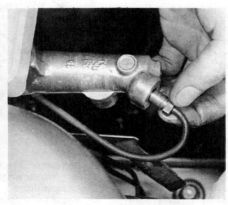

17.4 **A master cylinder hydraulic union**

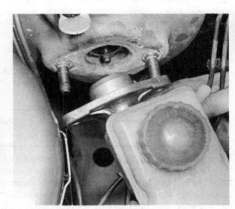

17.5 **Removing the master cylinder**

9

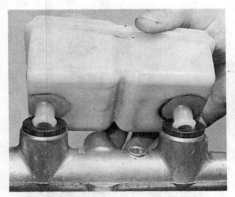

18.2   Removing the reservoir from the master cylinder

18.3   Remove the circlip to release the pistons

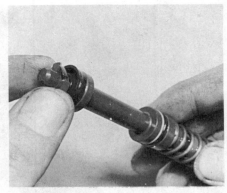

18.9A   Installing the spring seat . . .

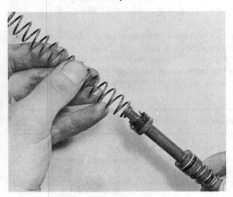

18.9B   . . . and the spring

18.9C   Installing the pistons into the master cylinder

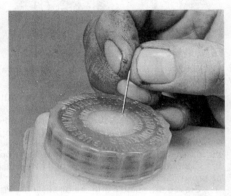

18.10   Clearing the reservoir cap breather hole

Non-ABS models

3   Depress the pistons and extract the circlip from the mouth of the cylinder (photo).
4   Shake the pistons, spring seat and spring out of the cylinder.
5   Inspect the master cylinder bore. If it is badly corroded or scratched, replace the cylinder complete. Light scoring or surface rust may be removed with steel wool and brake fluid.
6   Obtain a repair kit, which will contain new pistons with seals already installed.
7   Clean all parts not being replaced with clean brake fluid or brake cleaner. Blow through fluid passages with compressed air.
8   Lubricate the cylinder bore with clean brake fluid. Apply more fluid to the pistons and seals, or smear them with assembly lubricant if this is supplied in the kit.
9   Assemble the spring, spring seat and pistons. Make sure that all components are perfectly clean, then install the spring and pistons into the master cylinder. Depress the pistons and insert the circlip (photos).
10 Install the reservoir and seals; replace the seals if necessary. Make sure that the reservoir cap breather hole is clear (photo).

ABS models

11 The procedure is similar to that just described, but the pistons are retained by a roll pin as well as by a circlip.

19   Pressure differential warning valve — removal and installation

1   Seal the master cylinder reservoir by blocking the cap vent, or by tightening the cap over a piece of thin plastic film.
2   Clean the valve and its unions. It is located on the left-hand inner fender panel; access is not good (photo).
3   Disconnect the eight hydraulic unions for the valve, making notes for installation if there is any possibility of confusion. Be prepared for fluid spillage; cap open unions.

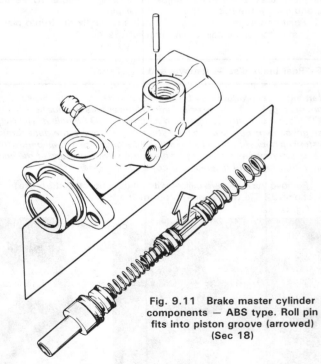

Fig. 9.11   Brake master cylinder components — ABS type. Roll pin fits into piston groove (arrowed) (Sec 18)

4   Disconnect the electrical lead from the valve.
5   Remove the single securing bolt and remove the valve. Do not drip fluid on the paint.
6   Install by reversing the removal operations. Bleed the complete hydraulic system on completion and check that the brake failure warning light operates correctly.

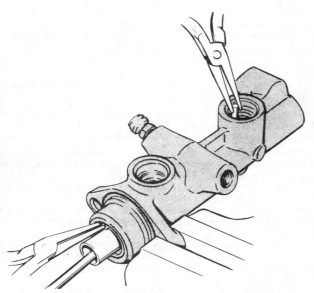

Fig. 9.12   Removing the roll pin and circlip from the ABS
type master cylinder (Sec 18)

19.2   The pressure differential warning valve

20 Pressure differential warning valve — overhaul

Note: *It is possible to carry out this procedure on the vehicle, but great care must be taken to keep dirt out of the hydraulic system.*

1   Thoroughly clean the outside of the valve.
2   Unscrew the switch from the top of the valve. Remove the spring and contact pin (photos).
3   Unscrew the two end plugs from the valve. Remove the O-rings.
4   Remove the piston, spring, plunger and O-rings. Note their installed order.
5   Clean all parts with brake fluid or brake cleaner and inspect them. If the valve bore is badly worn, rusty or scored, replace it. Otherwise, obtain a repair kit containing new O-rings (photo).
6   Install one end plug, using a new O-ring, and tighten it.
7   Assemble the piston, plungers and spring. Lubricate the piston and the new O-rings with clean hydraulic fluid. Install one of the O-rings to a plunger and insert the assembly into the valve bore, O-ring first.
8   Install the other O-ring into the bore and press it into place with a small tube or other suitable tool.
9   Install the other end plug and O-ring.
10 If the valve was removed for overhaul, install it.
11 Bleed the complete hydraulic system (Section 9), then check the success of the overhaul as follows.
12 Have an assistant depress the brake pedal hard for one minute. Watch the valve: if fluid emerges from the switch hole, replace the valve. If no fluid emerges, install the contact pin, spring and switch. Reconnect the switch.

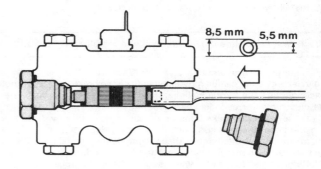

Fig. 9.13   Installing the second plunger O-ring to the
pressure differential warning valve. Tool dimensions as
shown (Sec 20)

21 Brake pedal — removal and installation

1   Remove the steering column/pedal trim.
2   Disconnect the brake pedal from the brake booster by removing the clevis pin.
3   Remove the pedal pivot bolt and nut. The return spring will force the pedal downwards. Remove the pedal, spring and pivot bolt.

20.2A   Unscrew the switch . . .

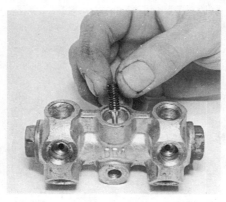

20.2B   . . . and recover the spring and
contact pin

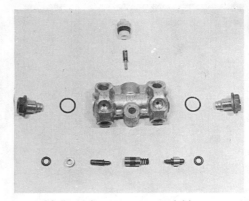

20.5   Valve components laid out
for inspection

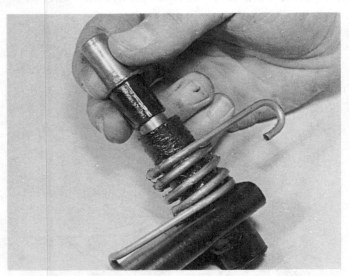

21.4   Removing the brake pedal sleeve and a bushing

4   The pedal sleeve and bushings may be replaced if required (photo). Grease the new bushings and sleeve before installing them.
5   Install by reversing the removal operations.

22   Power brake booster — removal and installation

1   Remove the brake master cylinder (Section 17). If care is taken, the master cylinder can be moved away from the brake booster without disconnecting the hydraulic lines. It will be necessary to disconnect the clutch master cylinder feed hose, however.
2   Disconnect the brake booster vacuum feed, either by disconnecting the hose or by levering out the check valve.
3   Inside the vehicle, remove the steering column/pedal trim. Disconnect the brake booster clevis from the brake pedal.
4   Remove the four nuts which secure the brake booster.
5   Withdraw the booster from the engine bay.
6   Install by reversing the removal operations. If a new brake booster is being installed, adjust the pushrod if necessary to give small clearance between the booster pushrod and the master cylinder piston in the resting position.
7   Bleed the hydraulic system on completion if necessary.

23   Power brake booster — overhaul

Even if parts are available, overhaul of the brake booster is not recommended. The peripheral components (check valve, seal and bellows) may be replaced if desired.

24   Vacuum pump — removal and installation

1   Disconnect the hose from the vacuum pump.
2   Remove the four securing nuts and lift off the pump (photo). Remove the gasket.
3   Install by reversing the removal operations, using a new gasket.

25   Vacuum pump — overhaul

1   Remove the pump top cover, which is secured by two screws. Remove the gasket, valve springs, valves and seals. Note which way the valves are installed.
2   Make alignment marks between the two halves of the pump. Remove the eight screws and separate the pump halves.
3   Remove the central screw which secures the diaphragm. Remove the diaphragm, washers and spring. Note the installed sequence of the washers.
4   Unscrew the four securing screws and remove the bottom cover.
5   Insert feeler gauges between the operating lever and the lever bearing arm to support the bearing arm. Drive out the lever pivot pin, then withdraw the feeler gauges.
6   Remove the operating rod and lever.
7   Clean all parts and replace as necessary. New gaskets and seals should be used as a matter of course.
8   Begin reassembly by installing the operating rod and lever to the pump body. Support the bearing arm with feeler gauges and drive in the pivot pin; apply a drop of locking fluid to the exposed ends of the pin. Withdraw the feeler gauges (photos).
9   Install the bottom cover, using a new gasket, and secure with the four screws (photo).
10   Assemble the diaphragm, spring, washers and screw. Hold the pump upside down and install the diaphragm assembly. Secure it with the screw (photos).
11   Install the top half of the pump, observing the alignment marks made when disassembling. Secure it with the eight screws.
12   Install the valves, using new seals. Make sure that the valves are installed the right way. Install the springs and the top cover, using a new gasket, and secure it with the two screws (photos).

26   Handbrake shoes — removal, inspection and installation

1   Loosen the handbrake cable adjuster (Section 7).
2   Remove the rear brake disc (Section 16).
3   Pry the shoes apart and displace the operating mechanism from them at the rear end, and the strut from them at the front (photos).
4   Unhook one of the return springs from one of the shoes, working through the hole in the axleshaft flange.
5   Free the shoes from the U-clips on the backplate and remove them and the springs (photo).
6   Inspect the shoes for wear, damage or oil contamination. Replace them if necessary and repair the source of any contamination. As with

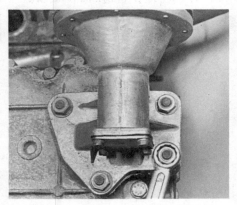

24.2   Vacuum pump securing nuts

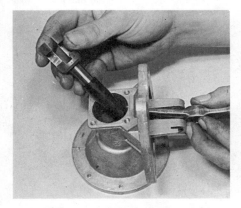

25.8A   Install the operating rod and lever . . .

25.8B   . . . and the lever pivot pin

25.8C   Support the arm with feeler gauges and tap the pin into place

25.9   Installing the pump bottom cover

25.10A   Installing the diaphragm spring

25.10B   Tightening the diaphragm screw. Circlip pliers are used to counterhold the washer

25.12A   Installing the valves (the right way up) . . .

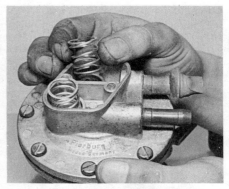

25.12B   . . . and the valve springs

25.12C   Install a new top cover gasket . . .

25.12D   . . . and the top cover itself

26.3A   Front of handbrake shoes, showing strut

26.3B   Disengaging the rear of the shoes from the operating mechanism

26.5   Handbrake shoe engaged in U-clip

9

the brake pads, the shoes must be replaced in axle sets.
7   Install by reversing the removal operations. Adjust the handbrake on completion.

---

27   Handbrake cables — removal and installation

Short (right-hand) cable

1   Remove the handbrake shoes on the right-hand side (Section 26).
2   Free the cable from the operating mechanism by pushing out the clevis pin.
3   Remove the clevis pin from the other end of the cable. Free the cable from the guides or retaining clips and remove it.
4   Check the condition of the rubber gaiter and replace it if necessary (photo).

Long (left-hand) cable

5   Inside the vehicle, loosen the handbrake adjustment as far as possible (Section 7). Release the cable from the lever.
6   Remove the handbrake shoes on the left-hand side (Section 26).
7   Free the cable from the operating mechanism by pressing out the clevis pin.
8   Release the cable from the brake backplate and from the rear axle.
9   Release the cable from the under-floor clamps and grommets and remove it. Transfer the grommets etc to the new cable. Replace the rubber boot if necessary.

Both cables

10   Install by reversing the removal procedure, noting the following points:
   a) Apply brake anti-seize compound to the operating mechanism and backplate rubbing surfaces. Keep the compound off brake friction surfaces
   b) Install the operating mechanism with the arrow visible and pointing up (photo).
   c) Adjust the handbrake on completion (Section 7)

---

28   Brake light switch — removal and installation

1   Remove the steering column/pedal trim.
2   Disconnect the wiring from the switch. Remove the locknut and unscrew the switch (photo).
3   When installing, screw the switch in so that it operates after 8 to 14 mm (0.32 to 0.55 in) movement of the brake pedal. Reconnect the wires and tighten the locknut.
4   Check for correct operation, then install the disturbed trim.

---

29   Handbrake warning switch — removal and installation

1   Remove the rear console (Chapter 11, Section 36).
2   Remove the switch securing screw (photo). Lift out the switch, disconnect the electrical connector from it and remove the switch.

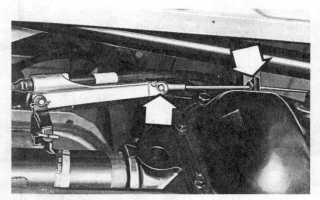

Fig. 9.14 Short handbrake cable attachments (arrowed) on rear axle (Sec 27)

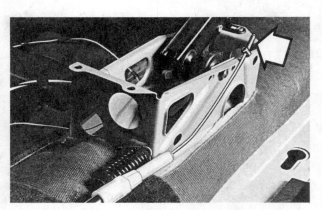

Fig. 9.15   Long handbrake cable end (arrowed) disengaged from the lever (Sec 27)

27.4   Handbrake cable showing rubber gaiter

27.10   Installing the handbrake mechanism — note arrow and UP marking

28.2   Brake light switch seen through a hole in the brake pedal bracket

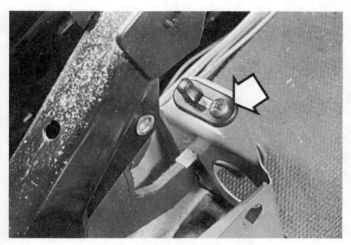

29.2 Handbrake warning switch — securing screw (arrowed)

3   Install by reversing the removal operations. Check for correct operation of the switch before installing the rear console.

30   Anti-lock brake system (ABS) — general information

When equipped, the anti-lock brake system monitors the rotational speed of the wheels under braking. Sudden deceleration of one wheel, indicating that lock-up is occurring, causes the hydraulic pressure to that wheel's brake to be reduced or interrupted momentarily. Monitoring and correction take place several times per second, giving rise to a pulsing effect at the brake pedal when correction is taking place. The system gives even inexperienced drivers a good chance of retaining control when braking hard on slippery surfaces.

The main components of the system are the sensors, the control unit and the hydraulic modulator.

One sensor is installed on each front wheel, picking up speed information from a pulse wheel carried on the brake disc. Rear wheel speed information is picked up from the speedometer sensor in the differential housing. For ABS purposes the rear wheels are treated as one unit.

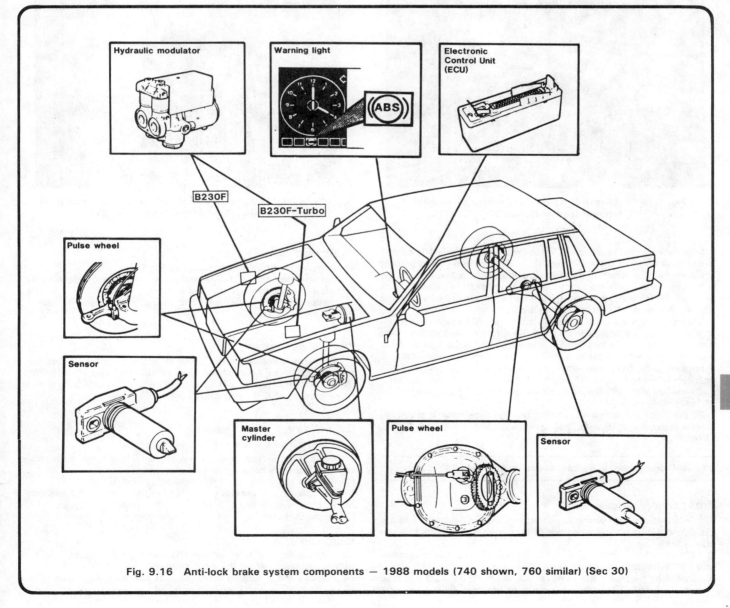

Fig. 9.16 Anti-lock brake system components — 1988 models (740 shown, 760 similar) (Sec 30)

Fig. 9.17 ABS front wheel sensor secured by an Allen screw (arrowed) (Sec 31)

Fig. 9.18   Pulling the pulse wheel off the brake disc (Sec 31)

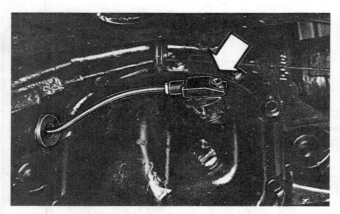

Fig. 9.19   ABS rear wheel sensor secured by an Allen screw (arrowed) (Sec 31)

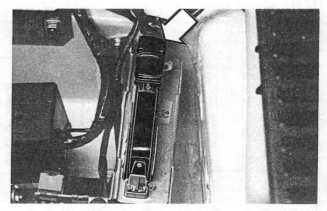

Fig. 9.20   ABS control unit (1987 and earlier models) — electrical connector arrowed (Sec 31)

Information from the sensors is fed to the control unit which is located in the trunk on 1987 and earlier models, and on the brake pedal bracket on later models. The control unit operates solenoid valves in the hydraulic modulator to restrict the supply to either front caliper or both rear calipers if necessary. The control unit also illuminates a warning light in the event of system malfunction.

The hydraulic modulator contains a pump as well as solenoid valves. It is a semi-active device, increasing the effort applied at the brake pedal. If the modulator fails, adequate braking effort will still be available from the master cylinder and brake booster, though the anti-lock function will be lost. The modulator is located in the trunk on 1987 and earlier models, or in the engine compartment on later models.

On models with ABS the hydraulic circuits are split front-rear instead of triangularly.

To avoid damage to the ABS control unit, do not subject it to voltage surges in excess of 16 volts, nor to temperatures in excess of 80° C (176° F).

---

31   ABS components — removal and installation

Front wheel sensor

1   Follow the sensor wiring back to the suspension turret. Separate the connector, push the wires out of it and feed them back into the wheel well.
2   Remove the Allen screw which secures the sensor to the steering knuckle. Withdraw the sensor and its wiring.
3   Install by reversing the removal operation. Apply a little grease (Volvo No 1 161 037-5, or equivalent) to the body of the sensor.

Front disc pulse wheel

4   Remove the front brake disc (Section 15).
5   Remove the pulse wheel from the disc with a two-legged puller. Be careful not to damage the hub oil seal.
6   Install the new pulse wheel and seat it with a piece of tube.
7   Install the brake disc.

Rear wheel sensor

8   This is the same as the speedometer sender (Chapter 12), but may be secured by an Allen screw instead of a ring nut. The running clearance for this sender is 0.35 to 0.75 mm (0.014 to 0.030 in) with a target value of 0.60 mm (0.024 in).

Control unit

1987 and earlier models

9   Make sure that the ignition is switched off. Disconnect the cable from the negative battery terminal.
10   Remove the cover from the right-hand well in the trunk.
11   Lift the control unit out of its bracket, disconnect the electrical connector and remove it.
12   Install by reversing the removal operations.

1988 models

13   From under the dash, unplug the electrical connector from the control unit (located on the panel bracket).
14   Remove the mounting screw and lift out the control unit.
15   Installation is the reverse of removal.

Fig. 9.21 ABS hydraulic modulator securing nuts
(arrowed) (Sec 31)

Hydraulic modulator

1987 and earlier models

16 Remove the cover from the right-hand well in the trunk.
17 Remove the modulator cover. Unplug the two relays and the electrical connector from the modulator. Unplug the ground wire.
18 Clean around the modulator hydraulic unions. Make identifying marks or notes.
19 Remove the three nuts from the modulator mountings.
20 Place some rags under the unit. Disconnect the hydraulic unions, being prepared for fluid spillage. Lift out the modulator. Plug or cap open unions.
21 If a new modulator is being installed, transfer the line connectors and the rubber mounts to it.
22 Install by reversing the removal operations. Bleed the complete hydraulic system on completion.

1988 models

23 Proceed as described above, but note that the modulator has been relocated under the hood, mounted on the left wheel well on the 740 Turbo and 760 V6 models, and on the right wheel well on all other models.

32 ABS — troubleshooting

1 In the event of an ABS fault, first check all fuses and wiring connectors. Besides the fuses in the central electrical unit (Nos 2 and 10), there is an 80A fuse on the front right-hand inner fender and a 10A fuse on the transient surge protector next to the control unit.
2 Switch off the ignition and disconnect the electrical connector from the control unit. Remove the cover from the electrical connector so that subsequent tests can be carried out through the side access holes. Do not insert meter probes into the front of the connectors.
3 Measure the resistance between ground and terminals 10, 20, 32 and 34 (Fig. 9.24). It should be zero in each case. If not, check the grounding point at the right-hand tail light. If terminal 32 is not grounded, try installing a new valve relay to the control unit.
4 Switch on the ignition. Measure the voltage at terminals 2, 3 and 4 of the transient surge protector (Fig. 9.25). It should be 12V. No voltage at terminal 3 may be due to a faulty surge protector; otherwise, lock for wiring damage.
5 Still with the ignition on, measure the voltage at the converter terminals (next to the control unit) (Fig. 9.26). If the result is not 12V at all terminals, replace the converter.
6 Returning to the control unit electrical connector, check the voltage between ground and terminals 1, 7, 9, 27 and 28. 12V should be obtained in each case. If not, there is a defect in the transient protector (terminal 1), the converter (7 and 9), the valve relay (27) or the pump relay (28).
7 Check the voltage between terminal 25 and ground while an assistant depresses the brake pedal. 12V should be obtained; if not, check the brake light switch and bulbs.

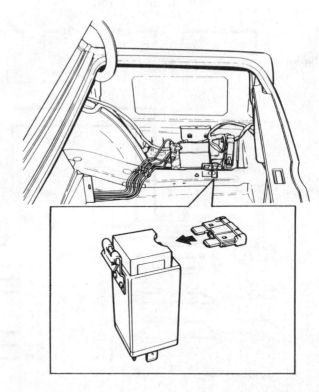

Fig. 9.22 Transient surge protector fuse (Sec 32)

8 Check the voltage between terminal 29 and ground. It should be 0.5 to 1.0V. If not, the solenoid valve relay is defective.
9 Switch off the ignition. Disconnect the hydraulic modulator electrical connector, then switch on the ignition again.
10 Check for 12V between ground and terminals 6, 7, 10 and 12 of the modulator plug. Absence of voltage suggests a blown No 2 fuse (terminal 6), blown ABS warning light bulb (No 7), faulty transient protector (No 10) or blown 80A fuse (No 12).
11 Switch off the ignition and reconnect the modulator electrical connector.
12 Measure the front sensor resistance across terminals 4 and 6, then 21 and 23, of the control unit electrical connector. Resistance should be 0.9 to 2.2 K-ohms. If not, check the resistance again at the connectors near the front suspension turrets. Replace the sensor (5) if the resistance is still incorrect.
13 Measure the rear sensor resistance between terminals 7 and 9. It should be 0.6 to 1.6 K-ohms. Recheck if necessary at the connector next to the fuel filter line.
14 Note that if the rear sensor is too far from the pulse wheel, the ABS will not operate and the warning light will come on. See Chapter 12.
15 As a further sensor check, verify that the measured resistance fluctuates if the wheel in question is rotated.
16 Check the resistance of the valve solenoids by measuring between terminal 32 and 2, 18 and 35. In each case the reading should be 0.7 to 1.7 ohms. If not, recheck at the hydraulic modulator (between terminals 4 and 1, 5 and 3). Repair the wiring or replace the modulator as necessary.
17 Switch on the ignition. Briefly ground terminal 28 of the control unit connector and check that the modulator pump runs. If not, try a new pump relay before condemning the pump.
18 With the ignition still on, connect the voltmeter between terminal 32 and ground. Connect pin 27 to ground: the voltmeter should read 12V. If not, replace the valve relay.
19 If no faults have been revealed, but the ABS is still not working, the fault must be in the control unit.
20 Switch off the ignition, disconnect the test gear and restore the original wiring connections.

9

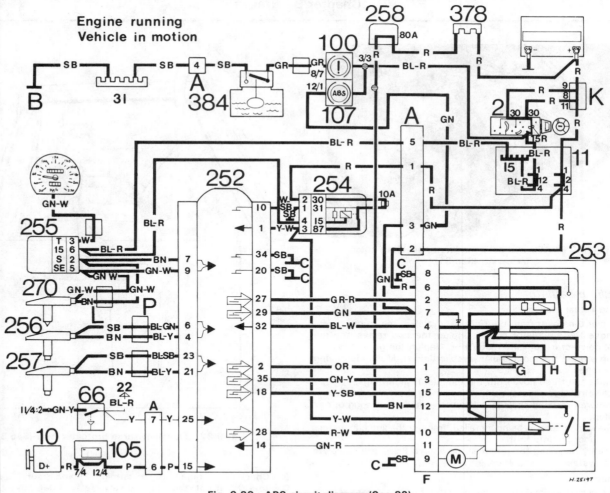

Fig. 9.23 ABS circuit diagram (Sec 32)

2	Ignition/starter switch	
10	Alternator	
11	Fusebox	
15	Connector (in central electrical unit)	
22	Brake light feed	
31	Ground point (in central electrical unit)	
66	Brake light switch	
85	Speedometer	
100	Brake failure warning light	

105	Ignition (no-charge) warning light
107	ABS warning light
252	Control unit
253	Hydraulic modulator
254	Transient surge protector
255	Converter
256	LH front wheel sensor
257	RH front wheel sensor
258	Fuse (80A)

270	Rear wheel/speedometer sensor
378	Positive terminal (in engine bay)
284	Brake fluid level sensor
A	Connector (RH A-pillar)
B	Ground point (RH A-pillar)
C	Ground point (RH tail light)
D	Solenoid valve relay
E	Pump motor relay

F	Hydraulic modulator multi-plug
G	LH front solenoid valve
H	RH front solenoid valve
J	Rear solenoid valve
K	Connector (LH A-pillar)
L	Connector (in boot)
M	Pump motor
N	Connector (RH front inner fender)
P	Connector (LH front inner fender)

Color code

B	Blue	GR	Grey	R	Red	W	White
BN	Brown	OR	Orange	SB	Black	Y	Yellow
GN	Green	P	Pink	VO	Violet		

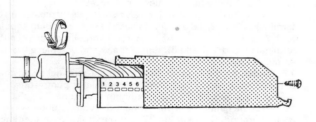
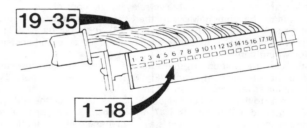

Fig. 9.24 Remove the electrical connector cover (left) for access to the numbered connectors (Sec 32)

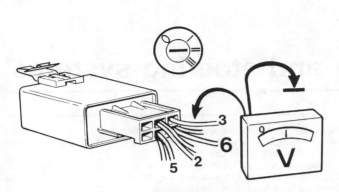

Fig. 9.25 Checking the voltage at the transient surge protector (Sec 32)

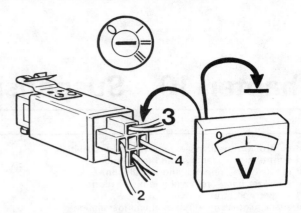

Fig. 9.26 Checking the voltage at the converter (Sec 32)

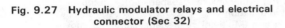

Fig. 9.27 Hydraulic modulator relays and electrical connector (Sec 32)

1 *Solenoid valve relay*
2 *Pump relay*
3 *Multi-plug*

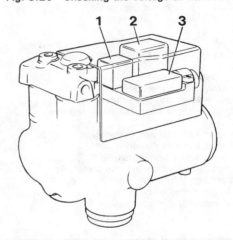

33 Troubleshooting — brake system

Symptom	Reason(s)
Pedal travel excessive	Air in system Leak in one hydraulic circuit Disc run-out excessive
Pedal spongy	Air in system Rubber hose(s) weak
Pedal sinks to floor during sustained application	Fluid leak Master cylinder seals leaking
Excessive pedal effort required	Power brake booster defective or disconnected Linings contaminated or incorrect grade New linings not yet bedded-in
Brakes pull to one side	Linings contaminated on one side Caliper piston seized Tire pressures incorrect Steering or suspension fault
Brakes grab	Linings wet (apply brakes to dry them) Linings worn out Disc worn or cracked Caliper loose Wheel bearing play excessive
Brakes bind	Booster pushrod incorrectly adjusted (too long) Master cylinder breather blocked Brake line crushed or blocked Caliper piston seized Air in system Handbrake over-adjusted, or cable seized

9

Chapter 10 Suspension and steering systems

Contents

Specifications

General

Front suspension type	Independent, MacPherson struts, with anti-roll bar
Rear suspension type	
1988 760 sedan models	Independent (Multi-link), coil springs, load leveling system
All others	Solid axle, coil springs and telescopic shock absorbers. Load levelling option on some models
Steering type	Rack-and-pinion, power-assisted
Toe-in	
1988 models	2.5 ± 0.5 mm (0.1 ± 0.04 in)
All others	2.0 ± 0.5 mm (0.08 ± 0.02 in)

Steering gear

Fluid type	See *Recommended lubricants and fluids*

Wheel rims

Lateral runout:	
Aluminum	0.8 mm (0.032 in) maximum
Steel	1.0 mm (0.039 in) maximum
Radial runout:	
Aluminum	0.6 mm (0.024 in) maximum
Steel	0.8 mm (0.032 in) maximum

Tire pressures (cold)*

	Front	Rear
Recommended pressures in psi:		
Sedan, up to 3 occupants	28	28
Sedan, fully laden	31	33
Wagon, up to 3 occupants	28	31
Wagon, fully laden	31	41
For sustained high speeds (over 72 mph) add	4	4
Space saver spare (see text):		
155/R15	51	51
165/14	41	41

* Refer to sticker on driver's door for confirmation

Torque specifications

	Nm	Ft-lbs
Front suspension		
Control arm balljoint stud nut	60	44
Balljoint to strut*:		
Stage 1	30	22
Stage 2	Tighten 90° further	Tighten 90° further
Track rod end ballpin nut	60	44
Control arm to crossmember*	85	63
Radius rod to control arm*	95	70
Radius rod to subframe*		
M12	85	63
M14	140	103
Strut top mount (to body)	40	30
Strut piston rod nut	150	111
Crossmember to body	95	70

* Use new fasteners every time

	Nm	Ft-lbs
Rear suspension (solid axle)		
Trailing arm to axle	45	33
Trailing arm bracket bolts	45	33
Trailing arm bracket nuts	85	63
Rear spring upper mount	48	35
Shock absorber mounts	85	63
Panhard rod bolts	85	63
Torque rods	140	103
Subframe front mount	85	63
Subframe rear bushing bracket	48	35

	Nm	Ft-lbs
Rear suspension (Multi-link)		
Lower link to wheel bearing housing	40 + 90° rotation	29 + 90° rotation
Lower link to differential support	25 + 90° rotation	18 + 90° rotation
Trailing arm to body	60 + 120° rotation	43 + 120° rotation
Trailing arm to wheel bearing housing	40 + 90° rotation	29 + 90° rotation
Upper link to wheel bearing housing	115	83
Upper link to differential support (front)	50 + 60° rotation	36 + 60° rotation
Upper link to differential support (rear)	85	61
Track rod to wheel bearing housing	85	61
Track rod to differential support	70	51
Wheel bearing hub nut	140 + 60° rotation	102 + 60° rotation

	Nm	Ft-lbs
Steering		
Steering wheel bolt	32	24
Steering column universal joints	21	16
Steering gear to crossmember	44	33
Tie rod end balljoint nut	60	44
Tie rod end locknut	70	52
Hydraulic union banjo bolts	42	31

	Nm	Ft-lbs
Wheels		
Wheel nuts	85	63

Fig. 10.1 Power steering gear components (Sec 1)

1 Intermediate shaft
2 Steering gear
3 Steering pump
4 Fluid reservoir
5 Tie-rod
6 Steering arm

10

---

1 General information

Steering is by power-assisted rack and pinion. Power assistance is derived from a hydraulic pump, belt-driven from the crankshaft pulley.

Front suspension is independent. MacPherson struts are used, located at their lower ends by control arms each carrying a balljoint.

The control arms are attached to the front crossmember, to a radius rod each and to the front stabilizer bar.

Rear suspension on most models is of the live rear axle type. The axle is supported by two trailing arms, two torque rods and a Panhard rod. The torque rods are attached to a central subframe. A coil spring

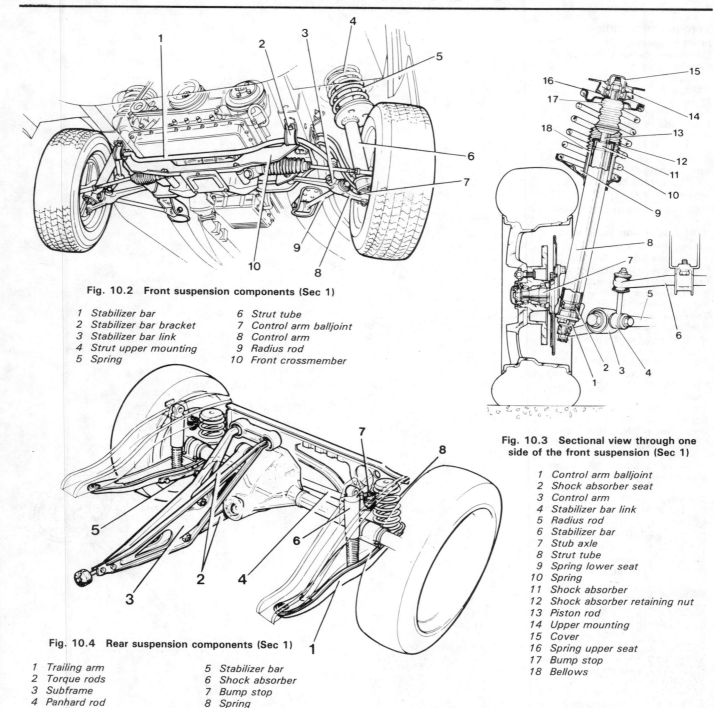

Fig. 10.2   Front suspension components (Sec 1)

1 Stabilizer bar
2 Stabilizer bar bracket
3 Stabilizer bar link
4 Strut upper mounting
5 Spring
6 Strut tube
7 Control arm balljoint
8 Control arm
9 Radius rod
10 Front crossmember

Fig. 10.3   Sectional view through one
side of the front suspension (Sec 1)

1 Control arm balljoint
2 Shock absorber seat
3 Control arm
4 Stabilizer bar link
5 Radius rod
6 Stabilizer bar
7 Stub axle
8 Strut tube
9 Spring lower seat
10 Spring
11 Shock absorber
12 Shock absorber retaining nut
13 Piston rod
14 Upper mounting
15 Cover
16 Spring upper seat
17 Bump stop
18 Bellows

Fig. 10.4   Rear suspension components (Sec 1)

1 Trailing arm
2 Torque rods
3 Subframe
4 Panhard rod
5 Stabilizer bar
6 Shock absorber
7 Bump stop
8 Spring

and a telescopic shock absorber are attached to each trailing arm. A stabilizer bar is installed on some models.

The rear suspension on 1988 760 sedan models is of an independent design. Unlike the ''live'' rear axles used on the other models, the rear driveaxles serve only to drive the rear wheels, and play no part in supporting the vehicle. This system, designated the ''Multi-link'' rear suspension, consists of two trailing arms (one per side), coil springs, shock absorbers, lower links, track rods, upper links, wheel bearing housings and the differential mounting member (see Fig. 10.5). The rear suspension allows camber and toe-in adjustments to be made (although these adjustments should be made by a Volvo dealer or alignment shop).

All 1988 models are equipped with sealed, non-serviceable front wheel bearings. The hub and brake disc are now two separate units.

2   Maintenance and inspection

1   Check the tire pressures frequently. See Section 32.
2   Every 6000 miles or six months, inspect the tires more thoroughly, again as described in Section 32. If the wheels are not removed for this check, at least check the tightness of the wheel nuts.
3   At the same intervals check the power steering fluid level (Section 3).
4   Every 12,000 miles or annually, check the front wheel bearing adjustment (Section 4).
5   At the same intervals examine all steering and suspension components for wear and damage. Pay particular attention to rubber gaiters, bellows etc (photo). Repair or replace as necessary.
6   To inspect the steering, have an assistant move the steering wheel back and forth with the wheels on the ground. Look for play in the

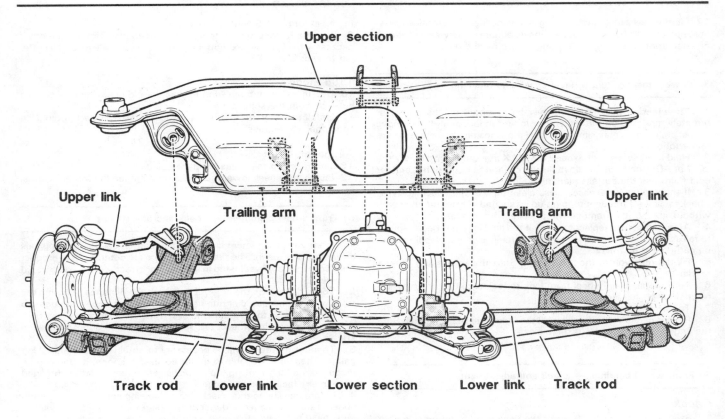

Fig. 10.5 Details of the Multi-link rear suspension system (Sec 1)

track rod end balljoints and in the rack itself. Radial play in a balljoint should not exceed 0.5 mm (0.020 in); play in the rack may be up to 2.0 mm (0.079 in).

7 Check for excessive play in the front control arm lower balljoints by levering them up and down, and by pushing and pulling the front wheel. Radial play (side-to-side) must not exceed 0.5 mm (0.020 in). Axial play (up-and-down) of up to 3 mm (0.118 in) is permitted. Do not confuse balljoint play with play in the strut top mounting or the control arm bushing.

8 Check for wear in front and rear suspension bushings by levering between the component and its attachment.

9 Inspect the shock absorbers visually for leakage or damage. Check their function by bouncing the vehicle at each corner in turn: it should come to rest within one complete oscillation. Continued movement, or squeaking and groaning from the shock absorbers, suggest that replacement is required (Section 21 or 27).

10 Check the security of attachment of the steering gear. Inspect the pipes and unions for leaks. Also check the tension and condition of the pump drivebelt (Chapter 2, Section 7).

11 At the first 12,000 mile service only, check-tighten (loosen and retighten to the specified torque) the following fastenings:

Rear axle-to-trailing arm nuts
Control arm-to-crossmember bolts
Radius rod-to-control arm bolts
Radius rod-to-subframe bolts
Steering gear-to-crossmember bolts
Front crossmember-to-body bolts

2.5 A split in a shock absorber bellows

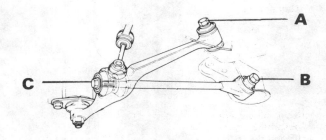

Fig. 10.6 Some of the front suspension bolts which must be checked/tightened (Sec 2)

A Control arm-to-crossmember   C Radius rod-to-control arm
B Radius rod-to-subframe

12 Front wheel alignment checking is not specified as a routine operation, but it should be carried out whenever abnormal tire wear is noticed, or after front wheel impact (hitting a curb or pothole at speed).

3   Power steering fluid — level check and bleeding

1   The steering fluid reservoir may be mounted on the pump, or remotely mounted on the radiator or inner fender panel. It may have a dipstick, or there may simply be level markings on a translucent container (photos).
2   Fluid level should not exceed the MAX mark, nor drop below the LOW or ADD mark. Some dipsticks are calibrated both for hot and for cold fluid: use the correct markings.
3   If topping-up is necessary, use clean fluid of the specified type. Check for leaks if frequent topping-up is required. Do not run the pump without fluid in it — remove the drivebelt if necessary.
4   After component replacement, or if the fluid level has been allowed to fall so low that air has entered the hydraulic system, bleeding must be carried out as follows.
5   Fill the reservoir to the MAX mark. Start the engine and allow it to idle.
6   Turn the steering wheel from lock to lock a couple of times. Do not hold it on full lock.
7   Top up the fluid if necessary.
8   Repeat paragraphs 6 and 7 until the fluid level ceases to fall. Stop the engine and install the reservoir cap.

4   Front wheel bearings — check and adjustment

Check

1   Raise and support the front of the vehicle with the wheels free.
2   Hold the wheel at top and bottom and try to rock it. Spin the wheel and listen for rumbling or grinding noises. Play should be barely perceptible and noise should be absent.
3   If play or noise is evident, adjust the bearings as follows. If adjustment does not improve matters, remove the bearings for examination (Section 15).

Adjustment

4   Loosen the front wheel nuts. Raise and support the front of the vehicle and remove the front wheel.
5   Pry or tap off the hub nut grease cap. Obtain a new cap if the old one is damaged (photo). On 1988 models, it is recommended that the cap always be replaced.

1987 and earlier models

6   Straighten the legs of the hub nut cotter pin: Remove the cotter pin; obtain a new one for reassembly.
7   Loosen the hub nut slightly, then tighten it to 57 Nm (42 ft-lbs), at the same time rotating the brake disc.
8   Loosen the nut half a turn, then retighten it using the fingers only

(nominal torque 1.5 Nm/1.1 ft-lbs).
9   Insert a new cotter pin to secure the hub nut. Tighten the nut if necessary to align the next cotter pin hole. Spread the legs of the cotter pin to secure it.

1988 models

10 Obtain a new hub nut (don't reuse the old one). Remove the old hub nut from the spindle.
11 Install the new nut and tighten it to 74 ft-lbs. Now tighten it an additional 45 degrees.

All models

12 Carefully tap the grease cap into place
13 Install the wheel, lower the vehicle and tighten the wheel lug nuts.

5   Front wheel alignment — check and adjustment

1   Front wheel alignment is defined by camber, caster, steering axis inclination and toe-in. The first three factors are determined in production; only toe can be adjusted in service. Incorrect toe will cause rapid tire wear.
2   Toe is defined as the amount by which the distance between the front wheels, measured at hub height, differs from the front edges to the rear edges. If the distance between the front edges is less than that at the rear, the wheels are said to toe-in; the opposite case is known as toe-out.
3   To measure toe, it will be necessary to obtain or make a tracking gauge. These are available in motor accessory shops, or one can be made from a length of rigid pipe or bar with some kind of threaded adjustment facility at one end.
4   Before measuring toe, check that all steering and suspension components are undamaged and that tire pressures are correct. The vehicle must be at approximately curb weight, with the spare wheel and jack in their normal position and any abnormal loads removed.
5   Park the vehicle on level ground and bounce it a few times to settle the suspension.
6   Use the tracking gauge to measure the distance between the inside faces of the front wheel rims, at hub height, at the rear of the front wheels. Record this distance; call it measurement A.

Fig. 10.7 Checking a front wheel bearing for wear (Sec 4)

3.1A   Power steering fluid reservoir — remote type with level marking

3.1B   Removing the dipstick from a pump-mounted reservoir

4.5   Removing the front hub grease cap

7   Push the vehicle forwards or backwards so that the wheels rotate exactly 180° (half a turn). Measure the distance between the front wheel rims again, this time at the front of the wheels. Record this distance; call it measurement B.

8   Subtract measurement B from measurement A. If the answer is positive it is the amount of toe-in; if negative it is the amount of toe-out. Permissible values are given in the Specifications.

9   If adjustment is necessary loosen the tie-rod end locknuts and the outer bellows clips, then rotate each tie-rod by equal amounts until the setting is correct. Hold the tie-rod ends in their horizontal position with a wrench while making the adjustment.

10   Tighten the locknuts and outer bellows clips.

11   Provided the tie-rods have been adjusted by equal amounts the steering wheel should be central when moving straight-ahead. The amount of visible thread on each track rod should also be equal to within 2 mm (0.08 in). If wheel alignment and track rod length are both correct but steering wheel positions is wrong, remove the steering wheel and reposition it (Section 12).

6   Tie-rod end — removal and installation

1   Remove the front wheel on the side concerned.

2   Counterhold the tie-rod and loosen the rod end locknut by half a turn.

3   Unscrew the rod end stud nut to the end of its threads. Separate the stud from the steering arm with a balljoint separator, then remove the nut and disconnect the tie-rod end ballstud from the arm (photo).

4   Unscrew the tie-rod end from the tie-rod, counting the number of turns needed to remove it. Record this number.

5   When installing, screw the tie-rod end on by the same number of turns noted during removal.

6   Engage the ballstud in the steering arm. Install the nut and tighten it to the specified torque.

7   Counterhold the tie-rod and tighten the locknut.

8   Install the front wheel, lower the vehicle and tighten the wheel lug nuts.

9   Have the front wheel alignment checked at the first opportunity (Section 5), especially if new components have been installed.

7   Steering gear boot — replacement

1   Remove the tie-rod end on the side concerned (Section 6). Also remove the rod end locknut.

2   Release the two clips which secure the boot. Peel off the boot (photos).

3   Clean out any dirt and grit from the inner end of the tie-rod and (when accessible) the rack. Apply fresh grease to these components.

4   Install and secure the new boot, then install the tie-rod end.

8   Steering gear — removal and installation

1   Raise and support the front of the vehicle. Remove the engine undertray.

2   Remove the cover panel from the middle of the front crossmember.

3   Remove the spring clips and loosen the pinch-bolts and nuts on the lower universal joint (photo). Slide the universal joint up the intermediate shaft to free it from the pinion.

4   Disconnect the tie-rod ends from the steering arms. See Section 6.

5   Clean around the fluid supply and return unions, then disconnect them (photo). Be prepared for fluid spillage. Plug or cap open unions to keep dirt out.

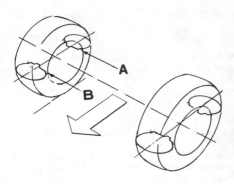

Fig. 10.8   Toe measurements. Arrow points forward; for A and B see text (Sec 5)

6.3   Using a balljoint separator on the tie-rod end

7.2A   Removing a steering gear boot clip . . .

7.2B   . . . and the boot

8.3   Intermediate shaft lower universal joint

8.5   Steering gear fluid supply and return unions (arrowed)

6   Remove the two mounting bolts and nuts. Remove the steering gear from the crossmember. It may be necessary to reposition the front stabilizer bar.
7   Install by reversing the removal operations, noting the following points:
   a) Tighten all fastenings to the specified torque
   b) Use new copper washers on the fluid unions
   c) Bleed the steering system (Section 3)
   d) Check the front wheel alignment (Section 5)

9 Steering gear — overhaul

Overhaul of the steering gear is not recommended, even if parts are available. Obtain a new or reconditioned unit from a Volvo dealer or other specialist.

10 Steering pump — removal and installation

1   Loosen the pump pivot and mounting strap nuts and bolts. Push the pump towards the engine and slip the drivebelt off the pulley (photos).
2   Disconnect the pump hydraulic pipes, either from below (remove the undertray) or from the back of the pump. Be prepared for fluid spillage.
3   Remove the pivot and strap nuts and bolts (photo).
4   Lift away the pump. On versions with a remote reservoir, either remove it with the pump or disconnect the hose from the pump.
5   If a new pump is to be installed, transfer the pulley and mounting brackets to it.
6   Install by reversing the removal operations, using new copper washers on the banjo unions.
7   Tension the drivebelt (Chapter 2, Section 7).
8   Refill the pump reservoir and bleed the system (Section 3).

11 Steering pump — overhaul

As with the steering gear, overhaul of the pump is not recommended for the home mechanic.

12 Steering wheel — removal and installation

1   Disconnect the battery negative cable.
2   Bring the steering wheel to the straight-ahead position.
3   Pry off the steering wheel center pad (photo).
4   Remove the steering wheel center bolt (photo).
5   If the steering column or steering gear may be moved while the

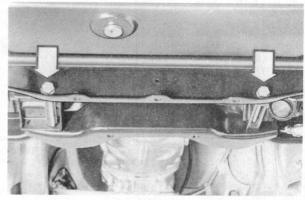

Fig. 10.9   Steering gear mounting bolts (arrowed) (Sec 8)

Fig. 10.10   Steering pump hydraulic pipes, seen from below (V6 engine, undertray removed) (Sec 10)

1 Supply   2 Return

wheel is removed, make alignment marks between the steering wheel and column.
6   Pull the steering wheel off its splines. If it is stuck, install the bolt by a few turns only and thump the wheel from behind with the hands. Do not use excessive force as the column may be damaged.
7   Install by reversing the removal operations, observing the alignment marks or the straight-ahead position of the wheel.

10.1A   Steering pump mounting strap — in-line engine

10.1B   Removing the steering pump drivebelt

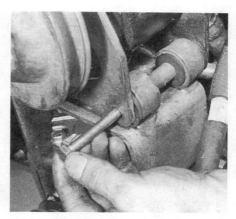

10.3   Removing the pump pivot bolt

12.3 Removing the steering wheel center pad

12.4 Removing the steering wheel center bolt

13.2 Intermediate shaft upper universal joint

13.3 Removing the horn contact ring

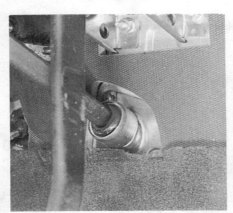

13.7 Steering column bottom bearing plate

13.8 The three bolts which secure the column top bearing to the crossmember

13 Steering column — removal and installation

1 Disconnect the battery negative cable.
2 Still under the hood, remove the clamp nut and bolt fom the top universal joint of the intermediate steering shaft. The nut is secured by a spring clip (photo).
3 Remove the steering wheel (Section 12) and the steering column switches, complete with baseplate and horn contact ring (photo).
4 Remove the trim panel from below the steering column. It is secured by two screws and two clips. Disconnect the heater duct as the panel is withdrawn.
5 Remove the switch panel to the right of the steering lock.
6 Disconnect the electrical connector from the ignition/starter switch.
7 Remove the three screws which secure the column bottom bearing plate to the firewall (photo).
8 Remove the two bolts which secure the column top bearing to the support crossmember (photo). In some markets shear-head bolts will be found here: remove them by drilling and inserting a stud extractor, or by turning them with a punch.
9 Remove the third bolt securing the top bearing. Recover the spacer tube (photo).
10 Remove the three bolts which secure the column support crossmember. To gain access to the right-hand bolts it will be necessary to remove the right-hand lower trim panel, disconnect the ECU (where applicable) and move the wiring harnesses aside.
11 Remove the steering lock and ignition/starter switch (Section 14).
12 Free the column and withdraw it into the vehicle. Recover the washer from the top bearing pin (photo).
13 The column bearings may now be removed if necessary. Be careful not to collapse the coupling in the upper section. The overall length of the column must be 727.2 ± 1 mm (28.63 ± 0.04 in).

14 Install by reversing the removal operations, noting the following points:
 a) Tighten nuts and bolts to the specified torque (when known)
 b) When shear-head bolts are used, only tighten them lightly at first. When satisfied that installation is correct, tighten the bolts until their heads break off

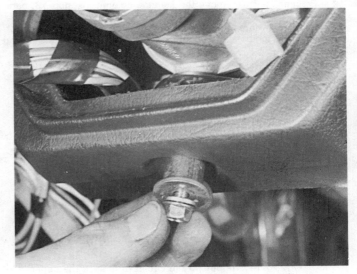

13.9 Removing the third bolt and spacer tube

10

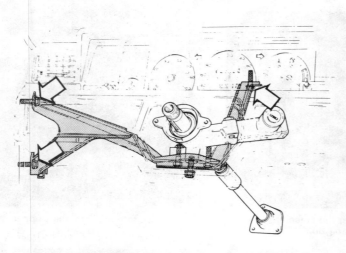

Fig. 10.11   Steering column crossmember support bolts (arrowed) (Sec 13)

13.12   Freeing the top bearing pin

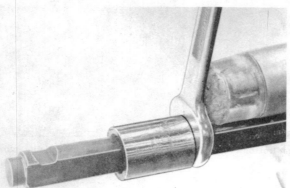

Fig. 10.12   Driving off the column lower bearing (Sec 13)

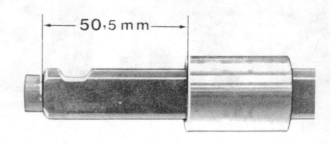

Fig. 10.13   Lower bearing installed dimension (Sec 13)

14   Steering lock — removal and installation

1   Proceed as if to remove the steering column (Section 13, paragraphs 1 and 3 to 10).
2   Remove the lock pinch-bolt from the top bearing housing (photo).
3   Insert the ignition key and turn it to position II. Depress the locking

ing button and begin to withdraw the lock from the bearing housing (photo).
4   The ignition key and lock barrel will obstruct removal by hitting the surrounding trim. Therefore remove the key and free the top bearing housing from the crossmember; do not lose the washer from the pin. By moving the bearing housing enough clearance can be gained to withdraw the steering lock complete with ignition/starter switch (photo).
5   Remove the switch from the lock by removing the two screws.
6   Install by reversing the removal operations.

Fig. 10.14   Removing the circlip to release the upper bearing components (Sec 13)

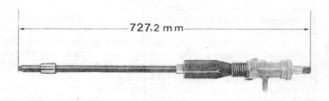

Fig. 10.15   Column overall length when undamaged (Sec 13)

14.2 Steering lock pinch-bolt (arrowed)

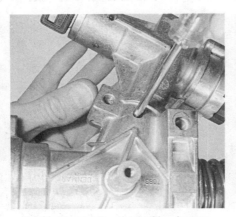

14.3 Depressing the locking button (column removed)

14.4 Withdrawing the steering lock — column installed. Locking button (arrowed) has just emerged

15 Front wheel bearings — removal, inspection and installation

1987 and earlier models

1 Remove the front brake disc (Chapter 9). Remove the bearings and discard the oil seal.
2 Clean the bearings and the races in the hub with solvent. Inspect them for roughness, blueing or other signs of damage.
3 When replacing bearings, note that the outboard bearing may be made by SKF or by Koyo. Bearings and races of different manufacture must not be mixed.
4 To remove the bearing races, tap them out of the disc hub using a hammer and a brass or copper drift (photo).
5 Clean the bearing race seats in the hub.
6 Tap the races into position in the hub, being careful to keep them square (photos). Use a socket or tube, or the old races, to drive them in.
7 Pack the bearing races with grease, working it well into the rollers by hand. Also put a few fingerfuls of grease into the space between the bearing races (photo).
8 Install the inboard race to the hub. Grease the lips of a new oil seal and install it so that it is flush with the hub (photo).
9 Install the hub/disc assembly to the stub axle, which should be well greased. Push the assembly home, then install the outboard race and the castellated nut (photo).
10 Adjust the bearings (Section 4).
11 Install the brake caliper and bracket (Chapter 9, Section 10).

1988 models

12 Following the procedure described in Chapter 9, remove the brake disc.
13 Using a hammer and punch, carefully knock the grease cap off the hub. It is not recommended that the cap be re-used.
14 Remove the hub nut and pull the hub and bearing assembly off

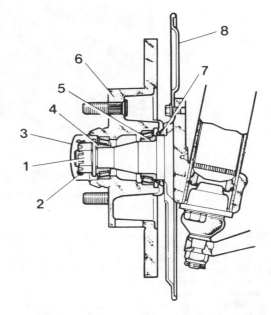

Fig. 10.16 Sectional view through the front hub (Sec 15)

1	Castellated nut	5	Inner bearing
2	Cotter pin	6	Brake disc
3	Grease cap	7	Oil seal
4	Outer bearing	8	Backplate

15.4 Driving out a bearing race

15.6A Installing a bearing race . . .

15.6B . . . and driving it into place

10

15.7   Pack the wheel bearing by working the grease into the rollers from the back side

15.8   Installing the oil seal

15.9   Installing the castellated nut

16.2   Control arm balljoint — cotter pin partly withdrawn

16.5   Control arm-to-crossmember bolt (arrowed)

the spindle. **Note:** *The hub and bearing assembly is a sealed unit — don't attempt to remove the bearings from the hub.*

15 If a new hub is being installed and the vehicle is equipped with ABS brakes, the pulse wheel must be transferred to the new hub assembly. This operation requires special equipment and should be left to a Volvo service department or other qualified shop.

16 Clean all traces of old grease from the spindle. Slide the new hub and bearing assembly onto the spindle and thread on a NEW nut. **Note:** *The hub and bearing assembly is pre-lubricated from the factory and no additional grease is required.*

17 Tighten the nut as directed in Section 4. Carefully tap a new grease cap onto the hub.

18 The remainder of installation is the reverse of the removal procedure.

16   Front control arm — removal and installation

1 Loosen the front wheel nuts, raise and support the front of the vehicle and remove the front wheel.

2 Remove the cotter pin and nut from the balljoint (photo). Obtain a new cotter pin for reassembly.

3 Unbolt the stabilizer bar link and the radius rod from the control arm. Obtain a new bolt for reassembly.

4 Separate the control arm from the balljoint, using a balljoint separator. Be careful not to damage the balljoint boot.

5 Remove the control arm-to-crossmember nut and bolt (photo). Remove the control arm from the crossmember. Obtain a new nut and bolt for reassembly.

6 Install by reversing the removal operations, but do not fully tighten the control arm-to-crossmember nut and bolt until the weight of the vehicle is back on its wheels. Rock the vehicle to settle the suspension, then tighten the nut and bolt to the specified torque.

17   Front control arm balljoint — removal and installation

1 Proceed as for control arm removal (Section 16, paragraphs 1 to 4) but without unbolting the radius rod.

2 Remove the two bolts which secure the balljoint to the strut (photo). Remove the balljoint.

17.2   Two bolts (arrowed) secure the balljoint to the strut (strut removed)

3   When installing, use new bolts to secure the balljoint and apply thread locking compound to them. Tighten the bolts in the specified stages, making sure that the balljoint is properly seated.
4   The remainder of installation is a reversal of the removal procedure.

18 Front radius rod — removal and installation

1   Loosen the front wheel nuts, raise and support the vehicle and remove the front wheel.
2   Unbolt the radius rod from the control arm and from the subframe. Remove the radius rod.
3   Install by reversing the removal operations, using new nuts and bolts to secure the radius rod. Do not fully tighten the radius rod-to-subframe nut and bolt until the weight of the vehicle is back on its wheels and it has been rocked a few times.

19 Front stabilizer bar — removal and installation

1   Raise the front of the vehicle and support it securely on jackstands.
2   Unbolt the two U-brackets which secure the stabilizer bar (photo).
3   Unbolt the stabilizer bar from its end links, or unbolt the end links from the control arms, as preferred (photo).
4   Install by reversing the removal operations. Replace the mounting rubbers as necessary. (The U-bracket rubbers are split and may be replaced without removing the stabilizer bar.)
5   Tighten the link upper nuts to achieve the dimension shown between the washers (Fig. 10.17).

20 Front suspension strut — removal and installation

1   Loosen the front wheel nuts, raise and support the front of the vehicle and remove the front wheel.
2   Remove the brake caliper (Chapter 9, Section 10), but do not disconnect the hydraulic hoses. Tie the caliper up so that the hoses are not strained.
3   On models with ABS, disconnect or remove the wheel sensor.
4   If the strut is to be replaced, remove the brake disc (Chapter 9, Section 15) and backplate (photo).
5   Remove the cotter pin from the suspension bottom balljoint nut. Unscrew the nut to the end of the threads. Free the balljoint stud from the control arm using a balljoint separator, then remove the nut.
6   Similarly separate the tie-rod end balljoint from the steering arm.
7   Lever the control arm downwards and free it from the bottom balljoint. If there is not enough movement to allow this, unbolt the stabilizer bar link.
8   Remove the cover from the strut top mounting. Note which way round the mount is installed: it is not symmetrical.
9   If the strut is to be disassembled, loosen the piston rod nut, at

19.2   A stabilizer bar U-bracket

19.3   A stabilizer bar link

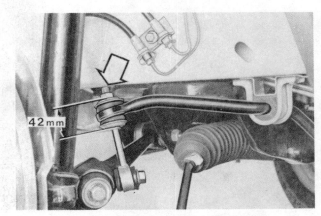

Fig. 10.17   Tighten the link nut (arrowed) to achieve the dimension shown (Sec 19)

42 mm

20.4   Unbolting the brake disc backplate

10

20.9   Releasing the piston rod nut (strut removed)

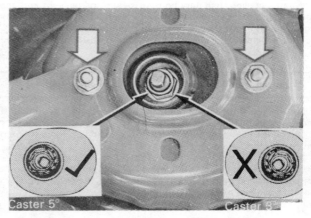

Fig. 10.18   Correct installation of strut gives correct castor (inset, left). Top mounting nuts arrowed; right-hand strut shown (Sec 20)

the same time counterholding the piston rod (photo). Do not remove the nut, just loosen it a turn or two.

10 Have an assistant support the strut. Check that all attachments have been removed, then remove the two top mounting nuts. Remove the strut through the wheel well.

11 Install by reversing the removal operations, noting the following points:

   a) Observe the correct installed direction of the top mounting (Fig. 10.18)
   b) Tighten all fasteners to their specified torques

21   Front suspension strut — overhaul

Warning: *Spring compressors of sound design and construction must be used during this procedure. Uncontrolled release of the spring may result in damage and injury.*

1   Remove the strut from the vehicle (Section 20). Alternately, the work can be carried out on the vehicle after the following preliminaries:

   a) Remove the wheel and separate the tie-rod end balljoint

   b) Unbolt the stabilizer bar link
   c) Unbolt the brake hose bracket from the inner fender panel
   d) Loosen the piston rod nut, then release the top mounting. Press the control arm down and swing the strut outwards, tying or wiring it to limit movement and to avoid strain on the brake hose

2   Install spring compressors to catch at least three coils of the spring. Tighten the compressors until the load is taken off the spring seats. Make sure that the compressors are secure.

3   Remove the piston rod nut (which should already have been loosened) and the strut top mount. Note the position of any washers (photos).

4   Remove the spring upper seat, the spring itself, the washer, bump stop and bellows. (With gas-filled shock absorbers there is no bump stop.) Do not drop or jar the compressed spring (photo).

5   Remove the rubber ring (if equipped) from the spring lower seat (photo).

6   Using an open-end wrench or similar tool, unscrew the shock absorber retaining nut (photo).

7   Pull the shock absorber out of its tube (photo).

8   Disassembly of the strut is now complete. Replace components as necessary, remembering that it is good practice to replace springs and shock absorbers in pairs.

9   If the spring is to be replaced, carefully remove the compressors from the old spring and install them to the new one.

10 Reassemble by reversing the disassembly operations. Note the relationship of the disc to the bellows on models with gas-filled shock absorbers (Fig. 10.19). Do not fully tighten the piston rod nut until the top mount has been secured to the vehicle.

21.3A   Removing the piston rod nut . . .

21.3B   . . . and the strut top mount

21.4 Removing the bump stop and bellows

21.5 Removing the rubber ring from the spring lower seat

21.6 Unscrewing the shock absorber nut with a spanner wrench

21.7 Removing the shock absorber

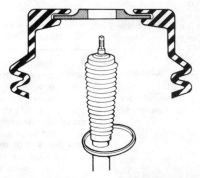

Fig. 10.19 Bellows and disc used with gas-filled shock absorbers (Sec 21)

23.2 Torque rod front mount

22 Suspension rubber bushings — replacement

1   The principle of bushing replacement is simple enough: the old bushing is pressed out and the new one is pressed in. The reality is slightly more difficult.
2   Various special tools are specified by the makers for bushing replacement. They are basically mandrels and tubes of different sizes which are used with a press and sometimes with V-blocks. The amateur may experiment with a bench vise and sockets or pieces of tubing, using liquid soap or petroleum jelly as a lubricant. If this is unsuccessful it will be necessary to have the bushing replaced by a workshop having press facilities.
3   Bushing replacement in the vehicle is not recommended.

23 Rear torque rods — removal and installation

Note: *This procedure does not apply to 1988 760 sedan models.*
1   Raise and support the rear of the vehicle.
2   Remove the front mounting bolts from both torque rods, even if only one is to be removed (photo).
3   Unbolt and remove the torque rods. Remove the X-link.

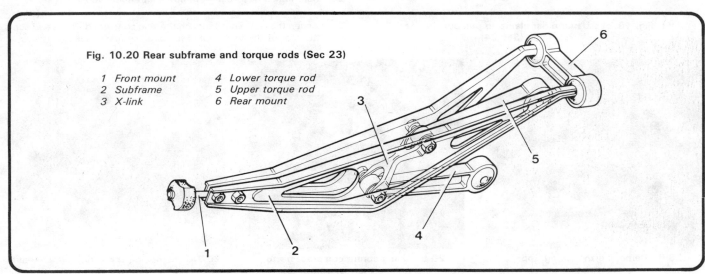

Fig. 10.20 Rear subframe and torque rods (Sec 23)

1 Front mount
2 Subframe
3 X-link
4 Lower torque rod
5 Upper torque rod
6 Rear mount

10

4   When installing, unbolt the subframe front mount to allow movement of the subframe. Install the torque rods to the rear axle first
without tightening the mounts, then attach them and the X-link to the
subframe.
5   Tighten the torque rod-to-subframe mounts to the specified torque.
6   Tighten the subframe front mount to the specified torque.
7   Get the weight of the vehicle back on the rear wheels, then tighten
the torque rod-to-axle mounts to the specified torque.

24   Rear subframe and mounts — removal and installation

Note: This procedure does not apply to 1988 760 sedan models.
1   Raise and support the rear of the vehicle.
2   Remove the subframe front mounting nuts and bolts.
3   The front mounting rubber and mounting bracket may now be
removed if desired, using a chisel and some lubricant around the rubber. Note the orientation of the rubber.
4   To remove the subframe completely, unbolt the torque rods and
X-link from it. Also release the handbrake cable from the subframe
bracket.
5   Install one of the front mounting bolts. Hook a bar-clamp behind
the bolt and use the clamp to pull the subframe out of the rear mountings (Fig. 10.21).
6   The rear mounting bracket can now be unbolted if required.
7   Install by reversing the removal operations, noting the following
points:

   a) Use petroleum jelly as a lubricant for the mounting rubbers
   b) Carry out the final tightening of the front mounting before that
       of the torque rods

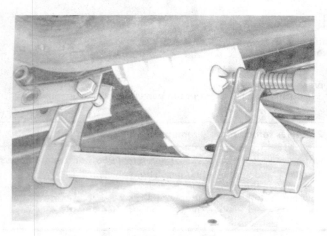

**Fig. 10.21 Using a bar-clamp to pull out the rear
subframe (Sec 24)**

25   Rear trailing arm — removal and installation

Note: This procedure does not apply to 1988 760 sedan models.
1   Proceed as if for rear spring removal (Section 26, paragraphs 1
to 3).
2   Disconnect the driveshaft from the pinion flange, making alignment marks for reference when installing.
3   Support the trailing arm below the spring pan with a jack.
4   Unbolt the stabilizer bar (if equipped) from both trailing arms. If
no stabilizer bar is installed, remove the shock absorber lower mounting bolt on the side concerned. Loosen the lower mounting on the other
side.
5   Lower the jack to release the spring tension.
6   Loosen the trailing arm-to-axle nuts crosswise. Remove the nuts,
axle clamp and mounting rubbers. Remove the stabilizer bar bracket,
if equipped.
7   Remove the trailing arm bracket nuts and bolts. Pry the front
mounting out of the body and remove the trailing arm.
8   Install by reversing the removal operations, tightening the various
fasteners to the specified torques.

26   Rear spring — removal and installation

1   Loosen the rear wheel nuts on the side concerned. Raise and support the rear of the vehicle so that both rear wheels hang free. Remove
the rear wheel.
2   Remove the two bolts which secure the rear brake caliper. Slide
the caliper off the disc and tie it up so that the flexible hose is not
strained. Obtain new bolts for reassembly.
3   If the exhaust system will be in the way, unhook it from its mounts
and lower it or move it aside.
4   Jack up the trailing arm slightly to take the load off the shock absorber. Remove the shock absorber lower mounting nut and bolt. Lower
the jack.
5   Remove the nut which secures the spring upper seat (photo).
6   Pull the trailing arm downwards as far as possible. Pull the top of
the spring downwards until the upper seat is clear of the mounting
stud, then remove the spring and seat rearwards. If difficulty is encountered, either use spring compressors to unload the spring, or disconnect the rear stabilizer bar to allow the trailing arm more downward
movement (photo).
7   Inspect the spring seat rubbers and replace them if necessary
(photos).
8   Install by reversing the removal operations, tightening the fasteners
to their specified torques. Use new bolts to secure the brake caliper.
9   Install the wheel, lower the vehicle and tighten the wheel lug nuts.

27   Rear shock absorber — removal and installation

1   Loosen the rear wheel nuts on the side concerned. Raise and support the rear of the vehicle and remove the rear wheel.

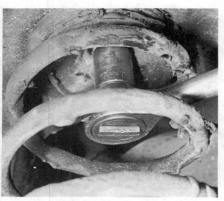

**26.5   Removing the spring upper
seat nut**

**26.6   Using spring compressors to
unload the rear spring**

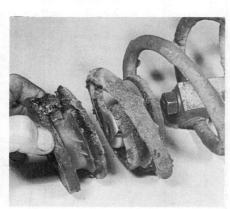

**26.7A   Removing the spring upper seat
rubber from the spring . . .**

26.7B . . . and the lower seat rubber from the trailing arm

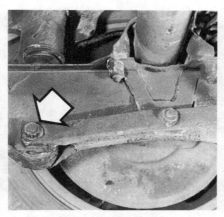

27.2 Rear shock absorber lower mounting bolt (arrowed)

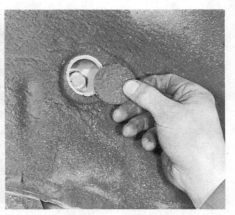

27.3 Exposing the shock absorber upper mounting bolt

2   Jack up the trailing arm slightly to take the load off the shock absorber. Remove the shock absorber lower mounting nut and bolt (photo). Lower the jack.
3   Remove the rubber cover in the wheel well which covers the shock absorber upper mounting bolt (photo). Remove the bolt.
4   Pull the shock absorber downwards and remove it.
5   Install by reversing the removal operations. Tighten the shock absorber mounting and the wheel nuts to the specified torque.

28 Rear stabilizer bar — removal and installation

1   Raise the rear of the vehicle and support it on jackstands.
2   Remove the two nuts and bolts on each side which secure the stabilizer bar. The forward bolts also secure the rear shock absorber lower mounts; it may be necessary to jack up under the trailing arms to take the load off these bolts.
3   Remove the stabilizer bar.
4   Install by reversing the removal operations.

29 Panhard rod — removal and installation

1   Raise and support the vehicle with the rear wheels free.
2   Unbolt the Panhard rod from the body, then from the rear axle (photo). Remove the rod.
3   If the rod bushings need replacing, have the old ones pressed out and new ones pressed in by a Volvo dealer or other specialist.
4   Install the rod and tighten the bolts to the specified torque, axle end first. Lower the vehicle.

30 Track rod (Multi-link rear suspension) — removal and installation

Note: This procedure applies to 1988 760 sedan models only.

1   Loosen the rear wheel lug nuts, raise the rear of the vehicle and support it securely on jackstands. Remove the wheel.
2   Using white paint or a sharp scribe, mark the position of the toe adjuster on the cam at the inner end of the track rod. This will insure that the rear wheel alignment will be the same upon installation.
3   Remove the bolt from each end of the track rod and pull the rod from the vehicle. If the rod sticks to the wheel bearing housing, pull it off with the aid of a two-jaw puller and a 50 mm long 12 mm bolt (Fig. 10.22).
4   To install the rod, position it on the vehicle and install the bolts, but don't tighten them fully yet.
5   Align the previously made matchmarks on the inner cam. A pair of large water pump pliers can be used to pull the rod into position,

29.2   Panhard rod attachment to the rear axle

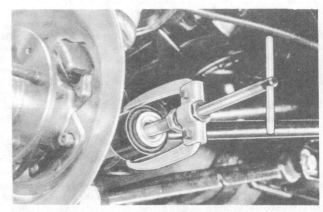

Fig. 10.22   Insert a bolt into the track rod bushing and push against it with a puller to remove the rod from the wheel bearing housing (Sec 30)

10

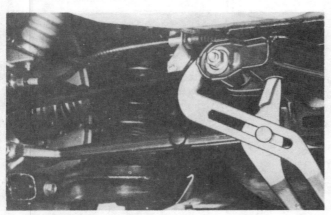

Fig. 10.23   Use a pair of large pliers to position the inner end of the track rod (Sec 30)

Fig. 10.24   A = Trailing arm-to-wheel bearing housing bolt
B = Lower link-to-wheel bearing housing bolt

if necessary (Fig. 10.23). Tighten the nut enough to hold this setting.
6   Place a floor jack under the trailing arm and raise it to simulate normal rear suspension ride height. Tighten the fasteners to the specified torque.
7   Install the wheel and lug nuts, lower the vehicle and tighten the lug nuts to the specified torque.
8   Drive the vehicle to a Volvo dealer or alignment shop to have the rear wheel alignment checked, and if necessary, adjusted.

31   Lower link (Multi-link rear suspension) — removal and installation

Note: *This procedure applies to 1988 760 sedan models only.*
1   Loosen the rear wheel lug nuts, raise the rear of the vehicle and support it securely on jackstands. Remove the wheel.
2   Support the trailing arm with a floor jack positioned under the spring seat area. Raise the jack just enough to take the spring pressure off the stop (**Note:** *The jack must remain in this position throughout the entire procedure).*
3   Remove the trailing arm-to-wheel bearing housing bolt (Fig. 10.24).
4   Mark the position of the adjusting cam on the inner end of the lower link to the differential support member, using white paint or a sharp scribe.
5   Unbolt the track rod from the wheel bearing housing and pull it off its mount (see the previous Section).
6   Unbolt the lower link from the wheel bearing housing.
7   Unbolt the inner end of the lower link from the differential support member. Pull the wheel bearing housing outward just far enough to allow removal of the lower link. **Caution:** *Don't pull the wheel bearing housing out too far, as the inner constant velocity joint on the driveaxle may become over-extended).*
8   Installation of the lower link is basically the reverse of the removal procedure, but before tightening the bolts to the specified torque, the match marks on the inner adjusting cam must be aligned and the suspension must be raised to simulate normal ride height.
9   Drive the vehicle to a Volvo dealer or an alignment shop to have the rear wheel alignment checked, and if necessary, adjusted.

32   Upper link (Multi-link rear suspension) — removal and installation

Note: *This procedure applies to 1988 760 sedan models only.*
1   Loosen the rear wheel lug nuts, raise the rear of the vehicle and support it securely on jackstands. Remove the wheel.
2   Position a floor jack under the trailing arm and raise it slightly, just enough to take the spring pressure off the stop. The jack must remain in this position during the entire procedure.
3   Remove the track rod-to-wheel bearing housing bolt and pull the rod from the housing (refer to Section 30 if necessary). Remove the

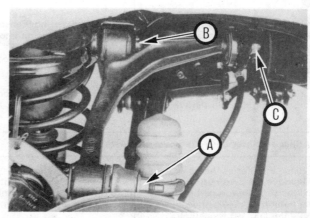

Fig. 10.25   After removing the upper link-to-wheel bearing housing nut (A), remove the upper link-to-differential support member fasteners (B and C) and remove the link from the vehicle

trailing arm-to-wheel bearing housing bolt.
4   Remove the nut that secures the upper link to the wheel bearing housing, and the fasteners that secure the upper link to the differential support member (Fig. 10.25). Pull the top of the wheel bearing housing to the rear just enough to remove the upper link mounting stud from its hole, then remove the link from the differential support member. Retrieve any spacers that may be present between the upper link and the wheel bearing housing. It may be necessary to pry between the support member and the link to free it.
5   Installation of the upper link is basically the reverse of the removal procedure, but before tightening the bolts to the specified torque the suspension must be raised to simulate normal ride height.
6   Drive the vehicle to a Volvo dealer or an alignment shop to have the rear wheel alignment checked, and if necessary, adjusted.

33   Trailing arm (Multi-link rear suspension) — removal and installation

Note: *This procedure applies to 1988 760 sedan models only.*
1   Loosen the rear wheel lug nuts, raise the rear of the vehicle and support it securely on jackstands. Remove the wheel.
2   Position a floor jack under the trailing arm, just ahead of the shock absorber. Place a block of wood on the jack head to serve as a cushion, then raise the jack just enough to take the spring pressure off of the stop.
3   Remove the shock absorber (Section 35).
4   Loop a length of chain up through the trailing arm (where the shock absorber used to be) and out through the coil spring, as near to the

top of the spring as is possible. Bolt the chain together, but leave enough slack for the spring to extend fully when the trailing arm is lowered. This precautionary measure will contain the spring should it accidently slip and "jump" out of its seat, which could cause severe injury.

5   Loosen the trailing arm-to-body bolt, then unbolt the trailing arm from the wheel bearing housing.

6   Slowly lower the jack until the coil spring is fully extended, then unbolt the chain and remove the spring.

7   Remove the nut and bolt from the forward end of the trailing arm and remove the arm from the vehicle.

8   To install the arm, position the forward end in its mount on the body and insert the bolt. Don't tighten it fully yet.

9   Place the coil spring between its upper and lower seats, making sure the spring seats are in place. Install the safety chain, then raise the trailing arm into position. Install the trailing arm-to-wheel bearing housing bolt, but don't tighten it fully at this time.

10 Install the shock absorber, tightening its fasteners securely.

11 Raise the trailing arm to simulate normal ride height, then tighten all fasteners to the specified torque.

12 Install the wheel and lug nuts, lower the vehicle and tighten the lug nuts to the specified torque.

34   Wheel bearing housing (Multi-link rear suspension) — removal and installation

Note: *This procedure applies to 1988 760 sedan models only.*

1   Loosen the rear wheel lug nuts, raise the rear of the vehicle and support it securely on jackstands. Remove the wheel.

2   Remove the rear brake caliper and suspend it with a piece of wire (Chapter 9). Slide the brake disc off the hub.

3   Remove the rear hub nut. Place a large pry bar between two of the wheel studs to prevent the hub from turning while loosening the nut. Discard the nut and obtain a new one for reassembly.

4   Position a floor jack under the trailing arm and raise it just enough to take the spring pressure off the stop. Unbolt the trailing arm from the wheel bearing housing.

5   Remove the track rod-to-wheel bearing housing bolt, then separate the rod from the housing (Section 30).

6   Unbolt the lower link from the wheel bearing housing (Section 31).

7   Remove the upper link-to-wheel bearing housing nut (Section 32) and rotate the top of the housing to the rear, separating it from the stud on the upper link. Be careful not to lose the shims on the upper link stud, if any are present.

8   Support the driveaxle outer constant velocity joint with one hand, then pull the wheel bearing housing off the end of the driveaxle (this may require an assistant). If the driveaxle is stuck in the hub, push it out with a two-jaw puller.

9   Inspect the bearings in the hub for sticking or rough operation. If they appear to be in need of replacement, take the wheel bearing housing to a Volvo dealer or other well-equipped shop to have the old bearings pressed out and the new ones pressed in.

10 Installation is the reverse of the removal procedure, but don't tighten the bolts to the specified torque until the suspension is raised to simulate normal ride height.

35   Shock absorber (Multi-link rear suspension) — removal and installation

Note: *This procedure applies to 1988 760 sedan models only.*

1   Loosen the rear wheel lug nuts, raise the rear of the vehicle and support it securely on jackstands. Remove the wheel.

2   Support the trailing arm with a floor jack positioned under the wheel bearing housing, but out of the way of the shock absorber lower mounting bolts. Raise the jack slightly. **Caution:** *The jack must remain in this position throughout the entire procedure.*

3   Remove the shock absorber-to-suspension carrier upper mounting bolt.

4   Remove the two shock absorber lower mounting bolts from the underside of the trailing arm. Pull the shock out through the hole in the trailing arm.

5   Installation is the reverse of the removal procedure.

36   Rear coil spring (Multi-link rear suspension) — removal and installation

Note: *This procedure applies to 1988 760 sedan models only.*

1   Refer to Section 33, Steps 1 through 6 to remove the coil spring, as it is part of the trailing arm removal procedure.

2   Inspect the spring for nicks, gouges and rust, which could cause premature failure. Inspect the spring upper and lower seats for hardness, cracking and general deterioration, replacing them if necessary.

3   To install the coil spring, again refer to Section 33, beginning with Step 9 and working through the end of that Section.

37   Rear suspension bushings (Multi-link rear suspension) — removal and installation)

Due to the special tools and adapters necessary for replacement of the various rear suspension bushings, this job should be reserved for a Volvo technician or a shop with the necessary equipment. The particular part containing the bushing can, however, be removed from the vehicle by the home mechanic, thereby saving the charge for removal and installation.

38   Self-leveling rear suspension — general information

Self-leveling rear suspension is used on some Wagon models. No information on this system was available at the time of writing.

39   Wheel studs — replacement

Front

1   Remove the front brake disc (Chapter 9, Section 15) or hub/bearing assembly (Chapter 10, Section 15).

2   Support the hub area and press or drive out the old stud. Invert the disc and press the new stud into place.

3   Install the disc (or hub/bearing assembly and brake disc) and adjust the hub bearings (Section 4).

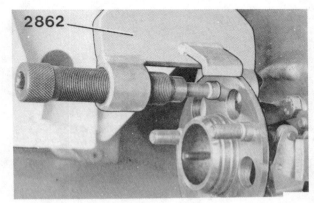

Fig. 10.26   Tool 2862 used to remove and install wheel studs on the vehicle (Sec 39)

Rear

4   Remove the handbrake shoes (Chapter 9).

5   If a pusher tool similar to that shown in Fig. 10.26 is available, stud replacement can be carried out on the vehicle. Otherwise, remove the axleshaft (Chapter 8) and proceed as for the front studs.

6   Install the axleshafts and/or handbrake shoes and other disturbed components.

10

40   Wheels and tires — general information

All vehicles covered by this manual are equipped with metric-sized fiberglass or steel belted radial tires. Use of other size or type of tires may affect the ride and handling of the vehicle. Don't mix different types of tires, such as radials and bias belted, on the same vehicle as handling may be seriously affected. It's recommended that tires be replaced in pairs on the same axle, but if only one tire is being replaced, be sure it's the same size, structure and tread design as the other.

Because tire pressure has a substantial effect on handling and wear, the pressure on all tires should be checked at least once a month or before any extended trips.

Wheels must be replaced if they are bent, dented, leak air, have elongated bolt holes, are heavily rusted, out of vertical symmetry or if the lug nuts won't stay tight. Wheel repairs that use welding or peening are not recommended.

Tire and wheel balance is important to the overall handling, braking and performance of the vehicle. Unbalanced wheels can adversely affect handling and ride characteristics as well as tire life. Whenever a tire is installed on a wheel, the tire and wheel should be balanced by a shop with the proper equipment.

41   Troubleshooting — steering and suspension

Symptom	Reason(s)
Excessive play at steering wheel	Worn tie-rod end balljoints Worn control arm balljoints Worn intermediate shaft coupling Worn steering gear
Vehicle wanders or pulls to one side	Uneven tire pressures Incorrect wheel alignment Worn tie-rod end balljoints Worn control arm balljoints Faulty shock absorber Accident damage
Steering heavy or stiff	Low tire pressures Seized balljoint Seized strut top bearing Incorrect wheel alignment Steering gear damaged or lacking lubricant Power steering fault (see below)
Lack of power assistance	Fluid level low Pump drivebelt slack or broken Pump or steering gear defective
Wheel wobble and vibration	Wheel nuts loose Wheels out of balance or damaged Wheel bearings worn Worn tie-rod end balljoints Worn control arm balljoints Faulty shock absorber
Excessive tire wear	Incorrect tire pressures Wheels out of balance Incorrect wheel alignment Faulty shock absorbers Driver abuse

Chapter 11 Body

Contents

1 General information

Body styles available are 4-door sedan and 5-door station wagon. The body and floorpan are of welded steel construction and form a very strong unit, with crumple zones at front and rear which will deform progressively in case of accident. The doors are also reinforced against side impacts. The tailgate on station wagon models is made of aluminum.

Stout bumpers are installed front and rear, with impact absorbers to protect against damage in low-speed collisions.

The front fenders bolt on for easy replacement. The hood has two opening positions: partly open for normal work, and fully open for major work.

2 Maintenance — body and undercarriage

1   The condition of your vehicle's body is very important, because the resale value depends a great deal on it. It's much more difficult to repair a neglected or damaged body than it is to repair mechanical components. The hidden areas of the body, such as the wheel wells, the frame and the engine compartment, are equally important, although they don't require as frequent attention as the rest of the body.
2   Once a year, or every 12,000 miles, it's a good idea to have the underside of the body steam cleaned. All traces of dirt and oil will be removed and the area can then be inspected carefully for rust, damaged

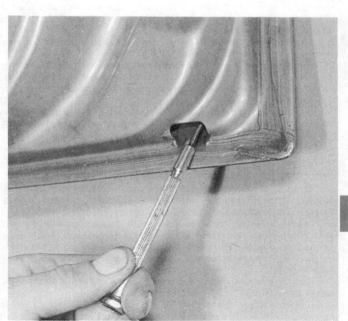

2.8 Clearing a door drain hole

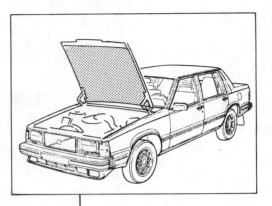

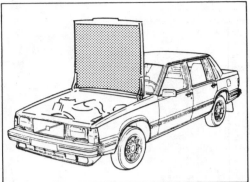

Fig. 11.1 Two opening positions of the hood (Sec 1)

H.25198

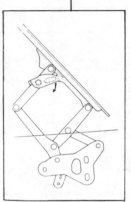

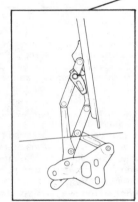

brake lines, frayed electrical wires, damaged cables and other problems. The front suspension components should be greased after completion of this job.

3   At the same time, clean the engine and the engine compartment with a steam cleaner or water soluble degreaser.

4   The wheel wells should be given close attention, since undercoating can peel away and stones and dirt thrown up by the tires can cause the paint to chip and flake, allowing rust to set in. If rust is found, clean down to the bare metal and apply an anti-rust paint.

5   The body should be washed about once a week. Wet the vehicle thoroughly to soften the dirt, then wash it down with a soft sponge and plenty of clean soapy water. If the surplus dirt is not washed off very carefully, it can wear down the paint.

6   Spots of tar or asphalt thrown up from the road should be removed with a cloth soaked in solvent.

7   Once every six months, wax the body and chrome trim. If a chrome cleaner is used to remove rust from any of the vehicle's plated parts, remember that the cleaner also removes part of the chrome, so use it sparingly.

8   Use a small screwdriver to clear the door drain holes (photo). This will prevent rust from forming along the lower edges of the doors.

3   Maintenance — upholstery and carpets

1   Every three months remove the carpets or mats and clean the interior of the vehicle (more frequently if necessary). Vacuum the upholstery and carpets to remove loose dirt and dust.

2   Leather upholstery requires special care. Stains should be removed with warm water and a very mild soap solution. Use a clean, damp cloth to remove the soap, then wipe again with a dry cloth. Never use alcohol, gasoline, nail polish remover or thinner to clean leather upholstery.

3   After cleaning, regularly treat leather upholstery with a leather wax. Never use car wax on leather upholstery.

4   In areas where the interior of the vehicle is subject to bright sunlight, cover leather seats with a sheet if the vehicle is to be left out for any length of time.

4   Minor body damage – repair

See color photo sequence

Repair of minor scratches

1   If the scratch is superficial and does not penetrate to the metal of the body, repair is very simple. Lightly rub the scratched area with a fine rubbing compound to remove loose paint and built up wax. Rinse the area with clean water.

2   Apply touch-up paint to the scratch, using a small brush. Continue to apply thin layers of paint until the surface of the paint in the scratch is level with the surrounding paint. Allow the new paint at least two weeks to harden, then blend it into the surrounding paint by rubbing with a very fine rubbing compound. Finally, apply a coat of wax to the scratch area.

3   If the scratch has penetrated the paint and exposed the metal of the body, causing the metal to rust, a different repair technique is required. Remove all loose rust from the bottom of the scratch with a pocket knife, then apply rust inhibiting paint to prevent the formation of rust in the future. Using a rubber or nylon applicator, coat the scratched area with glaze-type filler. If required, the filler can be mixed with thinner to provide a very thin paste, which is ideal for filling narrow scratches. Before the glaze filler in the scratch hardens, wrap a piece of smooth cotton cloth around the tip of a finger. Dip the cloth in thinner and then quickly wipe it along the surface of the scratch. This will ensure that the surface of the filler is slightly hollow. The scratch can now be painted over as described earlier in this section.

Repair of dents

4   When repairing dents, the first job is to pull the dent out until the affected area is as close as possible to its original shape. There is no point in trying to restore the original shape completely as the metal in the damaged area will have stretched on impact and cannot be restored to its original contours. It is better to bring the level of the dent up to a point which is about 1/8-inch below the level of the surrounding metal. In cases where the dent is very shallow, it is not worth trying to pull it out at all.

5   If the back side of the dent is accessible, it can be hammered out gently from behind using a soft-face hammer. While doing this, hold a block of wood firmly against the opposite side of the metal to absorb the hammer blows and prevent the metal from being stretched.

6   If the dent is in a section of the body which has double layers, or some other factor makes it inaccessible from behind, a different technique is required. Drill several small holes through the metal inside the damaged area, particularly in the deeper sections. Screw long, self tapping screws into the holes just enough for them to get a good grip in the metal. Now the dent can be pulled out by pulling on the protruding heads of the screws with locking pliers.

7   The next stage of repair is the removal of paint from the damaged area and from an inch or so of the surrounding metal. This is easily done with a wire brush or sanding disk in a drill motor, although it can be done just as effectively by hand with sandpaper. To complete the preparation for filling, score the surface of the bare metal with a screwdriver or the tang of a file or drill small holes in the affected area. This will provide a good grip for the filler material. To complete the repair, see the Section on filling and painting.

Repair of rust holes or gashes

8   Remove all paint from the affected area and from an inch or so of the surrounding metal using a sanding disk or wire brush mounted in a drill motor. If these are not available, a few sheets of sandpaper will do the job just as effectively.

9   With the paint removed, you will be able to determine the severity of the corrosion and decide whether to replace the whole panel, if possible, or repair the affected area. New body panels are not as expensive as most people think and it is often quicker to install a new panel than to repair large areas of rust.

10   Remove all trim pieces from the affected area except those which will act as a guide to the original shape of the damaged body, such as headlight shells, etc. Using metal snips or a hacksaw blade, remove all loose metal and any other metal that is badly affected by rust. Hammer the edges of the hole inward to create a slight depression for the filler material.

11   Wire brush the affected area to remove the powdery rust from the surface of the metal. If the back of the rusted area is accessible, treat it with rust inhibiting paint.

12   Before filling is done, block the hole in some way. This can be done with sheet metal riveted or screwed into place, or by stuffing the hole with wire mesh.

13   Once the hole is blocked off, the affected area can be filled and painted. See the following subsection on filling and painting.

Filling and painting

14   Many types of body fillers are available, but generally speaking, body repair kits which contain filler paste and a tube of resin hardener are best for this type of repair work. A wide, flexible plastic or nylon applicator will be necessary for imparting a smooth and contoured finish to the surface of the filler material. Mix up a small amount of filler on a clean piece of wood or cardboard (use the hardener sparingly). Follow the manufacturer's instructions on the package, otherwise the filler will set incorrectly.

15   Using the applicator, apply the filler paste to the prepared area. Draw the applicator across the surface of the filler to achieve the desired contour and to level the filler surface. As soon as a contour that approximates the original one is achieved, stop working the paste. If you continue, the paste will begin to stick to the applicator. Continue to add thin layers of paste at 20-minute intervals until the level of the filler is just above the surrounding metal.

16   Once the filler has hardened, the excess can be removed with a body file. From then on, progressively finer grades of sandpaper should be used, starting with a 180-grit paper and finishing with 600-grit wet-or-dry paper. Always wrap the sandpaper around a flat rubber or wooden block, otherwise the surface of the filler will not be completely flat. During the sanding of the filler surface, the wet-or-dry paper should be periodically rinsed in water. This will ensure that a very smooth finish is produced in the final stage.

17   At this point, the repair area should be surrounded by a ring of bare metal, which in turn should be encircled by the finely feathered edge of good paint. Rinse the repair area with clean water until all of the dust produced by the sanding operation is gone.

18   Spray the entire area with a light coat of primer. This will reveal any imperfections in the surface of the filler. Repair the imperfections with fresh filler paste or glaze filler and once more smooth the surface with sandpaper. Repeat this spray-and-repair procedure until you are satisfied that the surface of the filler and the feathered edge of the paint are perfect. Rinse the area with clean water and allow it to dry completely.

19   The repair area is now ready for painting. Spray painting must be carried out in a warm, dry, windless and dust free atmosphere. These conditions can be created if you have access to a large indoor work area, but if you are forced to work in the open, you will have to pick the day very carefully. If you are working indoors, dousing the floor in the work area with water will help settle the dust which would otherwise be in the air. If the repair area is confined to one body panel, mask off the surrounding panels. This will help minimize the effects of a slight mismatch in paint color. Trim pieces such as chrome strips, door handles, etc., will also need to be masked off or removed. Use masking tape and several thicknesses of newspaper for the masking operations.

20   Before spraying, shake the paint can thoroughly, then spray a test area until the spray painting technique is mastered. Cover the repair area with a thick coat of primer. The thickness should be built up using several thin layers of primer rather than one thick one. Using 600-grit wet-or-dry sandpaper, rub down the surface of the primer until it is very smooth. While doing this, the work area should be thoroughly rinsed with water and the wet-or-dry sandpaper periodically rinsed as well. Allow the primer to dry before spraying additional coats.

21   Spray on the top coat, again building up the thickness by using several thin layers of paint. Begin spraying in the center of the repair area and then, using a circular motion, work out until the whole repair area and about two inches of the surrounding original paint is covered. Remove all masking material 10 to 15 minutes after spraying on the final coat of paint. Allow the new paint at least two weeks to harden, then use a very fine rubbing compound to blend the edges of the new paint into the existing paint. Finally, apply a coat of wax.

5   Major body damage — repair

1   Major damage must be repaired by an auto body shop specifically equipped to perform unibody repairs. These shops have the specialized equipment required to do the job properly.

2   If the damage is extensive, the body must be checked for proper alignment or the vehicle's handling characteristics may be adversely affected and other components may wear at an accelerated rate.

3   Due to the fact that all of the major body components (hood, fenders, etc.) are separate and replaceable units, any seriously damaged components should be replaced rather than repaired. Sometimes the components can be found in a wrecking yard that specializes in used vehicle components, often at considerable savings over the cost of new parts.

6   Hood — removal and installation

1   Disconnect the battery negative cable.

2   Disconnect the windshield washer tube from the hood at the T-piece. Unclip the tube from the firewall.

3   Remove the under-hood light (if equipped) and disconnect the wire from it. Tie a piece of string to the wire, pull the wire through the hood cavity into the engine bay, then untie the string and leave it in the hood. This will make installation easier.

4   Mark around the hinge bolts with a soft lead pencil or white paint for reference when installing.

5   With the aid of an assistant, support the hood and remove the hinge bolts (photo). Lift off the hood (photo).

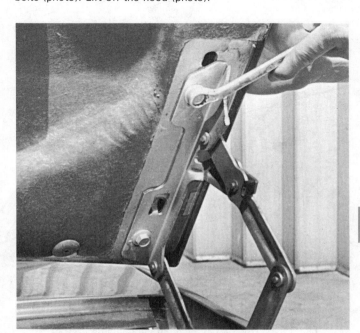

6.5A   Each hinge is attached to the hood with two bolts

11

6.5B Always use an assistant when removing the hood — don't attempt to do it on your own

6   When installing, place pads of rags under the corners of the hood near the hinges to protect the paint from damage.
7   Install the hood and insert the hinge bolts. Just tighten the bolts snugly in their previously marked positions.
8   Pull the light wire through with the string. Reconnect and install the light.
9   Reconnect the washer tube and clip it to the firewall.
10   Shut the hood and check its fit. The hinge-to-hood bolt holes control the fore-and-aft and left-right adjustment. Front height is adjusted by screwing the rubber bumpers in or out. Rear height is adjusted at the hinge mounting bolts near the wheel well.
11   Tighten the hinge bolts when adjustment is correct, and reconnect the battery.

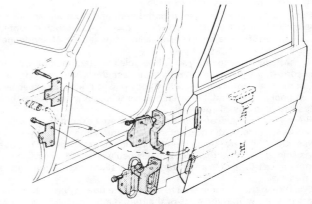

Fig. 11.2 Door hinge details (Sec 7)

7 Doors — removal and installation

1   Open the door. Support it with a jack or axle stand, using rags to protect the paint.
2   Disconnect the door electrical wiring, either by removing the door trim panel or the adjacent pillar trim. Feed the wiring through so that it hangs free.
3   Mark around the hinge bolts for reference when installing. With the aid of an assistant, remove the hinge bolts and lift away the door. Recover any hinge shims.
4   Install by reversing the removal operations. Adjust the fit of the door if necessary, using shims and/or the slotted hinge bolt holes. Do not try to adjust the position of the door lock striker for a good fit.

8 Trunk lid — removal and installation

1   Open the trunk. Disconnect the central locking system and/or trunk light wiring so that the trunk lid is free to be removed.
2   Mark around the hinge bolts. With the aid of an assistant, disconnect the trunk lid strut at the hinge end (photo), remove the hinge bolts and lift away the lid (photo).
3   Install by reversing the removal operations. If height adjustment is necessary, this is carried out at the rear by adjusting the lock bracket, and at the front by adjusting the hinges. Access to the hinge front bolts is via the covers in the rear window pillar trim.

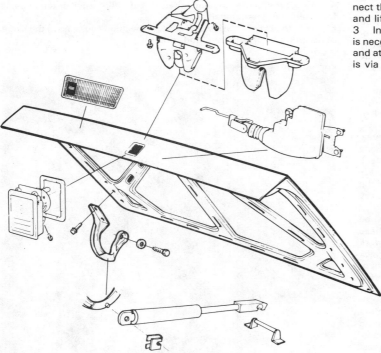

Fig. 11.3 Trunk lid and related components (Sec 8)

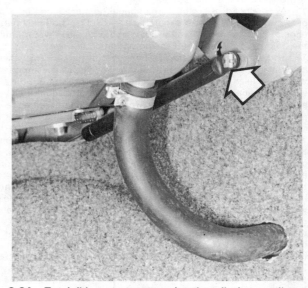

8.2A Trunk lid strut — removed spring clip (arrowed) at hinge end

8.2B   Trunk hinge bolts

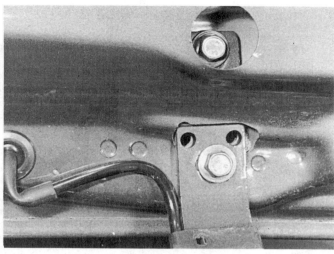

9.3   Tailgate hinge bolts

9.4   Trim panel fastener (arrowed) behind cargo area light

9.6   Disconnecting a tailgate strut

9.8   Tailgate side guide piece

9   Tailgate — removal and installation

1   Disconnect the battery negative cable.
2   Open the tailgate. Disconnect the washer tube at the junction next to the right-hand hinge.
3   Pry out the plugs which conceal two hinge bolts. Loosen the hinge bolts but do not remove them yet (photo).
4   Remove the trim panel from around the cargo area light. Besides the .visible fasteners, there is one concealed behind the light itself (photo).
5   Separate the wiring connectors exposed by removal of the trim panel, making notes for installation if necessary. Feed the wiring through to the tailgate.
6   Have an assistant support the tailgate. Disconnect the gas struts by removing the wire clips and separating the balljoints (photo).
7   Remove the hinge bolts and lift away the tailgate.
8   Install by reversing the removal operations. Only provisionally tighten the hinge bolts until satisfied with the fit of the tailgate. Adjust the lock striker and side guide pieces if necessary for a good fit (photo).

10   Hood release cable — removal and installation

1   Open the hood. If the cable is broken, the latch must be released from below.
2   Unbolt the release latch which is furthest from the release handle. Disconnect the cable from it (photos).

10.2A   Unbolt the hood release latch . . .

10.2B . . . and disconnect the cable

11

These photos illustrate a method of repairing simple dents. They are intended to supplement *Body repair - minor damage* in this Chapter and should not be used as the sole instructions for body repair on these vehicles.

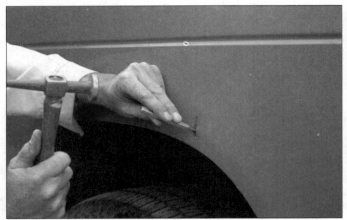

1   If you can't access the backside of the body panel to hammer out the dent, pull it out with a slide-hammer-type dent puller. In the deepest portion of the dent or along the crease line, drill or punch hole(s) at least one inch apart . . .

2   . . . then screw the slide-hammer into the hole and operate it. Tap with a hammer near the edge of the dent to help 'pop' the metal back to its original shape. When you're finished, the dent area should be close to its original contour and about 1/8-inch below the surface of the surrounding metal

3   Using coarse-grit sandpaper, remove the paint down to the bare metal. Hand sanding works fine, but the disc sander shown here makes the job faster. Use finer (about 320-grit) sandpaper to feather-edge the paint at least one inch around the dent area

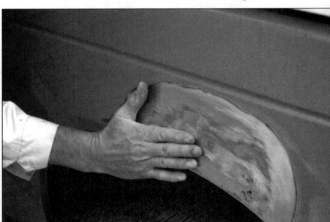

4   When the paint is removed, touch will probably be more helpful than sight for telling if the metal is straight. Hammer down the high spots or raise the low spots as necessary. Clean the repair area with wax/silicone remover

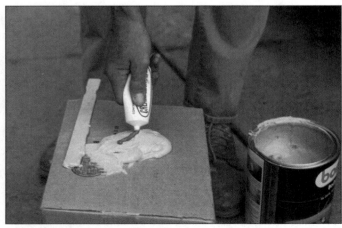

5   Following label instructions, mix up a batch of plastic filler and hardener. The ratio of filler to hardener is critical, and, if you mix it incorrectly, it will either not cure properly or cure too quickly (you won't have time to file and sand it into shape)

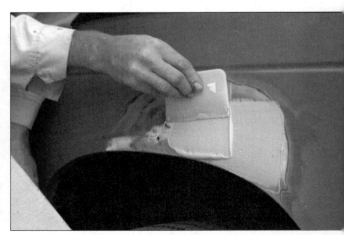

6   Working quickly so the filler doesn't harden, use a plastic applicator to press the body filler firmly into the metal, assuring bonds completely. Work the filler until it matches the original contour and is slightly above the surrounding metal

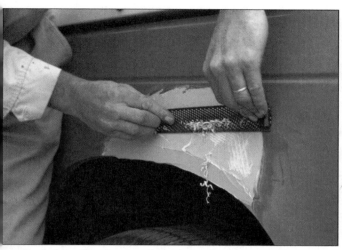

7   Let the filler harden until you can just dent it with your fingernail. Use a body file or Surform tool (shown here) to rough-shape the filler

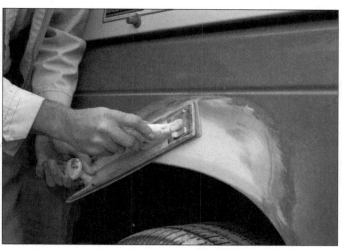

8   Use coarse-grit sandpaper and a sanding board or block to work the filler down until it's smooth and even. Work down to finer grits of sandpaper - always using a board or block - ending up with 360 or 400 grit

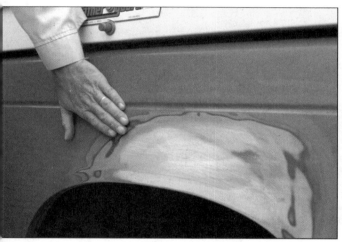

9   You shouldn't be able to feel any ridge at the transition from the filler to the bare metal or from the bare metal to the old paint. As soon as the repair is flat and uniform, remove the dust and mask off the adjacent panels or trim pieces

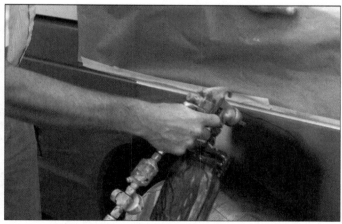

10   Apply several layers of primer to the area. Don't spray the primer on too heavy, so it sags or runs, and make sure each coat is dry before you spray on the next one. A professional-type spray gun is being used here, but aerosol spray primer is available inexpensively from auto parts stores

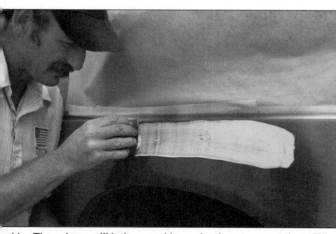

11   The primer will help reveal imperfections or scratches. Fill these with glazing compound. Follow the label instructions and sand it with 360 or 400-grit sandpaper until it's smooth. Repeat the glazing, sanding and respraying until the primer reveals a perfectly smooth surface

12   Finish sand the primer with very fine sandpaper (400 or 600-grit) to remove the primer overspray. Clean the area with water and allow it to dry. Use a tack rag to remove any dust, then apply the finish coat. Don't attempt to rub out or wax the repair area until the paint has dried completely (at least two weeks)

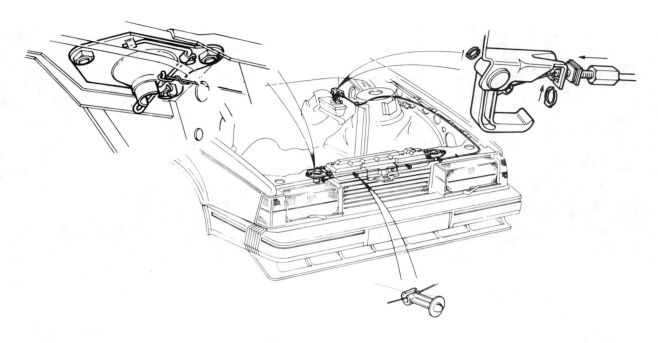

Fig. 11.4 Hood release cable fittings (Sec 10)

3   Release the cable casing from the other latch. Pull the cable free of the latches.
4   Inside the vehicle, release the cable from the lever by unhooking the cable and removing the slide clip from the casing.
5   Feed the cable into the engine bay and remove it.
6   Install by reversing the removal operations. Adjust the threaded section of the cable at the release lever end to take most of the slack out of the cable in the resting position.

11 Front door trim panel — removal and installation

Driver's door — pre-1985 models

1   Disconnect the battery negative cable.
2   Pry out the three screw plugs from the armrest. Remove the three screws (photo).
3   Unclip the door edge marker light lens, noting that the arrow points outwards.
4   Pry off the speaker grille. Remove the four screws which secure the speaker, pull it out of its cavity and disconnect the wires from it.

Also remove the fourth armrest screw now exposed.
5   Free the armrest from its clips by tugging firmly. Remove the switch panel from the armrest. Disconnect the edge marker light electrical connector and remove the armrest (photo).
6   Unscrew the interior lock button.
7   Pry out the two clips at the base of the main trim panel (photo). Free the panel from the door clips by tugging or prying and remove it.
8   Remove the large and small water deflectors (photos).
9   Install by reversing the removal operations.

Passenger's door — pre-1985 models

10 Proceed as above, but note that the door pull handle must be removed (two screws revealed by prying out the facing) at an early stage. There are also fewer switches to deal with.

1985 and later models

11 The armrest and trim panel cannot be separated. The combined panel and armrest appear to be retained by one screw.
12 Not all models have electrically-operated windows. When applicable it will be necessary to remove the window crank.

11.2 Removing an armrest screw plug

11.5 Removing the armrest

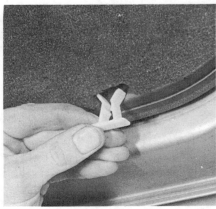

11.7 Door trim panel base clip

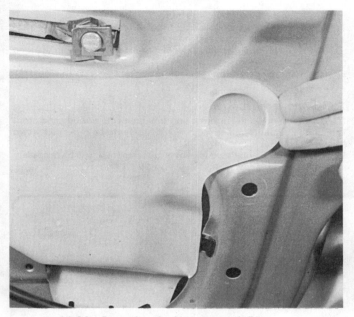

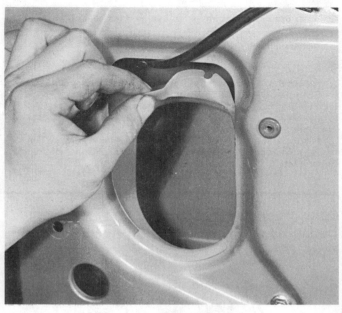

11.8A Removing the large water deflector . . .

11.8B . . . and the small one

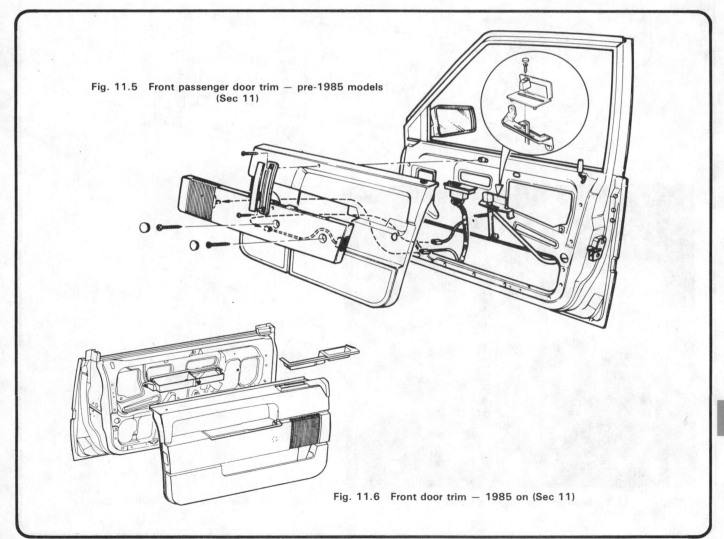

Fig. 11.5 Front passenger door trim — pre-1985 models
(Sec 11)

Fig. 11.6 Front door trim — 1985 on (Sec 11)

11

12 Rear door interior trim — removal and installation

1   Disconnect the battery negative cable.

Pre-1985 models

2   Pry out the two screw plugs from the armrest. Remove the screws.
3   Carefully pry the insert out of the pull handle to reveal two screws. Remove these screws and the pull handle (photo).
4   Pry off the speaker grille. Remove the speaker (if equipped) and two more armrest screws now exposed.
5   Pull the armrest off the door. Disconnect the window switch and the edge marker light electrical connector (as applicable) and remove the armrest.

6   Unscrew the interior lock button.
7   Release the trim panel clips by tugging firmly, or by prying with a putty knife. Lift and remove the trim panel.
8   The waterproof sheet may now be peeled off the door in the area to which access is desired.
9   Install by reversing the removal operations.

1985 and later models

10   On later models the armrest and trim panel cannot be separated. The combined panel and armrest would appear to be retained by two screws.
11   When manually-operated windows are installed, it will be necessary to remove the window crank.

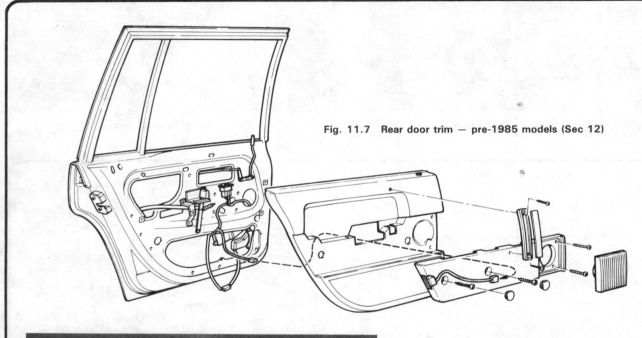

Fig. 11.7   Rear door trim — pre-1985 models (Sec 12)

12.3   Removing the pull handle insert

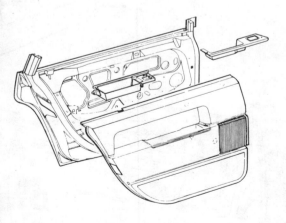

Fig. 11.8   Rear door trim — 1985 on (Sec 12)

13 Tailgate interior trim — removal and installation

1 Open the tailgate. From the bottom of the trim panel remove the four fasteners by turning them through 90° (photo).
2 Unclip the plastic trim from the interior handle. Remove the two screws now exposed, and the handle trim piece which they also secure (photo).
3 Slide the trim upwards (relative to the closed position of the tailgate) to free the keyhole fasteners along the top edge. Remove the trim panel.
4 Install by reversing the removal operations.

14 Windshield and other fixed glass — removal and installation

Special equipment and techniques are needed for successful removal and installation of the windshield, rear window and rear quarter windows. Have the work performed by a Volvo dealer or a glass shop.

15 Front door window — removal and installation

1 Remove the door interior trim (Section 11).
2 Raise or lower the window so that the lift arms are accessible. Remove the clip which secures each lift arm to the lift channel (photo).
3 Have an assistant support the window, or wedge or tape it in position. Disengage the lift arms from the channel and lift the glass out of the door.
4 If new glass is being installed, check whether or not it is supplied with the lift channel attached. If not, it will be necessary to transfer the old channel. The channel is removed and installed by careful use of a rubber mallet. Note the correct installed position (Fig. 11.9).
5 Install by reversing the removal operations.

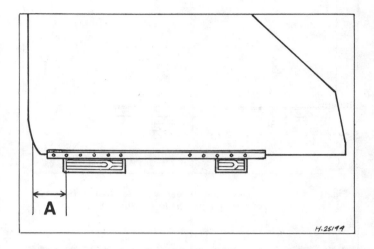

Fig. 11.9 Correct position of front window channel (Sec 15)

A = 17 to 19 mm (0.67 to 0.75 in)

13.1 Removing a tailgate trim fastener

13.2 Removing the tailgate interior handle trim

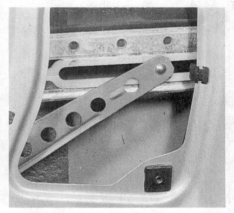

15.2 Window lift arm in the channel — clip is behind the end of the arm

16 Rear door windows — removal and installation

1 Remove the door interior trim (Section 12).
2 Remove the moveable glass as described for the front window (Section 15).
3 The fixed glass may now be removed after drilling out the blind rivets which secure the guide channel. Remove the guide channel and slide out the glass.
4 When installing the fixed glass, lubricate the weatherstrip with liquid soap.
5 Press the glass into position and install the guide channel, securing it with new blind rivets.
6 If installing a lift channel to the drop glass, refer to Fig. 11.11 for the correct installed position.
7 Install the moveable glass and the interior trim.

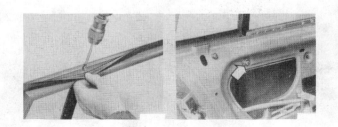

Fig. 11.10 Drilling out the guide channel top rivet (left). Lower rivet is arrowed, right (Sec 16)

11

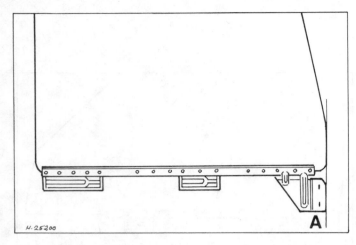

Fig. 11.11   Correct position of rear window channel (Sec 16)
A = 0 to 1 mm (0 to 0.04 in)

17   Window regulator — removal and installation

1   Proceed as for door window glass removal (Section 15 or 16), but do not remove the glass completely. Tape or wedge it in the fully raised position.

2   Remove the clip which secures the slide arm in its channel (photo).

3   In the case of electrically-operated windows, remove the motor connectors from the electrical connector, prying them out with a small screwdriver or scriber (photo). It is difficult to do this without damaging the connectors, but if a new motor is to be installed this does not matter.

4   Remove the nuts which secure the regulator to the inner door panel.

5   Push the regulator into the door cavity and remove it through the large hole at the bottom. It may be necessary to alter the position of the regulator to allow it to pass through the hole; with electrically-operated windows, do this by carefully connecting a battery to the connectors using jumper wires. Do not allow the connectors or the jumper wire clips to touch (photo).

6   The motor may be unbolted from the regulator if desired. Take great care that as the motor is removed, spring pressure does not allow the toothed quadrant to release suddenly, which could result in injury.

7   Install by reversing the removal operations. Before installing the door trim, adjust the stop screw as follows (photo).

8   Loosen the stop screw and press it forwards. Wind the window fully up, press the stop screw rearwards and tighten it.

17.2   The clip which secures the slide arm in the channel

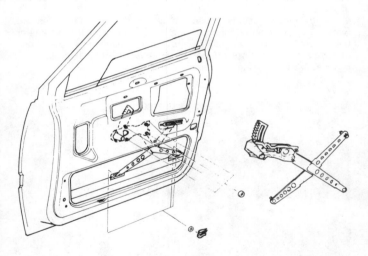

Fig. 11.12   Window lift mechanism — manual type shown (Sec 17)

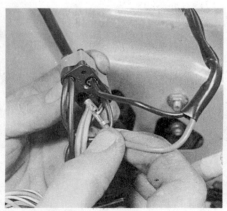

17.3   Removing the window motor connectors from the electrical connector

17.5   Using jumper wires to apply power to the window motor

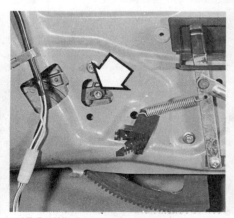

17.7   Window mechanism stop screw (arrowed)

18   Door handles, locks and latches — removal and installation

1   Remove the door interior trim (Section 11 or 12).

Lock cylinder

2   On early models, release the central locking switch from the cylinder by undoing the retaining clip.
3   Remove the two screws in the door rear edge which secure the lock barrel clip (photo).
4   Unhook the lock-to-latch rod, noting which way it is installed. Slide the clip off the lock and remove the lock and clip (photo).
5   When installing, make sure (when applicable) that the central locking switch groove engages with the lug on the lock.

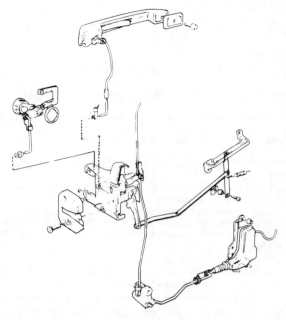

Fig. 11.13   Front door handle, lock and latch (Sec 18)

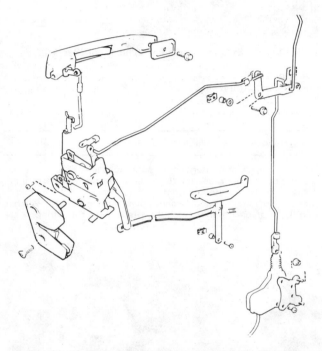

Fig. 11.14   Rear door handle, lock and latch (Sec 18)

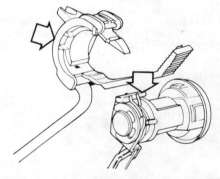

Fig. 11.15   Early type central locking switch. Groove and lug (both arrowed) must engage (Sec 18)

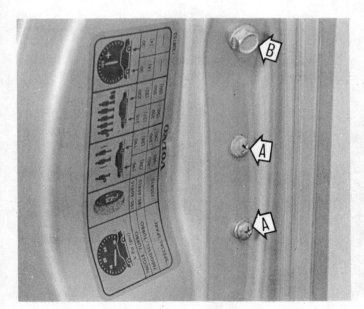

18.3   Lock cylinder clip screws (A). Screw B secures one end of the exterior handle

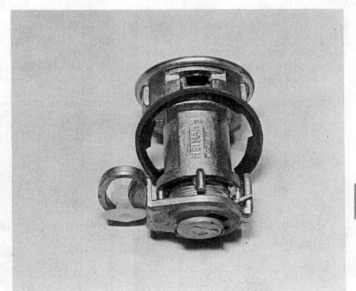

18.4   Door lock cylinder removed

11

Exterior handle

6   Remove the two bolts which secure the handle. Unhook the link rod and remove the handle (photos).

Latch mechanism

7   Disconnect the lock cylinder and exterior handle link rods from the latch.
8   Remove the latch from the door. It is secured by two Allen screws (photo).
9   Remove the single securing screw exposed by removal of the latch (photo).
10   Unclip the interior handle link and remove the latch mechanism (photo).

All items

11   Install by reversing the removal operations. Check for correct operation before installing the door trim.
12   Note that the exterior handle link rod contains an adjustable section. The length of the rod should be set so that the latch stop contacts its base, and the handle tongue protrudes at least 22 mm (0.87 in) (Fig. 11.16).

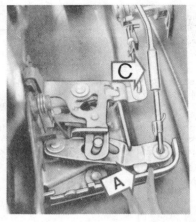
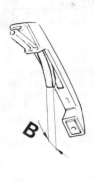

Fig. 11.16   Exterior handle link adjustment (Sec 18)

A   Latch stop   C   Adjuster
B   Tongue protrusion

19   Trunk lock — removal and installation

1   Remove the latch, and unhook the lock motor link rod from the latch driver (photo).
2   Remove the shear-head bolt which secures the lock, using a stud extractor or a hammer and punch.
3   Remove the lock from the trunk lid.
4   When installing, use a new shear-head bolt. Only tighten the bolt lightly until satisfied with the operation of the lock, then tighten the bolt until its head shears off.

20   Tailgate lock — removal and installation

1   Remove the tailgate interior trim panel (Section 13).
2   Disconnect the link rods from the exterior handle, the lock cylinder and (when applicable) the lock motor.
3   Remove the exterior handle/license plate light assembly, which is secured by two screws and two nuts. Disconnect the wiring.

18.6A   This bolt secures the other end of the exterior handle

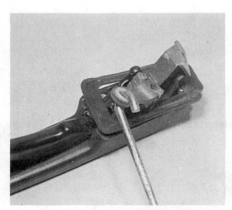

18.6B   The link rod engaged with the handle

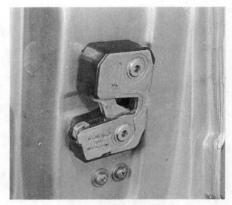

18.8   Remove the latch . . .

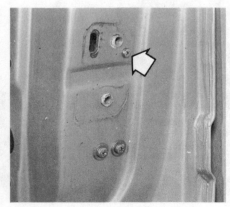

18.9   . . . to expose the latch securing screw (arrowed)

18.10   Removing the latch mechanism

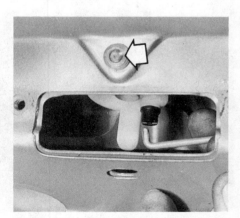

19.1   Unhooking the trunk lock motor link rod. Shear-head bolt is arrowed

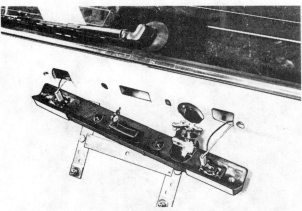

Fig. 11.17 Removal of the exterior handle/license plate
light assembly (Sec 20)

Fig. 11.18 Tailgate lock cylinder E-clip (A) and locking
plate (B) (Sec 20)

4   The lock cyclinder and levers can now be removed after releasing
the E-clip and locking plate.
5   Install by reversing the removal operation. Adjust the exterior handle link rod if necessary to give the handle approximately 3 mm (0.12
in) free play.

21 Central locking components — removal and installation

Driver's door switch

1   Remove the interior trim from the door (Section 11).
2   On early models, unclip the switch from around the lock barrel and
remove it. Note how the switch groove engages with the lug on the
lock.

3   On later models the switch is located next to the latch mechanism.
Remove the single securing screw and lift out the switch. Note how
the switch tongue engages with the latch rod (photos).
4   Disconnect the switch electrical connector. If other devices share
the same plug, pry out the appropriate connectors.
5   Install by reversing the removal operations.

Door lock motors

6   Remove the interior trim from the door (Section 11 or 12).
7   Unclip the motor link rod from the bellcrank (front door) or lock
button link rod (rear door) (photo).
8   Remove the motor securing nuts. Remove the motor and link rod
from the door. On some models the link rod is enclosed in a plastic
tube (photos).

21.3A Remove the securing screw . . . .

21.3B   . . . and lift out the switch

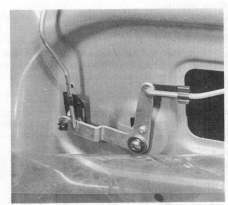

21.7 The lock motor link bellcrank

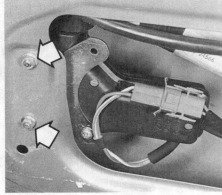

21.8A Lock motor securing nuts
(arrowed)

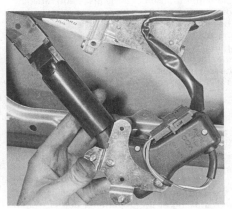

21.8B Removing the lock motor, link
rod and tube

11

9   Disconnect the electrical connector — see paragraph 4.
10 If a new motor is being installed, transfer the link rod, mounting plate and any other components to it.
11 Install by reversing the removal operations.

Trunk lock motor

12 Remove the latch cover. Unbolt and remove the latch (photos).
13 Unhook the lock motor link rod from the latch driver.
14 Remove the three securing nuts, disconnect the motor wiring and remove it (photo).
15 Install by reversing the removal operations. Adjust the position of the latch within the limits of the slotted holes to achieve satisfactory opening and closing.

Tailgate lock motor

16 Remove the tailgate interior trim (Section 13).
17 The lock motor may now be removed in a similar way to the trunk lock motor.

Relays

18 On 1982 and 1983 models, two relays in the central electrical unit control the locking and unlocking functions. See Chapter 12, Section 24.
19 On later models no relays are used in the central locking system.

---

22   Door mirror — removal and installation

Electrically-operated

1   Remove the door interior trim (Section 11).
2   Pry off the trim plate which covers the mirror mounting (photo).
3   Disconnect the mirror wiring electrical connector. Free the wiring harness from the door (photo).
4   Support the mirror and remove the mounting screw. Lift the mirror off its mounts.
5   Install by reversing the removal operations.

Manually-operated

6   The operations are similar to those just described, but since there are no wires to disconnect there should be no need to remove the door interior trim panel. No specific information is available.

---

23   Door mirror glass and motor — removal and installation

Note: *There is no need to remove the mirror from the door for these operations.*

1   Press the mirror glass inwards at the bottom until the retaining ring teeth are visible through the access hole.
2   Pry the teeth with a screwdriver to move the ring in a counter-clockwise direction (looking at the glass). This will release the retaining ring from the mounting plate (photo). Remove the glass and retaining ring. When applicable, disconnect the heating element wires.
3   The motor may now be removed after unscrewing the four retaining screws and disconnecting the wires from it. If the wires cannot be separated from the motor, remove the door interior trim and disconnect the mirror electrical connector (photo).
4   Install by reversing the removal operations. Observe the TOP marking on the motor, and the UNTEN (bottom) marking on the mirror glass (photos).

---

24   Door opening weatherstrip — removal and installation

---

1   Remove the kick panel from the door sill (photo).
2   Pry the weatherstrip free, starting at the bottom. Use a wide-bladed screwdriver and protect the paint by prying against a piece of wood.
3   Install the weatherstrip starting at the uppermost corner. Tap it into place with a rubber mallet.
4   Install the kick panel.

21.12A   Removing the trunk latch cover . . .

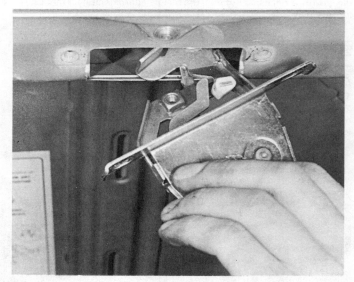

21.12B   . . . and the latch

21.14   Removing the trunk lock motor

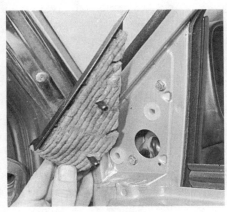

22.2 Removing the door mirror mounting trim plate

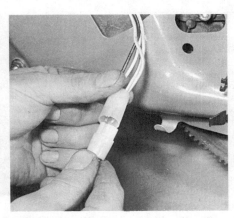

22.3 Disconnecting the mirror electrical connector

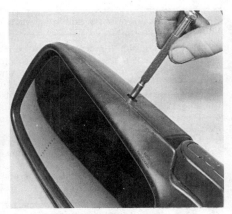

23.2 Releasing the mirror glass retaining ring

23.3 Mirror motor, showing the retaining screws

23.4A Mirror motor is marked 'TOP' . . .

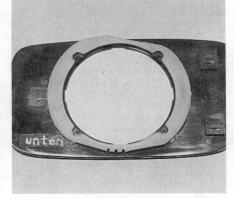

23.4B . . . and bottom of glass is marked 'unten'

24.1 Sill kick panel screw and cover

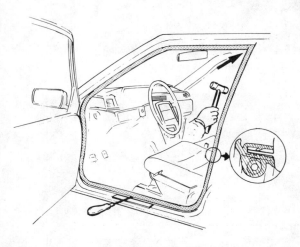

Fig. 11.19 Door opening weatherstrip removal and installation details. Start at the top corner (arrowed) (Sec 24)

11

25 Front seat — removal and installation

1   Remove the trim or storage pocket from the outboard side of the seat base. Unbolt the seat belt anchorage (photo).
2   Move the seat forwards. Remove the single bolt from the rear of each track — these may be concealed by trim covers (photo).
3   Move the seat rearwards. Remove any trim covers, then remove the single bolt from the front of each track (photo).
4   Disconnect the seat heater, seat belt switch and adjustment motor electrical connectors (as applicable).
5   Lift the front of the seat, pushing it rearwards at the same time, to free the tracks from their keyhole anchors in the floor. Remove the seat and tracks together.
6   Install by reversing the removal operations.

26 Rear seat — removal and installation

Sedan

1   Free the seat cushion from its retaining clips by pushing the front edge down and pulling it rearwards (photo). (On early models the clips are slightly different — Fig. 11.20. Lift out the cushion.
2   Straighten the tongues of the clips which secure the base of the seat back (photo). Thump the seat back upwards to free it from the top clips and remove it.
3   The armrest may now be unbolted and removed if necessary.
4   Install by reversing the removal operations.

Station wagon

5   Fold the seat cushions forwards. Remove the hinge retaining nuts and lift out the cushions (photo).
6   Fold down the seat backs. Pull the pins out of the center mounting (photo) and release the side mounting pins by turning them with pliers. Lift out the seat backs.
7   Install by reversing the removal operations.

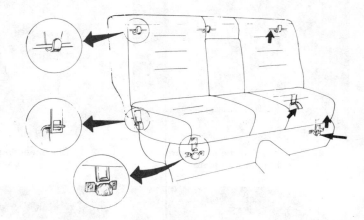

Fig. 11.20   Rear seat fastenings — models up to 1983 (Sec 26)

27 Head restraints — removal and installation

1   Press the front of the seat backrest about 90 mm (3.5 in) below the top edge, at the same time pulling the head restraint upwards to free it.
2   Pull the head restraint out of the guides and remove it.
3   When installing, push the head restraint firmly into place until it latches.

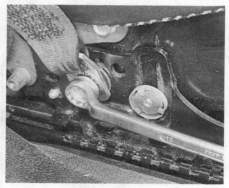

25.1   Unbolting the belt anchorage from the seat

25.2   A rear track bolt . . .

25.3   . . . and a front track bolt

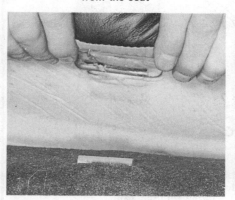

26.1   Unclipping the seat cushion front edge

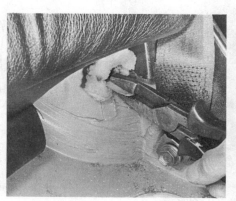

26.2   Straightening a seat back clip tongue

26.5   Two seat cushion hinges (Wagon)

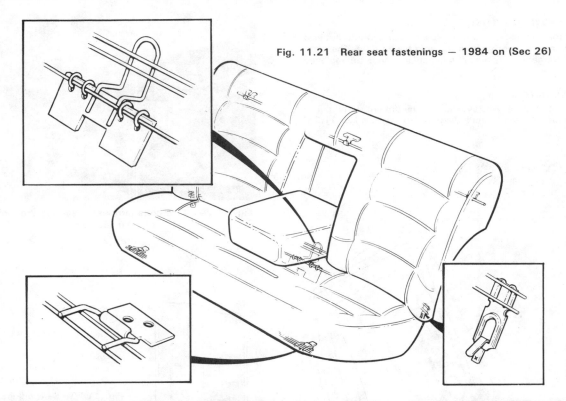

Fig. 11.21 Rear seat fastenings — 1984 on (Sec 26)

26.6 Seat back center mounting (Wagon) — pins arrowed

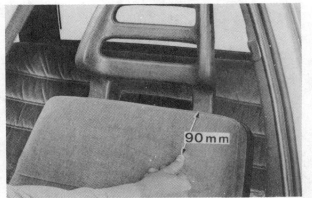

Fig. 11.22 Press where shown to release the head restraint (Sec 27)

28 Front seat position adjusters — removal and installation

1   Remove the seat and cushion (Sections 25 and 29).

Mechanical height adjusters

2   Raise the adjuster to its highest position. Remove the Allen screws which secure it to the seat.

3   Press the height adjuster lever towards the front of the seat and push downwards on the seat. Separate the seat from the rods.

4   The height adjuster components may now be replaced as necessary.

5   Install by reversing the removal operations. Insert the rods into the highest holes of the adjuster plates.

Fig. 11.23 Two Allen screws (arrowed) which secure one side of the height adjusters (Sec 28)

11

Mechanical reclining adjuster

6   Proceed as for backrest heater replacement (Section 29), but also unbolt the reclining mechanism from the seat base frame. The complete backrest frame and reclining mechanism must be replaced together.

Electrical adjusters

7   No specific information was available at the time of writing. The locations of the motors, and a circuit diagram, are given in Fig. 11.25.

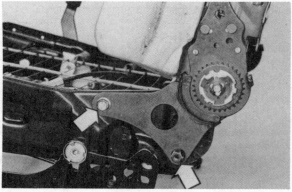

Fig. 11.24 Two bolts (arrowed) securing the reclining adjuster (Sec 28)

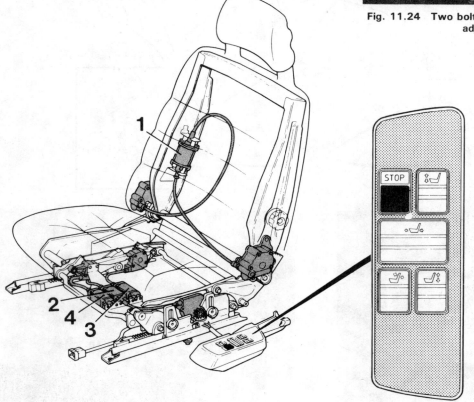

Fig. 11.25 Seat adjustment motor positions and circuit diagram (Sec 28)

1   Reclining motor
2   Fore-aft motor
3   Rear height motor
4   Front height motor
R1 Control relay
R2 Interlock relay
    For color code see main wiring diagrams

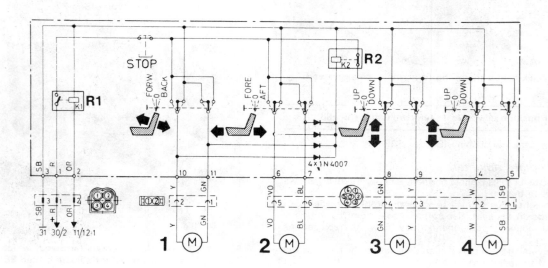

29 Seat heating elements — removal and installation

1   Remove the front seat (Section 25).
2   Recline the backrest as far as it will go. Invert the seat and free the wiring from the cable ties.

Backrest heater

3   Remove the head restraint (Section 27).
4   Remove the backrest adjuster knob, and the lumbar support adjuster knob and guide.
5   Remove the upholstery retaining rod. Cut the clamp rings which secure the bottom edge of the upholstery. Peel off the upholstery, freeing the center attachment clamps.
6   The heating element can now be removed.

Cushion heater

7   Remove the upholstery retaining rods. Unhook the side springs and remove the cushion (photo).
8   Cut the clamp rings which secure the upholstery. Peel off the upholstery, unhooking the center attachments (photo).
9   The heating element and thermostat can now be removed.

All heaters

10 Install by reversing the removal operations, using new clamp rings when necessary.

Fig. 11.26 Unscrew the special nut (arrowed) to remove the backrest adjuster knob (Sec 29)

Fig. 11.27 Backrest upholstery retaining rod (arrowed) (Sec 29)

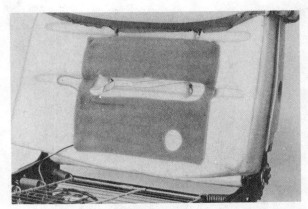

Fig. 11.28 Backrest heating element exposed (Sec 29)

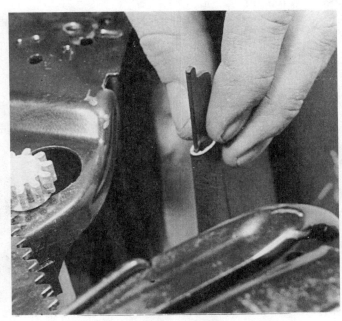

29.7 Unhooking an upholstery retaining rod

29.8 Cutting a clamp ring

11

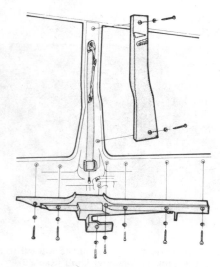

Fig. 11.29 Remove the trim panels for access to the front
seat belt (Sec 31)

31.4A Front belt upper guide

31.4B Unbolting an inertia reel unit

30 Seat belts — care and maintenance

1   Maintenance is limited to periodic inspection of the belts for fraying or other damage. Also check the operation of the buckles and
retractor mechanisms. In case of damage or malfunction the belt must
be replaced.
2   If it is necessary to clean the belts, use only an approved upholstery
cleaner or a weak solution of detergent, followed by rinsing with water.
Do not use solvents, strong detergents, dyes or bleaches. Keep the
belt extended until it is dry.
3   Belts which have been subjected to impact loads must be replaced.

31 Front seat belts — removal and installation

1   Move the front seat forwards. Remove the trim or storage pocket
from the outboard side of the seat base. Unbolt the seat belt anchorage.
2   Remove the B-pillar trim panel, which is secured by two screws
concealed by plugs. Free the belt guide from the slot in the trim.
3   Remove the reel cover/sill trim panel, which is secured by seven
concealed screws.
4   Unbolt the belt upper guide and the inertia reel unit, noting the
location of any washers and spacers. Remove the belt and reel (photos).
5   To remove the buckle, it is first necessary to remove the seat (Section 25).
6   Install by reversing the removal operations.

32 Rear seat belts — removal and installation

Sedan

1   Remove the rear seat (Section 26).
2   The buckles and floor anchorages can now be unbolted from the
seat pan (photo).
3   To gain access to the inertia reels it will first be necessary to remove
the parcel shelf speakers (if equipped). Access to their connectors and
fastenings is from inside the trunk.
4   Remove the parcel shelf securing clips and the parcel shelf itself
(photo).
5   Remove the reel cover clips and the reel covers (photo).
6   Unbolt and remove the inertia reels, noting the position of any
spacers (photo).
7   Install by reversing the removal operations.

Station wagon

8   Access to the buckles and floor anchorages is gained by tipping
the seat cushion forwards.

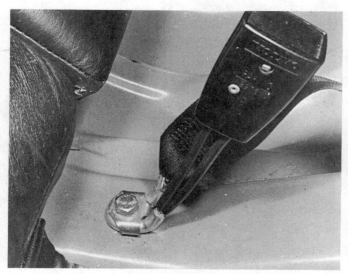

32.2 Rear seat belt buckle bolted to the floorpan

32.4 Removing a parcel shelf clip

32.5 Removing an inertia reel cover clip

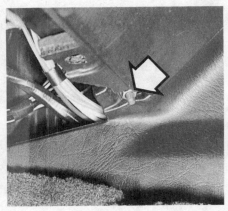

32.6 Rear inertia reel unit with cover removed

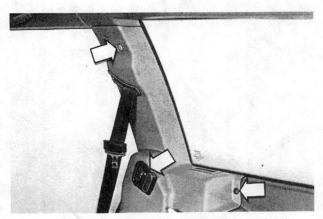

Fig. 11.30 C-pillar trim panel mounting points (arrowed) — Wagon (Sec 32)

9   The inertia reels are accessible after removing the C-pillar trim. This is attached by a screw at the top, by the seat back stop at the bottom and by a clip at the rear.

33   Steering column/pedal trim panel — removal and installation

1   The large trim panel below the steering column is secured by two screws and two clips (photo). Remove the screws and turn the clips

90° to release them.
2   Lower the trim panel and disconnect the heater duct from it. Remove the panel.
3   Install by reversing the removal operations.

34   Glovebox — removal and installation

1   Open the glovebox. Pry out the two trim pads from the edges of the glovebox and remove the two screws (photo).
2   Remove the trim panel from below the glovebox. This is secured by three clips which must be turned 90°.
3   Remove the nut at the base of the glovebox (towards the center of the vehicle) (photo).
4   Lower the glovebox, disconnect the wires from it and remove it.
5   Install by reversing the removal operations.

35   Center console — removal and installation

1   Disconnect the battery negative cable.
2   Remove the steering column/pedal trim (Section 33) and the glovebox (Section 34). This may not be essential but will improve access.
3   Remove the radio (Chapter 12).
4   Remove the ashtray and its carrier (photo).
5   Remove the cigarette lighter tray. This is secured by one or two screws, exposed by removing the lighter element and cover plate. Disconnect the lighter feed and withdraw the bulb holder as the tray

33.1   One of the clips and one of the screws which secure the steering column/pedal trim panel. D-shaped insert is of no significance

34.1   Removing a glovebox screw trim pad

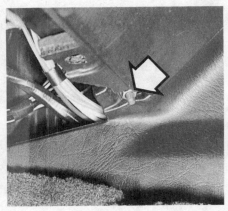

34.3   Glovebox base nut (arrowed)

35.4   Removing the ashtray carrier

35.6   Radio tray securing screw

35.7   Side panel screws (arrowed)
below the heater controls

35.8   Side panel rear edge screws

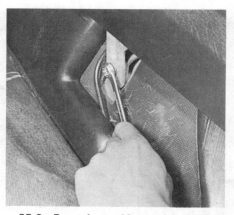

35.9   Removing a side panel forward
end screw

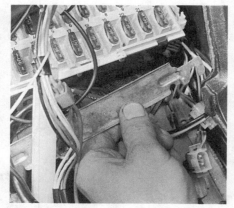

35.10   Removing the side panel
connecting strut

is withdrawn. (On some models the tray may contain audio equipment).

6   Remove the radio tray, which is secured by a single screw at the back (photo).

7   Remove the side panel screws from below the heater controls (photo).

8   Remove the screws (two on each side) which secure the rear edge of the center console side panels. It will be necessary to release the rear console and move it rearwards to gain access to these screws (photo).

9   Peel back the carpet from the forward end of the transmission tunnel and remove the two screws (one each side) which secure the forward ends of the side panels (photo).

10   Loosen the screws which secure the side panel connecting strut. Release the strut, which has slotted mounting holes (photo).

11   Remove the center console side panels.

12   Install by reversing the removal operations.

36   Rear console — removal and installation

1   Lift the armrest, empty the storage box and pry out the cover plate from the bottom of the box. Remove the two screws (photo).

2   On manual transmission models, remove the gear lever/handbrake trim. This is retained by two screws. Disconnect any switches.

3   On automatic transmission models, remove the selector lever trim. See Chapter 6.

36.1   Two screws in the bottom of the storage box

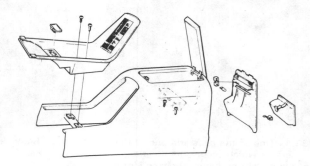

Fig. 11.31   Rear console installation details (Sec 36)

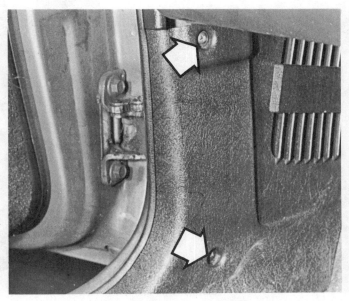

37.4 Footwell side trim panel screws (arrowed)

37.7 Removing the central air vent

4   Lift the rear console. Separate the rear ashtray/cigarette lighter/seat belt warning light panel from the console. Remove the console, leaving the panel behind.
5   Install by reversing the removal operations.

37 Dash panel — removal and installation

1   Disconnect the battery negative cable.
2   Remove the steering wheel, the steering column switches and the instrument panel. See Chapters 10 and 12.
3   Remove the steering column/pedal trim, the glovebox, the center console and the rear console. See Sections 33 to 36.
4   Remove the footwell side trim panels (photo). Also remove the A-pillar trim.
5   Disconnect the switch and lighting electrical connectors.
6   Remove the screw which secures the steering column top bearing to the dash panel. Recover the spacer tube.
7   Remove the central air vents (photo). Remove the air mix box retaining screw and disconnect the air ducts.
8   Unclip the wiring harness from the dash panel.

9   On vehicles with automatic climate control, remove the inner temperature sensor.
10   Remove the dash panel complete with switches, defroster vents, etc. Transfer components as necessary if a new panel is to be installed.
11   Install by reversing the removal operations.

38 Front spoiler — removal and installation

1   Have an assistant support the spoiler. Remove the six bolts and D-shaped washers which secure it to the bumper (photo).
2   Free the spoiler from the bumper side section and remove it.
3   Install by reversing the removal operations.

39 Front bumper — removal and installation

1   Remove the three nuts which secure each side section (photo). (Depending on equipment and model, it may be necessary to remove the battery, washer reservoir and/or air cleaner for access.)

38.1 A front spoiler bolt

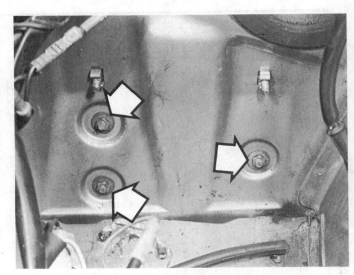

39.1 Three nuts (arrowed) which secure the bumper side section. Air cleaner has been removed for access

11

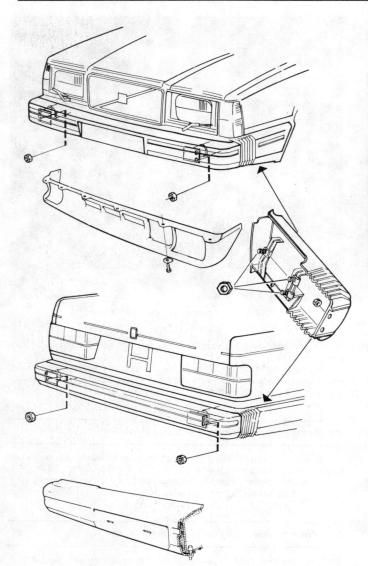

Fig. 11.32 Bumper installation details (Secs 39 and 40)

39.2   Removing the plug which secures the rear of the
bumper side section

2   Remove the single plug securing the rear edge of each side section (photo).
3   Remove the front spoiler (Section 38).
4   Disconnect or remove the auxiliary lights (if equipped).
5   From inside the bumper remove the four nuts which secure it to
the impact absorbers. Remove the bumper.
6   Install by reversing the removal operations.

40   Rear bumper — removal and installation

This is removed in a similar way to the front bumper, but access
to the side section nuts is gained from within the trunk or cargo area
wells.

41   Bumper impact absorbers — removal and installation

1   Remove the bumper (Section 39 or 40).
2   Remove the two nuts and bolts and the single nut securing the
impact absorber. The single nut is reached from the engine bay (front

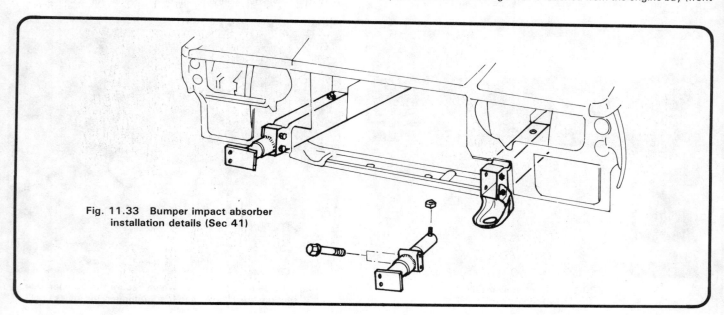

Fig. 11.33   Bumper impact absorber
installation details (Sec 41)

41.2A Front bumper impact absorber securing bolts
(arrowed) . . .

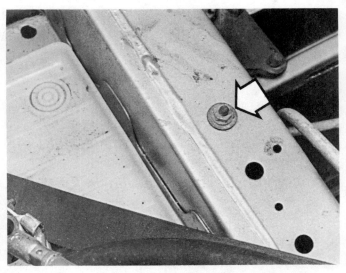

41.2B . . . and single nut in the engine compartment

bumpers) or from inside the trunk or cargo area (photos).
3   Pull the absorber out of its bracket.
4   Do not puncture the absorbers, or perform welding on or near them.
They contain gas under pressure which could cause injury if suddenly
released.
5   Install by reversing the removal operations.

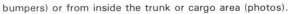

42 Front grille panel — removal and installation

1   Open the hood. Squeeze the grille panel top retaining clips and
remove them (photo).
2   Release the panel from its bottom mounts and remove it (photo).
3   Install by reversing the removal operations.

43 Engine undertray — removal and installation

1   Raise and support the front of the vehicle.
2   Remove the undertray securing screws and free it from the lugs
(photos). When a vacuum tank is installed in this area, it may share
some of the undertray screws.
3   Install by reversing the removal operations.

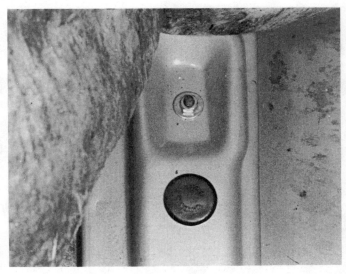

41.2C Rear bumper impact absorber nut in the trunk floor

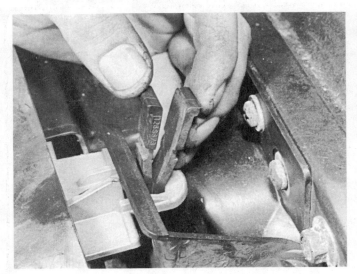

42.1 Removing a grille panel clip

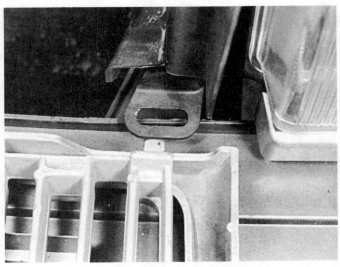

42.2 Grille panel bottom mount

11

43.2A   An undertray side securing screw

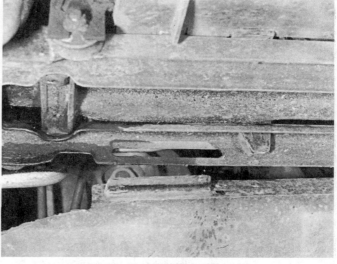

43.2B   Undertray lug and slot

44   Front fender — removal and installation

1   Remove the windshield wiper arms and the wiper spindle seals.
2   Open the hood to the fully raised position. Remove the cowl panel, which is secured by three screws and some clips.
3   Remove the bumper end section and the turn signal/parking light unit on the side concerned.
4   Remove the screws which secure the fender. Pull the fender off the inner panel and remove it.
5   Install by reversing the removal operations. Apply a suitable sealer (Volvo No 591 278-7, or equivalent) to the fender-to-wheel well joint.

45   Sunroof motor — removal and installation

1   Remove the motor cover securing screws and unclip the cover.
2   If a fabric headlining material is covering the motor, carefully cut it away, keeping inside the outline of the motor cover.

3   Remove the two screws and one nut which secure the motor.
4   Lower the motor off the drivegear and disconnect the wiring electrical connector (photo). If the electrical connector is deep in the headlining, either peel back the headlining for access, or cut the wires and install new connectors when installing.
5   Before installing the motor to the drivegear, run it backwards (to the fully open position), then forwards (to the fully closed position) until it stops.
6   Install and secure the motor and cover.

46   Sunroof — removal and installation

1   Open the sunroof to the ventilation position (rear edge raised). From outside, release the clips which secure the headliner to the rear edge.
2   Back inside, close the sunroof. Free the headlining from the front edge by jerking it rearwards, at the same time pulling down on the main headlining.
3   Release the sunroof spring retainers. Remove the side and front

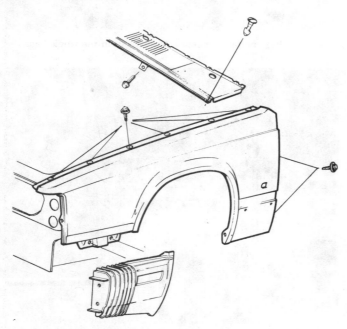

Fig. 11.34   Front fender installation details (Sec 44)

45.4   Removing the sunroof motor

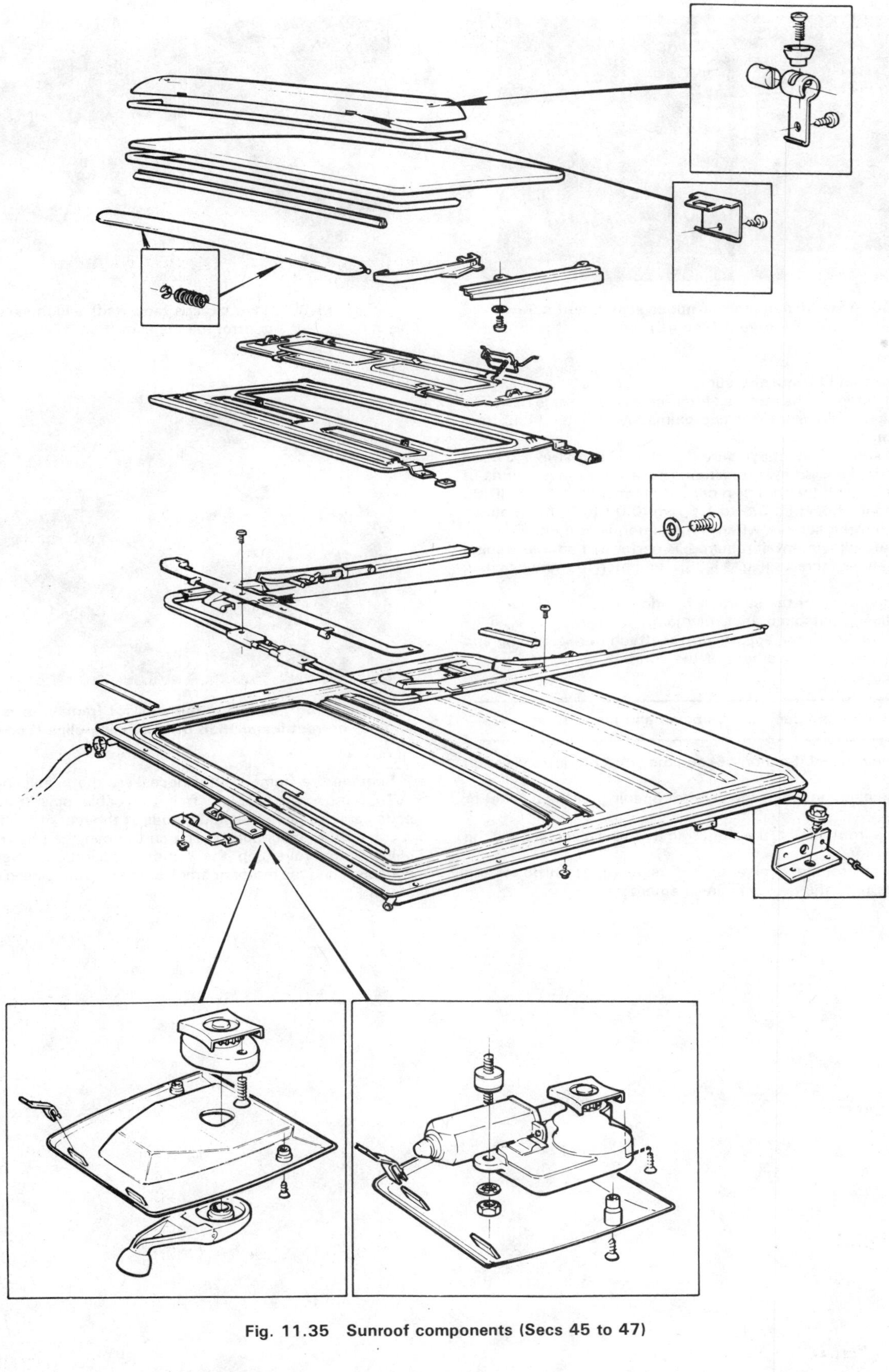

Fig. 11.35 Sunroof components (Secs 45 to 47)

Fig. 11.36   One of the sunroof upper adjustment screws
(arrowed) (Sec 46)

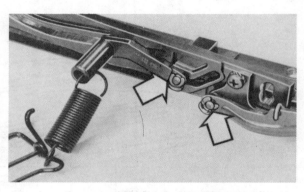

Fig. 11.37   Two circlips (arrowed) which secure the
control mechanism (Sec 47)

retaining screws and lift out the sunroof.
4   The sealing strip can be replaced after removing the side rails. The
joint in the strip should be located approximately 100 mm (4 in) from
the rear and on the left-hand side.
5   Install the sunroof and make sure that the sealing strip is a good
fit. Install the retaining screws, positioning the front outside edge of
the sunroof flush with the roof or recessed at most by 1.5 mm (0.06
in). The rear edge should be 0.5 to 1.5 mm (0.02 to 0.06 in) above
the roof. Tighten the screws when the position is correct.
6   Fore-and-aft adjustment, if required, is performed after loosening
the upper adjustment screws (Fig. 11.36). Retighten the screws when
adjustment is correct.
7   Test the operation of the sunroof, but do not run it too far back
with the headlining detached as it may jam.
8   When satisfied with the adjustment, reattach the headlining and
check the full range of movement of the sunroof.

47   Sunroof frame and cables — removal and installation

1   Remove the sunroof (Section 46) and the crank or motor (Section
45).
2   Protect the paint ahead of the sunroof opening with a blanket or
similar item.
3   Remove the front mount, the eight frame retaining screws and the
wind deflector.
4   Grasp the control mechanism on both sides. Press it down and
pull it forwards until the drain channels emerge.

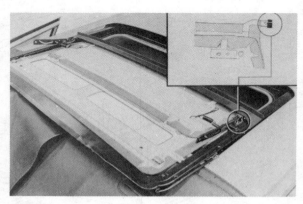

Fig. 11.38   Installing the sunroof frames. Inset shows
correct installation of headlining clips (Sec 47)

5   Remove the frame, and if necessary the headlining.
6   To remove the cables, free the cable pins from the control
mechanism. Remove the guide studs at the rear of the frame and pull
out the control mechanism. The cables can then be removed.
7   Install by reversing the removal operations. Set the control
mechanism and the motor or crank to the sunroof closed position when
installing.

Chapter 12 Electrical system

Contents

Specifications

General
System type	12 volt, negative ground
Battery type	Lead acid
Battery capacity	55 or 66 Ah

Alternator
Make and type	Bosch K1 or N1
Maximum output (at 14V):	
K1	55A
N1	70 or 90A
Brush minimum length	5.0 mm (0.2 in)
Slip ring diameter:	
New	28.0 mm (1.102 in)
Minimum — K2	26.8 mm (1.055 in)
Minimum — N1	27.0 mm (1.063 in)
Rotor resistance:	
K1 and N1 70A	3.4 to 3.7 ohms
N1 90A	2.8 to 3.1 ohms
Voltage regulator type	Integral with brushgear
Regulated voltage at 3000 (engine) rpm:	
5A load	13.8 to 14.9V
30 to 50A load	13.2 to 14.8V

Starter motor
Make and type	Bosch GF or DW, pre-engaged
Commutator minimum diameter:	
GF	33.5 mm (1.319 in)
DW	31.2 mm (1.228 in)
Brush minimum length:	
GF	13.0 mm (0.512 in)
DW	8.0 mm (0.315 in)
Armature endplay	0.1 to 0.3 mm (0.004 to 0.012 in)

Light bulbs (typical)

	Wattage	Pattern
Headlights		
Inner	50	Sealed beam
Outer	35/35	Sealed beam
Day running/parking lights	21/5	BAY 15d
Direction indicators — front	24/2.2cp	BAY 15d
Direction indicators — rear	21	VA 15s
Direction indicator side	5	W 2.1x9.5d
Front foglights/spotlights	55	PK 22s (H3)
Tail lights	5	BA 15s
Brake lights	21	BA 15s
Combined brake and tail	21/5	BA7 15d
Rear foglights/reversing lights	21	BA 15s
License plate light	5	BA 9s
Interior (courtesy) light	10	SV 8.5
Reading lights	5	W 2.1x9.5d
Engine bay/load area lights	10	SV 8.5
Glovebox light	2	BA 9s
Vanity mirror light	3	SV 7
Door edge marker light	3	W 2.1x9.5d
Indicator and warning lights	1.2	Integral holder
Instrument illumination	3	W 2.1x9.5d
Control illumination	1.2	W 2x4.6d

Fuses — 1982/83 models

Fuse No	Circuits protected	Rating (A)
1 (or 2)	Fuel pump (main)	25
2 (or 1)	Hazard warning, headlight flasher, central locking	25
3	Front foglights/spotlights	15
4	Brake lights	15
5	Clock, interior lighting, power aerial, radio (full-time), door edge marker lights	15
6	Cooling fan	25
7	Window motors	30
8	Direction indicators, constant idle system, overdrive relay	15
9	Heated rear window, sunroof motor	30
10	Instruments, reversing lights, seat heaters, seat belt reminder, fuel pump relay, window motor relay, cooling fan relay, air conditioning delay valve, oil level sensor, bulb failure warning	25
11	Day running lights, cruise control, heater blower (low speed), automatic climate control	25
12	Cigarette lighter, radio (ignition-controlled), mirror motors, seat motors	15
13	Horn, windshield wash/wipe, headlight wash/wipe	25
14	Heater blower (high speeds)	30
15	Fuel pump (auxiliary)	15
16	Rear foglights and relay	15
17	High beam (LH) and main beam pilot light	15
18	High beam (RH), front spotlight relay	15
19	Low beam (LH)	15
20	Low beam (RH)	15
21	Instrument and control lighting, tail/parking lights (LH), number plate light, warning buzzer, front ashtray	15
22	Rear ashtray light, transmission tunnel switch lighting, tail/parking lights (RH), front foglight relay	15

Fuses — 1984 models

Fuse No	Circuits protected	Rating (A)
1	Fuel pump (main), fuel injection system	25
2	Hazard warning, headlight flasher, ABS, central locking	25
3	Front foglights/spotlights	15
4	Brake lights	15
5	Clock, interior lighting, power aerial, radio (full-time), door edge marker lights	15
6	Cooling fan, seat belt reminder, seat heaters	25
7	Window motors	30
8	Day running lights, bulb failure warning, window motor relay, cooling fan relay	15
9	Heated rear window, sunroof motor, air conditioning	25
10	Instruments, reversing lights, ignition system, cruise control, oil level sensor, ABS	15 or 25
11	Direction indicators, overdrive relay, constant idle system, intake heater relay	15 or 25

Fuse No	Circuits protected	Rating (A)
12	Cigarette lighter, radio (ignition-controlled), mirror motors, seat motors	15
13	Horn, windshield wash/wipe, headlight wash/wipe	25
14	Heater blower, air conditioning	30
15	Fuel pump (auxiliary)	15
16	Rear foglights and relay	15
17	High beam (LH) and main beam pilot light	15
18	High beam (RH), front spotlight relay	15
19	Low beam (LH)	15
20	Low beam (RH)	15
21	Instrument and control lighting, tail/parking lights (LH), number plate light	15
22	Rear ashtray light, transmission tunnel switch lighting, tail/parking lights (RH), front foglight relay	15

Fuses — 1985 to 1988 models

Fuse No	Circuits protected	Rating (A)
1	Fuel pump (main), fuel injection system	25
2	Hazard warning, headlight flasher, ABS, central locking	25
3	Front foglights/spotlight relay, rear foglight relay	15
4	Brake lights	15
5	Clock, interior lighting, power aerial, radio (full-time),door edge marker lights	15
6	Seat heaters	15
7	Cooling fan	25
8	Window motors	30
9	Direction indicators, seat belt reminder, seat heater relay, window motor relay, air conditioning relay, cooling fan relay	15
10	Heated rear window, sunroof motor, heated mirrors	30
11	Fuel pump (auxiliary)	15
12	Reversing lights, oil level sensor, overdrive, ignition system, cruise control, ABS	15
13	Fuel injection system	15
14	Mirror motors, cigarette lighter, radio (ignition-controlled), rear window wiper	15
15	Horn, windshield wash/wipe, headlight wash/wipe	25
16	Heater blower, air conditioning	30
17	High beam (LH) and main beam pilot light	15
18	High beam (RH), front spotlights	15
19	Low beam (LH)	15
20	Low beam (RH)	15
21	Instrument lighting, tail/parking lights (LH), number plate lights	15
22	Rear ashtray light, transmission tunnel switch light, tail/parking lights (RH)	15
23	Seat motor relay	15
24	Spare	-
25	Day running lights	15
26	Seat motors	30

1 General information

The electrical system is of the 12 volt, negative ground type. Electricity is generated by an alternator, belt-driven from the crankshaft pulley. A lead-acid storage battery provides a reserve of power for use when the demands of the system temporarily exceed the alternator output, and for starting.

The battery negative terminal is connected to ground — vehicle metal — and most electrical system components are wired so that they only receive a positive feed, the current returning via vehicle metal. This means that the component mounting forms part of the circuit. Loose or corroded mountings can therefore cause apparent electrical faults.

Many semiconductor devices are used in the electrical system, both in the black boxes which control vehicle functions and in other components. Semiconductors are very sensitive to excessive (or wrong polarity) voltage, and to extremes of heat. Observe the appropriate precautions to avoid damage.

Although some repair procedures are given in this Chapter, some-times replacement of a well-used item will prove most satisfactory.

Before starting work on the electrical system, read the precautions listed in *Safety first* at the beginning of the manual.

2 Maintenance and inspection

1 Weekly, before a long trip, or when prompted by the appropriate warning light, check that all exterior lights are working. Replace blown bulbs as necessary (Section 13). Top up the washer reservoirs.
2 Every 6000 miles or six months, inspect the battery and check the electrolyte level as described in Section 3.
3 Every 12,000 miles or twelve months, or whenever poor output from the alternator is suspected, check the tension and condition of the alternator drivebelt(s). See Chapter 2, Section 7.
4 Periodically check the condition of the windshield, rear window and headlight wiper blades and arms. Replace as necessary (Section 29).
5 When a power-operated radio antenna is installed, lubricate it

12

regularly with water repellant/lubricant spray, and wipe it clean with a soft cloth. If the antenna is allowed to become dirty or corroded it will jam.

3   Battery check and maintenance

Warning: *Several precautions must be followed when checking and servicing the battery. Hydrogen gas, which is highly flammable, is always present in the battery cells, so keep lighted tobacco and all other open flames and sparks away from the battery. The electrolyte in the cells is actually dilute sulfuric acid, which will cause injury if splashed on your skin or in your eyes. It'll also ruin clothes and painted surfaces. When removing the battery cables, always detach the negative cable first and hook it up last!*

Check

1   Battery maintenance is an important procedure which will help ensure that you aren't stranded because of a dead battery. Several tools are required for this procedure.

 a) Face shield/safety goggles — When removing corrosion with a brush, the acidic particles can easily fly up into your eyes.

 b) Baking soda — A solution of baking soda and water can be used to neutralize corrosion.

 c) Petroleum jelly — A layer of this on the battery posts will help prevent corrosion.

 d) Battery post/cable cleaner — This wire brush cleaning tool will remove all traces of corrosion from the battery posts and cable clamps.

 e) Treated felt washers — Placing one of these on each post, directly under the cable clamps, will help prevent corrosion.

 f) Puller — Sometimes the cable clamps are very difficult to pull off the posts, even after the nut/bolt has been completely loosened. This tool pulls the clamp straight up and off the post without damage.

 g) Battery post/cable cleaner — Here is another cleaning tool which is a slightly different version of number 4 above, but it does the same thing.

 h) Rubber gloves — Another safety item to consider when servicing the battery; remember that's acid inside the battery!

2   The electrolyte level should be checked every week. To do this, remove all of the cell caps. If the level is low, add *distilled* water until it's above the plates. Most batteries have a split-ring indicator in each cell to help you judge when enough water has been added — don't overfill the cells!

Maintenance

3   Periodically clean the top and sides of the battery. Remove all dirt and moisture. This will help prevent corrosion and ensure that the battery doesn't become partially discharged by leakage through moisture and dirt. Check the case for cracks and distortion.

4   Check the tightness of the battery cable bolts to ensure good electrical connections. Inspect the entire length of each cable, looking for cracked or abraded insulation and frayed conductors.

5   If corrosion, which usually appears as white, fluffy deposits, is evident, remove tha cables from the terminals, clean them with a battery brush and reinstall them. Corrosion can be kept to a minimum by applying a layer of petroleum jelly to the terminals after the cables are in place.

6   Make sure the battery carrier is in good condition and the hold-down clamp is tight. If the battery is removed, make sure that nothing is in the bottom of the carrier when it's reinstalled and don't overtighten the clamp nuts.

7   The freezing point of electrolyte depends on its specific gravity. Since freezing can ruin a battery, it should be kept in a fully charged state to protect against freezing.

8   If you frequently have to add water to the battery and the case has been inspected for cracks that could cause leakage, but none are found, the battery is being overcharged; the charging system should be checked as described in Section 7.

9   If any doubt exists about the battery state of charge, a hydrometer should be used to test it by withdrawing a little electrolyte from each cell, one at a time.

10   The specific gravity of the electrolyte at 80°F will be approximately 1.270 for a fully charged battery. For every 10°F that the electrolyte

temperature is above 80°F, add 0.04 to the specific gravity. Subtract 0.04 if the temperature is below 80°F.

11   A specific gravity reading of 1.240 with an electrolyte temperature of 80°F indicates a half-charged battery.

12   Some of the common causes of battery failure are:

 a) Accessories, especially headlights, left on overnight or for several hours.

 b) Slow average driving speeds for short intervals.

 c) The electrical load of the vehicle being more than the alternator output. This is very common when several high draw accessories are being used simultaneously (such as radio/stereo, air conditioning, window defoggers, lights, etc.).

 d) Charging system problems such as short circuits, slipping drivebelt, defective alternator or faulty voltage regulator.

 e) Battery neglect, such as loose or corroded terminals or loose battery hold-down clamp.

3.1   Battery, showing positive (+) and negative (–) terminals

4   Battery — charging

1   In normal use the battery should not require charging from an external source, unless the vehicle is unused for long periods, when it should be recharged every six weeks or so. If vehicle use consists entirely of short runs at night it is also possible for the battery to become discharged. Otherwise, a regular need for recharging points to a fault in the battery or elsewhere in the charging system.

2   There is no need to disconnect the battery from the vehicle wiring when using a battery charger, but switch off the ignition and if possible leave the hood open. Don't jump-start the vehicle with a battery charger. The fuel injection and ignition control units could be damaged.

3   Domestic battery chargers (up to about 6 amps output) may safely be used overnight without special precautions. Make sure that the charger is set to deliver 12 volts before connecting it. Connect the leads (red or positive to positive terminal, black or negative to the negative terminal) before switching the charger on.

4   When charging is complete, turn the charger off before disconnecting it from the battery. Remember that the battery will be giving off hydrogen gas, which is very explosive.

5   Charging at a higher rate should only be carried out under carefully controlled conditions. Very rapid charging should be avoided if possible, as it is liable to cause permanent damage to the battery through overheating.

6   During any sort of charging, battery electrolyte temperature should never exceed 38°C (100°F). If the battery becomes hot, or the electrolyte is bubbling vigorously, charging should be stopped.

5   Battery — removal and installation

1   Disconnect the battery negative (ground) cable.

2   Disconnect the battery positive cables. These may be protected by a plastic cover. Do not allow the wrench to bridge the positive and negative terminals.

3   Release the battery hold-down clamps. Lift out the battery. Keep it upright and be careful not to drop it.

4   Begin installation by placing the battery in its tray, making sure it faces the right way. Secure it with the hold-down clamp.

5   Clean the battery terminals if necessary (Section 3), then reconnect them. Connect the positive cable first, then the negative cable.

6   Alternator — precautions

1   To avoid damage to the alternator and other components, the following precautions should be observed:
   a) Do not disconnect the battery or the alternator while the engine is running
   b) Do not allow the engine to turn the alternator when the latter is not connected
   c) Do not test for output from the alternator by touching the output lead to ground
   d) Do not use a battery charger of more than 12 volts output
   e) Disconnect the battery and the alternator before doing any arc welding on the vehicle
   f) Always observe the correct battery polarity

7   Alternator — check

1   Should it appear that the alternator is not charging the battery, check first that the drivebelt is intact and in good condition and that its tension is correct (Chapter 2). Always check the condition and security of the alternator electrical connections and the battery cables.
2   Accurate assessment of alternator output requires special equipment and a degree of skill. A rough idea of whether output is adequate can be gained by using a voltmeter (range 0 to 15 or 0 to 20 volts) as follows.
3   Connect the voltmeter across the battery terminals. Switch on the headlights (ignition on) and note the voltage reading: it should be between 12 and 13 volts.
4   Start the engine and run it at a fast idle (approx 2000 rpm). Read the voltmeter: it should indicate 13 to 14 volts.
5   With the engine still running at a fast idle, switch on as many electrical consumers as possible (heated rear window, heater blower etc). The voltage at the battery should be maintained at 13 to 14 volts. Increase the engine speed slightly if necessary to keep the voltage up.
6   If alternator output is low or zero, check the brushes, as described in Section 9. If the brushes are OK, seek expert advice.
7   Occasionally the condition may arise where the alternator output is excessive. Clues to this condition are constantly blowing bulbs; brightness of lights varying considerably with engine speed; overheating of alternator and battery, possibly with steam or fumes coming from the battery. This condition is almost certainly due to a defective voltage regulator, but expert advice should be sought.
8   Voltage regulator replacement is included in brush replacement (Section 9).
9   Later models vary the charge rate according to battery temperature (Fig. 12.1). In the event of failure or disconnection of the battery temperature sensor, the alternator will vary the rate according to its own internal temperature.

8   Alternator — removal and installation

Note: *On some models, access to the alternator is easiest from below. Remove the undertray if necessary.*

1   Disconnect the battery negative cable.

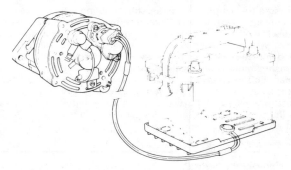

Fig. 12.1   Alternator with battery temperature sensor (Sec 7)

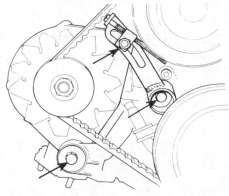

Fig. 12.2   Alternator pivot and adjusting strap nuts and bolts (arrowed) — Turbo model shown, others similar (Sec 8)

2   Loosen the alternator drivebelt(s) and slip them off the pulley (Chapter 2).
3   Disconnect the electrical wiring from the rear of the alternator — this may be a electrical connector or separate screw terminals. Make notes for reconnection if necessary (photo).
4   Support the alternator. Remove the pivot and adjusting strap nuts, bolts and washers, noting the installed positions of the washers. Lift out the alternator. Do not drop it, it is fragile.
5   Install by reversing the removal operations. Tension the drivebelt(s) (Chapter 2) before reconnecting the battery.

9   Alternator — brush replacement

Note: *Depending on model, it may be possible to replace the brushes without removing the alternator from the vehicle, but disconnect the battery negative cable first.*

1   From the rear of the alternator remove the two screws which secure the voltage regulator/brush carrier assembly. Withdraw the assembly (photos).

8.3   Alternator output terminal (arrowed) seen from below

9.1A   On this style alternator, the voltage regulator and brushes are contained in the same housing

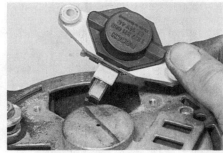

9.1B   Removing the voltage regulator/brush carrier

12

2   Measure the length of each brush protruding from the carrier. If they are worn down to, or below, the minimum specified, the old brushes will have to be unsoldered and new ones soldered into place. Some skill with a soldering iron will be required; excess heat from the soldering iron could damage the voltage regulator. When installed, the new brushes must move freely in their holders.
3   Clean the slip rings with a cloth moistened with rubbing alcohol. If they are badly burnt or damaged, seek expert advice.
4   Install the assembled brush carrier/voltage regulator and secure it with the two screws. If the alternator is on the vehicle, reconnect the battery negative cable.

10   Starter motor — check

1   If the starter motor fails to operate, first check that the battery is charged by switching on the headlights (ignition on). If the headlights do not come on, or rapidly become dim, the battery or its connections are at fault.
2   Check the security and condition of the battery and starter solenoid connections. Remember that the large wire to the solenoid is always live — disconnect the battery negative cable before using tools on the solenoid connections.

Solenoid check
3   Disconnect the battery negative cable, and all wires from the solenoid.
4   Connect a battery and a 3 watt test lamp between the solenoid body and the solenoid motor terminal (Fig. 12.3). The test lamp should light, if not, the solenoid windings are open-circuit.
5   Connect a battery and an 18 to 21 watt test lamp across the solenoid motor and battery terminals. Connect a wire from the battery positive terminal to the solenoid spade terminal (Fig. 12.4). The solenoid should be heard to operate and the test lamp should light: if not, the solenoid contacts are defective.

On load voltage check
6   Hook up the original connections to the solenoid and reconnect the battery negative cable. Connect a voltmeter across the battery terminals, then disconnect the low tension wire from the coil negative terminal and operate the starter by turning the ignition switch. Note the reading on the voltmeter which should not be less than 9.5 volts.
7   Now connect the voltmeter between the starter motor terminal on the solenoid and the starter motor body. With the coil low tension wire still disconnected, operate the starter and check that the recorded voltage is not more than 1 volt lower than that noted in paragraph 6. If the voltage drop is more than 1 volt a fault exists in the wiring from the battery to the starter.
8   Connect the voltmeter between the battery positive terminal and the motor terminal on the solenoid. With the coil low tension lead disconnected operate the starter for two or three seconds. Battery voltage should be indicated initially, then dropping to less than 1 volt. If the reading is more than 1 volt there is a high resistance in the wiring from the battery to the starter and the check in paragraph 9 should

be made. If the reading is less than 1 volt proceed to paragraph 10.
9   Connect the voltmeter between the two main solenoid terminals and operate the starter for two or three seconds. Battery voltage should be indicated initially, then dropping to less than 0.5 volt. If the reading is more than 0.5 volt, the solenoid and connections may be faulty.
10 Connect the voltmeter between the battery negative terminal and the starter motor body, and operate the starter for two or three seconds. A reading of less than 0.5 volt should be recorded; however, if the reading is more, the ground circuit is faulty and the ground connections to the battery and body should be checked.

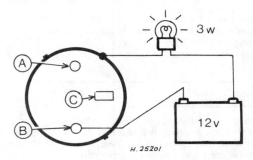

Fig. 12.3   Solenoid winding check (Sec 10)

A Battery terminal
B Motor terminal

C Spade terminal (normally connected to ignition/starter switch)

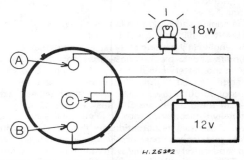

Fig. 12.4   Solenoid winding check. For key see Fig. 12.3 (Sec 10)

11   Starter motor — removal and installation

1   On some models, access to the starter motor is easier from below. Raise the front of the vehicle and support it securely on jackstands. Remove the undertray.
2   Disconnect the battery negative cable.
3   On the V6 engine, remove the oil filter (Chapter 1).

11.4   Starter solenoid connections

11.5   Starter motor securing bolts

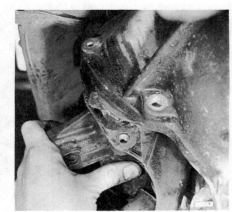

11.6   Removing a starter motor and adaptor plate

12.2A Removing the armature end cap to expose the E-clip and washer

12.2B Removing the armature washer

12.3 Removing the commutator cover screws

4 Disconnect the wires from the starter motor solenoid. Make notes or identifying marks if necessary (photo).
5 Support the starter motor and remove its securing bolts. If a tail bracket is installed, unbolt it first (photo).
6 Remove the starter motor. When present, recover the adaptor plate (photo).
7 Install by reversing the removal operations.

12 Starter motor — overhaul

1 Before undertaking the overhaul of a starter motor, check the cost and availability of spare parts. Replacement of a well worn motor may be more economial and more satisfactory than repair.

Bosch GF (direct drive)

2 Remove the armature and cap. Remove the E-clip and washer(s) from the end of the armature shaft (photos).
3 Remove the two through-bolts (or studs) and the two screws from the commutator cover. Pull off the cover (photo).
4 Disconnect the motor wire from the solenoid.
5 Hook up the brush springs and remove the brushes from their holders. Remove the brush carrier plate with the negative brushes, leaving the positive brushes soldered to the field coils.
6 Remove the yoke, with field coils and brushes, from the armature.
7 Unbolt and remove the solenoid, unhooking it from the operating

arm. Note the arrangement of any spring removed with the solenoid.
8 Remove the rubber plug from behind the operating arm pivot. Also remove the operating arm pivot nut and bolt (if equipped).
9 Remove the armature, operating arm and drive and components together. Unhook the operating arm from the drive.
10 To remove the pinion and clutch, clamp the armature lightly in a vise with padded jaws. Using a piece of tube, drive the stop ring down the shaft to expose the circlip (photo). Remove the circlip and stop ring, followed by the pinion and the one-way clutch.
11 Inspect all components for wear or damage and replace as necessary. The armature shaft bushings can be replaced: soak the new bushings in engine oil for at least half an hour before installing.
12 Simple continuity checks can be made on the armature and field windings using a multi-meter or a battery and test lamp. Special test equipment is required for thorough checking.
13 A burnt or damaged commutator can sometimes be saved by machining, provided the refinishing limit is not exceeded. This is specialist work. Be wary of using abrasives to clean the commutator, as particles may become embedded in the copper.
14 Replace the brushes if they are worn below the minimum specified. The new brush leads must be soldered to the tails of the old ones. Do not allow solder to run too far up the leads, or flexibility will be lost. It is good practice to replace the springs at the same time as the brushes. Make sure the brushes slide freely in their holders.
15 Replacement of the field coils and pole pieces must be left to a specialist.
16 Before beginning reassembly, apply grease or oil sparingly to the points shown in Fig. 12.5. Be careful not to get lubricant onto the commutator or brushes. Clean the commutator with rubbing alcohol.

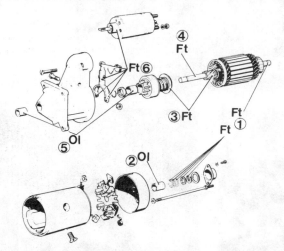

Fig. 12.5 Starter motor lubrication points (Sec 12)

1 Armature shaft and washers
2 Bushing
3 Spiral threads
4 Armature shaft
5 Bushings
6 Operating arm and solenoid plunger
Ft Grease
Ol Oil

12.10 Driving the stop ring down the shaft

12

17 Begin reassembling by installing the clutch, pinion and stop ring to the armature shaft. Install a new circlip into the shaft groove, then lever or pull the stop ring over it.

18 Engage the operating arm behind the clutch and install the assembly into the drive end housing. Install the pivot nut and bolt (if applicable) (photos).

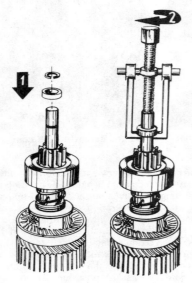

Fig. 12.6   Install the stop ring and circlip (1), then pull the stop ring over the circlip to keep it in the groove (2) (Sec 12)

19 Install the rubber plug behind the operating arm, then slide the yoke over the armature (photos).

20 Hook the solenoid onto the operating arm, making sure that the spring (when applicable) is correctly engaged. Install and tighten the solenoid securing bolts (photo).

21 Reconnect the motor wire to the solenoid (photo).

22 Install the brush carrier. Insert the brushes into their holders and hook the brush springs on top of them (photos).

23 Install the commutator cover and secure it with the through-bolts or nuts. Install the two screws also.

24 Install the washer(s) and E-clip to the armature shaft. Armature endplay is controlled by the thickness of the washer(s) — see Specifications for the desired value.

25 Install the armature end cap.

Bosch DW (reduction gear)

26 Overhaul procedures are similar to that for the Bosch GF starter, except that the armature can be withdrawn from the yoke leaving the reduction gears in place.

27 Permanent magnets may be used instead of field coils on the motor. These magnets are fragile: do not drop the yoke or clamp it in a vise.

28 Remove the cover plate and apply a little silicone grease to the reduction gears before reassembly (photos).

13   Exterior light bulbs — replacement

1   With all light bulbs, remember that if they have just been in use, they may be very hot. Switch off the power before replacing a bulb.

2   With quartz halogen bulbs (headlights and similar applications), do not touch the bulb glass with the fingers. Even small quantities of grease from the fingers will cause blackening and premature failure.

12.18A   Engage the operating arm . . .

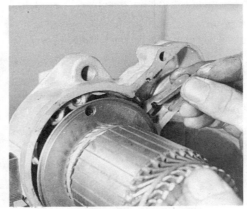

12.18B   . . . and fit the assembly to the drive end housing

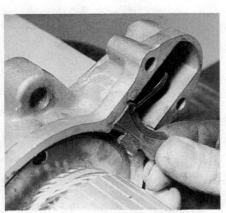

12.19A   Installing the rubber plug

12.19B   Installing the yoke over the armature

12.20   Installing the solenoid

12.21 Reconnecting the motor wire

12.22A Installing the brush carrier — the negative brushes are already in their holders

12.22B Hooking a brush spring onto a positive brush

12.28A Reduction gears with cover plate fitted

12.28B Reduction gears exposed

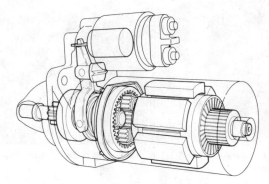

Fig. 12.7 Cutaway view of the reduction gear starter motor (Sec 12)

If a bulb is accidentally touched, clean it with rubbing alcohol and a clean rag.
3   Unless otherwise stated, install the new bulb by reversing the removal operations.

Headlight

4   Open the hood. Unclip the plastic cover from the rear of the headlight unit (photo). There is no need to disconnect the electrical connector.
5   Unplug the connector from the bulb. Release the retainer by pushing it and twisting it counterclockwise. Remove the retainer, spring and bulb (photos).
6   When installing the new bulb, do not touch the glass (paragraph

2). Make sure that the lugs on the bulb flange engage with the slots in the holder.
7   Observe the OBEN/TOP marking when reinstalling the plastic cover.

Auxiliary front light

8   Remove the lens/reflector unit, which is secured by two screws and retaining strips (photo).
9   Unplug the bulb wiring connector, release the spring clip and withdraw the bulb (photos).
10   Install the new bulb, being careful not to touch it with the fingers (paragraph 2). Reconnect the wiring.
11   Install the lens/reflector unit, observing the TOP marking.

Front direction indicator/day running/parking lights

12   Open the hood. Turn the appropriate bulb holder counterclockwise (without disconnecting it) and withdraw it (photo).
13   Remove the bulb from the holder (photo).
14   When installing the combined day running/parking light bulb, note that the pins are offset so it will only fit one way.

Direction indicator side repeater

15   Slide the lens forwards and free it from the rear. Withdraw the bulb holder from the lens without disconnecting the wiring.
16   When reinstalling, make sure that the rubber seal is seated in the hole.

Rear light cluster (sedan)

17   Open the trunk. Unscrew the knurled screw on the light unit cover and pivot the cover downwards.
18   Remove the appropriate bulb holder from the unit by twisting the holder counterclockwise and pulling it (photo).
19   Remove the bayonet fitting bulb from the holder (photo).

12

13.4   Unclipping the cover from the headlight unit (unit removed)

13.5A   Unplug the connector . . .

13.5B   . . . remove the retainer and spring . . .

13.5C   . . . and the bulb. Do not touch the bulb glass

13.8   Auxiliary light lens screw and strip

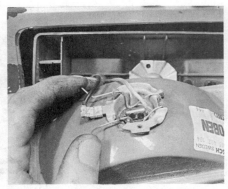

13.9A   Release the spring clip . . .

13.9B   . . . and withdraw the bulb

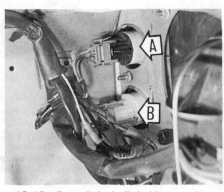

13.12   Front light bulb holders — day running light (A) and direction indicator (B)

13.13   Removing a day running/parking light bulb

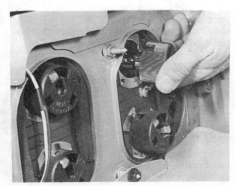

13.18   Remove the bulb and holder from the rear light cluster . . .

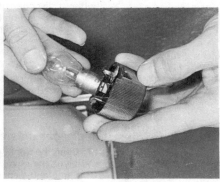

13.19   . . . then separate the two

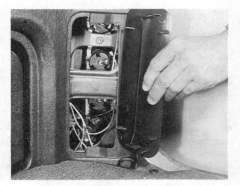

13.20   Rear light unit and cover — Wagon

Rear light cluster (wagon)

20 Open the tailgate. Unclip the light unit cover (photo), then proceed as for Sedan models.

License plate light

21 Unclip the light unit by sliding it rearwards.
22 Release the bulb by sliding the live contact off its tail. The bulb
can then be removed upwards (photo).

---

14 Exterior light units (except headlights) — removal and installation

1 Switch off the power before removing a light unit.
2 Except where noted, install by reversing the removal operations.

Auxiliary front light

3 Follow the wiring back from the light unit and unplug the connector.
4 Remove the nut which secures the light unit to the bracket, or unbolt the bracket complete with the light unit (photo).

Direction indicator/day running light unit

5 Open the hood. Disconnect the two electrical connectors from the
bulb holders on the rear of the unit.
6 Remove the single securing nut from the rear of the light unit. Free
it from the lugs on the side of the headlight and withdraw it (photo).

Rear light cluster (sedan)

7 Proceed as for light bulb replacement, but remove the hinged cover
completely. It is secured by two nuts.
8 Disconnect the cluster electrical connector (photo).
9 Remove the five flanged nuts and the single screw which secure
the unit. Note that the screw also secures ground tags.
10 Remove the cluster from the vehicle (photo).

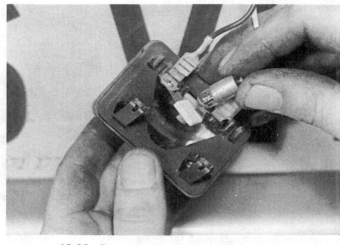

13.22 **Removing the license plate light bulb**

Rear light cluster (wagon)

11 Proceed as described for sedan models, making allowances for the
detail differences which will be found.

---

15 Headlight unit — removal and installation

1 Remove the front grille and the headlight wiper arm.
2 Disconnect the electrical connectors from the headlight and from
the day running light/direction indicator light unit (photo). Remove the
latter unit, which is secured by one nut.

14.4 **Auxiliary light showing securing nut**

14.6 **Disengaging the front light unit from the headlight**

14.8 **Disconnecting the rear light cluster electrical connector**

14.10 **Removing the rear light cluster**

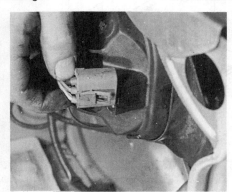

15.2 **Disconnecting a headlight electrical connector**

12

15.4A   Removing the trim strip . . .

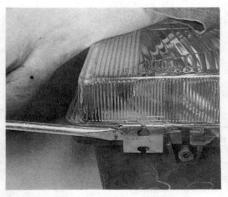

15.4B   . . . and a retaining clip

15.4C   Installing a new headlight seal

3   Remove the four nuts which secure the headlight unit. Disconnect the washer tube from the wiper arm, if not already done, and remove the headlight unit.
4   The lens and seal may now be replaced after removing the trim strip and the retaining clips (photos).
5   Install by reversing the removal operations. Remember to feed the washer tube through the trim strip.
6   Have the beam alignment checked on completion (Section 16).

16   Headlight beam alignment

1   Beam alignment should be carried out by a Volvo dealer or other specialist having the necessary optical alignment equipment.
2   In an emergency, adjustment may be carried out on a trial and error basis, using the two adjustment screws on the rear of each headlight unit.

17   Interior light bulbs — replacement

1   See Section 13, steps 1 and 3.
2   Some switch illumination/pilot bulbs are integral with their switches and cannot be replaced separately.

Courtesy/cargo area lights
3   Pull or pry the light unit from its mounts.
4   Replace the bulb(s), which may be bayonet or end clip fitting (photo).

Glovebox lights
5   Unclip the combined bulb holder/switch unit from the top of the glovebox for access to the bulb (photo).
6   When vanity mirror bulbs are installed, these are accessible after prying out the light diffuser strip (photo).

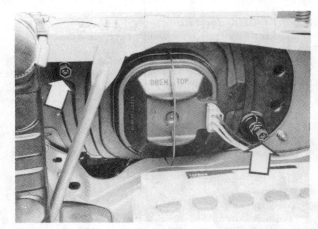

Fig. 12.8   Headlight beam alignment screws (arrowed) (Sec 16)

Fig. 12.9   Removing the front courtesy/map reading light (Sec 17)

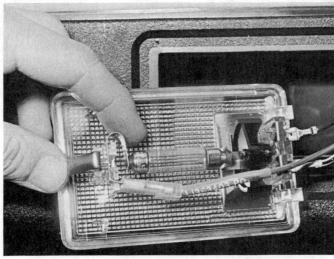

17.4   A cargo area light with an end clip fitting bulb

17.5 Glovebox light and switch (seen in a mirror)

17.6 Vanity mirror light bulbs exposed

17.7 Installing a door edge marker bulb

17.8 Extracting the automatic transmission selector light

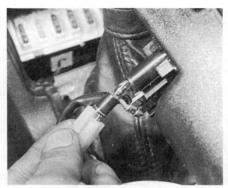

17.10 Removing a rear console switch light

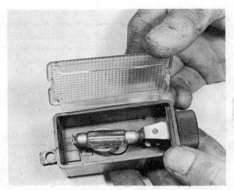

17.12 Under-hood light unit (removed)

Door edge marker lights

7   Pry off the lens for access to the bulb. The bulb is of the capless type, so it is a push fit (photo).

Automatic transmission selector light

8   Remove the selector quadrant as if for access to the starter inhibitor switch (Chapter 6). The bulb and holder can then be pulled out (photo).

Seat belt buckle light

9   Unclip the bulb holder from the buckle for access to the bulb.

Switch illumination bulbs

10   When these are separable from the switch, they simply pull out (photo).

Instrument panel bulbs

11   See Sections 20 and 21. (The reader with small hands and deft fingers may manage to replace bulbs in place after removing the steering column/pedal trim.)

Under-hood light

12   Pry off the lens with a screwdriver. The bulb is of the end clip fitting type (photo).

Cigarette lighter/ashtray light

13   See Section 33.

18 Ignition/starter switch — removal and installation

1   Disconnect the battery negative cable.
2   Remove the trim panel from below the steering column.
3   Disconnect the electrical connector from the switch (photo).
4   Remove the two screws which secure the switch to the steering lock. Withdraw the switch.
5   Install by reversing the removal operations. Note that the hole in the center of the switch is shaped so that it will only engage with the driving spindle in one position (photo).

Fig.12.10 The seat belt buckle light (Sec 17)

12

18.3   Disconnecting the ignition switch
electrical connector

18.5   Ignition switch and steering lock
showing driving hole and spindle

19.4   Removing a column shroud screw

19 Switches — removal and installation

1   Disconnect the battery negative cable, or assure yourself that there is no risk of short-circuit, before removing any switch.
2   Except where noted, a switch is installed by reversing the removal operations.

Steering column switches

3   Remove the steering wheel (Chapter 10).
4   Remove the column shrouds, which are secured by two screws each (photo).
5   Remove the switch in question. Each switch is secured by two screws. Remove the screws, pull the switch out and disconnect the electrical connector (photos).

Horn push switches

6   These are removed by prying them out of the steering wheel. They are difficult to remove without damage (photo).

Dash panel switches

7   Unclip the switch panel (and trim, if applicable) and withdraw it from the dash (photo).
8   Disconnect the switch electrical connectors, making identifying marks or notes if necessary (photo).
9   Remove the switch concerned by depressing its retaining lugs (photo).

Rear console switches

10 See Chapter 11.

19.5A   Removing a column
switch screw

19.5B   Disconnecting a column switch
electrical connector

19.6   Removing a horn push switch

19.7   Unclipping a switch panel from
the dash

19.8   Disconnecting a switch
electrical connector

19.9   Removing a switch from
the panel

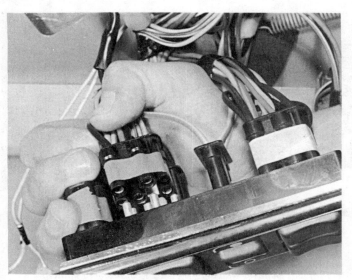

19.12 Disconnecting a window control switch

Window/mirror control switches

11 Remove the door armrest and separate the switch panel from it. See Chapter 11.

12 Disconnect the electrical connector from the switch in question (photo).

13 Carefully pry free the retaining lugs and remove the switch from the underside of the switch plate.

Door/tailgate switches

14 Open the door or tailgate. Remove the securing screw and withdraw the switch (photo).

15 Secure the wires with a clothes pin before disconnecting them so that they are not lost in the door pillar.

Other switches

16 Some switches will be found in the Chapter dealing with their system or equipment — for example, temperature-operated switches in Chapter 2, and transmission-operated switches in Chapter 6.

20 Instrument cluster — removal and installation

1 Disconnect the battery negative cable.

2 Remove the two screws at the bottom corners of the instrument cluster. These may be concealed by plastic covers, which will have to be pulled off first (photo).

3 Pull the cluster towards the steering wheel. (If difficulty is experienced, remove the steering column/pedal lower trim to gain access to the rear of the panel.)

4 Disconnect the electrical connectors from the rear of the cluster (photo).

5 Lift out the cluster. Do not drop or jar it.

6 Install by reversing the removal operations.

21 Instrument cluster — disassembly and reassembly

1 Remove the screws which secure the instrument cluster to the transparent panel and trim. Carefully remove the cluster.

2 Individual instruments can now be removed after unscrewing their securing nuts or screws (photo). Note that the screws are not identical: those which secure conductors are plated.

3 Bulb holders are removed by twisting them 90° and pulling. Some bulbs can be separated from their holders for replacement; others must be replaced complete with holder (photos).

4 The printed circuit can be replaced after removing all the instruments, bulbs and connectors. Be careful when handling the printed circuit, it is fragile.

19.14 Removing a door switch

20.2 Exposing an instrument cluster screw

20.4 Disconnecting an instrument cluster electrical connector

21.2 Removing the speedometer

21.3A Removing a bulb and holder from the printed circuit

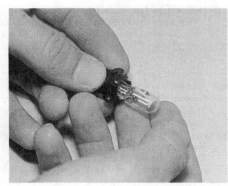

21.3B Separating the capless bulb and holder

12

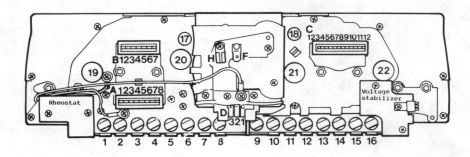

Fig. 12.11 Identification of instrument cluster bulbs — 1984 model shown. A to H are connectors (Sec 21)

1 Overdrive off light (AW 71)	6 Handbrake warning	12 Choke warning/Turbo boost warning	17 Direction indicator (RH)
2 Seat belt reminder	7 Brake failure warning		18 Direction indicator (LH)
3 Spare	8 High beam pilot light	13 Headlight pilot light	19 Instrument lighting
4 Low washer fluid warning	9 Overdrive on light (M 46)	14 Spare	20 Instrument lighting
5 Bulb failure warning	10 Battery charge failure warning	15 Engine oil level warning	21 Instrument lighting
	11 Engine oil pressure warning	16 Spare	22 Instrument lighting

22 Speedometer sender unit — removal and installation

1   Raise the rear of the vehicle and support it securely on jackstands.
2   Although not essential, it will improve access if the rear axle oil filler plug and the Panhard rod are removed. See Chapter 10, Section 29.
3   If there is a sealing wire on the sender connector, cut the wire and remove it.
4   Unplug the sender connector (photo).

Models without ABS
5   Unscrew the ring nut which secures the sender, using a pair of water pump pliers. This nut may be very tight: be careful not to crush it or it will be impossible to remove. As a last resort, the axle oil may be drained, the differential cover plate removed complete with sender unit, and the assembly dealt with on the bench.
6   Remove the sender unit and shim(s).
7   Install by reversing the removal operations. If a new sender unit is being installed, or if other related components have been removed, check the clearance between the sender unit and the toothed wheel as follows.
8   Working through the oil filler hole, place a feeler gauge between the sender unit and the toothed wheel and determine the clearance. The desired value is 0.85 mm ± 0.35 mm (0.033 ± 0.014 in). Adjust by adding or removing shims between the sender unit and the differential cover.
9   Install the oil filler plug and reconnect the sender unit connector. Check the sender for correct operation before installing a new seal.

Models with ABS
10   Proceed as above, but note the following:
  a) The sender may be secured with an Allen screw, not a ring nut
  b) The desired clearance is 0.60 mm (0.024 in), with a tolerated range from 0.35 to 0.75 mm (0.014 to 0.030 in)

23 Fuses — general information

1   The fuses are located on the sloping face of the central electric unit, behind the front ashtray. Access is gained by removing the ashtray, then unclipping the ashtray carrier by pressing up the section marked electrical fuses — press.
2   If a fuse blows, the electrical circuit(s) protected by that fuse will cease to operate. Lists of the circuits protected are given in the Specifications; a sticker behind the ashtray gives details for the particular vehicle.
3   To check for a blown fuse, either remove the fuse and inspect its

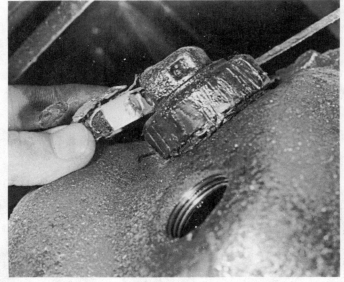

22.4 Disconnecting the speedometer sender

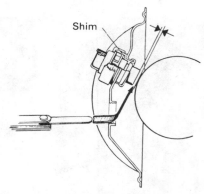

Fig. 12.12 Checking the speedometer sender unit clearance (Sec 22)

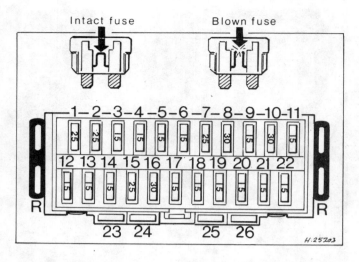

Fig. 12.13 Fuse numbering (1985 model shown) and identification of a blown fuse (Sec 23)

Fig. 12.14 Checking for a blown fuse using a test light (Sec 23)

wire link, or (with the power on) connect a 12 volt test light between ground and each of the fuse terminals. If the test light comes on at both terminals, the fuse is OK; if it comes on at one terminal only, the fuse is blown.

4 To replace a blown fuse, pull out the old fuse either with the fingers or with the special tool provided. Press in a new fuse of the correct rating (indicated by color and by a number on the fuse). Spare fuses are provided at each side of the central electrical unit.

5 Never install a fuse of a higher rating than that specified, nor bypass a blown fuse with wire or metal foil. Serious damage or fire could result.

6 Persistent blowing of a particular fuse indicates a fault in the circuit(s) protected. Where more than one circuit is involved, switch on one item at a time until the fuse blows, so showing in which circuit the fault lies.

7 Besides a fault in the electrical component concerned, a blown fuse can also be caused by a short-circuit in the wiring to the component. Look for trapped or frayed wires allowing a live wire to touch vehicle metal, and for loose or damaged connectors.

24 Relays — general information

1 Relays are electrically-operated switches. They are used for two main reasons:
  a) A relay can switch a heavy current at a distance, allowing the use of lighter gauge control switches and wiring
  b) A relay can receive more than one control input, and can in some circumstances perform logic functions

2 In addition, some relays have a timer function — for instance the intermittent wiper relay.

3 If a circuit which includes a relay develops a fault, remember that the relay itself could be faulty. Testing is by substitution of a known good relay. Do not assume that relays which look similar are necessarily identical for purposes of substitution.

4 Most relays are located on the central electrical unit, in front of the fuses. For identification see Fig. 12.15. For access, remove the

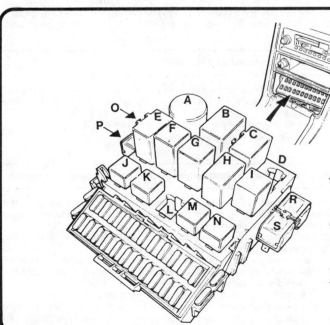

Fig. 12.15 Relay identification in central electrical unit. Not all relays are installed in all models (Sec 24)

A Bulb failure warning sensor
B Seat belt reminder or torque limiter (B23FT)
C Windshield wiper delay
D Tailgate wiper delay
E Continuous injection system
F Impulse relay (1982) or front foglights
G Flasher unit
H Main lighting relay (1983)
I Overdrive relay
J Window winders/elecric fan
K Central locking (unlocking)/main lighting relay (1984 on)
M Auxiliary lights
N Rear foglights
O Vacant
P Vacant
R Vacant/ignition advance
S Oil level sensor

12

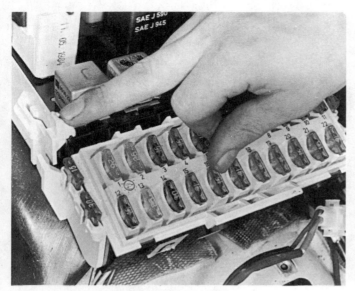

24.4A   Release the clips . . .

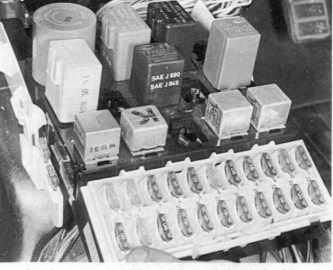

24.4B   . . . and withdraw the central electrical unit.
(Center console has been removed)

ashtray and ashtray holder, then release the clips and pull the unit into the vehicle (photos).

5   Other relays relating to the fuel and ignition systems are found under the hood. These are considered in Chapters 3 and 4. Two air conditioning relays are located behind the dash panel.

25   Bulb failure warning system — general information

The bulb failure warning sensor is a special kind of relay. It is mounted on the central electrical unit.

The sensor contains a number of reed switches surrounded by coils of wire. Current to each bulb covered by the system travels through one coil. The coils are arranged in pairs, one pair carrying the current for one pair of bulbs.

When both bulbs of a pair are lit, the magnetic fields produced by the two coils cancel each other out. If one bulb fails, the coil remaining in circuit will produce an uncancelled magnetic field. The magnetic field operates the reed switch, which illuminates the warning light.

From the above it will be realized that no warning will be given if a pair of bulbs fails simultaneously. False alarms may result if bulbs of different wattage, or even of different make, are installed.

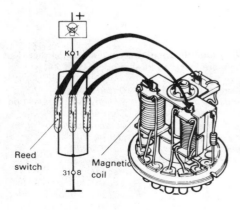

Fig. 12.16 Construction of the bulb failure warning sensor
(Sec 22)

Wiring for trailer lighting must be connected upstream of the bulb failure warning sensor, otherwise it may be damaged by excessive current flow. Consult a Volvo dealer or an auto-electrician.

26   Direction indicator system — troubleshooting

1   The direction indicator system consists of the flasher unit, control switch, external and repeater lights and the associated wiring. The hazard warning system shares the same flasher unit.

2   If the direction indicators operate abnormally fast or slowly on one side only, check the bulbs and wiring on that side. Incorrect wattage bulbs, dirty bulb holders and poor ground connections can all cause changes in the flashing rate.

3   If the directon indicators do not work at all, check the fuse before suspecting a flasher unit. If the hazard warning system works but the indicators do not, the flasher unit is almost certainly not faulty.

4   The flasher unit occupies position G among the relays on the central electrical unit. Testing is by substitution of a known good unit.

27   Horn — removal and installation

1   Raise the front of the vehicle and support it securely on jackstands.

2   Working under the front bumper, disconnect the wires from the horn (photo).

3   Unbolt the horn from its bracket and remove it.

4   Install by reversing the removal operations.

28   Windshield/headlight/tailgate washers — general information

1   The washer systems share a common reservoir, located under the hood. For access to the pump(s) and level indicator it will be necessary to remove the air cleaner unit.

2   The level indicator is a float-operated switch which can be removed after unscrewing its retaining ring (photo).

3   To remove a washer pump, unplug its electrical connector, disconnect the hose from it and pull the pump out of its locating spigot (photo). Be prepared for fluid spillage.

4   If a pump malfunctions it must be replaced.

5   Only use clean water, and an approved windshield washer additive in the washer reservoir. Use an additive with antifreeze properties (not engine antifreeze) in freezing conditions.

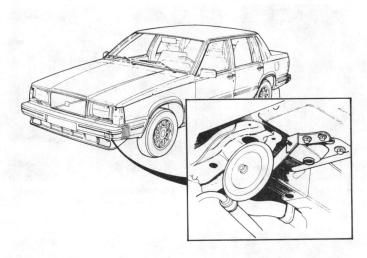

Fig. 12.17 Horn location under the front bumper (Sec 27)

29 Wiper blades and arms — removal and installation

1 To remove a blade alone, unhook or unclip it from the arm. In the case of headlight wiper blades, also disconnect the washer tube (photos).

2 Before removing an arm end blade, mark the parked position of the blade on the glass with tape or crayon.
3 Remove the nut at the base of the wiper arm and pull the arm off the splines (photo).
4 Install by reversing the removal operations. In the case of the headlight wiper blades, note that the longer end goes towards the grille.
5 Bias the headlight wiper arms by reinstalling them with the blades just below the stops (motors parked). Secure the arms, then lift the blades over the stops.

30 Windshield wiper motor and linkage — removal and installation

1 Remove the windshield wiper arms and spindle seals (photo).
2 Raise the hood to its fully open position.
3 Remove the cowl panel, which is secured by three bolts and some clips (photo). Close the hood.
4 Unclip the heater air intake cover and disconnect the wiper motor electrical connector (photo).
5 Remove the two bolts and lift out the wiper motor, linkage and cover (photo).
6 The motor may be removed from the linkage by unscrewing the spindle nut and the three securing screws (photo). Do not attempt to disassemble the motor; spare parts are unlikely to be available.
7 Other components of the linkage, including the cable, may be replaced as necessary. There is a tensioning nut at one end of the cable (photo).
8 Install by reversing the removal operations. Before reinstalling the wiper arms, switch the wipers on and off to bring the motor into the parked position.

27.2 Horn wiring connectors (arrowed)

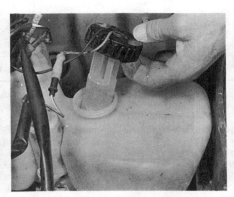

28.2 Washer reservoir level indicator

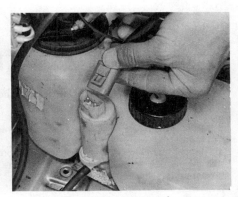

28.3 Disconnecting a washer pump

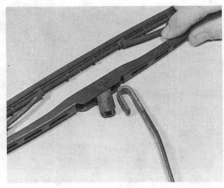

29.1A Unhooking a windshield wiper blade

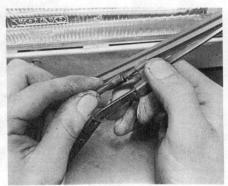

29.1B Disconnecting the washer tube from a headlight wiper blade

29.3 Removing a wiper arm nut

12

30.1 Removing a wiper arm spindle seal

30.3 Removing one of the cowl panel bolts

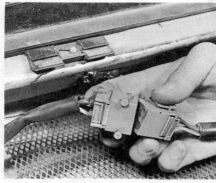

30.4 Disconnecting the wiper motor electrical connector

30.5 Unbolting the wiper assembly

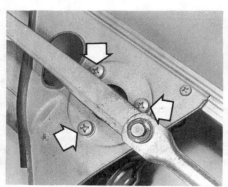

30.6 Wiper motor securing screws (arrowed)

30.7 Part of the wiper linkage — cable tensioning nut is arrowed

31 Headlight wiper motor — removal and installation

1   Remove the headlight unit on the side concerned (Section 15).
2   Follow the wiper motor wiring back to the electrical connector and disconnect it.
3   Remove the two nuts which secure the motor (photo). Withdraw the motor.
4   Install by reversing the removal operations. If there is any doubt that the motor is in the parked position, operate the wipers and washers before reinstalling the wiper arm.

32 Rear wiper motor — removal and installation

1   Remove the tailgate interior trim (Chapter 11, Section 13).
2   Pry the link balljoint off the wiper motor crank arm (photo).
3   Remove the three bolts which secure the motor. Withdraw the motor (it may be necessary to rotate the crank arm) and disconnect the wiring from it (photo).
4   Install by reversing the removal operations. Check the operation of the motor before reinstalling the trim.

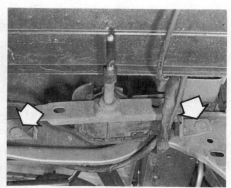

31.3 Headlight wiper motor exposed. Securing nuts are behind the two studs (arrowed)

32.2 Rear wiper motor showing crank arm balljoint (arrowed) and securing bolts

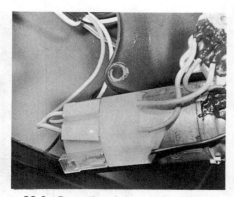

32.3 Removing the rear wiper motor

33 Cigarette lighter — removal and installation

1 Make sure the ignition is switched off.

Front

2 Remove the lighter element and unclip the trim from around the aperture.
3 Remove the screws now exposed (photo).
4 Remove the lighter and tray, disconnecting the wiring feed and bulb holder from the rear (photo). Also disconnect any audio equipment which may be occupying the tray.
5 The lighter may now be removed from the tray.
6 Install by reversing the removal operations.

Rear

7 This is covered in removal of the rear console (Chapter 11).

34 Heated rear window — general information

1 All models are equipped with a heated rear window. Heating is achived by passing current through a resistive grid bonded to the in-side of the rear window.
2 Do not allow hard or sharp items of luggage to rub against the heating grid. Use a soft cloth or chamois to clean the inside of the win-dow, working along the lines of the grid.
3 Small breaks in the grid can be repaired using special conductive paint, obtainable from auto parts stores. Use the paint as directed by the manufacturer.
4 The heated rear window draws a high current, so it should not be left switched on longer than necessary. On some models a so-called delay relay is incorporated into the circuit in order to switch the window off after a few minutes.

5 When heated door mirrors are installed, their heaters are controlled by the heated rear window switch.

35 Radio/cassette player (original equipment) — removal and installation

1 The radio/cassette player seen in the accompanying photo is removed as follows.
2 Disconnect the battery negative cable.
3 Pull the control knobs off the front of the instrument (photo).
4 Using a hook made of a piece of bent wire, retract the side securing clips, working through the control knob apertures. As the clips are retracted, draw the unit out of its mounting (photos).
5 Withdraw the unit fully and disconnect the wiring.
6 When reinstalling, reconnect the wiring, then push the unit in until the clips snap into place.
7 Install the control knobs and reconnect the battery.

36 Radio antenna (original equipment) — removal and installation

Note: *Two types of original equipment antenna are shown here. There may be others.*

Sedan (automatic, in trunk)

1 Disconnect the battery negative cable.
2 Open the trunk and remove the left-hand side trim.
3 Remove the nut and cover which secure the antenna tube to the rear fender (photo).
4 Disconnect the antenna signal and power wires (photos).
5 Remove the tube and drive securing nuts and bolts. Withdraw the antenna into the trunk.

33.3 Loosening a cigarette lighter screw

33.4 Removing the lighter bulb and holder. This also serves the ashtray

35.3 Pulling off a radio knob

35.4A Insert a wire hook . . .

35.4B . . . to retract the side clip (unit removed to show clip)

35.4C Removing the radio/cassette unit

36.3   Removing the antenna tube nut and cover

36.4A   Disconnect the antenna cable . . .

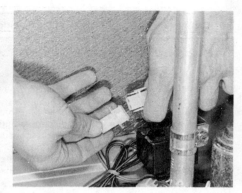

36.4B   . . . and the power feed

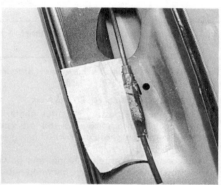

36.7   Antenna cable connector (Wagon) wrapped in tape

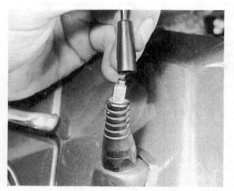

36.8   Unscrewing the antenna rod from the stub

Wagon (fixed, on rear pillar)

6   Open the tailgate. Unclip the trim panel which covers the antenna mount and wiring.

7   Disconnect the antenna cable (photo).

8   Outside the vehicle, unscrew the antenna rod from the stub (photo). Remove the spacer.

9   Unscrew the tube securing nut. Remove the lower spacer and seal and withdraw the antenna into the vehicle (photos).

All types

10   Install by reversing the removal operations, but check for correct operation before installing the trim that was removed.

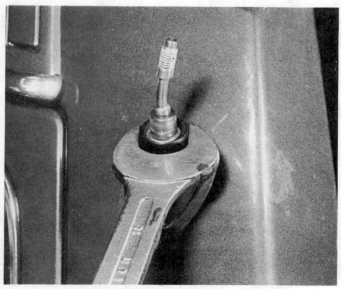

36.9A   Remove the antenna tube nut . . .

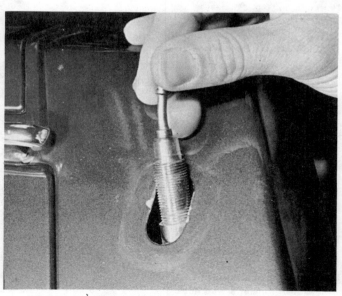

36.9B   . . . and withdraw the antenna into the vehicle

37 Troubleshooting — electrical system

Symptom	Reason(s)
Starter motor does not turn — no voltage at motor	Battery terminals loose or corroded Battery discharged or defective Starter motor connections loose or broken Starter switch or solenoid faulty Automatic transmission not in P or N Automatic transmission inhibitor switch faulty
Starter motor does not turn — voltage at motor	Starter motor internal defect
Starter motor turns very slowly	Battery nearly discharged or defective Battery terminals loose or corroded Starter motor internal defect
Starter motor noisy or rough	Mounting bolts loose Pinion or flywheel ring gear teeth damaged or worn
Alternator not charging battery	Drivebelt slipping or broken Alternator brushes worn Alternator connections loose or broken Alternator internal defect
Alternator overcharging battery	Alternator regulator faulty
Battery will not hold charge	Short-circuit (continual drain on battery) Battery defective internally Battery case dirty and damp
Gauge or speedometer gives no reading	Sender unit defective Wire disconnected or broken Fuse blown Gauge or speedometer defective
Fuel or temperature gauge reads too high	Sender unit defective Wire grounded Gauge faulty
Horn operates continuously	Horn button stuck down Cable to horn button grounded
Horn does not operate	Fuse blown Cable or connector broken or loose Switch, slip ring or brush dirty or defective
Lights do not come on	Battery discharged Fuse(s) blown Light switch faulty Bulbs blown Relay defective (when applicable)
Lights give poor illumination	Lenses or reflectors dirty Bulbs dirty Incorrect wattage bulbs fitted
Wiper motor fails to work	Fuse blown Connections loose or broken Relay defective Switch defective Motor defective

12

37   Troubleshooting — electrical system (continued)

Symptom	Reason(s)
Wiper motor works slowly and draws little current	Brushes badly worn Commutator dirty or burnt
Wiper motor works slowly and draws heavy current	Linkage seized or otherwise damaged Motor internal fault
Wiper motor works, but blades do not move	Linkage broken or disconnected Motor gearbox badly worn
Defect in any other components	Fuse blown Relay faulty (when applicable) Supply wire broken or disconnected Switch faulty (when applicable) Ground return faulty (check for loose or corroded mountings) Component itself faulty

Key to Figs. 12.18 to 12.27   Not all items are applicable to all models; some systems do not apply to US models

No	Item	Grid ref*	No	Item	Grid ref*
1	Battery	B2	37	Gear selector light (auto)	H4
2	Ignition switch	D3	38	Instrument illumination	F3, F4
3	Instrument panel connector (3-pole)	N3	39	Engine bay light	B2
4	Ignition coil	B4	40	Boot light	H4
5	Distributor	B3	41	Door edge marker light	L3, L4
6	Spark plugs	C3	42	Heater control illumination	F3, F1
7	Instrument panel connector (7-pole)	N3	43	Vanity mirror light	M5
8	Instrument panel connector (8-pole)	M3	45	Driver's belt lock tight	H3, L3
9	Starter motor	B3	46	Passenger's belt lock light	H3
10	Alternator and voltage regulator	B3	47	Windscreen wiper switch	F2
11	Fusebox	B1, E1, H1	48	Light switch	F3
12	Instrument panel connector (12-pole)	M3	49	Direction indicator/hazard warning/dip switches	F3
13	Headlight main beam	A2, A4, A5	50	Horn switch	B4
14	Headlight dipped beam	A2, A5	51	Heated rear window switch	J3
15	No 15 terminal (in central electrical unit)	K4	52	Rear foglight switch	H5
16	Parking light	A2, A5, J2, J5	53	Passenger seat heater switch	H3
17	Day running light	A2, A5	54	Overdrive switch (auto)	M3
18	Direction indicators	A1, A2, A5, B5, J2, J5	55	Heater blower switch	N1
19	Reversing light	J2, J5	56	Window switch (driver's door)	O3
20	Rear foglight	J2, J5	57	Window switch (front passenger's door)	P4
21	Tail light	J2, J5	58	Window switch (RH rear)	P4
22	Stop-light	J5	59	Window switch (LH rear)	O4
23	Front foglight/spotlight	N5, O5, Q1	60	Door mirror switch (driver's door)	N4
24	Number plate light	J3, J4	61	Door mirror switch (passenger's door)	O4
25	Interior light unit	H3	62	Central locking link rod switch	O4
26	Map reading lights	H3	63	Central locking key switch	O4
27	Courtesy light	H3	64	Sunroof switch	M2
28	Rear reading lights	H3, H4	65	Front foglight/spotlight switch	N5, P5, Q1
29	Positive terminal	C2	66	Stop-light switch	F3
30	No 30 terminal (in central electrical unit)	K4	67	Choke control switch (not UK)	D2
31	Earth connection (in central electrical unit)	K2	68	Handbrake switch	D2
32	Glovebox light	D2, E2, M4	69	Brake failure warning switch	E2
33	Front ashtray light	E2	70	Reversing light switch	H5
34	Rear ashtray light	H4	71	Starter inhibitor switch (auto)	B2
35	Switch illumination	H4	72	Driver's door switch	H5, L4
36	Switch illumination	H4	73	Passenger's door switch	H2, J5, L3
			74	Rear door switches	J2, M3

Color code

BL Blue	GR Grey	R Red	W White
BN Brown	OR Orange	SB Black	Y Yellow
GN Green	P Pink	VO Violet	

Key to Figs. 12.18 to 12.27 (continued)   Not all items are applicable to all models; some systems do not apply to US models

No	Item	Grid ref*	No	Item	Grid ref*
75	Passenger's seat contact	H3	114	Seat belt reminder (rear)	H3, L3
71	Overdrive switch (manual)	H2	115	Bulb failure sensor	G3
78	CIS microswitch	K1, N3	116	Seat belt buzzer	F3, L2
79	Lambdasond microswitch (not UK)	L2	117	Wiper delay relay	F3
80	Thermal time switch	C5	119	Fuel pump relay	D4
81	Air conditioner pressure sensor	N2, O1	120	Fuel injection impulse relay	D5
82	ACC control panel sensor	O1	121	Flasher unit	F3
83	ACC coolant thermal switch	O2	122	Exhaust temperature sensor (Japan)	N5
85	Speedometer	E3, N3	123	Overdrive relay	H3
86	Tachometer	D3	124	Window winder/cooling fan relay	P3
87	Clock	D3, D4	125	Central locking relay – opening	N3
88	Coolant temperature gauge	E3	126	Central locking relay – closing	O3
89	Fuel gauge	F3	127	Auxiliary light relay	O5, P5, Q2
90	Voltmeter	E4	129	Foglight relay (Sweden)	O5, Q1
91	Oil pressure gauge	E3	130	Glow plug relay (Diesel)	L4
92	Ambient temperature gauge	D3	131	Heater blower relay	N1, P1
93	Instrument voltage regulator	E3	132	Air conditioning delay relay	N1, O1
94	Panel light rheostat	E3	133	Oil level relay	D3
95	Panel illumination	E3	136	Overdrive relay (auto)	M4
96	Oil level warning light	D3	137	Main beam relay	F4
97	Oil pressure warning light	D3	138	Driver's seat heater	H4
98	Choke warning light (not UK)	D3	139	Driver's backrest heater	H4
99	Handbrake warning light	D3	140	Passenger's seat heater	H2
100	Brake failure warning light	E3	141	Passenger's backrest heater	H2
101	Washer fluid level warning light	E3	142	Seat heater thermostats	H2, H4
102	Spare	E3	143	Loudspeaker – LH front	M1
103	Bulb failure warning light	E3	144	Loudspeaker – RH front	M1
104	Preheater pilot light (Diesel)	E3	145	Loudspeaker – LH rear	M1
105	Ignition (no charge) warning light	D4	146	Loudspeaker – RH rear	M1
106	Overdrive pilot light (auto)	D4	147	Aerial (static)	L1
107	Exhaust temperature light (Japan)	D4	148	Aerial (power-operated)	M1
108	Direction indicator pilot light (LH)	D4	149	Radio	L1
109	Main beam pilot light	E4	150	Window motor – driver's door	P3
110	Direction indicator pilot light (RH)	E4	151	Window motor – passenger's door	P4
111	Lambdasond light (not UK)	E4	152	Window motor – RH rear	P4
112	Overdrive pilot light (manual)	E4	153	Window motor – LH rear	O4
113	Seat belt reminder (front)	E4, L3	154	Driver's door mirror	N4

Key to Figs. 12.18 to 12.27 (continued)   Not all items are applicable to all models; some systems do not apply to US models

No	Item	Grid ref*	No	Item	Grid ref*
155	Passenger's door mirror	P4	193	Hot start injector	B2
156	Cooling fan motor	K1	194	Idle up solenoid	K4
157	Headlight wiper motor	A3, A4	195	Fuel cut-off solenoid	B2
158	Sunroof motor	M3	196	CIS idle valve	O3
159	Locking motor – passenger's door	N4	197	Oil pressure sensor	D2
160	Locking motor – RH rear	N4	199	Temperature sensor (Diesel)	L5
161	Locking motor – LH rear	N4	200	Air conditioning compressor solenoid	K5
162	Locking motor – boot	N4	201	Overdrive solenoid	H2, N4
163	Windscreen wiper motor	F3	202	Heater control	N2
164	Windscreen washer motor	F3	203	ACC temperature control	O2
165	Heater blower motor	N1, P1	204	ACC ambient temperature sensor	O2
166	Capacitor (interference suppression)	B3	205	ACC cabin temperature sensor	O2
167	Interference suppressors – spark plugs	C3	206	ACC programmer	P2
168	Ignition ballast resistor	B3	207	Horn	A4
169	Heater blower resistor	N1, P1	208	Glow plugs (Diesel)	L4
170	Catalyst element (Japan)	M5	210	Tank pump	H2
171	Lambdasond thermostat (not UK)	L2	211	Main fuel pump	C5
173	Interior light delay	H3	212	Starter cranking contact	C2
174	Oil level control unit	C3	219	Lambdasond test point (not UK)	L2
175	Ignition system control unit	C4	220	CIS test point	N3
176	CIS control unit	O2	221	Heated rear window	J3
177	Lambdasond control unit (not UK)	L2	222	Cruise control speedometer connection	E3
178	Washer fluid level sensor	E2	223	Cigarette lighter	E2
179	Oil level sensor	C4	224	Fan thermoswitch	K1
180	Speedometer sender	E5	225	Cruise control switch	K1
181	Coolant temperature sensor	E5	226	Cruise control control unit	K2
182	Fuel gauge sender	E5	227	Vacuum pump	K2
183	TDC sensor	P4	228	Clutch switch	K2
184	CIS temperature sensor	N3	229	Brake switch	K2
187	Lambda sensor (not UK)	L2	231	Rear foglight relay	O5, Q1
188	Start injector	C5	233	Turbo pressure sensor (Diesel)	D2
189	Control pressure regulator	B5	236	Pressure sensor relay (Diesel)	K1
190	Auxiliary air valve	C5	237	Pressure sensor (Diesel)	K1
191	Frequency valve	L2	250	Auxiliary tank fuel gauge sender	E4
192	Pressure differential switch	M2	251	Connector	D4

UTOM means except

*The grid references given here are correct for the 1982 wiring diagram. On the 1983 diagram there is extra information regarding relocated components. eg 157 Headlight wiper motor. In Fig. 12.23, grid box A3, there is a note to the effect that 157 is now at grid reference A2.

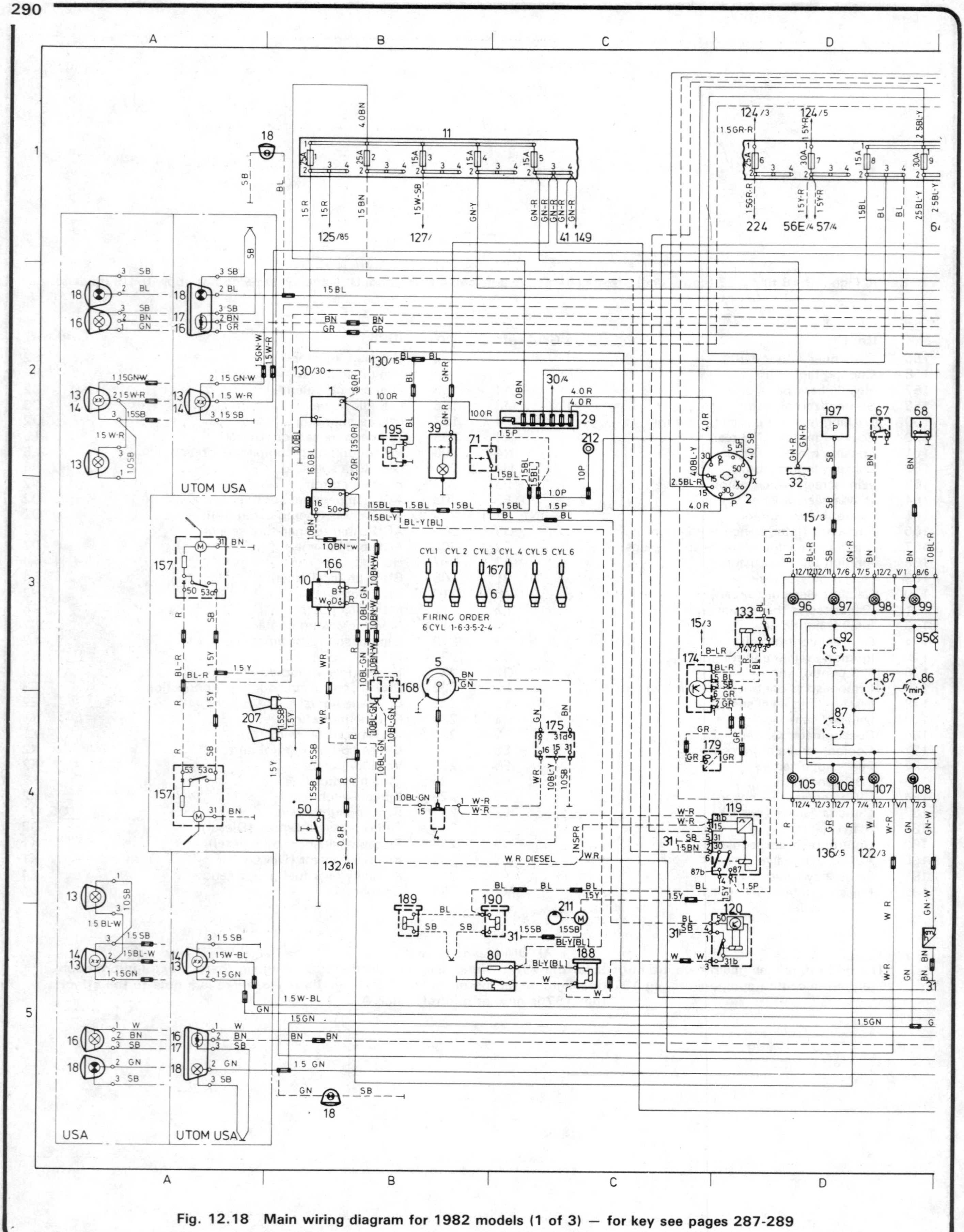

Fig. 12.18 Main wiring diagram for 1982 models (1 of 3) — for key see pages 287-289

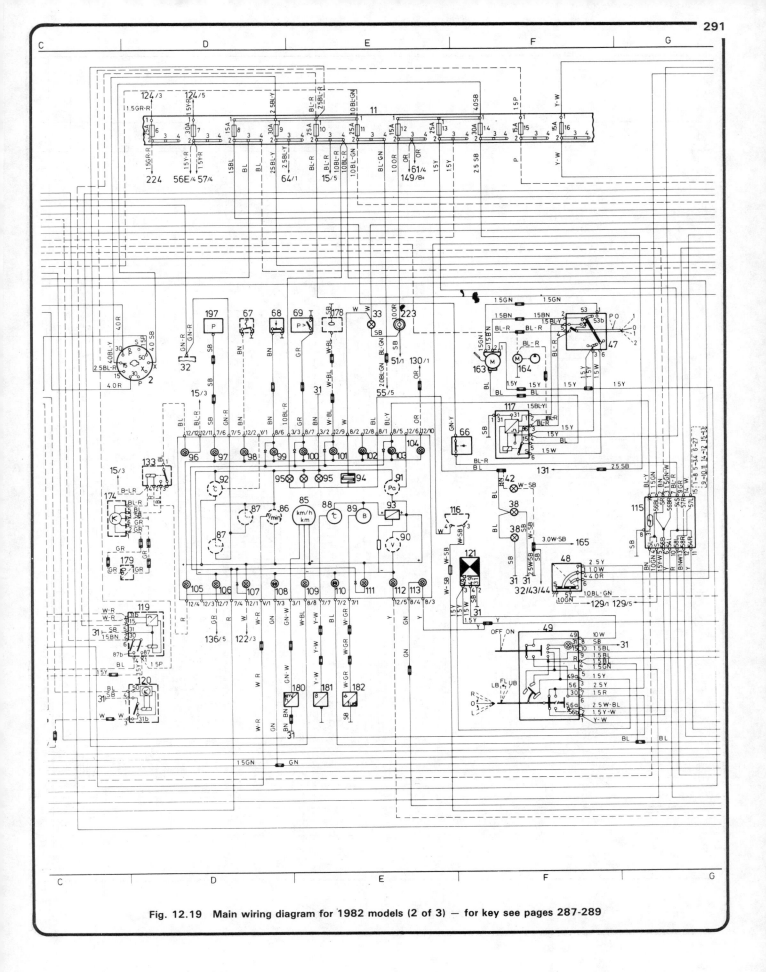

Fig. 12.19 Main wiring diagram for 1982 models (2 of 3) — for key see pages 287-289

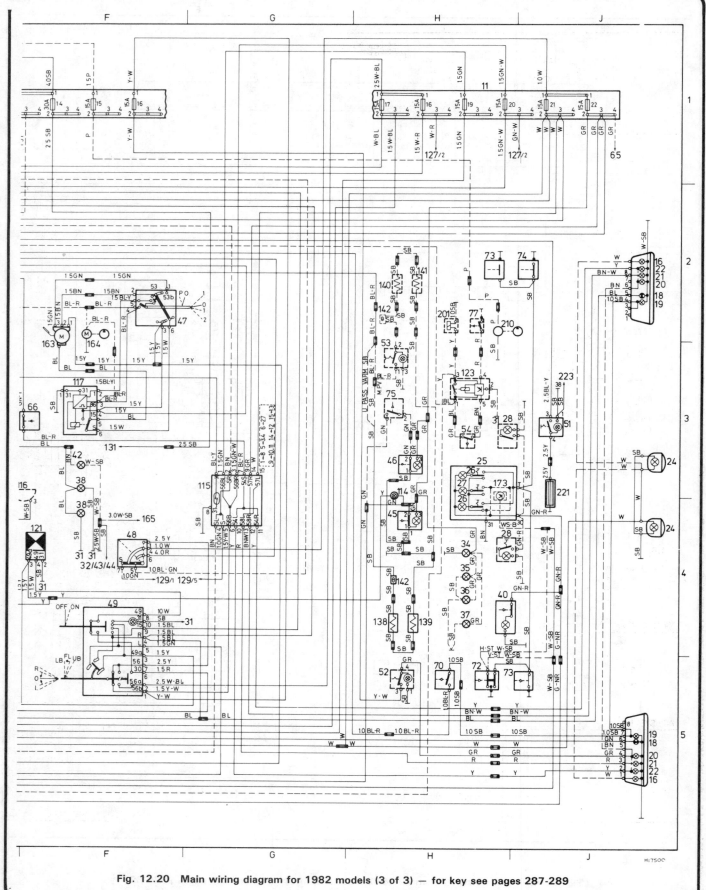

Fig. 12.20 Main wiring diagram for 1982 models (3 of 3) — for key see pages 287-289

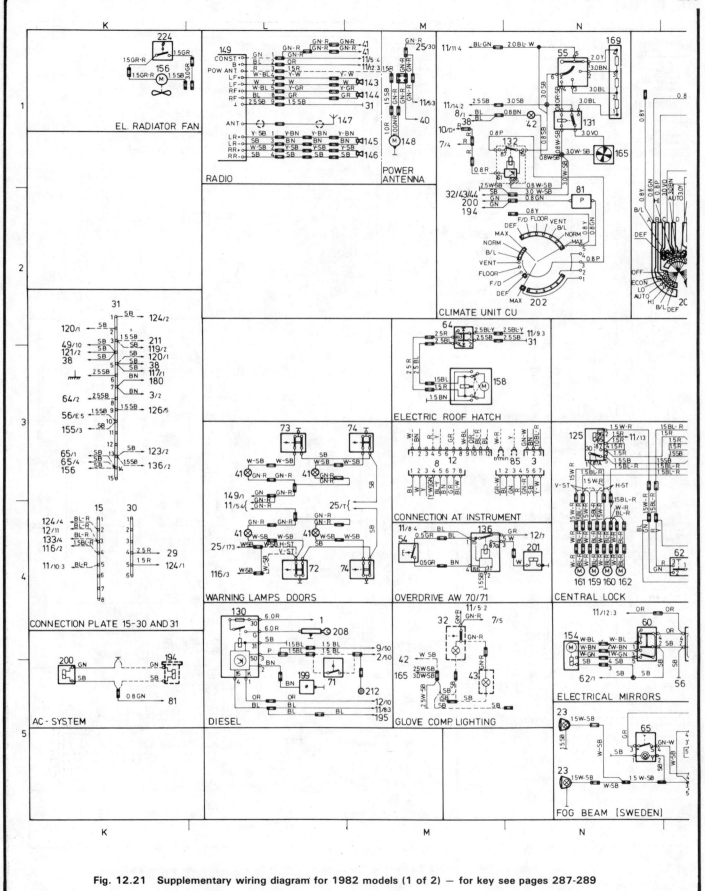

Fig. 12.21 Supplementary wiring diagram for 1982 models (1 of 2) — for key see pages 287-289

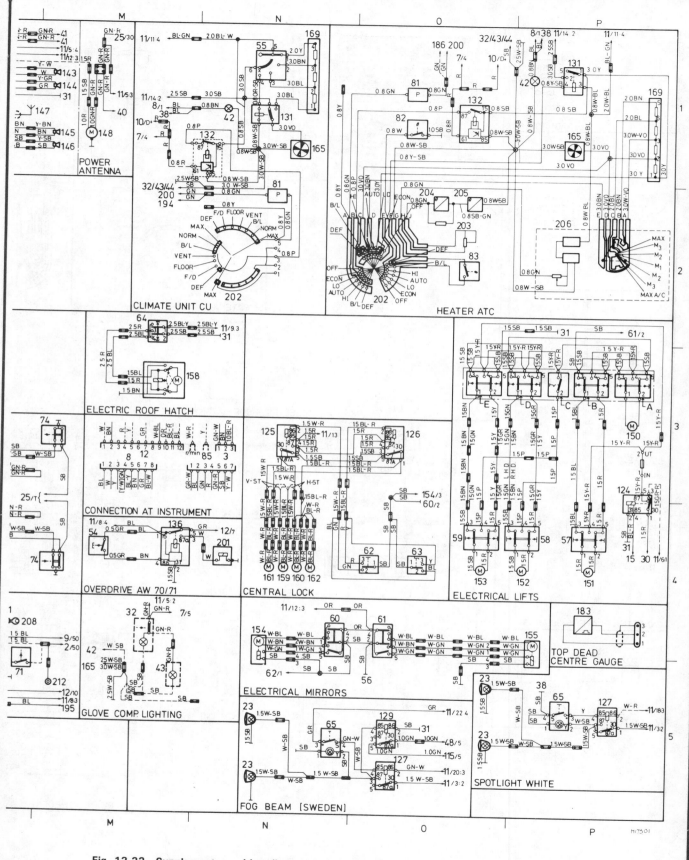

Fig. 12.22 Supplementary wiring diagram for 1982 models (2 of 2) — for key see pages 287-289

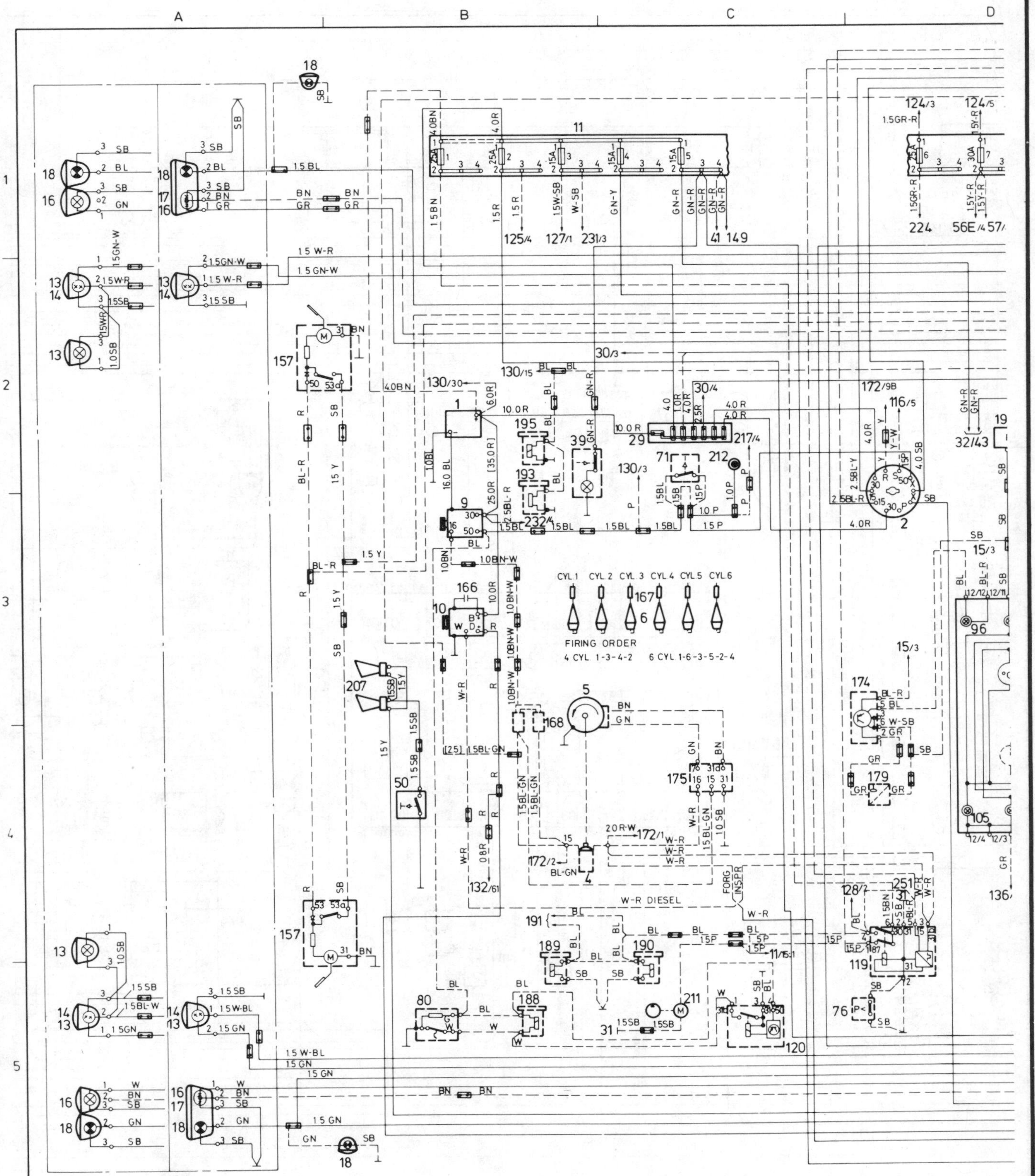

Fig. 12.23 Main wiring diagram for 1983 models (1 of 3) — for key see pages 287-289

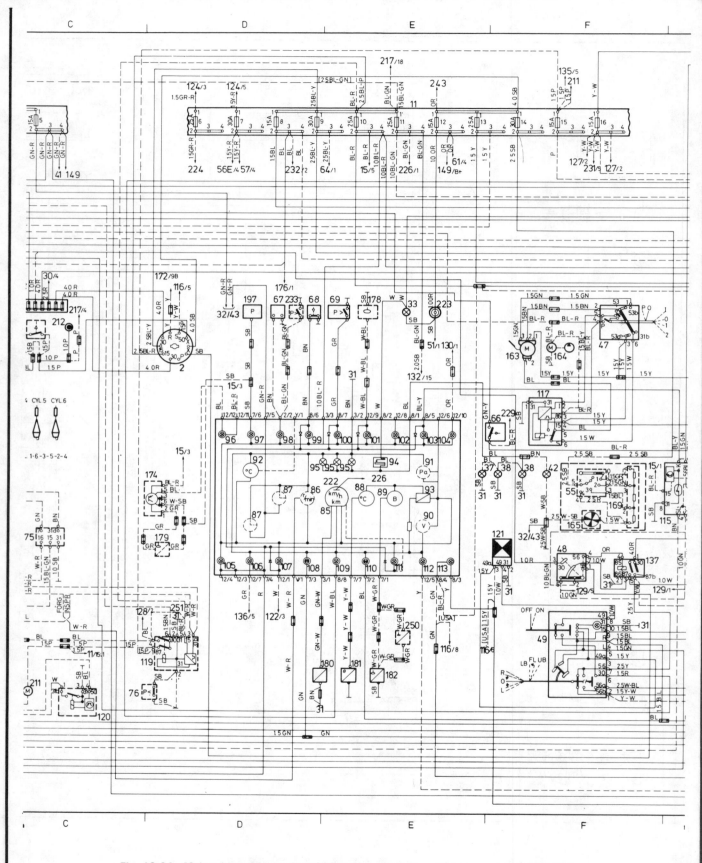

Fig. 12.24 Main wiring diagram for 1983 models (2 of 3) — for key see pages 287-289

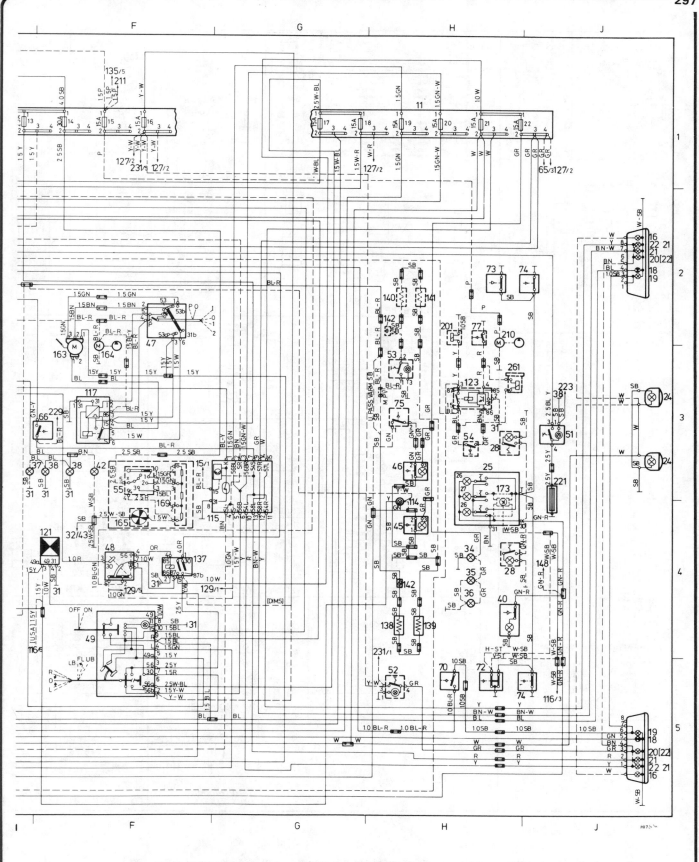

Fig. 12.25 Main wiring diagram for 1983 models (3 of 3) — for key see pages 287-289

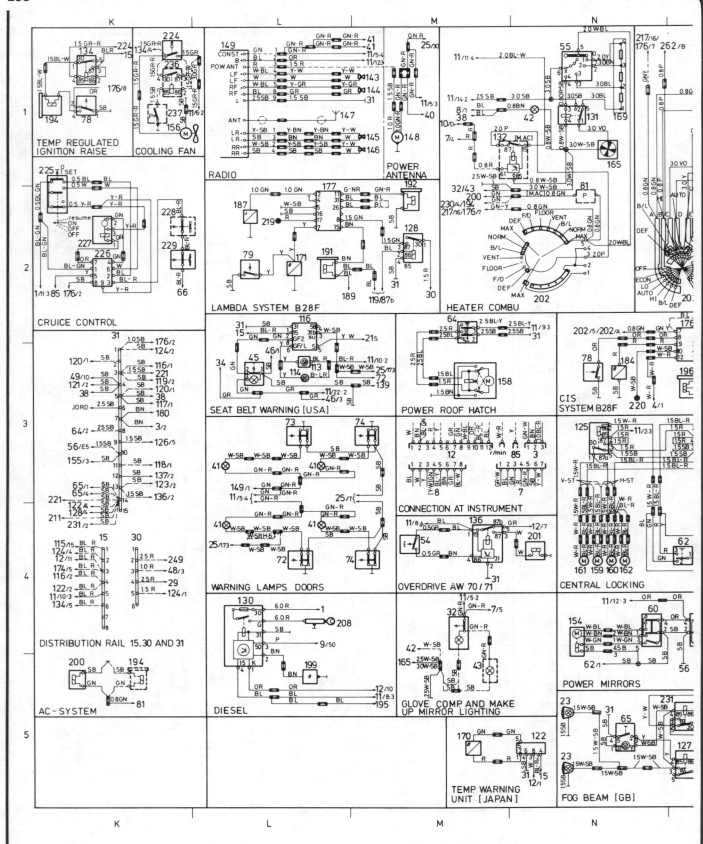

Fig. 12.26 Supplementary wiring diagram for 1983 models (1 of 2) — for key see pages 287-289

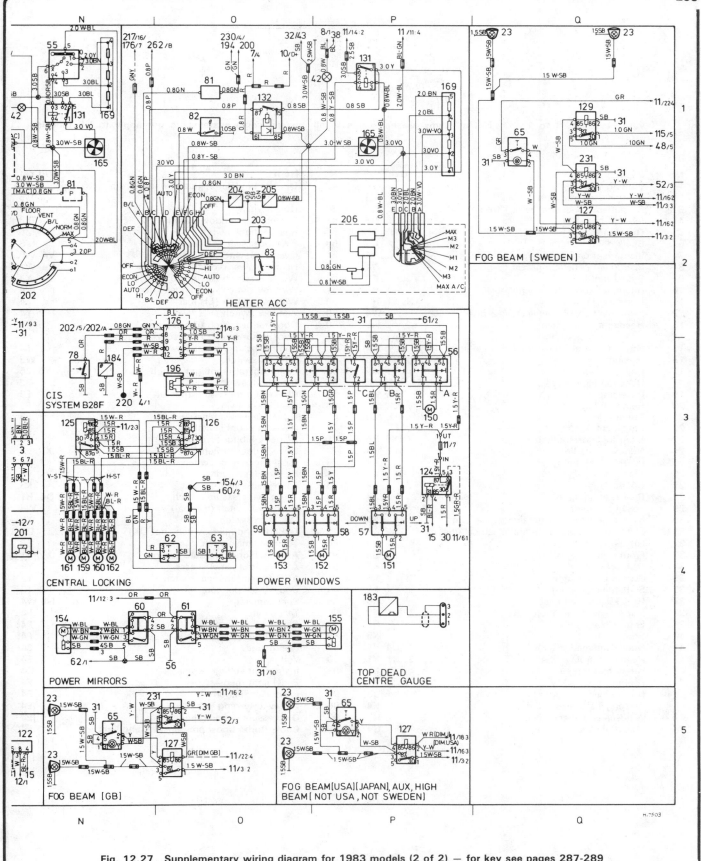

Fig. 12.27 Supplementary wiring diagram for 1983 models (2 of 2) — for key see pages 287-289

Key to Figs. 12.28 to 12.33   Not all items are applicable to all models; some systems do not apply to US models

No	Item	Grid ref	No	Item	Grid ref
1	Battery	C2	49	Direction indicator/hazard warning/dip switches	G5
2	Ignition/starter switch	E3	50	Horn switch	B4
3	Instrument panel connector (3-pole)	W4	51	Heated rear window switch	L3
4	Ignition coil	C5, N3	52	Rear foglight switch	X6, Z6
5	Distributor	C4, M5, N3, 55	53	Passenger seat heater switch	J3
6	Spark plugs	C4	54	Overdrive switch	V4, W6
7	Instrument panel connector (7-pole)	W4	55	Heater blower switch	G4, W1
8	Instrument panel connector (8-pole)	W4	56	Window switch (driver's door)	Y3
9	Starter motor	C3	57	Window switch (passenger's door)	Z4
10	Alternator and voltage regulator	B3	58	Window switch (LH rear)	Z4
11	Fusebox	C1, E1, H1	59	Window switch (RH rear)	Y4
12	Instrument panel connector (12-pole)	W4	60	Door mirror switch (driver's door)	X4
13	Headlight main beam	A2, A5, A6	61	Door mirror switch (passenger's door)	X4
14	Headlight dipped beam	A2, A6	62	Central locking link rod switch	Y4
15	No 15 terminal (in central electrical unit)	T4	64	Sunroof switch	W3
16	Parking light	A1, A6, L1, M6	65	Front foglight/spotlight switch	Y6, Z6
17	Day running light	A1, A6	66	Stop-light switch	G3
18	Direction indicators	A1, B1, L1, M1, M6	67	Choke control switch (not UK)	E3
19	Reversing light	L1, M1, M6	68	Handbrake switch	F3
20	Rear foglight	L1, M1, M6	69	Brake failure warning switch	F3
21	Tail light	L1, M1, M6	70	Reversing light switch	K5
22	Stop-light	L1, M1, M6	71	Starter inhibitor switch (auto)	D3
23	Front foglight/spotlight	X6, Y6	72	Driver's door switch	K5, V5
24	Number plate light	M3, M4	73	Passenger's door switch	K2, V4
25	Interior light unit	K4	74	Rear door switch	K5, V4, V5
26	Map reading light	K4	75	Passenger's seat contact	K3
27	Courtesy light	K4	76	Turbo overpressure switch	D6, R1
28	Rear reading lights	K4	77	Overdrive switch (manual)	W5
29	Positive terminal	D3	78	CIS microswitch	T1, X3
30	No 30 terminal (in central electrical unit)	T4	79	Lambdasond microswitch (not UK)	U2
31	Earth connection (in central electrical unit)	T3	80	Thermal time switch	B6
32	Glovebox light	K3	81	Air conditioner pressure sensor	X2, V1
33	Front ashtray light	G3	82	ACC control panel sensor	Y1
34	Rear ashtray light	K5	83	ACC coolant thermal switch	Y2
35	Switch illumination	F3	84	Coolant temperature sensor	R2, T3
36	Switch illumination	K5	85	Speedometer	F4, W4
37	Gear selector light (auto)	K5	86	Tachometer	F4
38	Instrument illumination	F3	87	Clock	F4
39	Engine bay light	C2	88	Coolant temperature gauge	F4
40	Boot light	K5	89	Fuel gauge	E4
41	Door edge marker light	U4, V4	90	Voltmeter	E4
42	Heater control illumination	G3, W1, Y1	93	Instrument voltage regulator	G4
43	Vanity mirror light	K3	94	Panel light rheostat	F4
44	Fuel injectors	N2, T2, T3, T4	95	Panel illumination	F4
45	Driver's belt lock light	K4, U3	96	Oil level warning light	E4
46	Passenger's belt lock light	K4	97	Oil pressure warning light	E4
47	Windscreen wiper switch	H3	98	Choke/turbo boost pressure warning light	E4
48	Main light switch	G4			

Key to Figs. 12.28 to 12.33 (continued)   Not all items are applicable to all models; some systems do not apply to US models

No	Item	Grid ref	No	Item	Grid ref
99	Handbrake warning light	F4	150	Window motor – driver's door	Z4
100	Brake failure warning light	F4	151	Window motor – passenger's door	Z5
101	Washer fluid level warning light	E3	152	Window motor – RH rear	Y5
102	Gearshift indicator	F4	153	Window motor – LH rear	Y5
103	Bulb failure warning light	F4	154	Driver's door mirror	L3, X4
104	Preheater pilot light (Diesel)	G4	155	Passenger's door mirror	L3, Z5
105	Ignition (no charge) warning light	E5	156	Cooling fan motor	U1
106	Overdrive pilot light (auto)	E5	157	Headlight wiper motor	B2, B5
107	Exhaust temperature light (Japan)	E5	158	Sunroof motor	W3
108	Direction indicator pilot light (LH)	F5	159	Locking motor – passenger's door	Y5
109	Main beam pilot light	F5	160	Locking motor – LH rear	W4
110	Direction indicator pilot light (RH)	F5	161	Locking motor – RH rear	W5
111	Lambdasond light (not UK)	F5	162	Locking motor – boot or tailgate	W4
112	Overdrive pilot light (manual)	F5	163	Windscreen wiper motor	G3
113	Seat belt reminder (front)	G5, V3	164	Windscreen washer motor	G3
114	Seat belt reminder (rear)	V3, J4	165	Heater blower motor	G4, X1, Z1
115	Bulb failure sensor	H4	166	Capacitor (interference suppression)	C3
116	Seat belt reminder (not UK)	V3	167	Interference suppressors – spark plugs	C3
117	Windscreen wiper delay relay	G3	168	Ignition ballast resistor	C4
118	Tailgate wiper delay relay	P4	169	Heater blower resistor	X1, Z1
119	Fuel pump relay	E5	170	Catalyst element (not UK)	Z5
120	Fuel injection impulse relay	D6	171	Lambdasond thermostat (not UK)	V2
121	Flasher unit	G4	173	Interior light delay	K4
122	Exhaust temperature sensor (Japan)	Z5	174	Oil level control unit	D4
123	Overdrive relay (manual)	W5	175	Ignition system control unit (Bosch)	D4
124	Window winder/cooling fan relay	Z4	176	CIS control unit	X3
127	Auxiliary light relay	Y6, Z6	177	Lambdasond control unit (not UK)	R5, V2
128	Lambdasond relay (not UK)	V2	178	Washer fluid level sensor	F3
130	Glow plug relay (Diesel)	V5	179	Oil level sensor	E4
131	Heater blower relay	X1, Z2	180	Speedometer sensor	F5
132	Air conditioning delay relay	W1, Y1	181	Coolant temperature sensor	F5
133	Ignition control unit (T2 28)	N3, R6	182	Fuel gauge sender	F5
134	Ignition advance relay (not UK)	T1	184	CIS temperature sensor	X3
135	Motronic/LH Jetronic relay	R2, R5	185	Charge air temperature sensor	52
136	Overdrive relay (auto)	W4	186	Airflow meter	T1
137	Main beam relay	H5	187	Lambda sensor (not UK)	R4, U2
138	Driver's seat heater	J5	188	Start injector	C6
139	Driver's backrest heater	K5	189	Control pressure regulator	C5
140	Passenger's seat heater	J3	190	Auxiliary air valve	C5
141	Passenger's backrest heater	K3	191	Frequency valve	V2
142	Seat heater thermostats	J3, K5	192	Pressure differential switch	V2
143	Loudspeaker – LH front	V1	193	Hot start injector	C3
144	Loudspeaker – RH front	V1	194	Idle up solenoid	T5, T1
145	Loudspeaker – LH rear	V1	195	Fuel cut-off solenoid	C3
146	Loudspeaker – RH rear	V1	196	CIS idle valve	R4, X3
147	Aerial (Static)	V1	197	Oil pressure sensor	E3
148	Aerial (power-operated)	V1	198	Throttle switch (LH Jetronic)	54
149	Radio	U1	199	Temperature sensor (Diesel)	V5

Key to Figs. 12.28 to 12.33 (continued)   Not all items are applicable to all models; some systems do not apply to US models

No	Item	Grid ref	No	Item	Grid ref
200	Air conditioning compressor solenoid	T6	253	ABS modulator	Q3
201	Overdrive solenoid	V5, W4	254	ABS surge protector	Q2
202	Heater control	W3, X3	255	ABS converter	Q1
203	ACC temperature control	Y2	256	ABS sensor – LH front	P2, Q1
204	ACC ambient temperature sensor	P5, Y2	257	ABS sensor – RH front	P2, Q1
205	ACC cabin temperature sensor	Y2	258	ABS fusebox	Q2
206	ACC programmer	Z2	259	Charge pressure sensor	R4
207	Horn	B4	260	Ignition system control unit (EZ-K)	S6
208	Glow plugs (Diesel)	V5	261	EGR solenoid (not UK)	W5
210	Tank pump	K2	262	ACC vacuum valve	X1
211	Main fuel pump	D6	263	Overdrive oil pressure switch	S3
212	Starter cranking contact	D3	264	Charge pressure switch	S3
213	Throttle switch (Motronic)	S1	265	Torque limiter relay	P2, S3
214	Crankshaft position sensor	R1	266	Heated rear window timer	L3
215	Engine speed sensor	R1	267	EZ-K test point	S6
216	Motronic control unit	S1	268	Gear position sensor	R3
217	LH-Jetronic control unit	S3	270	ABS speedometer sensor	Q1
218	Knock sensor	56	271	Fuel shut-off valve	V6
219	Lambdasond test point (not UK)	U2	272	Throttle pedal switch	S6
220	CIS test point	S4, X3	273	EZ-K temperature sensor	S6
221	Heated rear window	L2	274	EGR relay (not UK)	Q6
223	Cigarette lighter	F3	275	EGR idling switch (not UK)	Q5
224	Fan thermoswitch	U1	277	EGR 3-way valve (not UK)	R5
225	Cruise control switch	T1	278	Aneroid switch (not UK)	P6
226	Cruise control control unit	T2	279	Altitude compensation solenoid valve (not UK)	P6
227	Vacuum pump	T2	280	Driver's seat heater relay	J3
228	Clutch switch	U2	284	Air mass meter	S4
229	Brake switch	G3, U2	286	ETC sensor – LH rear	N1
231	Rear foglight relay	X6	287	ETC sensor – RH rear	N1
232	Hot spot relay	T5	288	ETC pressure sensor	P1
233	Turbo pressure sensor (Diesel)	E3	289	ETC power stage	N1, T3
234	Hot spot thermostat	U5	290	ETC control unit	P1
235	Hot spot PTC resistor	U5	292	Idle advance solenoid valve	T6, W6
236	Pressure sensor relay (Diesel)	U1	293	Idle advance relay	P5, T6, U6, V6, W6
237	Pressure sensor (Diesel)	U1	295	Gearshift indicator relay	Q5
238	Rear washer pump	P4	298	ETC relay	N1
239	Rear wiper connector	P3	349	Instrument connector (6-pole)	P5
240	Rear wash/wipe switch	P3	375	Seat heater switch	J5
241	Rear wiper motor	P3	376	Ballast resistor (Jetronic)	N1, S2
242	Power seat emergency stop	Q4	378	Positive terminal (engine bay)	C2
243	Power seat 'on' switch	Q4	379	Trip computer electronic unit	P5
244	Power seat control unit	Q3	384	Brake fluid level sensor	Q1, F3
245	Power seat motor – fore/aft	R4	395	ETC switch	P1
246	Power seat motor – up/down (front)	R3	403	Battery temperature sensor	C3
247	Power seat motor – up/down (rear)	R3	404	Vacuum switch	R6
248	Power seat motor – backrest inclination	R4	405	Choke heater	C3
250	Auxiliary tank fuel gauge sender	F5	406	Renix ignition unit (not UK)	P5
251	Connector	E5	407	Renix impulse sender (not UK)	P5
252	ABS control unit	R1	408	Gearshift indicator switch	Q5

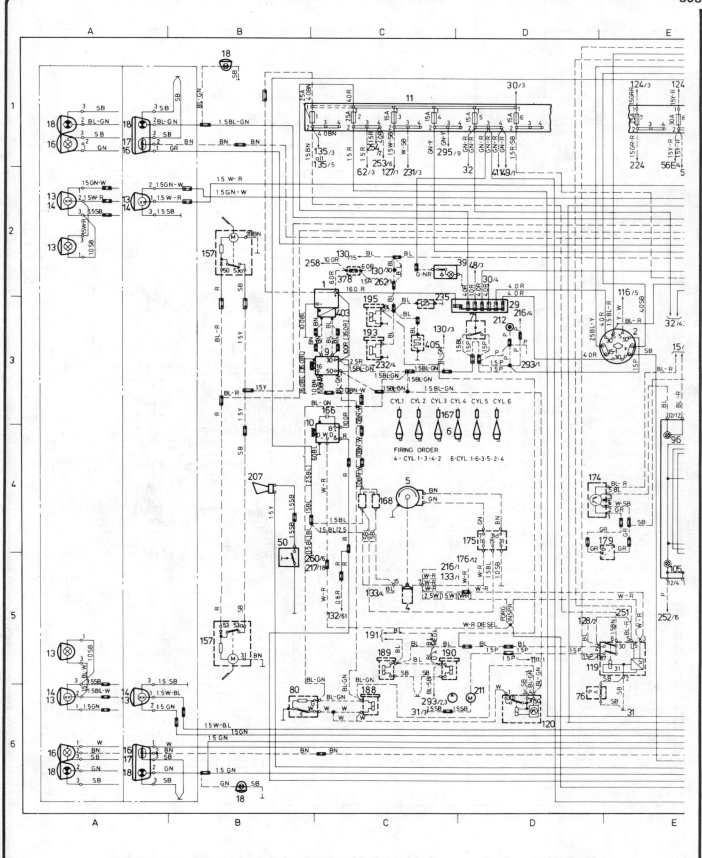

Fig. 12.28 Main wiring diagram for 1984 thru 1986 models (1 of 3) — for key see pages 300-302

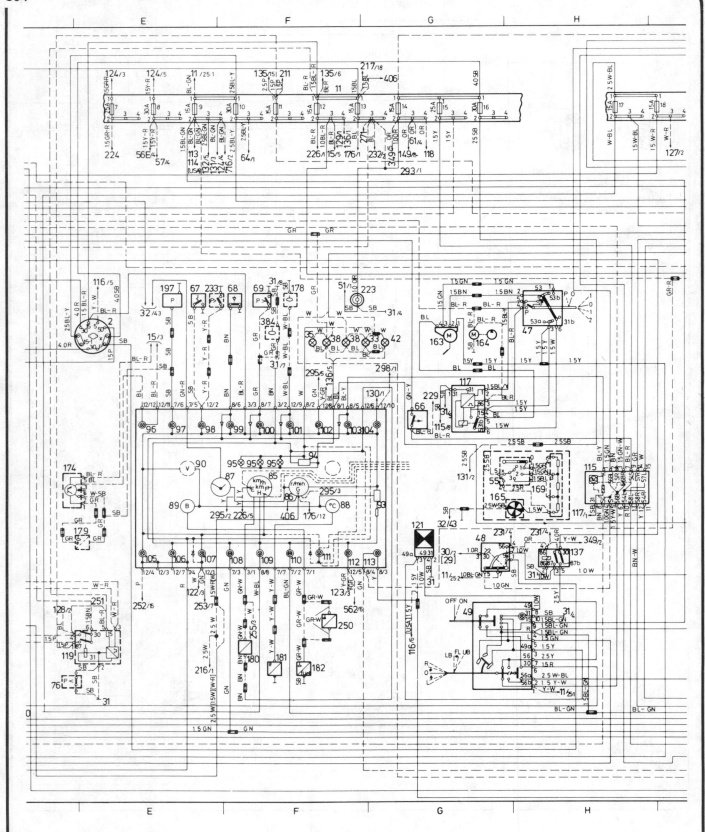

Fig. 12.29 Main wiring diagram for 1984 thru 1986 models (2 of 3) — for key see pages 300-302

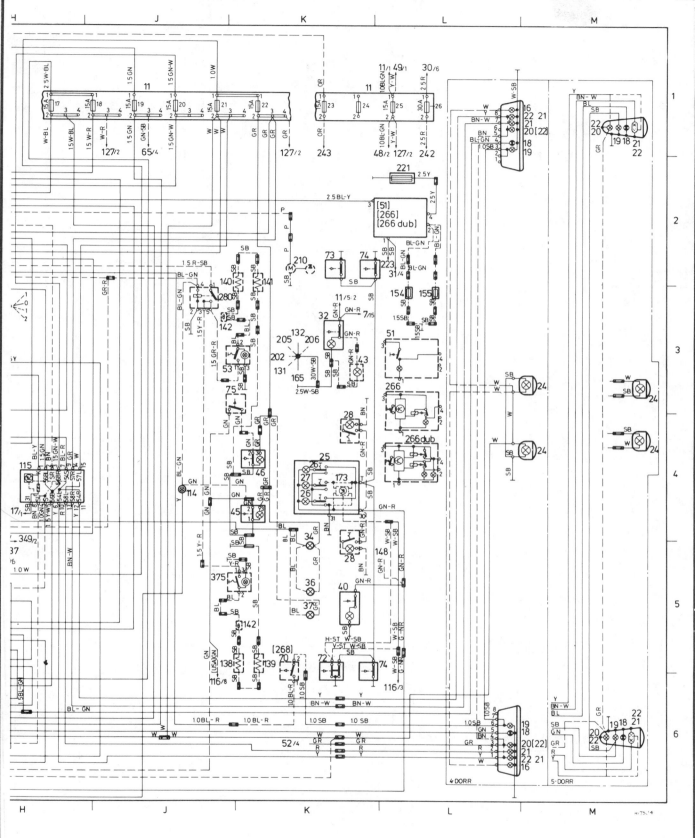

Fig. 12.30 Main wiring diagram for 1984 thru 1986 models (3 of 3) — for key see pages 300-302

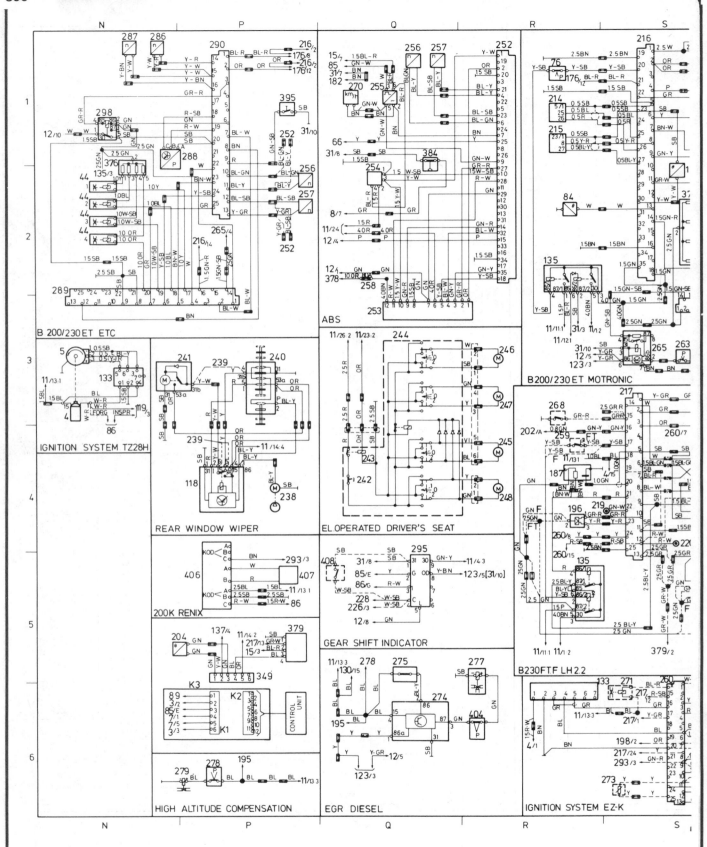

Fig. 12.31 Supplementary wiring diagram for 1984 thru 1986 models (1 of 3) — for key see pages 300-302

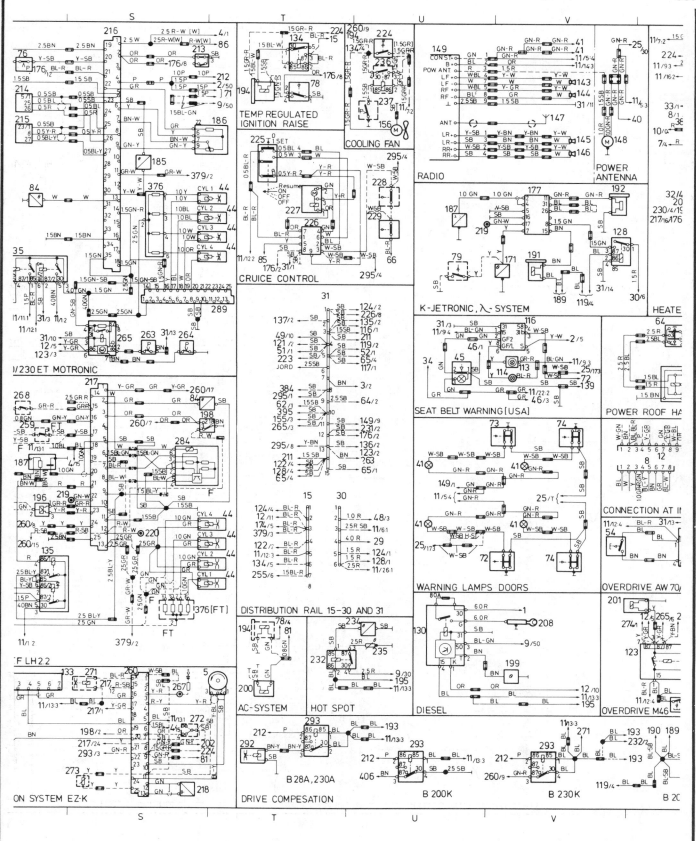

Fig. 12.32 Supplementary wiring diagram for 1984 thru 1986 models (2 of 3) — for key see pages 300-302

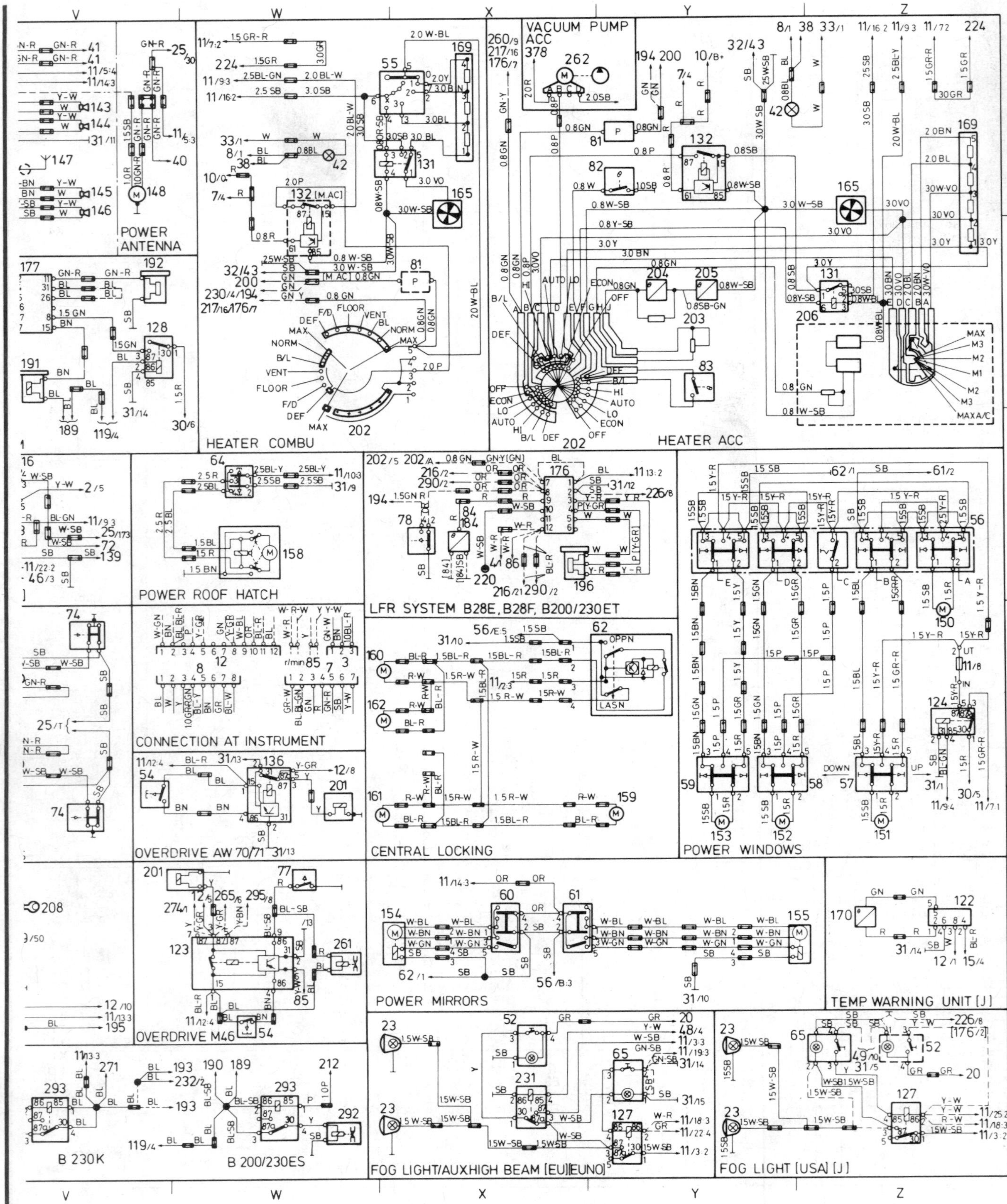

Fig. 12.33 Supplementary wiring diagram for 1984 thru 1986 models (3 of 3) — for key see pages 300-302

Key to Figs. 12.34 to 12.36

1	Battery	C2
2	Ignition switch	E3
3	Instrument connection, 3-pole	Z4
4	Ignition coil, 12 A	C5
5	Distributor	C4, R4
6	Spark plug	C4
7	Instrument connection, 7-pole	Z4
8	Instrument connection, 8-pole	Y4
9	Starter motor	C3
10	Alternator with built-in regulator	B3
11	Fusebox	C1, E1, H1
12	Instrument connection, 12-pole	Y4
13	Main beam bulb, 60 W	A2, A5, A6
14	Dipped beam bulb, 55 W	A2, A6
15	Central electrical unit, terminal 15	W4
16	Parking light, 4 cp/5 W (USA: also tail)	A1, A6, L1, L6
17	Day running light, 32 cp/21 W	A1, A6
18	Turn signal 32 cp/21 W	A1, A6, L1, L6, M1, M6
19	Back-up (reversing) light 32 cp/21 W	L1, L6, M1, M6
20	Rear foglight, 32 cp/21 W	L1, L6, M1, M6
21	Tail light 4 cp/5 W	L1, L6, M1, M6
22	Brake light, 32 cp/21 W	L1, L6, M1, M4, M6
23	Foglight (spotlight), 55 W	Z6, AA6
24	Numberplate light, 4 cp/5 W	M3, M4
25	Courtesy light	P5
26	Reading light, front	P5
27	Courtesy light	P5
28	Reading light, rear	N5, P5
29	Positive terminal	D3
30	Central electrical unit, terminal 30	W4
31	Ground connection, central electrical unit	W3
32	Glove box light	N4
33	Ashtray light, front	F3
34	Ashtray light, rear	K4
35	Sun roof switch light	F3
36	Passenger seat heater switch	K4
37	Gear selector light (automatic)	J4
38	Instrument and panel lighting	F3
39	Engine compartment light	C2
40	Boot (trunk) light	N5
41	Door open warning light	N5, P5
42	Heater control panel	G3, Z1, BB1
43	Vanity mirror light	P4
45	Seat belt, light, driver	K5, X2
46	Seat belt light, passenger	K4
47	Windscreen wiper switch	H3
48	Main light switch	G4
49	Turn signal switch (hazard warning lights)	G5
50	Horn	A5
51	Heated rear window switch	K3
52	Rear foglight switch	Z6, BB6
53	Heater pads, passenger seat switch	J3, Q3
54	Overdrive switch	Y4, Y6
55	Heater switch	G4, Z1
56	Power windows, driver side switch	AA3
57	Power windows, passenger side switch	BB4
58	Power windows, driver side, rear	BB4
59	Power windows, passenger side, rear	AA4
60	Power mirrors, driver side	Z5
61	Power mirror, passenger side	AA5
62	Central lock switch (link rod)	Z4
64	Power sun roof switch	Y3
65	Fog/spotlamp switch	AA6, BB6
66	Brake light switch	G3
67	Choke switch	E3
68	Handbrake switch	F3
69	Brake failure warning switch	F3
70	Reversing (back-up) light switch	K5
71	Start inhibitor switch (automatic)	D3
72	Driver door switch	N4
73	Passenger door switch	P4
74	Rear door switch	N6, P6
75	Passenger seat contact	K4
76	Charge air overpressure switch (turbo)	U4
77	Overdrive switch (M 46)	Y5
80	Thermal time switch	B6
81	AC pressure switch	Z2, AA1
82	ACC heater fan pressure switch	AA2
83	In-car temperature sensor	AA2
84	Water temperature sensor	Q1, Q5, U2, V3
85	Speedometer	F4
86	Tachometer	F4
87	Clock	E4
88	Coolant temperature gauge	F4
89	Fuel gauge	E4
90	Voltmeter	E4
93	Voltage regulator	G4
94	Rheostat, instrument and control lighting	F4
95	Instrument lighting	F4
96	Oil level lamp	E4
97	Oil pressure lamp	E4
98	Choke/turbo boost lamp (exhaust gas temp)	E4
99	Handbrake lamp	F4
100	Brake failure warning lamp	F4
101	Washer fluid level lamp	F4
102	Gear shift indicator lamp/AW 70/71 overdrive lamp	F4
103	Bulb failure lamp	F4
104	Glow plug/ETC sensor lamp	F4
105	Battery charge lamp	E5
106	Not connected	E5
107	Exhaust gas temp., ABS	E5
108	Direction indicator lamp, left	F5
109	High beam lamp	F5
110	Direction indicator lamp, right	F5
111	Indicator lamp, EGR	F5
112	Overdrive (M 46) indicator lamp	F5
113	Fasten seat belt light, front	F5, X2
114	Fasten seat belt light, rear	J5, X2
115	Bulb failure warning sensor	H4
116	Seat belt reminder	X2
117	Relay for windscreen intermittent wipe	G3
118	Relay for tailgate intermittent wipe	S4
119	Fuel pump relay	D5
121	Flasher device	G4
122	Exhaust gas temperature sensor (Japan)	BB5
123	Overdrive relay (M 46)	Y5
124	Relay, power windows + electric cooling fan	BB4
125	Central lock relay	Z4
127	Auxiliary light relay	AA6, BB6
130	Glow plug relay (diesel)	R5
131	Fan relay	Z1, BB2
132	AC compressor delay relay	Y1, AA1
135	Motronic & LH-Jetronic system relay	U2, U5
136	Overdrive relay, AW 70/71	Y4
137	High beam relay	H5
138	Heater pad, set 30/120 W	J5, K2, Q3
139	Heater pad, backrest 30/120 W	K2, K5, Q3
142	Overheating protection device	J3, K5, Q3
143	Loudspeaker, front left door 4 ohms	Y1
144	Loudspeaker, front right door 4 ohms	Y1
145	Loudspeaker, rear left 4 ohms	Y1
146	Loudspeaker, rear right 4 ohms	Y2
147	Aerial	X1
148	Power aerial 3 A	Y1
149	Radio	X1
150	Power window motor, driver door 5 A	BB4
151	Power window motor, passenger door 5 A	BB5
152	Power window motor, driver side rear 5 A	BB5
153	Power window motor, passenger side rear 5 A	AA5
154	Power door mirror, driver side	L3, Z5
155	Power door mirror, passenger side	L3, BB5

Key to Figs. 12.34 to 12.36 (continued)

Key to Figs. 12.37 to 12.40

1	Battery	C2
2	Ignition switch	E3
3	Instrument connection, 3-pole	Z4
4	Ignition coil, 12 A	C5
5	Distributor	C4, R4
6	Spark plug	C4
7	Instrument connection, 7-pole	Z4
8	Instrument connection, 8-pole	Y4
9	Starter motor	C3
10	Alternator with built-in regulator	B3
11	Fusebox	C1, E1, H1
12	Instrument connection, 12-pole	Y4
13	Main beam bulb, 60 W	A2, A5, A6
14	Dipped beam bulb, 55 W	A2, A6
15	Central electrical unit, terminal 15	W4
16	Parking light, 4 cp/5 W (USA: also tail)	A1, A6, L1, L6
17	Day running light, 32 cp/21 W	A1, A6
18	Turn signal 32 cp/21 W	A1, A6, L1, L6, M1, M6
19	Back-up (reversing) light 32 cp/21 W	L1, L6, M1, M6
20	Rear foglight, 32 cp/21 W	L1, L6, M1, M6
21	Tail light 4 cp/5 W	L1, L6, M1, M6
22	Brake light, 32 cp/21 W	L1, L6, M1, M4, M6
23	Foglight (spotlight), 55 W	Z6, AA6
24	Numberplate light, 4 cp/5 W	M3, M4
25	Courtesy light	P5
26	Reading light, front	P5
27	Courtesy light	P5
28	Reading light, rear	N5, P5
29	Positive terminal	D3
30	Central electrical unit, terminal 30	W4
31	Ground connection, central electrical unit	W3
32	Glove box light	N4
33	Ashtray light, front	F3
34	Ashtray light, rear	K4
35	Sun roof switch light	F3
36	Passenger seat heater switch	K4
37	Gear selector light (automatic)	J4
38	Instrument and panel lighting	F3
39	Engine compartment light	C2
40	Boot (trunk) light	N5
41	Door open warning light	G3, Z1, BB1
42	Heater control panel	G3, Z1, BB1
43	Vanity mirror light	P4
45	Seat belt, light, driver	K5, X2
46	Seat belt light, passenger	K4
47	Windscreen wiper switch	H3
48	Main light switch	G4
49	Turn signal switch (hazard warning lights)	G5
50	Horn	A5
51	Heated rear window switch	K3
52	Rear foglight switch	Z6, BB6
53	Heater pads, passenger seat switch	J3, Q3
54	Overdrive switch	Y4, Y6
55	Heater switch	G4, Z1
56	Power windows, driver side switch	AA3
57	Power windows, passenger side switch	BB4
58	Power windows, driver side, rear	BB4
59	Power windows, passenger side, rear	AA4
60	Power mirrors, driver side	Z5
61	Power mirror, passenger side	AA5
62	Central lock switch (link rod)	Z4
64	Power sun roof switch	Y3
65	Fog/spotlamp switch	AA6, BB6
66	Brake light switch	G3
67	Choke switch	E3
68	Handbrake switch	F3
69	Brake failure warning switch	F3
70	Reversing (back-up) light switch	K5
71	Start inhibitor switch (automatic)	D3
72	Driver door switch	N4
73	Passenger door switch	P4
74	Rear door switch	N6, P6
75	Passenger seat contact	K4
76	Charge air overpressure switch (turbo)	U4
77	Overdrive switch (M 46)	Y5
80	Thermal time switch	B6
81	AC pressure switch	Z2, AA1
82	ACC heater fan pressure switch	AA2
83	In-car temperature sensor	AA2
84	Water temperature sensor	Q1, Q5, U2, V3
85	Speedometer	F4
86	Tachometer	F4
87	Clock	E4
88	Coolant temperature gauge	F4
89	Fuel gauge	E4
90	Voltmeter	E4
93	Voltage regulator	G4
94	Rheostat, instrument and control lighting	F4
95	Instrument lighting	F4
96	Oil level lamp	E4
97	Oil pressure lamp	E4
98	Choke/turbo boost lamp (exhaust gas temp)	E4
99	Handbrake lamp	F4
100	Brake failure warning lamp	F4
101	Washer fluid level lamp	F4
102	Gear shift indicator lamp/AW 70/71 overdrive lamp	F4
103	Bulb failure lamp	F4
104	Glow plug/ETC sensor lamp	F4
105	Battery charge lamp	E5
106	Not connected	E5
107	Exhaust gas temp., ABS	E5
108	Direction indicator lamp, left	F5
109	High beam lamp	F5
110	Direction indicator lamp, right	F5
111	Indicator lamp, EGR	F5
112	Overdrive (M 46) indicator lamp	F5
113	Fasten seat belt light, front	F5, X2
114	Fasten seat belt light, rear	J5, X2
115	Bulb failure warning sensor	H4
116	Seat belt reminder	X2
117	Relay for windscreen intermittent wipe	G3
118	Relay for tailgate intermittent wipe	S4
119	Fuel pump relay	D5
121	Flasher device	G4
122	Exhaust gas temperature sensor (Japan)	BB5
123	Overdrive relay (M 46)	Y5
124	Relay, power windows + electric cooling fan	BB4
125	Central lock relay	Z4
127	Auxiliary light relay	AA6, BB6
130	Glow plug relay (diesel)	R5
131	Fan relay	Z1, BB2
132	AC compressor delay relay	Y1, AA1
135	Motronic & LH-Jetronic system relay	U2, U5
136	Overdrive relay, AW 70/71	Y4
137	High beam relay	H5
138	Heater pad, set 30/120 W	J5, K2, Q3
139	Heater pad, backrest 30/120 W	K2, K5, Q3
142	Overheating protection device	J3, K5, Q3
143	Loudspeaker, front left door 4 ohms	Y1
144	Loudspeaker, front right door 4 ohms	Y1
145	Loudspeaker, rear left 4 ohms	Y1
146	Loudspeaker, rear right 4 ohms	Y2
147	Aerial	X1
148	Power aerial 3 A	Y1
149	Radio	X1
150	Power window motor, driver door 5 A	BB4
151	Power window motor, passenger door 5 A	BB5
152	Power window motor, driver side rear 5 A	BB5
153	Power window motor, passenger side rear 5 A	AA5
154	Power door mirror, driver side	L3, Z5
155	Power door mirror, passenger side	L3, BB5

Key to Figs. 12.37 to 12.40 (continued)

156	Electric cooling fan motor 13 A	W1
157	Headlight wiper motor 1 A	B2, B5
158	Power sun roof motor	Y3
159	Central lock motor, passenger door	AA4
160	Central lock motor, driver side rear	Z5
161	Central lock motor, passenger side rear	AA5
162	Central lock motor, boot (trunk)/tailgate	Z5
163	Windshield wiper motor 3.5 A	G3
164	Windshield washer motor 2.6 A	G3
165	Heater fan	G4, Z2, BB1
166	Capacitor	C3
169	Heater fan resistor	Z1, BB1
170	Catalytic converter	BB5
173	Delay unit for courtesy light	P5
176	CIS control unit	AA3
178	Washer level sensor	F3
180	Speedometer transmitter	F5
181	Coolant temperature sensor	F5
182	Fuel level sensor	F5
185	Charge air temperature sensor	V2
186	Air flow meter	V1
187	Lambdasond (heated)	U4
188	Start injector	C6
189	Control pressure regulator	C5
190	Auxiliary air valve	C5
193	Hot start valve	B5
194	Solenoid valve for AC compensation/ignition advance	V5
195	Solenoid valve (carb), fuel valve (diesel)	C3, T6
196	Air control valve	U4, AA3
197	Oil pressure sensor	E3
198	Throttle switch, LH-Jetronic	V4
199	Temperature sensor, diesel	S5
200	AC compressor solenoid 3.9 A	V6
201	Overdrive solenoid	Y5, Z4
202	CU heater control panel	Z3, AA3
203	ACC temperature control	AA2
204	ACC ambient temperature sensor	AA2
205	ACC in-car temperature sensor	AA2
206	ACC programmer	BB2
207	Horn 15 A	A4
208	Glow plug	S5
210	Tank pump 1.6 A	K2
211	Fuel pump 6.5 A	D6
212	Test point for cranking starter motor	D3, S5, W6, X6
213	Motronic throttle switch	V1
214	Crankshaft position sensor	U1
215	Engine rpm sensor	U1
216	Motronic control unit	V1
217	LH-Jetronic	U3
218	Knock sensor	Q2, R6
219	Lambdasond test point	U4
220	CIS test point	V4, Z3
221	Heated rear window 140 W	L2
223	Cigar lighter 7 A	F3
224	Electric cooling fan thermal switch	W1
225	Cruise control switch	W1
226	Cruise control switch	W2
227	Vacuum pump	W2
228	Bridge connector	W2
229	Brake pedal switch	W2
231	Rear fog light relay	Z6
232	Hot spot relay	X5
233	Pressure sensor, turbo-diesel	S6
234	Hot spot thermostat	X5
235	Hot spot PTC resistor	X5
238	Tailgate washer motor	S4
239	Tailgate wiper bridge connector	S4
240	Tailgate wash/wipe	S3
241	Tailgate wiper motor	S3
242	Emergency stop, power seat	T4
243	Power seat, on-off switch	T4
244	Power seat control unit	T3
245	Power seat motor, fore-aft	U4
246	Power seat motor, up-down, front	U3
247	Power seat motor, up-down, rear	U3
248	Power seat motor, backrest rake	U4
250	Fuel level sensor, increased capacity tank	F5
251	Kick down inhibitor	Z5
252	ABS control unit	U1
253	ABS modulator	T3
254	ABS transient surge protector	T2
255	ABS converter	T1
256	ABS/ETC sensor, front left	S2, T1
257	ABS/ETC sensor, front right	S2, T1
258	ABS 80 A fuse	T3
260	Ignition system (EZ-K) control unit	Q1, Q4
262	ACC vacuum pump	AA1
266	Heated rear window, time-delay relay	K3, K4
267	Test point, EZ-K	R5
270	ABS speedometer transmitter	T1
271	Fuel shut-off valve	Q4
272	Accelerator pedal microswitch	R5
274	EGR relay	T6
275	EGR idling switch	T5
277	EGR 3-way valve	T5
278	Aneroid switch	T6
279	Altitude compensation solenoid valve	T6
280	Heater pad relay, driver seat	Q3
284	Air mass meter	V4
286	ETC sensor, rear left	R1
287	ETC sensor, rear right	R1
288	ETC pressure sensor	S2
289	ETC power stage	R3, V3
290	ETC control unit	S1
292	Solenoid valve (idling advance)	Z6
293	Relay (idling advance)	W6, X6, Y6
295	Gear shift indicator relay	T5
298	ETC relay	R1
346	Roof light, cargo	N6
347	Tailgate light contact	P6
361	Injector No 1	R2, V2, V6
362	Injector No 2	R2, V2, V6
363	Injector No 3	R2, V2, V6
364	Injector No 4	R2, V2, V5
365	Injector No 5	V5
366	Injector No 6	V5
375	Heated seat switch	K5, Q3
376	Ballast resistor (LH-Jetronic)	U6
377	PTC resistor	C3
384	Brake fluid level sensor	F3, T2
395	ETC switch	S1
403	Temperature sensor, battery	B3
404	Vacuum-controlled microswitch	T6
405	Choke (semi-automatic heated type)	B5
406	Control unit, Renix	R3
407	Impulse sender, Renix	R3
408	Gear shift indicator switch	T5
410	Crankcase ventilation, heated	D2
413	Impulse sender, EZ-K	Q1
416	HT lead sensor	P2
417	EZ-K service socket	Q2
419	Power stage, EZ-K	Q1, Q4
424	Solenoid valve, charge pressure	S6
425	Temperature sensor, charge pressure limiter	S6
438	Seat heater contact	K3
464	Radio interference suppression relay	R2, U6, V3
479	DIM-DIP regulator	G5
490	Power aerial switch	Y1
886	Bridge connector	V4
928	Air bag	B4
929	Ignition module	B5

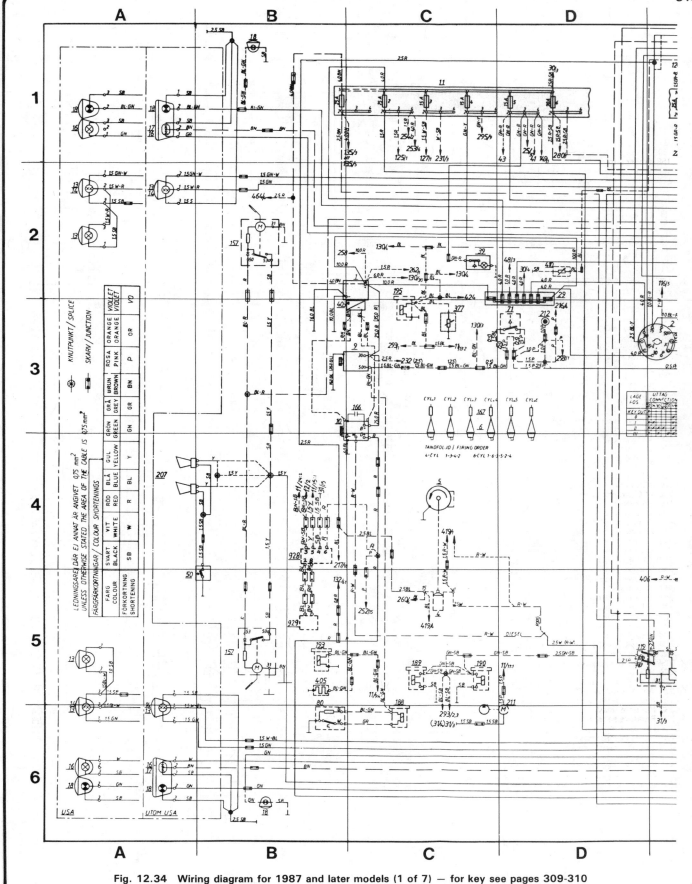

Fig. 12.34 Wiring diagram for 1987 and later models (1 of 7) — for key see pages 309-310

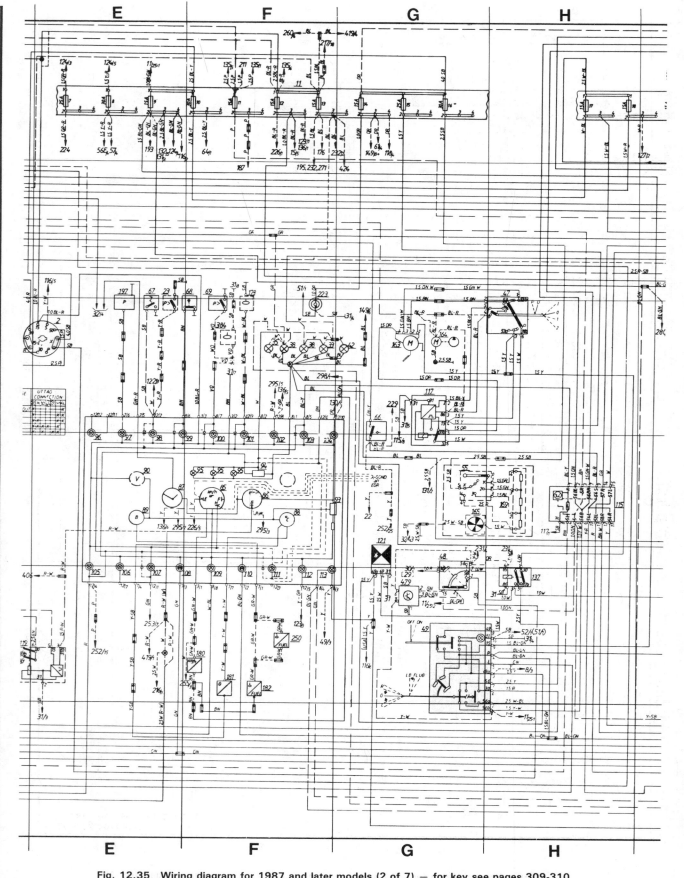

Fig. 12.35 Wiring diagram for 1987 and later models (2 of 7) — for key see pages 309-310

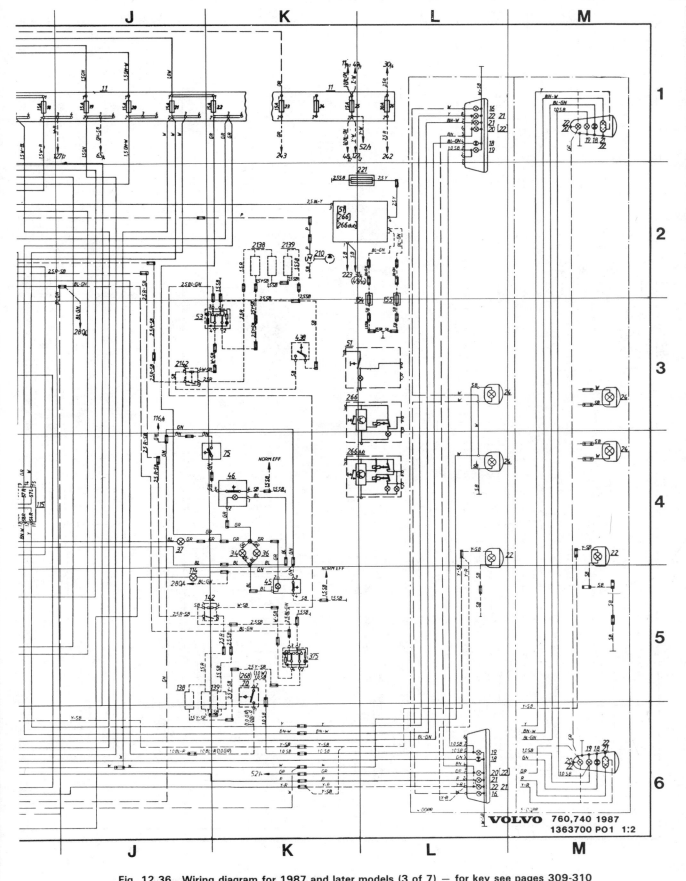

Fig. 12.36 Wiring diagram for 1987 and later models (3 of 7) — for key see pages 309-310

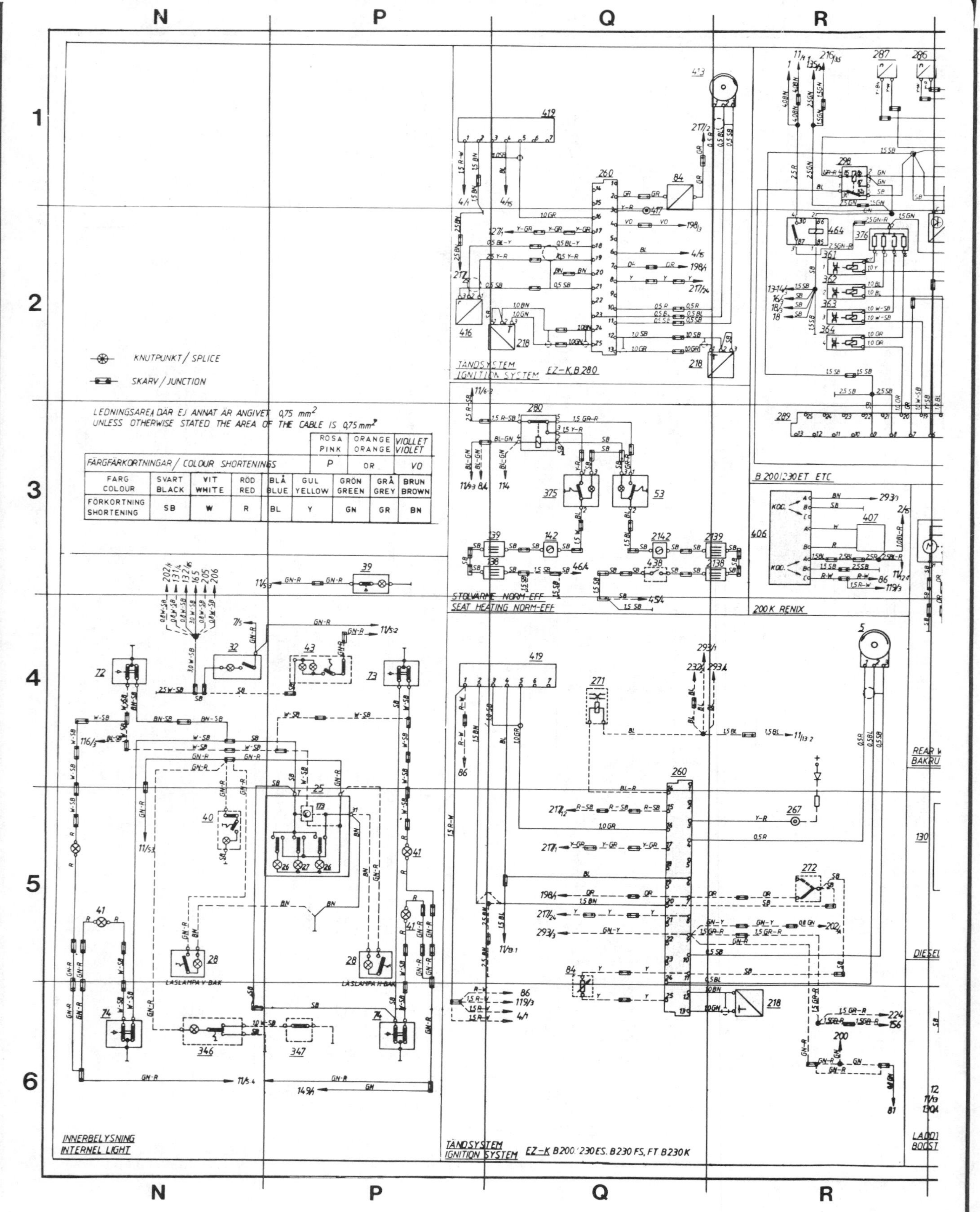

FÄRGFÄRKORTNINGAR / COLOUR SHORTENINGS	ROSA PINK	ORANGE ORANGE	VIOLLET VIOLET
	P	OR	VO

FARG COLOUR	SVART BLACK	VIT WHITE	RÖD RED	BLÅ BLUE	GUL YELLOW	GRÖN GREEN	GRÅ GREY	BRUN BROWN
FÖRKORTNING SHORTENING	SB	W	R	BL	Y	GN	GR	BN

Fig. 12.37 Wiring diagram for 1987 and later models (4 of 7) — for key see pages 311-312

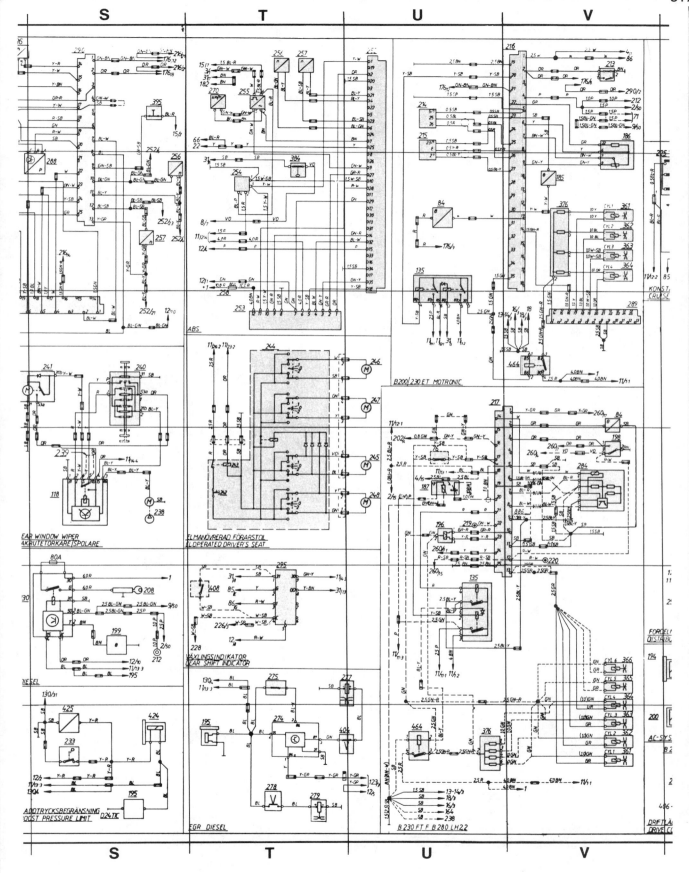

Fig. 12.38 Wiring diagram for 1987 and later models (5 of 7) — for key see pages 311-312

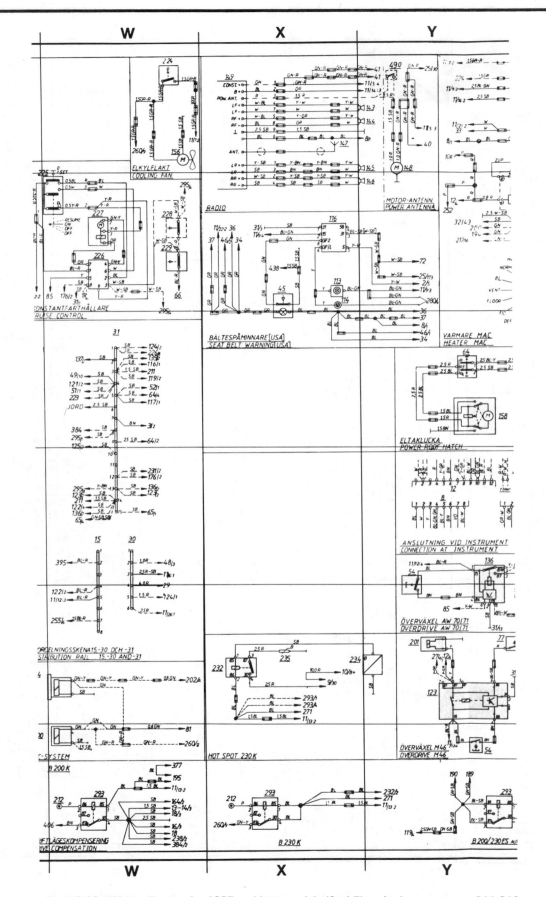

Fig. 12.39 Wiring diagram for 1987 and later models (6 of 7) — for key see pages 311-312

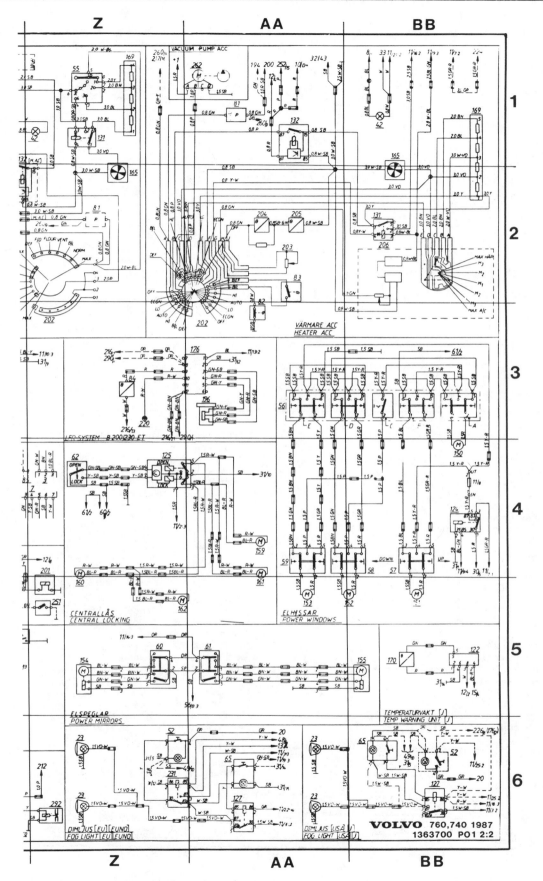

Fig. 12.40 Wiring diagram for 1987 and later models (7 of 7) — for key see pages 311-312

Index

HAYNES AUTOMOTIVE MANUALS

NOTE: New manuals are added to this list on a periodic basis. If you do not see a listing for your vehicle, consult your local Haynes dealer for the latest product information.

ACURA
*1776   **Integra & Legend** '86 thru '90

ALFA-ROMEO
531   **Alfa Romeo Sedan & Coupe** '73 thru '80

AMC
    Jeep CJ – see JEEP (412)
694   **Mid-size models,** Concord, Hornet, Gremlin & Spirit '70 thru '83
934   **(Renault) Alliance & Encore** all models '83 thru '87

AUDI
615   **4000** all models '80 thru '87
428   **5000** all models '77 thru '83
1117   **5000** all models '84 thru '88
207   **Fox** all models '73 thru '79

AUSTIN
    Healey Sprite – see MG Midget Roadster (265)

BLMC
527   **Mini** all models '59 thru '69
*646   **Mini** all models '69 thru '88

BMW
276   **320i** all 4 cyl models '75 thru '83
632   **528i & 530i** all models '75 thru '80
240   **1500 thru 2002** all models except Turbo '59 thru '77
348   **2500, 2800, 3.0 & Bavaria** '69 thru '76

BUICK
    Century (front wheel drive) – see GENERAL MOTORS A-Cars (829)
*1627   **Buick, Oldsmobile & Pontiac Full-size (Front wheel drive)** all models '85 thru '90
    Buick Electra, LeSabre and Park Avenue; Oldsmobile Delta 88 Royale, Ninety Eight and Regency; Pontiac Bonneville
*1551   **Buick Oldsmobile & Pontiac Full-size (Rear wheel drive)**
    Buick Electra '70 thru '84, Estate '70 thru '90, LeSabre '70 thru '79
    Oldsmobile Custom Cruiser '70 thru '90, Delta 88 '70 thru '85, Ninety-eight '70 thru '84
    Pontiac Bonneville '70 thru '86, Catalina '70 thru '81, Grandville '70 thru '75, Parisienne '84 thru '86
627   **Mid-size** all rear-drive **Regal & Century** models with V6, V8 and Turbo '74 thru '87
    Regal – see GENERAL MOTORS (1671)
    Skyhawk – see GENERAL MOTORS J-Cars (766)
552   **Skylark** all X-car models '80 thru '85

CADILLAC
*751   **Cadillac Rear Wheel Drive** all gasoline models '70 thru '90
    Cimarron – see GENERAL MOTORS J-Cars (766)

CAPRI
296   **2000 MK I Coupe** all models '71 thru '75
205   **2600 & 2800 V6 Coupe** '71 thru '75
375   **2800 Mk II V6 Coupe** '75 thru '78
    Mercury Capri – see FORD Mustang (654)

CHEVROLET
*1477   **Astro & GMC Safari Mini-vans** all models '85 thru '91
554   **Camaro V8** all models '70 thru '81
*866   **Camaro** all models '82 thru '91
    Cavalier – see GENERAL MOTORS J-Cars (766)
    Celebrity – see GENERAL MOTORS A-Cars (829)

625   **Chevelle, Malibu & El Camino** all V6 & V8 models '69 thru '87
449   **Chevette & Pontiac T1000** all models '76 thru '87
550   **Citation** all models '80 thru '85
*1628   **Corsica/Beretta** all models '87 thru '90
274   **Corvette** all V8 models '68 thru '82
*1336   **Corvette** all models '84 thru '91
704   **Full-size Sedans** Caprice, Impala, Biscayne, Bel Air & Wagons, all V6 & V8 models '69 thru '90
    Lumina – see GENERAL MOTORS (1671)
319   **Luv Pick-up** all 2WD & 4WD models '72 thru '82
626   **Monte Carlo** all V6, V8 & Turbo models '70 thru '88
241   **Nova** all V8 models '69 thru '79
*1642   **Nova and Geo Prizm** all front wheel drive models, '85 thru '90
*420   **Pick-ups '67 thru '87** – Chevrolet & GMC, all full-size models '67 thru '87; Suburban, Blazer & Jimmy '67 thru '91
*1664   **Pick-ups '88 thru '90** – Chevrolet & GMC all full-size (C and K) models, '88 thru '92
*1727   **Sprint & Geo Metro** '85 thru '91
*831   **S-10 & GMC S-15 Pick-ups** all models '82 thru '92
*345   **Vans** – Chevrolet & GMC, V8 & in-line 6 cyl models '68 thru '92

CHRYSLER
*1337   **Chrysler & Plymouth Mid-size** front wheel drive '82 thru '89
    K-Cars – see DODGE Aries (723)
    Laser – see DODGE Daytona (1140)

DATSUN
402   **200SX** all models '77 thru '79
647   **200SX** all models '80 thru '83
228   **B-210** all models '73 thru '78
525   **210** all models '78 thru '82
206   **240Z, 260Z & 280Z** Coupe & 2+2 '70 thru '78
563   **280ZX** Coupe & 2+2 '79 thru '83
    300ZX – see NISSAN (1137)
679   **310** all models '78 thru '82
123   **510 & PL521 Pick-up** '68 thru '73
430   **510** all models '78 thru '81
372   **610** all models '72 thru '76
277   **620 Series Pick-up** all models '73 thru '79
    720 Series Pick-up – see NISSAN Pick-ups (771)
376   **810/Maxima** all gasoline models '77 thru '84
124   **1200** all models '70 thru '73
368   **F10** all models '76 thru '79
    Pulsar – see NISSAN (876)
    Sentra – see NISSAN (982)
    Stanza – see NISSAN (981)

DODGE
*723   **Aries & Plymouth Reliant** all models '81 thru '89
*1231   **Caravan & Plymouth Voyager Mini-Vans** all models '84 thru '91
699   **Challenger & Plymouth Saporro** all models '78 thru '83
236   **Colt** all models '71 thru '77
610   **Colt & Plymouth Champ (front wheel drive)** all models '78 thru '87
*556   **D50/Ram 50/Plymouth Arrow Pick-ups & Raider** '79 thru '91
*1668   **Dakota Pick-up** all models '87 thru '90
234   **Dart & Plymouth Valiant** all 6 cyl models '67 thru '76
*1140   **Daytona & Chrysler Laser** all models '84 thru '89
*545   **Omni & Plymouth Horizon** all models '78 thru '90
*912   **Pick-ups** all full-size models '74 thru '91
*1726   **Shadow & Plymouth Sundance** '87 thru '91
*1779   **Spirit & Plymouth Acclaim** '89 thru '92
*349   **Vans** – Dodge & Plymouth V8 & 6 cyl models '71 thru '91

FIAT
080   **124 Sedan & Wagon** all ohv & dohc models '66 thru '75
094   **124 Sport Coupe & Spider** '68 thru '78
479   **Strada** all models '79 thru '82
273   **X1/9** all models '74 thru '80

FORD
*1476   **Aerostar Mini-vans** all models '86 thru '92
788   **Bronco and Pick-ups** '73 thru '79
*880   **Bronco and Pick-ups** '80 thru '91
268   **Courier Pick-up** all models '72 thru '82
789   **Escort & Mercury Lynx** all models '81 thru '90
*2021   **Explorer & Mazda Navajo** '91 thru '92
560   **Fairmont & Mercury Zephyr** all in-line & V8 models '78 thru '83
334   **Fiesta** all models '77 thru '80
754   **Ford & Mercury Full-size,** Ford LTD & Mercury Marquis ('75 thru '82); Ford Custom 500, Country Squire, Crown Victoria & Mercury Colony Park ('75 thru '87); Ford LTD Crown Victoria & Mercury Gran Marquis ('83 thru '87)
359   **Granada & Mercury Monarch** all in-line, 6 cyl & V8 models '75 thru '80
773   **Ford & Mercury Mid-size,** Ford Thunderbird & Mercury Cougar ('75 thru '82); Ford LTD & Mercury Marquis ('83 thru '86); Ford Torino, Gran Torino, Elite, Ranchero pick-up, LTD II, Mercury Montego, Comet, XR-7 & Lincoln Versailles ('75 thru '86)
*654   **Mustang & Mercury Capri** all models including Turbo '79 thru '92
357   **Mustang V8** all models '64-1/2 thru '73
231   **Mustang II** all 4 cyl, V6 & V8 models '74 thru '78
649   **Pinto & Mercury Bobcat** all models '75 thru '80
*1670   **Probe** all models '89 thru '92
*1026   **Ranger & Bronco II** all gasoline models '83 thru '92
*1421   **Taurus & Mercury Sable** '86 thru '91
*1418   **Tempo & Mercury Topaz** all gasoline models '84 thru '91
1338   **Thunderbird & Mercury Cougar/XR7** '83 thru '88
*1725   **Thunderbird & Mercury Cougar** '89 and '90
*344   **Vans** all V8 Econoline models '69 thru '91

GENERAL MOTORS
*829   **A-Cars** – Chevrolet Celebrity, Buick Century, Pontiac 6000 & Oldsmobile Cutlass Ciera all models '82 thru '90
*766   **J-Cars** – Chevrolet Cavalier, Pontiac J-2000, Oldsmobile Firenza, Buick Skyhawk & Cadillac Cimarron all models '82 thru '92
*1420   **N-Cars** – Buick Somerset '85 thru '87; Pontiac Grand Am and Oldsmobile Calais '85 thru '90; Buick Skylark '86 thru '90
*1671   **GM:** Buick Regal, Chevrolet Lumina, Oldsmobile Cutlass Supreme, Pontiac Grand Prix, all front wheel drive models '88 thru '90
*2035   **GM:** Chevrolet Lumina APV, Oldsmobile Silhouette, Pontiac Trans Sport '90 thru '92

GEO
    Metro – see CHEVROLET Sprint (1727)
    Prizm – see CHEVROLET Nova (1642)
    Tracker – see SUZUKI Samurai (1626)

GMC
    Safari – see CHEVROLET ASTRO (1477)
    Vans & Pick-ups – see CHEVROLET (420, 831, 345, 1664)

(continued on next page)

---

* Listings shown with an asterisk (*) indicate model coverage as of this printing. These titles will be periodically updated to include later model years – consult your Haynes dealer for more information.

Haynes North America, Inc., 861 Lawrence Drive, Newbury Park, CA 91320 • (805) 498-6703

HAYNES AUTOMOTIVE MANUALS

(continued from previous page)

NOTE: New manuals are added to this list on a periodic basis. If you do not see a listing for your vehicle, consult your local Haynes dealer for the latest product information.

HONDA
351	**Accord CVCC** all models '76 thru '83
*1221	**Accord** all models '84 thru '89
160	**Civic 1200** all models '73 thru '79
633	**Civic 1300 & 1500 CVCC** all models '80 thru '83
297	**Civic 1500 CVCC** all models '75 thru '79
*1227	**Civic** all models '84 thru '91
*601	**Prelude CVCC** all models '79 thru '89

HYUNDAI
*1552	**Excel** all models '86 thru '91

ISUZU
*1641	**Trooper & Pick-up**, all gasoline models '81 thru '91

JAGUAR
*242	**XJ6** all 6 cyl models '68 thru '86
*478	**XJ12 & XJS** all 12 cyl models '72 thru '85

JEEP
*1553	**Cherokee, Comanche & Wagoneer Limited** all models '84 thru '91
412	**CJ** all models '49 thru '86
*1777	**Wrangler** all models '87 thru '92

LADA
*413	**1200, 1300. 1500 & 1600** all models including Riva '74 thru '86

LAND ROVER
529	**Diesel** all models '58 thru '80

MAZDA
648	**626** Sedan & Coupe (rear wheel drive) all models '79 thru '82
*1082	**626 & MX-6** (front wheel drive) all models '83 thru '90
*267	**B1600, B1800 & B2000 Pick-ups** '72 thru '90
370	**GLC Hatchback** (rear wheel drive) all models '77 thru '83
757	**GLC** (front wheel drive) all models '81 thru '86
460	**RX-7** all models '79 thru '85
*1419	**RX-7** all models '86 thru '91

MERCEDES-BENZ
*1643	**190 Series** all four-cylinder gasoline models, '84 thru '88
346	**230, 250 & 280** Sedan, Coupe & Roadster all 6 cyl sohc models '68 thru '72
983	**280 123 Series** all gasoline models '77 thru '81
698	**350 & 450** Sedan, Coupe & Roadster all models '71 thru '80
697	**Diesel 123 Series** 200D, 220D, 240D, 240TD, 300D, 300CD, 300TD, 4- & 5-cyl incl. Turbo '76 thru '85

MERCURY
See FORD Listing

MG
111	**MGB** Roadster & GT Coupe all models '62 thru '80
265	**MG Midget & Austin Healey Sprite** Roadster '58 thru '80

MITSUBISHI
*1669	**Cordia, Tredia, Galant, Precis & Mirage** '83 thru '90
*2022	**Pick-ups & Montero** '83 thru '91

MORRIS
074	**(Austin) Marina 1.8** all models '71 thru '80
024	**Minor 1000** sedan & wagon '56 thru '71

NISSAN
1137	**300ZX** all Turbo & non-Turbo models '84 thru '89
*1341	**Maxima** all models '85 thru '91
*771	**Pick-ups/Pathfinder** gas models '80 thru '91
*876	**Pulsar** all models '83 thru '86
*982	**Sentra** all models '82 thru '90
*981	**Stanza** all models '82 thru '90

OLDSMOBILE
	Custom Cruiser – *see BUICK Full-size (1551)*
658	**Cutlass** all standard gasoline V6 & V8 models '74 thru '88
	Cutlass Ciera – *see GENERAL MOTORS A-Cars (829)*
	Cutlass Supreme – *see GENERAL MOTORS (1671)*
	Firenza – *see GENERAL MOTORS J-Cars (766)*
	Ninety-eight – *see BUICK Full-size (1551)*
	Omega – *see PONTIAC Phoenix & Omega (551)*

PEUGEOT
663	**504** all diesel models '74 thru '83

PLYMOUTH
425	**Arrow** all models '76 thru '80
	For all other PLYMOUTH titles, see DODGE listing.

PONTIAC
	T1000 – *see CHEVROLET Chevette (449)*
	J-2000 – *see GENERAL MOTORS J-Cars (766)*
	6000 – *see GENERAL MOTORS A-Cars (829)*
1232	**Fiero** all models '84 thru '88
555	**Firebird** all V8 models except Turbo '70 thru '81
*867	**Firebird** all models '82 thru '91
	Full-size Rear Wheel Drive – *see Buick, Oldsmobile, Pontiac Full-size (1551)*
	Grand Prix – *see GENERAL MOTORS (1671)*
551	**Phoenix & Oldsmobile Omega** all X-car models '80 thru '84

PORSCHE
*264	**911** all Coupe & Targa models except Turbo & Carrera 4 '65 thru '89
239	**914** all 4 cyl models '69 thru '76
397	**924** all models including Turbo '76 thru '82
*1027	**944** all models including Turbo '83 thru '89

RENAULT
141	**5 Le Car** all models '76 thru '83
079	**8 & 10** all models with 58.4 cu in engines '62 thru '72
097	**12 Saloon & Estate** all models 1289 cc engines '70 thru '80
768	**15 & 17** all models '73 thru '79
081	**16** all models 89.7 cu in & 95.5 cu in engines '65 thru '72
	Alliance & Encore – *see AMC (934)*
984	**Fuego** all models '82 thru '85

SAAB
247	**99** all models including Turbo '69 thru '80
*980	**900** all models including Turbo '79 thru '88

SUBARU
237	**1100, 1300, 1400 & 1600** all models '71 thru '79
*681	**1600 & 1800** 2WD & 4WD all models '80 thru '89

SUZUKI
*1626	**Samurai/Sidekick and Geo Tracker** all models '86 thru '91

TOYOTA
*1023	**Camry** all models '83 thru '91
150	**Carina Sedan** all models '71 thru '74
229	**Celica ST, GT & liftback** all models '71 thru '77
437	**Celica** all models '78 thru '81
*935	**Celica** all models except front-wheel drive and Supra '82 thru '85
680	**Celica Supra** all models '79 thru '81
1139	**Celica Supra** all in-line 6-cylinder models '82 thru '86
361	**Corolla** all models '75 thru '79
961	**Corolla** all models (rear wheel drive) '80 thru '87
*1025	**Corolla** all models (front wheel drive) '84 thru '91
*636	**Corolla Tercel** all models '80 thru '82
230	**Corona & MK II** all 4 cyl sohc models '69 thru '74
360	**Corona** all models '74 thru '82
*532	**Cressida** all models '78 thru '82
313	**Land Cruiser** all models '68 thru '82
200	**MK II** all 6 cyl models '72 thru '76
*1339	**MR2** all models '85 thru '87
304	**Pick-up** all models '69 thru '78
*656	**Pick-up** all models '79 thru '91

TRIUMPH
112	**GT6 & Vitesse** all models '62 thru '74
113	**Spitfire** all models '62 thru '81
028	**TR2, 3, 3A, & 4A** Roadsters '52 thru '67
031	**TR250 & 6** Roadsters '67 thru '76
322	**TR7** all models '75 thru '81

VW
159	**Beetle & Karmann Ghia** all models '54 thru '79
238	**Dasher** all gasoline models '74 thru '81
*884	**Rabbit, Jetta, Scirocco, & Pick-up** all gasoline models '74 thru '91 & **Convertible** '80 thru '91
451	**Rabbit, Jetta & Pick-up** all diesel models '77 thru '84
082	**Transporter 1600** all models '68 thru '79
226	**Transporter 1700, 1800 & 2000** all models '72 thru '79
084	**Type 3 1500 & 1600** all models '63 thru '73
1029	**Vanagon** all air-cooled models '80 thru '83

VOLVO
203	**120, 130 Series & 1800 Sports** '61 thru '73
129	**140 Series** all models '66 thru '74
244	**164** all models '68 thru '74
*270	**240 Series** all models '74 thru '90
400	**260 Series** all models '75 thru '82
*1550	**740 & 760 Series** all models '82 thru '88

SPECIAL MANUALS
1479	**Automotive Body Repair & Painting Manual**
1654	**Automotive Electrical Manual**
1480	**Automotive Heating & Air Conditioning Manual**
1762	**Chevrolet Engine Overhaul Manual**
1736	**Diesel Engine Repair Manual**
1667	**Emission Control Manual**
1763	**Ford Engine Overhaul Manual**
482	**Fuel Injection Manual**
1666	**Small Engine Repair Manual**
299	**SU Carburetors** thru '88
393	**Weber Carburetors** thru '79
300	**Zenith/Stromberg CD Carburetors** thru '76

See your dealer for other available titles

Over 100 Haynes motorcycle manuals also available

* Listings shown with an asterisk (*) indicate model coverage as of this printing. These titles will be periodically updated to include later model years – consult your Haynes dealer for more information.

7-1-92

Haynes North America, Inc., 861 Lawrence Drive, Newbury Park, CA 91320 • (805) 498-6703